Inside CorelDRAW!™ 4.0, Special Edition

Daniel Gray
with
John Shanley
John Cornicello
Ed Fleiss

Inside CorelDRAW! 4.0, Special Edition

By Daniel Gray

Published by:
New Riders Publishing
11711 N. College Ave., Suite 140
Carmel, IN 46032 USA
(317) 573-2500

Printed in the United States of America 1 2 3 4 5 6 7 8 9 0
Library of Congress CIP Data is not available.

New Riders Publishing, Carmel, Indiana

Publisher
Lloyd J. Short

Associate Publisher
Tim Huddleston

Marketing Manager
Brad Koch

Manager of Acquisitions
Cheri Robinson

Acquisitions Editor
Rob Tidrow

Managing Editor
Matthew Morrill

Production Coordinator
Lisa D. Wagner

Senior Editor
Nancy Sixsmith

Editors
JoAnna Arnott
Geneil Breeze
John Kane
Rob Lawson
Steve Weiss
Lisa Wilson
Phil Worhtington

Technical Editor
John Cornicello

Aquisitions Coordinator
Stacey Beheler

Publisher's Assistant
Melissa Keegan

Editorial Assistant
Karen Opal

Imprint Manager
Kelli Widdifield

Book Design and Production
Lisa Daugherty
Denny Hager
Carla Hall-Batton
Michael Mucha
Roger Morgan
Juli Pavey
Angela Pozdol
Michelle M. Self
Barbara Webster
Alyssa Yesh

Proofreaders
Mitzi Foster Gianakos
Linda Koopman
Sean Medlock
Tonya R. Simpson
Suzanne Tully
Dennis Wesner
Donna Winter
Lillian Yates

Indexer
John Sleeva

Composed in Poster Bodoni, MCPdigital and
Palatino by Prentice Hall Computer Publishing

About the Author

Daniel Gray is a journeyman artist who has been involved in both traditional and electronic publishing for more than 10 years. Dan's electronic publishing experience includes stints at the drawing board, in the darkroom, in systems management, and with personal computers. Dan has worked on dozens of publications including *The Princeton Packet* and *Women's Wear Daily*. He founded and publishes *Banzai Wire*, America's only independent journal for Suzuki automobile owners.

Dan is currently a Graphic Systems Analyst for the Continental Corporation and uses both MS-DOS and Macintosh platforms to publish a wide range of periodicals, from simple newsletters to four-color magazines.

Readers are invited to contact Daniel Gray through CompuServe. His CIS number is 71210,667.

Acknowledgments

Once upon a time, Inside CorelDRAW! was a cool little book about a great little illustration program. Over the past few years, both this book and CorelDRAW! have grown to huge proportions. I have been very lucky to work with a fine group of people throughout the process.

To all my fellow New Riders, my heartfelt (and gut-wrenching) thanks. This is no easy business we're in, but together we've had a great ride. This would have never happened if not for Rusty Gesner taking the initial chance on me. In kind, many thanks to Christine Steel for her guidance on the first and second editions. A tip of the hat to Cheri Robinson, Brad Koch, Stacey Beheler, Lisa Wagner, and everyone else at New Riders, both in Carmel and Gresham.

This "NYC Metro" edition of Inside CorelDRAW! would not have been possible without the fine work of a great bunch of contributing authors. Thanks to John Shanely for the Move and Show chapters, as well as his update of the Windows appendix (not to mention compiling disks); John Cornicello for updating the Printing Considerations chapter and for his diligent technical editing; and Ed Fleiss for penning the Photo-Paint chapter.

At Corel Corporation, thanks for the continuing support. In particular, many thanks to Vivi Nichol, Bill Cullen, Rus Miller, Janie Sullivan, and Fiona Rochester.

My deepest gratitude to Gary Cartwright for his humor, insight, and for teaching me (way back in 1990) the right way to engineer an electronic illustration.

Debbie and Allie, you still deserve the most thanks of all.

Trademark Acknowledgments

New Riders Publishing has made every attempt to supply trademark information about company names, products, and services mentioned in this book. Trademarks indicated below were derived from various sources. New Riders Publishing cannot attest to the accuracy of this information.

Adobe, Adobe Illustrator, and PostScript are a registered trademarks of Adobe Systems, Inc.

Ami Professional is a trademark of SAMNA Corporation.

Apple and Microsoft TrueType are registered trademarks of Apple Computer, Inc.

CorelDRAW!, CorelMOVE!, CorelSHOW!, and CorelTRACE! are registered copyrights of Corel Systems Corporation.

CompuServe is a registered trademark of CompuServe, Inc.

FontMonger is a trademark of Ares Software Corporation.

FreeHand and PageMaker are registered trademarks of Aldus Corporation.

IBM/PC/XT/AT, IBM PS/2, and PC DOS are registered trademarks of the International Business Machines Corporation.

Linotype is a registered trademark of Linotype-Hell Company.

Lotus is a registered trademark of Lotus Development Corporation.

Macintosh is a registered trademark of Apple Computer, Inc.

Microsoft is a registered trademark and Word for Windows is a trademark of Microsoft Corporation.

MS and MS-DOS are registered trademarks, and Windows and Windows/386 are trademarks of Microsoft Corporation.

Pantone, Inc. is the copyright owner of PANTONE Color Computer Graphics and Software, which is licensed to Corel Systems Corporation to distribute for use only in combination with CorelDRAW!. PANTONE Computer Video Simulations used in this publication may not match PANTONE-identified solid color standards. Use current PANTONE Color Reference Manuals for accurate color.

QuarkXPress is a registered trademark of Quark, Inc.

Ventura Publisher is a trademark of Ventura Software, Inc.

Trademarks of other products mentioned in this book are held by the companies producing them.

Warning and Disclaimer

This book is designed to provide information about the CorelDRAW! computer program. Every effort has been made to make this book as complete and as accurate as possible, but no warranty or fitness is implied.

The information is provided on an "as is" basis. The author and New Riders Publishing shall have neither liability nor responsibility to any person or entity with respect to any loss or damages arising from the information contained in this book or from the use of the disks or programs that may accompany it.

Contents at a Glance

Contents

2 Creating and Drawing 51

14 CorelSHOW!   591

Part Five: Appendixes

A Working with Windows   621

Introduction

orelDRAW! is the best-selling graphics software
package for the Microsoft Windows environment.
The program has an intuitive interface that makes it
easy to learn but tricky to master. When you master
CorelDRAW!, however, you can use your Windows-
based computer to create publication-quality artwork—a domain formerly ruled exclusively by the
Apple Macintosh.

CorelDRAW! version 4.0 is an incremental improvement over
version 3.0, despite the moniker. The package includes one new
module, CorelMOVE!, a vector-based animation program. This
new module—along with the latest editions of CorelDRAW!,
CorelMOSAIC!, CorelTRACE!, CorelPHOTO-PAINT!,
CorelCHART!, and CorelSHOW!—form a powerful toolkit that
meets many of the demands of both graphic artists and business
people.

CorelDRAW!, the cornerstone program in the package, is an
object-oriented drawing program. In many ways, it is more similar to computer-aided design (CAD) programs—such as
AutoCAD—than it is to many PC-based graphics programs.
CorelDRAW! might seem akin to paint programs such as
CorelPHOTO-PAINT!, PC Paintbrush, or Windows Paint, but the
differences are clear. Paint programs use bit-mapped graphics and
give the illusion of painting on canvas or working with pencils.

Although you draw in both genres, the process of producing an image in CorelDRAW! is more like building a collage.

The Theory Behind Object-Oriented Drawing Programs

Vector-based (rather than bit-mapped) programs such as CorelDRAW! are the electronic artist's tool of choice for print media. The two major benefits of an object-oriented drawing program are precision and flexibility. Because you define objects with vector coordinates—think of it as working with mathematical equations—you can operate with output-device and resolution independence. Bézier curves are infinitely scalable in size, giving you the flexibility to reduce or enlarge artwork without losing quality.

Where CorelDRAW! Fits into the DTP Arsenal

CorelDRAW! 4.0 is perhaps the most full-featured graphics program that a PC-based artist can use, and it is a good complement to such programs as Aldus PageMaker, Ventura Publisher, or Quark Xpress. The program's combination of powerful features and ease-of-use put it ahead of the pack—PC or Macintosh. CorelDRAW! also fits well in a workgroup environment.

What's New in CorelDRAW! version 4.0?

The folks up in Ottawa have been very busy. In short, they've crammed even more features into Draw, added a brand new multimedia module (CorelMOVE!), and unified the user interface across all the modules. Corel's engineers have pulled off yet another amazing revision. In addition, Corel has licensed a huge number of typefaces from Bitstream and the International Typeface Corporation (ITC), bringing the total number of fonts shipped with CorelDRAW! 4.0 up to an incredible 750 typefaces.

The Bitstream and ITC fonts are a welcome change. Earlier versions of CorelDRAW!—while they came with a good number of fonts—were lacking in type quality when compared to commercial offerings from the commercial foundries (such as Adobe and Bitstream). The font load alone is worth the price of the upgrade (or the street price of the full package, for that matter).

Corel didn't stop there. It also beefed up the number of clip art images and animations, which you find on CD-ROM. In fact, the program now comes with two CD-ROM disks … even more reason to buy a CD-ROM drive if you don't already have one. In fact, the majority of the fonts and clip art are accessible only from CD-ROM.

If you are upgrading to version 4.0, perhaps the first thing you will notice is the evolution of the interface. "Roll-up menus" are everywhere, from the Node Edit roll-up to the Envelope roll-up, continuing the transformation that began in version 3.0. Purists take heart—the program's basic interface still has not changed much from the original version 1.0.

Changes to CorelDRAW!: Cool Tools!

The changes to Draw itself will please the artist in you. The Pencil tool has been enhanced with the PowerLine option. *PowerLines* enable you to create drawings with a traditional woodcut look. Drawing a PowerLine is like carving out a line with a chisel, and you can choose from dozens of chisels right out of the box or create your own custom PowerLines. Following the lead of Aldus Freehand, CorelDRAW! 4.0 enables you to use a pressure-sensitive drawing tablet to create object art. If you are lucky, you might even create an *object d'art*!

Object fill choices also are enhanced. CorelDRAW! 4.0's cupboard of tasty fillings is stuffed with lots of yummy new flavors. For starters, they've added a Conical option to the fountain fill feature, along with custom fountain fills and fountain fill presets. You also can create blend-like fills with the Contour fill, in which each level of gradient actually is an object. The most amazing new fill feature, however, is Fractal Texture Fills. If you've ever had the pleasure of working with fractals, you will be in a state of nirvana. If you haven't, you'll find yourself in a state of shock. Fractals are nothing short of incredible.

The program offers 44 different default fractal texture fills in countless variations. Although the program includes only a finite number, you won't find yourself running out of different looks. The color section of this book displays all 44 default fractal fills so that you can choose a fill without waiting for your system to generate them.

Precision Drawing

Are you obsessed with perfection? These changes are for you! Node editing mavens will appreciate the changes that Corel has made to the Shape tool. For instance, you now can select a number of nodes and, with one click, autoreduce (or simplify) the selection. This results in tighter, cleaner objects that print faster and require less memory. You also can edit lines in ways you never could before: just click and drag the curve rather than manipulating the nodes and control points.

Technical illustrators will make quick use of the dimensioning feature. You can add scale to your drawings without resorting to a slide rule. This feature is great for everything from landscape design to office planning to product design specification.

Welding and Cloning are timesaving power tools. Weld is a boon to those who create typefaces with CorelDRAW!. It acts in a manner similar to combining, but you really have to see the results to understand them. Cloning, on the other hand, is best described as hyperduplication. When you use the Clone tool, not only do you duplicate an object, you create an object that is tied to the original object. When you make a change to the original object, such as altering the fill or outline, the changes also appear on the clone.

CorelDRAW! Turns into a Page Layout Package

This latest version of Draw contains features previously found only in such page layout packages as Aldus PageMaker, Quark-Xpress, and Ventura Publisher. For the very first time, you can create multipage CorelDRAW! documents—up to 999 pages. This capability makes it possible to complete a project entirely within the CorelDRAW! environment without exporting any files.

The program also enables you to create styles—for objects as well as text—which greatly enhance production flow. With a click, you can tag a block of text or an object with a specific style … no more copying attributes or adjusting individual settings. Just set them up once, then point and shoot!

All of the modules now share a common printing engine. This high-end feature promises to make color separation a more exact science. Although you might not need this feature, power users will appreciate the capability to apply Gray Component Replacement (GCR) as well as Undercolor Removal (UCR) to their color-separated images.

Corel PHOTO-PAINT!

CorelDRAW!'s bit-map paint program has many enhancements. The program now sports a true Corellian look, with the familiar left-side toolbox and mondo roll-up menus. For the first time, Photo-Paint offers scanner support, so you can ditch the lame software that came with your scanner. Although it still is not in the same league as Adobe Photoshop, the program now offers beefed-up masking and a new cadre of filters.

With Photo-Paint, once again, Corel aims to please the artist in you. Stealing a cue from Fractal Design Painter, the program includes Van Gogh and Seurat filters and brushes, as well as a number of canvas choices.

CorelCHART!

When Corel introduced CorelCHART! in version 3.0, it rushed the module to market. In that form, the program was in its infancy, and as such, was not very popular. There's good news here, however, because Corel's engineers have been hard at work squashing bugs and adding features. Chart now has access to all of Draw's fills.

CorelSHOW!

Interactivity and Per Object Transitions.

CorelTRACE!

Most power users will tell you that CorelTRACE! is one of their most-used modules in the package. Once again, Corel has been listening to its users and has implemented a number of changes. Although the first thing you might notice is the new interface, if you poke a little deeper you will find lots of depth. This latest version of Trace includes Optical Character Recognition (OCR), which enables you to turn a scanned page (or a PC fax) into a text file.

CorelMOSAIC!

CorelMOSAIC!, the visual file manager, now includes cataloging as well as drag-and-drop file management.

CorelMOVE!

Have you ever had the latent desire to become a filmmaker, or at least an animator? Using CorelMOVE!, you can create spiffy little two-dimensional animations that will wow your friends and amuse your coworkers. This module won't turn you into Walt

Disney (or even Ralph Bakshi), but it might be just the thing you need to turn your next business presentation into a big success.

About This Book

To make the most of this book, both you and your computer need to be properly set up. To run CorelDRAW!, you need a DOS-based personal computer equipped with the minimum of an 80386 processor, a hard disk, a printer, a high-resolution monitor (VGA or better), and a Windows-supported pointing device such as the Microsoft Mouse. Microsoft Windows must be installed on the computer, and you should be familiar with its interface. It is suggested that you have Windows 3.1. Part Three provides you with some more specific guidelines for setting up your system.

Using This Book

Inside CorelDRAW! is a tutorial meant for you to use as you sit at the computer. You will find that the immediate visual feedback you get by trying commands as you read about them provides a most effective means of learning.

This book is neither a substitute for, nor a restatement of, the program's documentation. It was written as a learning tool—a doorway into the program, if you will. The CorelDRAW! reference manual and on-line help, along with the other material you received in your CorelDRAW! 4.0 package, are necessary as reference material.

What Lies Ahead

Inside CorelDRAW! is divided into five parts, which present a logical progression of information for inexperienced as well as seasoned CorelDRAW! users. Each chapter builds on previously covered topics. This approach is intended to shorten your learning curve and to help you enjoy using the program from the first time you boot up.

Part One: The Basics

In Part One, you start with the simplest of maneuvers and progress through the essentials of creating artwork. Chapter 1, "Getting Up and Running," covers the basics of image manipulation. You open an existing CorelDRAW! clip-art file and stretch, scale, and rotate it. You learn to save files and to use the Page Setup dialog box to adjust page size and other parameters. You also learn to use the Zoom tool to take a closer look at your image. You finish the chapter by printing the modified clip-art image.

Chapter 2, "Creating and Drawing," gets into the specifics of Draw's tools and guides you through the completion of your first drawing. You learn to use the Pencil tool to draw straight and curved lines and to understand the difference between open- and closed-path objects. The secrets behind the precise use of the Ellipse and Rectangle tools, as well as the Skew function, are revealed when you turn on the grid to build a box kite.

As you move on to Chapter 3, "Editing and Manipulating," your work begins to get more complex. You begin by learning the way CorelDRAW! implements Bézier curves, using the Shape tool to tweak the nodes and control points of different node types. The exercises cover the concepts of layering work by building groups as you construct some simple playing cards. Along the way, you learn to round corners on a rectangle, set up and use the Duplicate command, and create special characters such as hearts, spades, and clubs.

Part Two: Putting CorelDRAW! to Work

After you get into Part Two, you are ready to roll up your sleeves and put yourself to the task of creating some real-world graphics.

This book's emphasis is to make you proficient with Draw so that you can use the program to help pay the rent rather than to merely entertain.

Chapter 4, "Basic Typography," explains the concepts behind Draw's typographic conventions as you build a quick-and-dirty flyer for the proprietor of an imaginary used car lot. In the process, this chapter covers the basics of Draw's Text tool, and you pick up tips about bringing in text from other programs.

Chapter 5, "Advanced Typography," picks up where Chapter 4 ends and gets into a more complex typographical project. It deals with the aesthetic aspects of typesetting while designing an intricately formed logo design. The type is kerned and converted to curves, enabling you to work on the actual character outlines as objects rather than as text. You learn to use nonprinting guidelines to help you align objects properly. You also investigate two of CorelDRAW!'s most powerful effects, Envelope and Extrude, as well as Version 4.0's new paragraph formatting options.

Chapter 6, "Outline, Fill, and Color," ambitiously covers the theories behind Draw's Outline and Fill tools. You learn about spot and process (the two different types of printed color) and about Draw's powerful fountain fill capabilities. To illustrate these concepts, you build a 35mm slide image, importing and colorizing a piece of black-and-white art along the way.

While Draw is primarily object-oriented, Chapter 7, "Working with Bit Maps in Draw," shows how the program can work with bit-mapped artwork from a variety of sources. You learn that bit maps can be created with Windows Paintbrush or CorelPHOTO-PAINT!, brought in through an optical scanner, or imported as existing BMP, PCX, or TIFF files. You create a bit map using Paintbrush, then import it into Draw and use it with a mask to create some pleasantly filled logotype. CorelTRACE! and autotracing also are discussed as you use the process to convert a bit-mapped clip-art file into a vector image.

Building on many of the concepts presented throughout the book, Chapter 8, "Assembling Complex Images," shows you ways to create an intricately engineered monarch butterfly. Your object here is to create a lean, mean, working drawing that is complex yet compact. You see the powerful nature of Draw's Combine command as you craft the drawing for reduced redraw time and imaging. Blend and Perspective, two of Draw's fabulous effects, are used in hands-on exercises. Draw's streamlined file format is explored, and you also learn file management and screen preview strategies. Draw 4.0's snazzy new PowerLines effect is used, as are Welding and Cloning.

Want to wow your boss and amaze your friends? Chapter 9, "Special Type Effects," consists of a series of step-by-step procedures for creating distinctive drawings and typographical illustrations. Everything from the plain-vanilla drop shadow through chromed and beveled effects is thoroughly detailed. This chapter is the one you will turn to when you get stuck for a new idea or design solution.

Part Three: Past Your Own PC

Part Three focuses on what you need besides your PC and CorelDRAW! to get your electronic art projects done. Chapter 10, "The Windows DTP Arsenal," contains exercises that delve into exporting and interfacing your images with other programs. It also presents a number of sources for acquiring everything from actual fonts to typographic information and inspiration. CorelMOSAIC!, Corel's visual file manager, also is discussed.

Chapter 11, "Printing Considerations," is where you finally get all your images into print—whether on paper, slides, or vinyl. This chapter covers the intricacies of Draw's Print command and discusses how you can use CorelDRAW! to trap artwork.

Part Four: OLE... Fighting the Bull

Part Four dives into the newest additions to the Corel family. In this section, you learn to use Windows's object linking and embedding (OLE) capabilities to supercharge your work.

Chapter 12, "CorelPHOTO-PAINT!," covers Corel's new bit-mapped paint program. You might already be familiar with Photo-Paint, because this module is really just a reworked version of ZSoft's PHOTO-FINISH. This chapter sheds light on many aspects of the program, including setup, filters, conversion, and image retouching.

Chapter 13, "CorelMOVE!," takes you step by step as you create a cool little animation—complete with sound—using Corel's latest addition to its graphics toolkit.

Chapter 14, "CorelSHOW!," buys you a ticket to the hottest show in town. Show is an OLE-aware multimedia application that enables you to use sound and graphics for everything from tradeshow exhibits to boardroom presentations. In this chapter, you complete a presentation for Rippin' Surfboards, using files created in the two previous chapters, along with an animation supplied on the CorelDRAW! distribution disks.

Part Five: Appendixes

Part 5 includes six appendixes—including a glossary—that provide you with a wealth of practical information about CorelDRAW!. System integration is covered in Appendix A, "Working with Windows." You learn to fine-tune your system, including information in the CORELDRW.INI file. Relatively unknown features are placed in a new light, and you find out what Windows files you can remove if you are running with little disk space to spare.

More information is contained in Appendixes B, D, and E, which cover a variety of subjects, from drawing tablets to clip-art vendors to keyboard shortcuts. Appendix C is a glossary of electronic and conventional graphic art terms.

Using the Exercises

To take full advantage of this book, you need to understand the way the exercises are presented. When you use CorelDRAW!, you are, in fact, creating PostScript programs that run on your laser printer. You do not find any IFs, THENs, or GO TOs in this book or in your drawings, but your drawings are uncompiled programs. If they are not properly composed, you will have problems when you try to print them.

To this end, the exercises are organized in a straightforward manner, so they are easy to follow and to use as a reference. The exercises are set apart from the text with horizontal rules and are set up in a two-column format. To complete an exercise, follow the commands and instructions in the left hand column and watch the right column for commentary. Here is a short example of an exercise:

Opening a File

Click on File	The File menu appears
Click on **O**pen	The Open File dialog box appears
Click on BOXKITE.CDR	Specifies the drawing file you want to open
Click on OK	The drawing opens on the screen

Conventions Used In This Book

Throughout this book, certain conventions are used to help you distinguish the various elements of Windows, DOS, their system files, and sample data. Before you look ahead, you should spend a moment examining these conventions:

- Shortcut keys are normally found in the text where appropriate. In most applications, for example, Shift-Ins is the shortcut key for the **P**aste command.

- Key combinations appear in the following formats:

Key1-Key2 When you see a hyphen (-) between key names, you should hold down the first key while you press the second key. Then release both keys. If you see "Press Ctrl-F2," for example, hold down the Ctrl key and press the F2 function key once, then release both keys.

Key1,Key2 When a comma (,) appears between key names, you should press and release the first key, then press and release the second key. "Alt,S" means press the Alt key once and then press S once.

Hot Keys On the screen, Windows underlines the letters on some menu names, file names, and option names. For example, the File menu is displayed on-screen as Ｆile. This underlined letter is the letter you can type to choose that command or option when it appears on the screen. (In this book, however, such letters are displayed in bold, underlined type: **F**ile.)

- Information you type is in **boldface**. This applies to individual letters and numbers as well as to text strings. This convention, however, does not apply to special keys, such as Enter, Tab, Esc, or Ctrl.

- New terms appear in *italic*.

- Text that is displayed on-screen, but which is not part of Windows or a Windows application—such as DOS prompts and messages—appears in a `special typeface`.

- In the text, function keys are identified as F1, F2, F3, and so on.

The book repeatedly uses terms that refer to mouse techniques. These terms are: *click, double-click, shift-click*, and *marquee-select*. *Clicking* on an object or menu item selects the object or item. *Double-clicking* usually performs a function, without the need to click an OK button. *Shift-clicking* is used to select more than one object. By holding down Shift, objects are added to the already selected objects. *Dragging a marquee* is like throwing a lasso around a number of objects to select them in one swoop.

Finally, note that this book often refers to the CorelDRAW! program by its popularly used nickname, Draw.

Margin Notes

Throughout this book, you find many notes, tips, and warnings. These passages are set in the outside margins of the book so that you can instantly recognize their significance and so that you can easily find them for future reference. You can see examples of these items on this page.

New Riders Publishing

The staff of New Riders Publishing is committed to bringing you the very best in computer reference material. Each New Riders book is the result of months of work by the authors and staff, who research and refine the information contained within its covers.

As part of this commitment to you, the NRP reader, New Riders invites your input. Please let us know if you enjoy this book, if you have trouble with the information and examples presented, or if you have a suggestion for the next edition.

Please note, however, that the New Riders staff cannot serve as a technical resource for CorelDRAW! or CorelDRAW! application-related questions, including hardware- or software-related problems. Refer to the documentation that accompanies your CorelDRAW! package for help with specific problems.

If you have a question or comment about any New Riders book, please write to NRP at the following address. We will respond to as many readers as we can. Your name, address, or phone number will never become part of a mailing list or be used for any other purpose than to help us continue to bring you the best books possible.

New Riders Publishing
Attn: Associate Publisher
11711 N. College Avenue
Carmel, IN 46032

NOTE

A *note* includes "extra" information that you should find useful, but which complements the discussion at hand instead of being a direct part of it.

TIP

A *tip* provides quick instructions for getting the most from CorelDRAW! as you follow the steps outlined in the general discussion. A tip might show you ways to conserve memory, speed up a proce-dure, or avoid problems with your software and hardware.

Shortcut

A *shortcut* reminds you of the keys or key combinations you can use to quickly access an option or execute a command, such as "Press Ctrl-S to save the file."

If you prefer, you can fax New Riders Publishing at (317) 571-3484 or call the product director at (317) 573-2588. We also welcome your CompuServe electronic mail; our ID is 70031,2231.

Meet Joe DeLook and DeLook Design

The book's imaginary hero is Joe DeLook, proprietor of DeLook Design, a small design firm in a seaside resort town. Joe is an experienced graphics designer, but a fledgling electronic artist. He has just purchased CorelDRAW! for the same reason everybody did—it is the best PC-based illustration package on the market.

Throughout this book, you learn CorelDRAW! alongside Joe DeLook—a novel idea in a tutorial! This approach provides a unique perspective and helps you grasp the bigger picture of the way you can use CorelDRAW! to do your job in the real world. If you are ready, get yourself a glass or mug of your favorite beverage and get comfortable. You are about to take a trip *Inside CorelDRAW!*.

Part One

The Basics

1

Getting Up and Running

o function efficiently within the CorelDRAW! environment, you need to know how to handle all the basics. Even if you already are familiar with the program's basic operation, you still should look through this chapter. You are bound to pick up a hint or two along the way.

This chapter lays the foundation on which you build in the following chapters. To begin, you learn to start CorelDRAW! and open an existing Draw file. (Throughout this book, the name "CorelDRAW!" is shortened to just "Draw.") After you open the file, you learn to use the program's Select, Move, Size and Stretch, Rotate, and Zoom features. Finally, you learn to save your file, open a new file, adjust the page setup, and import some clip art.

As you move through the exercises, you learn the ways in which CorelDRAW! clusters multiple functions within a single tool. This organization runs throughout the program and is crucial to Draw's uncluttered appearance and functionality.

The tutorial exercises in this book are written with the assumption that your hard disk is drive C and that your floppy disk is inserted into drive A. If your computer is set up differently, substitute your own drive letters as appropriate. The book assumes that you are using CorelDRAW! version 4.0 or newer.

You should have a basic knowledge of Microsoft Windows and be familiar with buttons, windows, scroll bars, and so on. If not, check the documentation that comes with the Windows program or read Appendix A.

Getting Rolling with DeLook Design

In the imaginary village of Seaside, Joe DeLook has loaded CorelDRAW! on his PC's hard disk, and he is ready to take the plunge into the world of electronic art.

It is well past closing time on Friday afternoon, and everyone has left except for Joe. Rather than sitting with his friends at the bar, Joe is sitting at his PC. He is intent on learning to use CorelDRAW!

Joe has little experience with personal computers, but he has a solid background in graphic design. Although the PC has been in the studio for a few months, it has been used mostly for book-keeping—not design work. Sitting at the PC, Joe has been aim-lessly flipping through the book of symbol and clip-art libraries that came with the CorelDRAW! package. Leafing through the transportation section, he pauses at a picture of a 1953 Chevrolet Corvette—his dream car, and a far cry from the junker he drives now. Joe notes that the file is called 1953_VET.CDR, and he de-cides to see if he can load it into Draw.

Before you begin, make sure that CorelDRAW! is properly in-stalled. The installation process is easy to follow, although it can take upwards of an hour to install the full program. The install procedure includes options that enable you to install the program and its associated files according to your preferences. You can, for instance, choose whether to install the clip-art files. To perform many of the exercises in this book, you need to have the clip art handy.

For best results, load pre-existing artwork (such as existing clip art or a file you have created and saved on floppy disk) onto your computer's hard disk while you are outside the CorelDRAW! program. By default, Corel's installation program creates a C:\CORELDRW\CLIPART directory, within which you can find a number of different subdirectories separated by theme. Load your clip-art libraries into these subdirectories or create a subdirectory of your own.

You can find most of Draw's clip art on the CD-ROM disks. A number of clip-art files, however, are loaded when you install Draw from the distribution disks. If you did not load the clip art when you installed CorelDRAW!, you need to run Draw's Setup program now. You can find this program on Disk 1 of the CorelDRAW! distribution disks.

Before you begin image manipulation, you must get Draw up and running—a very easy task. Start this exercise at the Windows Program Manager. The CorelDRAW! icon should be located in the Corel Graphics window. If this icon is not present on your screen, double-click on CORELDRW.EXE at the File Manager.

Booting Draw

Double-click on the CorelDRAW! icon	Your computer loads CorelDRAW!. The opening screen greets you, and a clean page appears.

Manipulating Images

Now that you have the program running, see about getting that Corvette image to work with. If you have had the chance to look at Draw's *Symbol and Clip-Art Libraries* booklet, you know that CorelDRAW! comes with a bounty of clip-art files from a variety of manufacturers. These files offer a good sampling of what is available in the commercial clip-art marketplace.

Opening a File

The Open Drawing dialog box provides a powerful interface for searching, previewing, and loading artwork. When you work through the following steps and load the Corvette file that comes with Draw, you see that you easily can choose files by name or by face. As you scroll through the clip-art files, click once on the file name; the preview window displays a thumbnail view of the file's contents.

Like many other dialog boxes, the Open Drawing dialog box expands with a click of a button. When you click on the Options button, the dialog box nearly doubles in size as well as functionality. The Sort by feature enables you to sort files by file name or file creation date. You can do keyword searches and review notes without using the Mosaic utility program. Access to Mosaic, however, is only a button click away.

As you open the Corvette file in the following exercise, notice the features hidden behind the Options button.

Opening a Clip-Art File

Click on **F**ile	The File menu appears
Click on **O**pen	The Open Drawing dialog box appears (see fig. 1.1)

Most likely, the directory that first appears is not the one you want. The Open Drawing dialog box, like other Corel dialog boxes, remembers where you left it. You need to switch to the correct directory, library, and file type.

Change the directory to
C:\CORELDRW\CLIPART\TRANSPO

Click on **O**ptions	The dialog box expands
Click on 1953_VET.CDR	A Corvette appears in the preview window
Click on OK	The 1953_VET.CDR file opens

SPEED TIP: If you prefer, you can forgo clicking on OK and simply double-click on the file name to open the file.

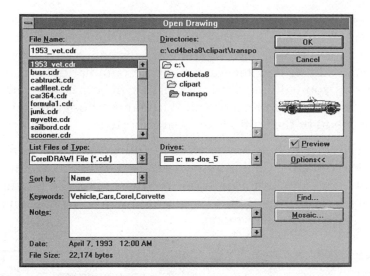

Figure 1.1:
The Open Drawing
dialog box.

The two basic reasons to preload your clip art are safety and speed. Try to avoid working with a clip-art file on an original disk—if you ruin the file, you have no way to get it back to its original form. Always work with a backup. In addition, loading a file directly into Draw from a floppy disk is slow and can take more than three times as long as loading from your hard disk. Loading times vary with your computer's speed and the type and size of your hard disk.

Of course, the size of your hard disk is a major factor in deciding where to keep your clip-art files and libraries. If your hard disk has plenty of room to spare, you can keep the clip-art files there. If not, back up the files to a second set of floppy disks.

You can load a file directly from a floppy disk into Draw, but if you preload, you safeguard your original disks. Preloading is a good habit to get into. If Draw already is running, switch to the Windows File Manager to load files to your hard disk before you use the File menu's Open command.

Shortcut

Press Ctrl-O to open a file.

Full-Color or Wireframe Mode?

When you open the Corvette file, it appears on your computer screen in either Full-Color or Wireframe mode. CorelDRAW! 4.0

provides full-color editing capabilities. Many electronic artists prefer Full-Color mode editing, but this convenience can take a toll on system performance—particularly on complex images. Wireframe editing is faster—in many cases, dramatically so. For this reason, you will find yourself working in both editing modes. To switch between Full-Color and Wireframe editing, use the Display menu or the Shift-F9 keyboard shortcut.

Shortcut

Press Shift-F9 to switch between Full-Color and Wireframe editing.

In the following exercises, you work in Full-Color mode. A check mark next to the words Edit Wireframe on the Display menu indicates that Draw is in Wireframe mode (see fig. 1.2). If a check mark appears, click on Edit Wireframe to remove the check mark and change to Full-Color mode.

Figure 1.2:

The Display menu with Edit Wireframe selected.

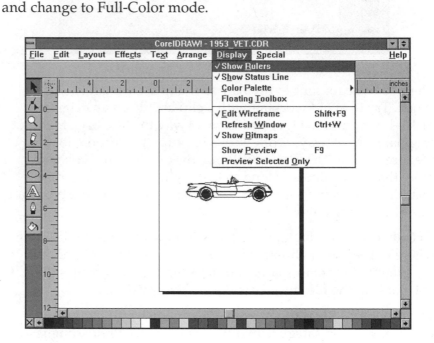

Selecting an Object

Now that the Corvette file is loaded, you can start exploring Draw. When you place your pointer on the Corvette and click, you see eight black boxes surrounding the car. These boxes are called *handles*. They indicate that the Corvette is selected. The black box handles designate that the object is in Stretch/Scale mode. An object must be selected before you can manipulate it.

Start out by moving the Corvette around the page. When you click and drag, be sure to position the cursor on the selected object. In Wireframe mode, the Pick tool's tip must touch one of the lines in the selected object. If you don't click directly on a selected line, you deselect the object and have to reselect it. In Full-Color mode, however, you can simply click anywhere on an object to select it.

As you drag the mouse up, notice that a blue dashed outline box appears (see fig. 1.3). The cursor turns into a four-headed arrow, indicating that you are in the Move mode. Don't be surprised when the image of the Corvette does not appear to move while you are dragging. After you release the mouse button, the original Corvette disappears and the image appears in its new position.

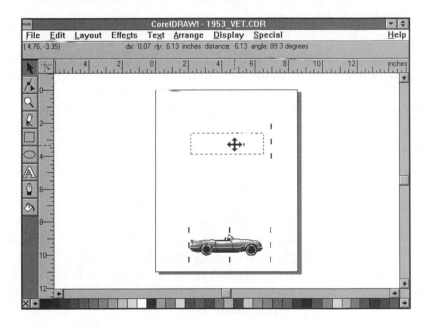

Figure 1.3:

The status line changes as you move the selected object.

Moving an Object

As you move the image around, watch the numbers change on the status line at the top of the window. If you do not see a status line, it has been turned off. Pull down the Display menu and look at the Show Status Line option. A check mark indicates that the status line is operational. If no check mark appears, click on Show Status Line now.

Selecting and Moving the Corvette

Click on the Corvette	The eight handles appear
Drag the Corvette upward	The handles disappear and a dashed outline box appears
Drag the box to top of the page	
Release the mouse button	The image reassembles itself in its new position

It might take a few moments for your computer to reassemble the image. Notice that it redraws object by object. After you become more familiar with Draw, you might want to dissect the Corvette to learn how it was built.

Simple images redisplay much faster than complex images. As with loading files, your hard disk type affects the speed at which Draw operates. A fast hard disk, an accelerated graphics card, and a fast computer—a speedy 80486 or Pentium processor—greatly improve Draw's operating speed. If you never wanted a faster computer before, you might after you spend a few hours working with complex graphics.

During the process of moving an object, the status line shows you four things: cursor coordinates, object position, distance, and angle. The *cursor coordinates* (shown in parentheses) tell you the exact position of the cursor relative to the horizontal and vertical rulers. The numbers denoted by *dx:* and *dy:* refer to the amount of horizontal and vertical distance, respectively, that you have moved the object from its original position. *Distance* also is a linear measurement, denoting the amount of diagonal movement. *Angle* refers to the number of degrees of movement.

As you discover in subsequent exercises, the status line has different gauges to record different functions. As you perform your own screen maneuvers, keep an eye on the status line.

Stretching an Object

To stretch an object, you must pull on the correct handle. Stretching is controlled by any one of the four center handles at an object's top, sides, or bottom.

The top or bottom handles make the object taller or shorter. The side handles make the object wider or thinner. As you stretch an object, it is anchored to the side opposite the one you are dragging.

Stretching the Corvette

Watch the status line as you stretch the Corvette. The status line reports the percentage of stretch.

Click on the Corvette	The eight handles appear
Place the cursor on the bottom center handle	The cursor arrow becomes a +
Drag the bottom center handle down	The handles are replaced by a blue box
Release the mouse button at the bottom of the page	A tall 'Vette appears (see fig. 1.4)

Figure 1.4:
A tall Corvette.

Fixing a Mistake

Every artist needs an eraser to fix those occasional "Oops!" situations. Draw's eraser is the Undo command in the Edit menu. Before you do anything else to your graphic, give Undo a try.

Shortcut

Press Alt-Backspace to invoke the Undo command.

Using Undo and Redo

The eight handles still should be around the Corvette graphic. If not, you might not be able to undo the last change.

Click on **E**dit, *click on* **U**ndo	The car returns to its original proportions
Click on **E**dit, *click on* **R**edo	Returns the graphic to its pre-undo state
Click on **E**dit, *click on* **U**ndo	The car is restored to its original proportions

Shortcut

Press Alt-Enter to invoke the Redo command.

If you want, try stretching the car with its top and side handles. Return the car to its original state by using Undo after each move. CorelDRAW! 4.0 allows up to 99 levels of Undo, meaning you can "erase" up to 99 of your last steps. You can specify the number of levels of Undo in the Preferences dialog box. For high Undo level settings, however, you need plenty of RAM memory.

Stretching versus Scaling

If you are working with realistically rendered, finished graphics, you might need to *scale* (enlarge or reduce in size) them. In most cases, you want to scale the picture proportionally rather than anamorphically.

When you scale *proportionally*, the width and length of an object enlarge or reduce in direct symmetry to each other but maintain their width-to-length aspect ratio.

When you pulled on the bottom handle of the Corvette, the image was scaled anamorphically. In other words, you enlarged (or reduced) the vertical (or horizontal) length (or width) without altering the other axis. This action is *asymmetrical* or *anamorphic scaling*. Draw simply refers to it as *stretching*.

Enlarge the Corvette by scaling it proportionally. As you do the next exercise, watch the status line. It tells you by what percentage you are reducing or enlarging the selected object.

Scaling the Corvette Proportionally

Click on the Corvette	The eight handles appear
Put the cursor on the bottom right handle	The cursor becomes a +
Drag the bottom right handle down and right	Handles are replaced by a blue dashed box that expands as you pull down
Release the mouse button at the bottom of the page	A large 'Vette appears (see fig. 1.5)

In figure 1.5, the drawing is enlarged beyond the CorelDRAW! page. If you try to print right now, only the part of the drawing actually in the page area (defined by the shadowed box) prints.

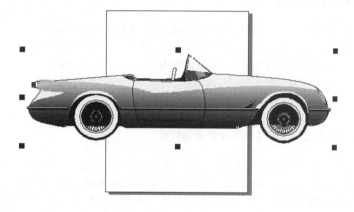

Figure 1.5:
A big proportional Corvette.

Leaving an Original

Draw includes options that can make your sizing and scaling more efficient. In three cases, these options involve pressing a key while you drag the selected object's handles. The fourth option uses a simple dragging procedure. You can use all four options in combination or in unison.

Shortcut

Click the right mouse button or press + on the numeric keyboard as you drag, scale, stretch, or mirror to create a new object and leave the original untouched.

Scaling a Copy

The first option enables you to create a new, stretched object without altering the original. If you press and release + during the stretching or scaling operation, Draw creates a new object and leaves the original object untouched. (You must use the + key on the numeric keypad, not on the top line of the standard keyboard.) You also can use + to duplicate an object while dragging. Clicking the right mouse button yields the same results.

If you press + as you pull on any of the handles, the status line reports the stretching or scaling percentage and includes the words Leave Original.

Exponential Scaling

Shortcut

Press Ctrl while scaling, stretching, or mirroring to scale, stretch, or mirror in 100-percent increments.

The second option enables you to scale objects exponentially. By holding down Ctrl, you can scale in 100-percent increments. This feature makes it easy to make an object exactly twice as large as the original, for example.

Scaling from the Center Point

Shortcut

Press Shift while scaling or stretching to scale or stretch from an object's center point.

You might have noticed that until now, the selected object has been stretched or scaled from its sides or corners. The third option makes it possible to stretch or scale from an object's center point. By holding down Shift, you can stretch or scale from the middle of a selected object.

Creating a Mirrored Image

The fourth and final option enables you to *reverse*, or flip over, an object. Draw refers to this action as *mirroring*. By pulling the bottom handles over the top handles or the left side handles over the right side handles (or vice versa in both cases), you can create a mirrored version of the original object. In addition to simply changing orientation, the mirroring process can be very useful when you want to create cast shadows and similar effects.

In the following exercise, you practice the stretching, scaling, and mirroring options on the Corvette.

Using the Stretch/Scale Options

Press + as you drag the bottom right handle down and right	The new car is scaled; the original remains untouched

Caution: Press and release the + key quickly, or you create more than one copy.

Press Del	Removes the new image

Now, scale the Corvette in 100-percent increments:

Press Ctrl as you drag the bottom right handle down and right	
Release the mouse button and then Ctrl	The image is scaled in 100-percent increments
Press Del	Removes the new image

Next, combine the commands and leave the original while scaling in 100-percent increments:

Hold down Ctrl, press and release the + key as you drag the bottom right handle down and right	
Release the mouse button, then Ctrl	
Press Del	Removes the new image

Finish this exercise with a mirror and leave the original.

Press and release the + key as you drag the top left handle down; release the mouse button	A mirrored Corvette appears
Press Del	Removes the new image

Remember that if you press and release + as you move, stretch, scale, or mirror, Draw creates a new object and leaves the original untouched. If you hold down Ctrl, Draw enables you to stretch, scale, or mirror in 100-percent increments. If you hold down Shift, Draw stretches, scales, or mirrors from an object's center point. You can mirror the object by dragging a handle across the opposite side of an object. You can mirror in any direction, but you must drag the handle over the opposite side.

The modifiers Ctrl, Shift, and + commonly are used in combination. Take the time to try a few maneuvers on your own.

Rotating an Object

You can rotate objects as well as size them. To rotate an object, you must select an object twice to display the Rotate/Skew handles. If the object already is selected, just click on it again.

The black box handles turn into double-headed arrows. The object now is ready to be rotated or skewed. Each time you click on an already selected object, you switch between the two types of handles.

As you begin to rotate the Corvette, notice that the cursor turns into a rotation symbol. When you rotate the Corvette, remember to watch the status line. It tells you the amount of rotation in degrees. This reading is important, because you see only the blue dashed box.

To rotate an object precisely, it helps to specify the number of degrees of rotation. A protractor can serve as a handy guide.

Rotating the Corvette

Click on the Corvette	The eight handles appear
Click on the Corvette again	Arrows replace the handles
Position the cursor over the bottom right handle	The cursor arrow becomes a +
Drag the bottom right handle up and left	Arrow handles are replaced by a blue dashed box. The status line shows the amount of rotation in degrees
Release the mouse button at the top of the page	A rotated sports car appears
Click on Undo	Back on all four wheels

Look at the center of the selected Corvette. A small circle with a dot should be in the center of the Corvette. This dot marks the *center of rotation*; it controls the point around which the object rotates. The first time you invoke the Rotate/Skew handles on an object, the center of rotation is horizontally and vertically centered on the object. You can change the center of rotation by moving the marker (see fig. 1.6).

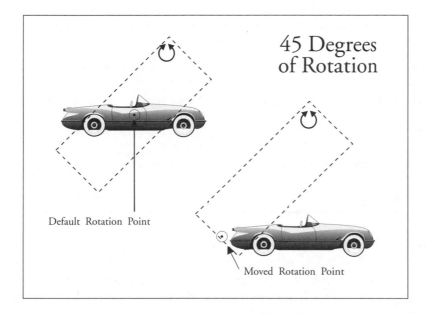

Figure 1.6:

The default and moved rotation point.

The center of rotation can be hard to see if the screen is not zoomed in. The program, however, enables you to select and move the center of rotation even if you cannot see it! The center of rotation's default position is the absolute center of the selected object. In this case, it is located in the middle of the Corvette's door. As you move the cursor over the center of rotation, the pointer tool turns into a + symbol, letting you know that the center of rotation is selectable. You then can click and drag it to a new location. Unlike previous versions of Draw, after you move an object's center of rotation, Draw 4.0 "remembers" where you left it.

Changing the Rotation Point

Click on the Corvette	The eight handles appear
Click on the Corvette again	Arrows replace the handles
Position the cursor over the center of rotation	
Drag the center of rotation to just behind the taillight	The rotation point moves

Now rotate the Corvette again. The sports car rotates on its taillight rather than its center.

Position the cursor over the bottom right handle	The cursor's pointer becomes a +
Drag the bottom right handle up and left	Arrow handles are replaced by a blue dashed box. The status line shows the amount of rotation in degrees
Release the mouse button at the top of the page	A rotated 'Vette appears
*Click on **U**ndo*	Back on all four wheels

Shortcut

Press + while rotating to rotate the object and leave the original untouched.

Shortcut

Press Ctrl as you rotate to limit movement to 15-degree increments.

In addition to having control over the rotation point, you also can use + and Ctrl while rotating objects. The + key works as it does when scaling—it leaves an untouched original behind. These features are useful if you want to build things such as spokes on a wheel or blades on a propeller.

Using Ctrl as you rotate offers yet another advantage. Rotating with Ctrl pressed *constrains* movement to 15-degree increments with Draw's default setting (this increment can be changed in the Preferences dialog box). Once again, this function can be useful for building objects that spiral from a given point.

Zooming In with the Zoom Tool

Use the Zoom tool to get a good look at the precision work involved in the Corvette drawing.

This feature enables you to magnify your view (hence the magnifying glass icon), giving you ultimate control over your precision work. Zoom works in typical Draw fashion; its features are clustered in a single tool.

Using Zoom

Follow these steps to zoom in:

Click on the Zoom tool	The Zoom fly-out menu appears (see fig. 1.7)
Click on the + tool	The cursor is now a Zoom tool
Click the mouse button and drag across the front wheel	The blue dashed marquee appears
Release the mouse button	The screen displays a magnified view of the front wheel

Follow these steps to zoom out:

Click on the Zoom tool	The Zoom fly-out menu appears
Click on the − tool	The view returns to its prior state

The other functions available on the Zoom menu are Actual Size (the 1:1 icon), which provides a close-to-actual-size view; Fit in Window (denoted by a peculiar group of polygons), which displays every item on the page and surrounding pasteboard; and a Full Page view (represented by an icon that looks like a page), which enables you to view everything on the page itself.

Two convenient shortcuts also can be used with the Zoom tool. If you want to zoom in a hurry, just press F2; the cursor changes to the Zoom In tool, enabling you to immediately marquee a selected area. To zoom out quickly, use F3.

Shortcut

Press F2 to access the Zoom In tool.

Shortcut

Press F3 to zoom out.

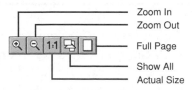

Zoom In
Zoom Out
Full Page
Show All
Actual Size

Figure 1.7:

An annotated Zoom fly-out menu.

Saving Files

Although the process of saving files might seem obvious, you can save files two different ways: Save or Save As. Using the wrong one at the wrong time can wipe out a file.

If you look at the title bar at the top of your screen, notice that it reads COREL DRAW - 1953_VET.CDR. This line tells you that you are running the CorelDRAW! program and that your current file is 1953_VET.CDR. If you use the Save command now to save the current screen, you overwrite the original file that you loaded at the beginning of the session.

To maintain the originally loaded file, save the current version using the Save As command. The program then enables you to name the new file. If you enter the same name as a file already stored on your computer, the program asks if you want to over-write the old file.

To save your current version with a new name without writing over the previous version, you must use Save As.

Saving a File By Using the Save As Command

Click on **F**ile	The File menu appears
Click on Save **A**s	The Save Drawing dialog box appears (see fig. 1.8)
Type **MYVETTE** *and press Enter*	A new file is saved as MYVETTE.CDR. The title bar reads COREL DRAW - MYVETTE.CDR

Shortcut

Press Ctrl-S to save a file.

The Save Drawing dialog box enables you to save information along with a file, which can make it easier to organize, retrieve, exchange, and catalog your work. The Save Drawing dialog box has fields for keywords (which you can use to search through files by client, for example) and notes (which can be handy for job-specific reminders, such as production information, print-runs, or even phone numbers).

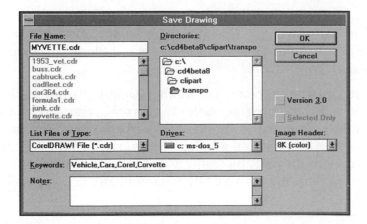

Figure 1.8:
The Save Drawing
dialog box.

The Image Header option gives you a number of choices for previewing thumbnails. You have your choice of None, 1K (monochrome), 2K (monochrome), 4K (color), and 8K (color). The higher the Image Header setting, the larger the file.

If you are working with someone who has an earlier version of Draw, you can save files as a version 3.0 format. You must choose this option for backwards compatibility. Unfortunately, CorelDRAW! 4.0 cannot save files as 2.x format files. In the event you need to save a 4.0 file in 2.x format, you must save it first as a 3.0 file, then open that file in Draw 3.0 and save it as a 2.x file.

When you are constructing a drawing, get into the habit of saving your files frequently. You can do this simply by pressing Ctrl-S to save the file without using the mouse or menus. If you want to save using the mouse, you can access the Save command from the File menu. When you save a new drawing for the first time, Ctrl-S accesses the Save As dialog box.

Saving your files frequently is a good habit to develop. Try to save after every involved maneuver. This step limits your exposure to disaster. The longer you go between saves, the more time it takes for you to re-create your work in case of a computer crash or power failure.

CorelDRAW! version 2.0 introduced Timed AutoBackup. This convenient feature saves files without any intervention on your part. The program is shipped with a default Save File setting of every 10 minutes. By editing the CORELDRW.INI file, however, you can change the AutoBackup frequency to your liking. A setting of 0 disables Timed AutoBackup. INI file settings are covered in Appendix A.

As added insurance, Draw has another backup feature. Each time you save a file, the program saves the current version with a CDR extension and automatically saves the earlier version with a BAK file extension. Should you accidentally overwrite a file, you easily can go back to the BAK file. Simply go to the File Manager and rename the BAK file with a CDR extension, and you are back in business.

Setting Up a New File

In this section, you learn how to open a new file, work with the Page Setup dialog box, and import files of different formats. Once again, these steps are basic program functions that you should be familiar with before you proceed to more complex subjects.

You already learned to open and save an existing file. Draw uses the file extension CDR when it saves drawing files. Each Draw file must use the CDR extension; otherwise, the program does not recognize the file as a CorelDRAW! file.

To use a clip-art file stored in a format other than CDR, you must import the file. *Importing* converts the file from its native format to Draw's internal format. CorelDRAW! supports many popular image file formats. (See table 1.2 later in this chapter for a list of file formats that Draw can import.)

Creating a New File

Shortcut

Press Ctrl-N to create a new file.

To open a blank page and begin a new drawing, use the File menu's New option. Creating a new file is similar to opening an existing file. If an unsaved file is on the screen, the Save Changes dialog box asks whether you want to save your work. Respond appropriately to this query and the subsequent Save Drawing dialog box (if you are actually saving a file).

Opening a New File

Click on **F**ile	The File menu appears
Click on **N**ew	A blank file, UNTITLED.CDR, appears

You now have a blank page on your screen. It might not be the proper size page for your drawing, however. To change the page specifications, you must use the Page Setup dialog box.

Get into the habit of defining your desired page setup before you begin composing your images. Otherwise, you might need to make changes to your image in midstream to accommodate a new page size or orientation.

Using Page Setup/Paper Size

Draw's default mode presents you with an 8 1/2 by 11-inch page in portrait orientation each time you open a new file. This arrangement suits most people most of the time. Certain projects, however, require paper sizes other than 8 1/2 by 11 inches. They also might require a different orientation. Use the Page Setup dialog box (see fig. 1.9) to set the desired page size and orientation to suit the situation.

Shortcut

Double-click on a page border to access the Page Setup dialog box.

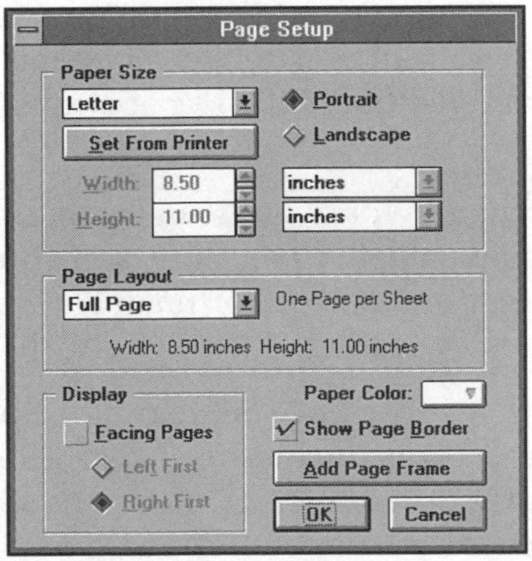

Figure 1.9:

The Page Setup dialog box.

Page orientation is an either/or choice, offering a portrait or a landscape orientation. *Portrait* (vertical or "tall") and *landscape* (horizontal or "wide") refer to the way a page is laid out, both on your screen and as it is output from your printer. Think of a page with portrait orientation as standing up (like you might paint a portrait of someone) and a page with landscape orientation as lying on its side (like you might draw a picture of a landscape). Call up the Page Setup dialog box and see what all this means. To start, change the orientation from portrait to landscape.

Changing the Page Orientation

Click on Layout   The Layout menu appears

Click on Page Setup   The Page Setup dialog box appears

Letter size is selected, and the Portrait button is highlighted. The Width and Height are dimmed but read 8.50 and 11.00, respectively.

Click on Landscape   The Width and Height entries are still
                                                   dimmed, but have reversed themselves, and
                                                   now read 11.00 and 8.50, respectively

Click on OK

Look at the page on your screen. You have changed it from a letter-sized (8 1/2 x 11 inches) portrait page to a letter-sized landscape page.

When you are finished changing between portrait and landscape, investigate the second feature of the Page Setup dialog box: Paper Size.

Although the majority of work you do in Draw can be accomplished with the standard letter page size, sometimes you will need something larger or smaller. Fortunately, Draw enables you to change paper sizes as needed.

The Paper Size section of the Page Setup dialog box offers eighteen predefined paper sizes (including envelopes). In addition, you can choose the Custom option to specify paper size up to a maximum of 30 inches by 30 inches. You also can change the measurement units from inches to centimeters or picas and points.

You can probably get away with using the letter, legal (8 1/2 × 14), and tabloid (11 × 17) sizes for most of your work. On certain occasions, however, you need the flexibility that the Custom option provides.

Changing the Paper Size to Legal

Click on Layout	The Layout menu appears
Click on Page Setup	The Page Setup dialog box appears. Letter size is selected, and the Portrait button is highlighted
Roll down, click on Legal	The Width and Height entries are still dimmed, but now read 8.50 and 14.00, respectively
Click on OK	

The page on your screen should now be a legal-sized portrait page. Try changing back to different paper sizes by calling up the Page Setup dialog box and clicking on the various predefined choices.

The predefined paper sizes (in inches) are shown in table 1.1.

Table 1.1
Predefined Paper Sizes (in Inches)

Paper Size	Horizontal	Vertical
Letter	8.50	11.00
Legal	8.50	14.00
Tabloid	11.00	17.00
Slide	11.00	7.33
Statement	8.50	5.50
Executive	10.50	7.25
Fanfold	14.88	11.00
A3	11.70	16.50

continues

Table 1.1
continued

Paper Size	Horizontal	Vertical
A4	8.27	11.70
A5	5.83	8.27
B5	6.90	9.80
Envelope #9	8.88	3.38
Envelope #10	9.5	4.13
Envelope #11	10.38	4.50
Envelope #12	11.00	4.00
Envelope #14	11.50	5.00
Envelope Monarch	7.50	3.88

Sometimes you want to use the Paper Size's Custom option instead of choosing a predefined size. Imagine, for example, that you are designing a wedding invitation with a finished size of 4.25 by 5.50 inches. You could lay out the piece on any of the pre-defined paper sizes, but that is not the smartest nor fastest way to go. Instead, choose Custom. When Custom is selected, the Width and Height edit boxes become black instead of gray so that you can enter the dimensions you want.

To change the Width and Height entries, you can highlight the current entry in the edit box and type in your new size or use the entry window buttons to roll through the sizes.

After you click on Custom, press Tab to move your cursor to the Width edit box. The current size is highlighted, enabling you to type in the new size immediately. After you enter the new size, two more tabs bring you to the Height edit box.

Changing to a Custom Page Size

Click on Layout   The Layout menu appears

Click on Page Setup	The Page Setup dialog box appears

The Portrait and letter buttons should be lit. The width and height entries are dimmed. (If they are not, do not worry—you are changing to a custom size anyway.)

Roll down, click on Custom	The width and height entries are now active
Tab to the <u>W</u>idth *entry*	A black bar appears over the entry
Type **4.25**	Changes the width of the page
Tab twice to the Height entry	A black bar appears over the entry
Type **5.5**	Changes the height of the page
Click on OK	

The page on your screen should now be 4 1/4 inches wide and 5 1/2 inches tall. Go ahead and experiment with different paper sizes by using the Custom paper size option. When you are finished, reset the paper size to Letter and the orientation to Portrait.

Using Page Layouts

If you look just below the Paper Size section of the Page Setup dialog box, you will notice that CorelDRAW! 4.0 has introduced the capability to use predefined page layouts. This handy addition makes it easy to create booklets, tent cards, and other items directly from your desktop printer. Figure 1.10 illustrates the six different page layouts.

Those of you who are familiar with printing terms will understand this next concept. If you are not, pay attention because this next section can save you a great deal of time, money, and frustration.

Using Crop Marks

Crop marks are the lines used by print shops to position artwork on a printing press. At this writing, Draw can generate crop marks for you, but only if you are using a PostScript printer.

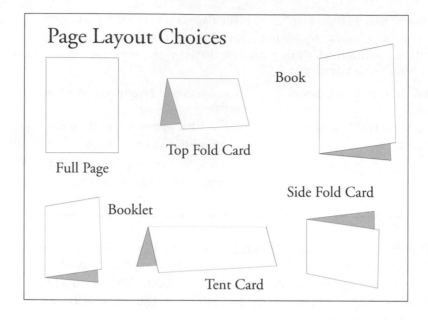

Page Layout Choices

Book

Top Fold Card

Full Page

Side Fold Card

Booklet

Tent Card

If you are using process colors and want to make your own specialized crop marks, simply assign them an outline color of 100 percent cyan, 100 percent yellow, 100 percent magenta, and 100 percent black. That way, a crop mark prints on every color separation.

Think of a view finder on a camera. When you take a picture, the camera records what is in the frame at the moment you click on the shutter button. The view finder controls where things are positioned in your picture.

Crop marks are your view finder. When you bring in your artwork to be printed, your printer assumes that you have positioned the crop marks so that what you placed on the page is exactly where you want to see it reproduced.

To avoid misplacing the crop marks, allow Draw to make them for you. Just click on Crop Marks in the Print Options dialog box (see fig. 1.11). Crop marks (or what printers refer to as *registration marks*) are placed automatically on your PostScript printout. (They cannot be printed on any other type of output device.) Crop marks are not visible on the computer screen.

A section on the basics of printing follows. For an in-depth look at the subject of printing, see Chapter 11.

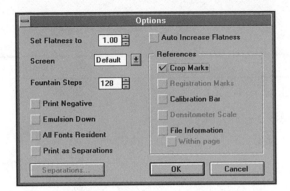

Figure 1.11:
The Print Options dialog box with Crop Marks selected.

Importing Art: A Brief Look

CorelDRAW! can import a wide range of graphic file formats, which is marvelous—most commercial clip art is not available in CDR format. CorelDRAW constantly is adding to the list—even more options might be available by the time you read this than are listed here. If you need to import a file in a format other than one of the following formats, contact Corel technical support for more information. Table 1.2 is a list of graphic file formats supported by CorelDRAW!'s import feature as of this writing.

Table 1.2
Graphic File Formats for Importation

Format	Extension(s)
AutoCAD	DXF
CompuServe (Bit Maps)	GIF
Computer Graphics Metafile	CGM
CorelDRAW!	CDR
CorelPHOTO-PAINT!	PCX
CorelTRACE!	EPS
EPS (Thumbnail)	EPS, PS, AI
GEM	GEM

continues

Table 1.2
continued

Format	Extension(s)
Hewlett-Packard (HPGL)	PLT
IBM PIF (GDF)	PIF
Illustrator 1.1, 88, 3.0	AI, EPS
JPEG (Bit Map)	JPG, JFF, JFT, CM
Kodak Photo-CD	PCD
Lotus PIC	PIC
Macintosh (PICT)	PCT
Micrographx 2.x, 3.x	DRW
PC Paintbrush (Bit Maps)	PCX, PCC
Targa (Bit Maps)	TGA, VDA, ICB
TIFF 5.0 (Bit Maps)	TIF
Windows Bit Maps	BMP
Windows Metafiles	WMF
Word Perfect Graphic	WPG

You might notice that Draw's native CDR format is included in the list. Why would you want to import a file that you can open directly? An excellent example comes to mind.

Imagine that you are producing an advertisement. You have finished the layout and have set all the type. Now you want to place a piece of electronic clip art into the file. Importing artwork enables you to assemble pieces from a number of different sources.

Import the same Corvette file that you experimented with earlier in this chapter. Only this time, import the file into the file you already have open.

Importing a CDR File

Click on **F**ile	The File menu appears
Click on **I**mport	The Import dialog box appears
Click on CorelDRAW.CDR	
Change the directory to C:\CORELDRW\CLIPART\TRANSPO	
Double-click on 1953_VET.CDR	The Corvette assembles itself on the screen

You have just imported an existing clip-art file into an open file. You can import many files into one drawing. Be advised, however, that the more complex a file is, the more time it takes to print and the more room it takes up on your hard disk. A file that has had multiple files imported into it saves as one (large) file.

Importing files from other programs is just as easy. As the preceding table shows, Draw provides a healthy cadre of import filters. Just designate the appropriate drive, double-click on the appropriate file format in the Import dialog box, and follow the same steps as before.

Although all the clip art supplied with CorelDRAW! version 4.0 is in the native CDR format, most commercial clip art is not. Appendix E, the "Clip Art Compendium," features a list of companies that sell a wide variety of electronic illustrations, in various formats.

If you are looking for more clip art, the first place you should look is on the CD-ROM disks that come with CorelDRAW 4.0. You will find an abundance of clip art. Of course, you need a CD-ROM drive to access it. The prices of CD-ROM drives have dropped dramatically and might not be as expensive as you might expect.

Printing

The final thing you need do in this chapter is print out the Corvette. The Print dialog box might look big and scary at first, but all you have to do for now is click on OK. The subject of printing is covered in depth in Chapter 11.

Producing output is CorelDRAW!'s reason for existing. A pretty screen file does you no good if you cannot print it. Furthermore, you cannot tell what a piece really looks like until it rolls off the printer.

You can access the Print function in one of two ways. The first is through the File menu. The easiest way is to use the shortcut, Ctrl-P. This shortcut (along with Ctrl-S for Save) will eventually become automatic keystrokes for you. Your brain will think "print," and your fingers will press Ctrl-P.

Printing the Corvette

Click on **F**ile	The File menu appears
Click on **P**rint	The Print File dialog box appears
Click on OK	The file is sent to the printer

Try to get in the habit of saving your file with Ctrl-S before you walk away from your PC. Although the program always asks whether you want to save your file before you quit, and the program has Timed AutoBackup, it is still a good idea to save as frequently as possible. Always save a file before you print it. You will be covered if your system "hangs" while printing.

Quitting

You have one last thing to do before you take a break. You must learn how to quit the Draw program. You can quit in one of two ways, either from the File menu or by using a shortcut.

Shortcut

Press Alt-F4 to quit CorelDRAW!.

If you have an unsaved file on your screen when you quit, the program asks if you want to save the file before you exit. Pay attention to this dialog box—it can save you a lot of work!

Quitting CorelDRAW!

Click on **F**ile	The File menu appears
Click on **Q**uit	

If you have a file on your screen that you want to save, save it now.

Summary

In this chapter, you learned some important things about CorelDRAW! You started out by getting up and running, and you opened an existing file. After investigating how to select, scale, rotate, and zoom, you opened a new file and adjusted the page size and orientation. After seeing that the Page Setup dialog box offers predefined Paper Sizes, you set up an odd-sized page (4.25 inches by 5.5 inches), fiddled with Page Layouts, and learned about automatic crop marks. Finally, you learned a little about importing files and printing.

In the next chapter, you start getting into the exciting stuff. Take a break, get some air, or, like Joe, wrap it up and go home for a well-deserved supper. In the next chapter, you explore creating and drawing, and you tackle a real project.

2

Creating and Drawing

n the last chapter, you learned about some of the Draw basics. Chapter 1 covered the essential file functions: opening, importing, saving, and printing. You also learned to select, move, scale, and rotate an object. Along the way, you found out how to set up a page and how to use Zoom and Preview. What you did not learn was how to draw with CorelDRAW!. That is what this chapter is all about.

You are going to open up Draw's toolbox (see fig. 2.1) and use it to do your first project, a letterhead.

As you experiment with Draw's various tools, you see that most of them do double duty. First, you use the Pencil tool, noting how you can use it to draw either straight or curved lines. Next, you use the Ellipse tool to produce perfect circles and ovals, and you find that the Rectangle tool works in much the same way. For more precision, you set up and use the grid. You learn the basics of Outline and Fill to finish the drawing. Finally, a quick look at the Text tool gives you a chance to complete your first project.

Figure 2.1:
The CorelDRAW!
toolbox.

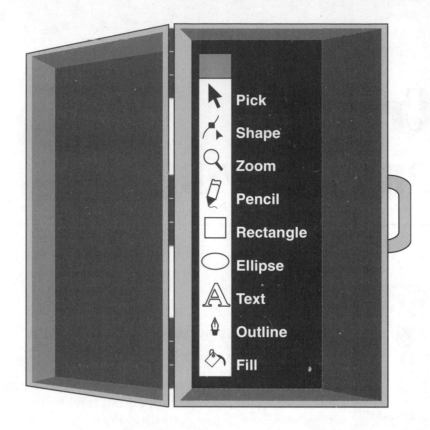

Designing DeLook's First Project

On Saturday morning, Joe DeLook is at it again. Today, he is determined to conquer Draw's design tools. He promised to create a letterhead for his girlfriend, Katie, for her kite store.

Joe needs a simple drawing of a kite, along with a line or two of type. Nothing fancy, just serviceable. With a fresh pot of coffee in the galley, Joe shoves off into the uncharted waters of electronic design.

Drawing with the Mouse

If you have never drawn anything with a mouse, you are not in for a treat. Freehand drawing with a mouse is like filleting a fish with a chain saw. It is not a pretty sight. Some excellent alternatives to the mouse are available; the most notable among them is the graphics tablet. Appendix B reviews one of the best graphics tablets, the Wacom SD-420.

After you have used a graphics tablet, you will not want to go back to using a mouse. You might choose to purchase and use a tablet; for clarity's sake, however, this book still refers to it as a mouse.

This chapter begins with a blank page in CorelDRAW!. It soon fills up with all kinds of wonderful shapes and doodles. Your pages might become overly doodle-filled, but don't worry—you also learn how easy it is to remove unwanted objects.

Using the Pencil Tool

The drawing tool to start with is the Pencil tool. The Pencil tool can draw straight lines or curved objects, depending on how you use it. Producing an image with CorelDRAW! is akin to building a collage; you assemble your drawings by using different shapes. Keep this philosophy in mind as you plan your drawings.

Remember, too, that Draw is not a bit-mapped paint program. If you are not sure of the differences between paint and draw programs, reread the introduction to this book.

The Pencil tool has two drawing modes: Freehand and Bézier. Each mode has its place, but for the purposes of these next exercises, use the Freehand mode. The Bézier mode is explored in the next chapter, after you understand how Bézier curves work.

Drawing Straight Lines (Open Path)

The Pencil tool can draw either straight or curved lines. You begin by drawing some straight lines, then you connect them to build closed-path objects. As you draw, watch the status line; it tells you some important information.

The technique used to draw straight lines is quite simple. It consists of a position, a click, a second position, and a second click. As you move the cursor around the page, the status line informs you of the dx: and dy: change in position, distance (length), the angle of the line segment you are drawing, and the line segment's starting and ending points. The dx: and dy: entries are Cartesian coordinates for horizontal and vertical position, respectively.

Drawing a Straight Line

Click on the Pencil tool	The cursor becomes a +
Click the mouse button near the top of the page	A line appears, with a node where you clicked. The status line becomes active
Move the cursor to bottom of the page	The line pivots around its node
Click the mouse button	This action creates a line with a node at each end (see fig. 2.2)

Try this a few times to get the feel of it.

Figure 2.2:

A single line.

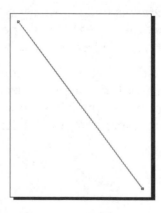

You can use two methods to draw a diagonal line. As you have probably seen, you can use the preceding technique to draw a diagonal line at any angle. In addition, you can constrain the angle to 15-degree increments by holding down Ctrl as you draw the line. Try drawing a few constrained-angle lines by using Ctrl. (You must release the mouse button before you release Ctrl.) You can adjust the constrain increment to your liking by changing the Constrain Angle option in the Preferences dialog box. You can access the Preferences dialog box from the Special menu or by using the Ctrl-J shortcut.

The lines you have just drawn are *open paths*. Although they can be outlined, they cannot be filled with any color or pattern. *Closed-path* objects are constructed from groups of connected lines, and they can be filled (more on this later).

Shortcut

Press Ctrl-J to access the Preferences dialog box.

Drawing Straight Lines (Closed Path)

An open path is like a lobster trap with an open lid. To keep the lobsters in the trap, you must close the lid. Closing an open path is like shutting the lid on a lobster trap. How do you close this open path? You play a simple game of connect the dots. The dots are called *nodes*.

You can connect the dots and close the path in several ways. The first method is to draw a line segment from one node to another. The simplest way to do this is by drawing one line with two nodes, then starting the second line directly from one of the first line's nodes.

Connecting Straight Lines

Draw a single horizontal line segment:

Click on the last node drawn	A new line segment is initiated, connected to the node
Move the cursor up and to the left	
Click the mouse button	A second line segment is drawn, connected to the first line segment

Now two line segments are connected.

Objects other than ovals or circles usually consist of at least three segments. As you do this next exercise, you create a closed path to see a variation on the last exercise. The Pencil tool immediately starts a new line segment with the same node when you double-click rather than single-click.

Double-Clicking on Connected Straight Lines To Close a Path

Click on the Pencil tool	The cursor becomes a + with a gap in the center
Click the mouse button at the bottom left of the page	
Move the cursor to the right	A line appears. Maintain a 0-degree angle
Double-click the mouse button	Creates a line with nodes at each end, and a new line segment is started
Move the cursor up and to the left	
When you reach a 135-degree angle, double-click the mouse button	A connected diagonal line is drawn, and a new line segment starts
Position the cursor over the initial node	
Click the mouse button	A triangular closed path is created (see fig. 2.3)

Figure 2.3:
Connected lines.

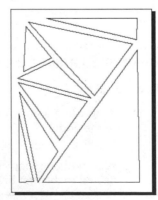

Snapping to Nodes Using AutoJoin

If you cannot seem to get those pesky little lines to connect, you can try an easier way to get them to snap to each other. A feature called *AutoJoin* controls the Pencil tool's "magnetic" node-connection range.

AutoJoin settings are altered through the Curves option in the Preferences dialog box (see fig. 2.4), which you access from the Special menu. In this dialog box, scroll buttons enable you to set AutoJoin in a range from 1 (lowest) to 10 (highest). AutoJoin's default setting is 5. The lower settings make it difficult to connect nodes. Reserve those settings for intricate work where lines need to be close without touching. The maximum setting of 10 greatly facilitates node-connection—you can almost feel the pencil snapping to the node. But be careful—it can snap when you do not intend it to. A high setting can give you haphazard autojoining.

Right now, use a few different AutoJoin settings to draw polygons

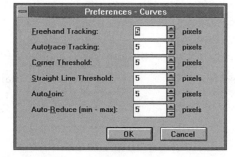

Figure 2.4:

The Preferences-Curves dialog box.

Connecting Lines Using Different AutoJoin Settings

Click on **S**pecial   The **S**pecial menu appears

Click on Pr**e**ferences   The Preferences dialog box appears

Click on C**u**rves   The Curves dialog box appears

Set Auto**J**oin *to* 1

Click on OK

Click on OK again

continues

With AutoJoin set at 1, you might find it difficult to connect lines, but keep trying.

Click on the Pencil tool

Draw a single line segment

Click on the last node

Draw a second connected line segment

Draw a few more connected line segments to close the path

Now make it easier. Set AutoJoin to an ultra-sticky 10. Feel the cursor's magnetic attraction.

*Click on **S**pecial*

*Click on Pr**e**ferences* The Preferences dialog box appears

*Click on C**u**rves* The Curves dialog box appears

Set AutoJoin to 10

Click on OK

Click on OK again

Draw a single line segment

Click on the last node

Draw a second connected line segment

Draw a few more connected line segments to close the path

Return AutoJoin to its default setting of 5 and try just a few more.

*Click on Pr**e**ferences* The Preferences dialog box appears

*Click on C**u**rves* The Curves dialog box appears

Set AutoJoin to 5

Click on OK

Click on OK again

Draw a single line segment

Click on the last node

Draw a second connected line segment

Draw a few more connected line segments to close the path

In addition to AutoJoin settings, the Preferences dialog box offers many choices to help make your life with Draw a pleasant experience. Shortly, you learn about one of those: freehand tracking.

After all that, you should understand how to draw a closed path by connecting the nodes. Although you have been working with straight lines, the concept of connecting nodes works curved lines as well.

By now, your screen is probably full of triangles and other assorted polygons. Take some time to clean up the screen by deleting some of the objects. You can do this in a variety of ways.

Deleting Objects

The simplest way to delete an object is to select it with the Pick tool, and then delete it. You can use at least three other ways, however, to rid your screen of unwanted objects. This section takes a look at all four procedures:

- Click/Delete
- Shift-Click/Delete
- Marquee/Delete
- Select All/Delete

Deleting a Triangle (Click/Delete)

You should have plenty of lines (open paths) and triangles (closed paths) on the screen from the last exercise. If you do not have any, create a few.

Click on the Pick tool	The pointer is activated
Click on the triangle you want to delete	The handles appear. The triangle is selected
Press Del	The triangle is deleted

If you did not really want to delete the object, you can get it back by choosing Undo from the Edit menu (or by pressing Alt-Backspace).

Draw provides a way to select objects without using the mouse at all. With the Pick tool selected, you can cycle through objects by pressing Tab. CorelDRAW! refers to this wonderful feature as *Select Next*. You also can select objects in reverse order by pressing Shift and Tab at the same time.

Shortcut

Press Tab to select the next object.

Shortcut

Press Shift-Tab to select the previous object.

Try this time-saver right now. You should have plenty of objects on the screen to tab through.

Tabbing through Objects on the Screen

Click on the Pick tool	Activates the pointer
Click on a polygon	Selects the polygon
Press Tab	Selects the next object
Press Tab again	Selects the next object
Press Tab again	Selects the next object

If you want, try reversing through the objects by pressing Shift-Tab.

Sometimes you want to remove several objects at a time. The next three procedures enable you to delete a number of objects selectively. By shift-clicking (holding down Shift while clicking), for example, you can select several objects at a time. Watch the status line for the number of objects selected.

Selectively Deleting Several Lines (Shift-Click/Delete)

Click on the Pick tool	Activates the pointer
Click on the first object you want to delete	The handles appear. The object is selected
Shift-click on the next object to delete	The handles expand to include both objects. The status line indicates two objects have been selected on layer 1
Shift-click on the other object to delete	The handles continue to expand to include all selected lines. The status line shows the number of lines selected
Shift-click on one of the selected objects	Deselects the line. The status line reflects the selection
Press Del	The selected lines are deleted

A variation on the last select/delete is the marquee select/delete. Marquee-selecting is like throwing out a big net.

Deleting Using the Marquee (Marquee/Delete)

If you have run out of lines or triangles to delete, draw some more. Then take the following steps to delete them:

Click on the Pick tool	Activates the pointer
Position the cursor above and to the left of the lines to be deleted	
Drag the cursor below and to the right of the lines to be deleted	A blue dashed box appears around the lines
Release the mouse button	Handles appear that surround all the selected lines. The status line reflects the total number of objects selected
Shift-click on a selected object	Deselects the object
Press Del	The objects are deleted

If you want to erase all the objects on your page, the following exercise shows you the slickest way to do it.

Deleting All Objects (Select All/Delete)

Click on the Pick tool	Activates the pointer
Click on **E**dit	The Edit menu appears
Click on Select **A**ll	All objects are selected
Press Del	All objects are deleted

By learning to delete multiple objects, you also have learned the principles behind selecting multiple objects. You soon see that you can use the shift-click, marquee-select, and select-all techniques to apply fills, outlines, and transformations on groups of objects.

Now that you have finished playing Search and Destroy, you can start filling up the screen with doodles again. Take your mouse in hand and get ready to draw some curves.

Shortcut

Press Alt-E, then A, then Del to delete all objects.

Drawing Curves Freehand

As mentioned earlier, the Pencil tool can create curved lines as well as straight ones. Like straight lines, curved lines can be open or closed paths. You can create closed paths composed entirely of curves or in combination with straight lines. In this section, use the Pencil tool to draw curves and create some simple clouds.

The more you work with Draw, the more you realize that the curves you draw using a mouse do not always turn out exactly the way you envisioned them. This fact is largely due to the imprecise drawing capabilities of the common mouse. A mouse can be a difficult tool to use for freehand drawing.

Nevertheless, try drawing some simple curves. Most likely, they do not look all that great at close inspection. Fear not. Through a process known as tweaking, you can refine your curves to a more suitable form. The actual process of tweaking is covered in Chapter 3.

The technique to use when you want to draw curved lines is different from the one to use when drawing straight lines. Drawing curved lines requires a click-and-drag technique. Hold the mouse button down while drawing your curve. When you release the mouse button, CorelDRAW! takes a few seconds to plot your curve. When it is done, nodes appear along the path of the line (see fig. 2.5).

Drawing a Curved Line

Click on the Pencil tool	The cursor becomes a +
Click and drag the mouse in a curving line	A curved line is drawn
Release the mouse button	After a few moments, nodes are added to the line

Drawing a curved line is not too difficult. Notice that the status line reads Curve on Layer 1 Open Path. This message means that the selected object is not a closed path and cannot be filled.

If you do not like the way your object looks while you are in the midst of drawing, you can erase part of it without starting from scratch. Press the Shift key as you draw a curved line to "back up" and erase the line. When you release Shift, you resume drawing.

Shortcut

Press Shift as you draw to back up and erase.

Next, draw a curved closed path following much the same procedure. To close the path, you need to end your line on top of the node where you began the line. This procedure is almost exactly like creating the triangular closed path, except this time you are working with curves. When you have finished drawing and your nodes are plotted, the status line should read Curve on Layer 1.

When working in Full-Color mode (as opposed to Wireframe mode), you see the immediate results of closing a path—the object is filled with the default fill. If, however, No Fill is the default, you might not notice a difference. If you are not sure whether the object is filled, just remember that the status line always tells you if it is an open or closed path.

Drawing a Curved Closed Path

Click on the Pencil tool

Drag the mouse in curving cloud shape   A cloud shape is drawn

Bring the cursor back to where the line began

continues

Release the mouse button	After a few moments, nodes are added to the cloud

If the status line reads `Open Path`, you did not close the path. (It can be tricky!) If you have an open path, try the exercise again. It might take a few tries for you to get your path closed.

What if you have drawn the ultimate cloud but failed to create a closed path? You can very simply join the nodes and close the path. In the next exercise, you use a new menu: the Node Edit menu. Node Edit is introduced here; Chapter 3 covers this feature in more detail.

This next exercise is similar to the last, except that you should try *not* to connect the end nodes when you lay down the drawing.

Leave plenty of room between the first and last nodes.

Closing an Open Path

Click on the Pencil tool	
Drag the mouse in a curving cloud shape	
Bring the cursor back almost to where the line began	
Release the mouse button	After a few moments, nodes are added to the cloud (see fig. 2.6). The status line should read `Curve on Layer 1 Open Path. Number of Nodes: X` (where X is the number of nodes)
Click on the Shape tool	The status line should read `Curve: X nodes` (where X is the number of nodes)
Shift-click on the first and last nodes	
Release the mouse button	The selected nodes turn black. The status line reads `2 selected nodes`
Double-click on a selected node	The Node Edit roll-up menu appears (see fig. 2.7)
Click on Join	The status line reads `First node of a closed curve` (see fig. 2.8)
Click on Pick tool	The status line reads `Curve on Layer 1 Number of Nodes: X`

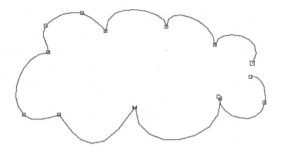

Figure 2.6:
A curve (open path).

Figure 2.7:
The Node Edit roll-up menu.

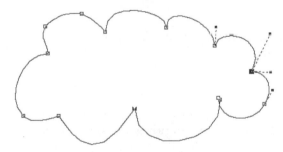

Figure 2.8:
A curve (closed path).

You have joined the first and last nodes of an open path by using Node Edit to form a closed path. If you were not successful in creating a closed path, you might have selected more than two nodes. Only two nodes can be joined. Deselect the nodes and try again. You also can try marquee-selecting instead of shift-clicking.

Drawing Smooth Lines

Do your lines seem really jagged or, conversely, far too smooth? If so, you can change a setting in the Preferences dialog box to alter the precision that the program uses when it converts mouse movements to Bézier curves. CorelDRAW! refers to this function as *Freehand Tracking*.

Like AutoJoin, Freehand Tracking can be set in a range from 1 (lowest) to 10 (highest). The default setting is 5. Lower settings enable the program to follow the line with far more precision, but can render too many nodes and give the line a jagged appearance. High settings give the line fewer nodes and a smoother curve, but with a corresponding loss of precision. Take a look at what different Freehand Tracking settings do to your freehand drawings. Try drawing a few more clouds.

Adjusting Freehand Tracking

Click on **S**pecial	The **S**pecial menu appears
Click on Pr**e**ferences	The Preferences dialog box appears
Click on C**u**rves	The Curves dialog box appears
Set **F**reehand Tracking *to* 1	
Click on OK	
Click on OK again	

With the **F**reehand Tracking set at 1, you get more precision, more nodes, and more jaggedness.

Click on Pencil tool

Draw a cloud

That looks pretty rough. Smooth out your technique by setting **F**reehand Tracking to 10. Notice the loss of precision, as shown in figure 2.9.

Click on **S**pecial	
Click on Pr**e**ferences	The Preferences dialog box appears
Click on C**u**rves	The Curves dialog box appears
Set **F**reehand Tracking *to* 10	
Click on OK	
Click on OK again	
Draw a cloud	

Return **F**reehand Tracking to its default setting of 5 and try one more setting.

Click on **S**pecial	
Click on Pr**e**ferences	The Preferences dialog box appears
Click on C**u**rves	The Curves dialog box appears
	Set **F**reehand Tracking *to* 5

Click on OK
Click on OK again
Draw a cloud

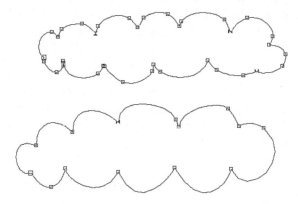

Now is a good time to practice drawing with the Pencil tool. You might find it difficult to draw with precision, but have no fear— you can tweak those curves soon enough.

Draw several clouds. (Imagine that a storm front is moving in!) Delete all the clouds you are less than happy with and save your three favorites. Drag them to the top of the page—you are going to use them in your first drawing!

At this point, save your drawing. Use the file name BOXKITE.CDR. If you cannot recall how to save a file, refer to Chapter 1.

Drawing Ellipses and Rectangles

The Ellipse and Rectangle tools are as straightforward as you could hope a pair of drawing tools to be. Anyone who has ever tangled with mechanical compasses, plastic templates, and technical pens will be ecstatic over the Ellipse tool's ease of use. In fact, you probably will hang up your compass, put away your templates, and clean your pens for the last time, abandoning them in favor of working exclusively with CorelDRAW!'s superior electronic versions. You do not need to worry about ink splats or smudge marks. If you draw something the wrong size or shape, simply undo it and try again!

By using these tools in conjunction with Draw's Snap To Grid and Guidelines features (both of which are covered shortly), as well as the program's rulers, you can draw ellipses and rectangles of precise proportions. If the rulers are not already showing on your screen, select Show **R**ulers from the **D**isplay menu.

The Ellipse and Rectangle tools offer flexibility that even the largest collection of templates and technical pens could not hope to match. While you are drawing these objects, look to the status line for immediate feedback.

The Ellipse Tool

The Ellipse tool works in one of two modes to produce either ovals or circles. By clicking and dragging, you can draw ovals of infinitely variable proportions. To draw a perfect circle, hold down Ctrl as you click and drag. You can draw an ellipse or a circle from its center point by holding down Shift. Figure 2.10 shows some samples of what you might draw. Remember to watch the status line as you draw—it shows the ellipse's exact height and width as well as the starting, ending, and center points.

Figure 2.10:

A variety of circles and ellipses.

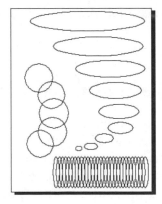

Drawing Ovals and Circles

Click on the Ellipse tool	Cursor changes into a +
Click and drag the cursor diagonally	An oval grows as you move the cursor
Release the mouse button	An oval is drawn

That was too easy. Now try a circle. With the Ellipse tool still selected, take the following steps:

Press Ctrl as you click and drag the cursor	A circle grows as you move the cursor
Release the mouse button, then release Ctrl	A circle is drawn

Now draw an ellipse from its center point:

Press Shift as you click and drag the cursor	An ellipse grows from its center point as you move the cursor
Release the mouse button, then release Shift	An ellipse is drawn

Try drawing a few more ovals and circles. When you are finished, delete them by using one of the methods described earlier in this chapter. Try using both Ctrl and Shift to draw a circle from its center point. Attempt to draw to exact proportions, using the status line. After you complete an object and release the mouse button, the status line displays the dimensions and the page position of its center point.

The Rectangle Tool

The Rectangle tool works just like the Ellipse tool; it creates either rectangles or squares (see fig. 2.11). By clicking and dragging, you can draw a rectangle of infinitely variable proportions. To draw a perfect square, hold down Ctrl as you draw. If you want to draw from a center point, hold down Shift.

Figure 2.11:

A variety of squares and rectangles.

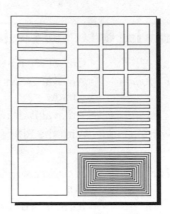

Drawing Rectangles and Squares

Click on the Rectangle tool	The cursor changes to a +
Drag the cursor diagonally	A rectangle grows as you move the cursor. The status line shows the width and height of the rectangle
Release the mouse button	A rectangle is drawn

Now that you have drawn a rectangle, draw a square. With the Rectangle tool still selected, take the following steps:

Press Ctrl as you click and drag the cursor	A square grows as you move the cursor
Release the mouse button, then release Ctrl	A square is drawn

Next, draw a rectangle from its center point:

Press Shift as you click and drag the cursor	A rectangle grows from its center point as you move the cursor
Release the mouse button, then release Shift	A rectangle is drawn

As you have seen, the Ellipse and Rectangle tools originate (or pull) objects from their corners or from a center point depending on whether you press Shift. If you want, try drawing a few more ellipses, circles, rectangles, and squares using different combinations until you are comfortable with the tools. When you are done, delete them to clear the page.

Using the Grid and Guidelines for Precision

You easily can make your objects fit a particular size by using CorelDRAW!'s grid and guidelines. The *grid* forces the cursor to snap to a predefined spacing pattern. You also can place *guidelines* at specific points on the page; these guidelines exhibit similar magnetic snap qualities. If you are familiar with Aldus PageMaker, you should find these features similar to PageMaker's Snap To Rulers and Snap To Guidelines options.

Draw's Grid Setup dialog box (see fig. 2.12) controls the horizontal and vertical Grid Frequency and the Grid Origin point. It also enables you to display the grid on the screen. If you have the grid set for a high frequency, the screen display does not show all the grid intersection points unless you magnify the drawing. The closer in you zoom, the more detailed the grid display becomes.

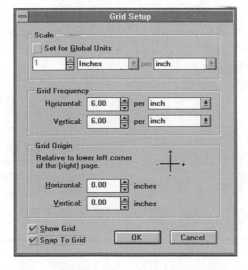

Figure 2.12:
The Grid Setup dialog box.

The variable options provided by the Grid Setup dialog box make setting up such (formerly difficult) tasks as business forms that require 1/10-inch horizontal spacing and 1/6-inch vertical spacing a snap!

Shortcut

Double-click on a ruler to access the Grid Setup dialog box.

The Grid and Guideline functions in CorelDRAW! version 4.0 include layering controls. The grid and guidelines are now placed on their own individual layers. The Layers Roll-Up window provides control over grid and guideline (non-printing) colors. Both the grid and guidelines can be turned on or off through either the Display menu or the Layers Roll-Up window. The Layers function is covered in depth in Chapters 3 and 8.

Begin by setting up a simple grid. You use the guidelines shortly.

Setting Up the Grid

Click on Layout	The Layout menu appears
Click on Grid Setup	The Grid Setup dialog box appears
At Grid Frequency, do the following:	
Adjust the Grid Frequency to 6 per inch	
Click on the Horizontal units *edit box, adjust to* inches	Sets the unit of measurement
Repeat for Vertical units	
Click on Horizontal Grid Frequency, *adjust to* 6.00	Sets the number of grid points per unit
Repeat for Vertical frequency	
Click on Show Grid	Designates that the feature is active. If the item already is checked, do not click on it—you will turn off the feature
Click on Snap to Grid	Designates that the feature is active. If the item already is checked, do not click on it—you will turn off the feature

NOTE

Always set the units before you set the frequency, because Draw automatically adjusts the frequency to the new units.

If you do not happen to be in the Grid Setup dialog box, you can use the Ctrl-Y shortcut to turn on and off Snap to Grid.

Shortcut

Press Ctrl-Y to turn the grid on and off.

Now that you have turned on the grid, take a look at what it does. When the grid is turned on, the cursor snaps to the defined grid intersection points like a magnet snaps to a refrigerator. You can set the Grid Frequency to a maximum of 72 units per inch, conveniently echoing the number of points per inch. Current grid settings are saved with your drawings.

Grid Origin enables you to place the grid's zero point anywhere on your page or pasteboard. You can change this setting with numerical precision by using the Grid Setup dialog box or change it visually by clicking on the ruler intersection point and dragging it to the new origin. You might want to set the zero point at the upper left hand corner of the page, for example.

Aligning Objects to the Grid

For the last series of exercises, set up a coarse grid with six grid lines per inch. This setup translates to one grid line per pica. This size grid helps you develop a simple box kite. You build the box kite at three times its finished size and reduce it later.

Before you start this next section, try drawing a few rectangles with the grid on. Pull the rectangle out to the right, to the left, up, and down. Notice how the grid feature enables you to position your beginning and ending points precisely. It does not let you place a node at anything other than a grid intersection point

After you are comfortable with the way the grid works, start the exercise. Begin by drawing three connected rectangles, as shown in figure 2.13, which you use to form the sides of your box kite. It is important to watch the status line when sizing your rectangles.

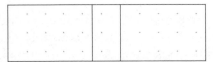

Figure 2.13:
Three connected rectangles.

Building a Box Kite Using the Grid

Click on the Rectangle tool

At the center of the page, do the following:

Drag the mouse down and to the right to form a rectangle	Make the rectangle two inches wide by one inch high
Release mouse button	The status line reads Rectangle on Layer 1

continues

These rectangles form the back of the box kite. Now draw the sides. Notice that you can draw a rectangle to the left or the right, and up or down.

Position the cursor on bottom left node of the rectangle	
Drag the cursor up and to the left to form a new rectangle 1-1/2 inches wide by 1 inch high	Makes a new rectangle
Release the mouse button	The status line reads `Rectangle on Layer 1`
Position the cursor directly on the top right node of the first (largest) rectangle	
Drag the cursor down and to the left to form a new rectangle 1-1/2 inches wide by 1 inch high	
Release the mouse button	The status line reads `Rectangle on Layer 1`

Are you looking at this collection of three connected rectangles and wondering how you are going to turn this into a box kite? This is where you start to have fun.

Using Skew

You are going to use a feature called *Skew* to bend the rectangles into more suitable polygons. When you apply Skew to an object, you impart a leaning look to it. You can use this tilting to create rudimentary cast shadows, or, as in the case of this box kite, a sort of pseudo-perspective.

Skew can be invoked directly from the object. Double-click to display the Rotate/Skew handles. These handles are the same ones you used to turn the Corvette on end in the first chapter—yet another example of CorelDRAW!'s tool-clustering philosophy.

This next step gives your box kite some semblance of perspective.

Skewing the Sides of the Box Kite

Click on the Pick tool

Double-click on the left rectangle	The Rotate/Skew handles appear
Position the cursor on the left vertical two-headed arrow	The cursor becomes a +
Drag the cursor down	The handles are replaced by a skew symbol and a blue dashed skew box. The status line reports on the number of degrees of horizontal skew
Position the cursor for approximately 34 degrees of skew; align the top node with the lower node	
Release the mouse button	The side is skewed
Double-click on the right rectangle	The Rotate/Skew handles appear
Position the cursor on the left vertical two-headed arrow	The cursor becomes a +
Drag the cursor downward	
Position the cursor for 34 degrees of skew	
Release the mouse button	The second side is skewed
Draw another rectangle; connect it to the front edges of the skewed sides (see fig. 2.14)	

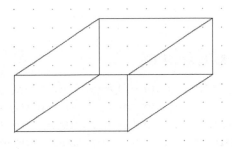

Figure 2.14:

A partially finished box kite.

You can skew any object or piece of text. Like Rotate, you can constrain a skew angle by pressing Ctrl. Be careful not to overdo the skew on typography—just because Draw enables you to make any typeface oblique does not mean that you should.

By now, you should see something beginning to resemble a box kite. With a few more steps, you add the bottom of the kite by duplicating what you have already drawn. Then you build its frame. You use a shortcut that you picked up in the last chapter, Drag-Duplicate, to clone the top of the kite.

Because the grid is still on, you easily can place the duplicate precisely. Remember to press + from the numeric keypad to make a duplicate and leave the original object untouched. Use the status line to place the duplicate three inches below and horizontally centered under the original.

Finishing the Box Kite

Marquee-select the rectangles

*Press + as you drag the rectangles down
3 inches below the originals*

*Draw four rectangles to form the frame; make them
17 inches wide by 4 inches tall*

Marquee-select the box kite

Rotate the box kite to a more realistic angle

Now that you have the kite together, save your drawing if you have not already done so. Remember, the more often you save, the less work you have to redo in the event of a power failure or file mishap.

Pulling in the Guidelines

Earlier, you read a little bit about Draw's guideline feature. Take a moment to draw guidelines to position your artwork on the page. Because Island Printing (Joe DeLook's cousin, actually) usually asks for lots of gripper space and good-sized margins, draw half-inch horizontal and vertical guidelines.

You can lay down guidelines in CorelDRAW! very easily. If you are familiar with Aldus PageMaker, this procedure is old hat. Position your cursor over a ruler (horizontal ruler for horizontal guidelines, vertical ruler for vertical guidelines) click, and drag your guideline into position.

Dragging Guidelines

If the rulers are not showing on your screen, activate them by clicking on
Show **R**ulers on the Display menu.

Position the cursor over the horizontal ruler

Drag the guideline 0.5 inch from the top of the page

Position the cursor over the vertical ruler

Drag the guideline 0.5 inch from the left side of the page

Position the cursor over the vertical ruler

Drag the guideline 0.5 inch from the right side of the page

You easily can tell whether a guideline is in the exact position.
Draw provides a convenient dialog box to handle it (see fig. 2.15).
By double-clicking on a guideline, you display the Guidelines
dialog box, in which you can check a guideline's position and
change it if necessary.

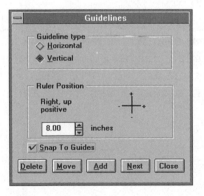

Figure 2.15:
The Guidelines
dialog box.

The Guidelines dialog box enables you to move, add, and delete
guidelines with precision. After the dialog box opens, you can use
the **N**ext button to pop from guideline to guideline. Try changing
the horizontal (gripper) guideline to three-quarters of an inch
(0.75).

In the next section, you use CorelDRAW!'s Group and Copy
functions as you draw the kite's tail.

Shortcut

Double-click on a
guideline to access
the Guidelines dialog
box.

Forming, Copying, and Pasting a Group

As you learn in the next chapter, CorelDRAW!'s Group function is a great time-saver and a vital tool. Although this chapter only touches on the subject here, it is imperative that you understand and use the concepts behind grouping. Make sure that you work through the Deck of Cards exercises in Chapter 3 for a thorough lesson.

Shortcut

Press Ctrl-C (or Ctrl-Ins) to copy to the Clipboard.

Shortcut

Press Ctrl-V (or Shift-Ins) to paste from the Clipboard.

CorelDRAW! implements the standard Microsoft Windows Cut, Copy, and Paste commands. You can access these commands from the Edit menu as well as through keyboard shortcuts.

When you cut or copy an object (or a group of objects), it is held in the Windows Clipboard until it is replaced by the next cut or copied object or until you exit Windows.

The Clipboard can hold only one object or group of objects at a time. When you paste an object from the Clipboard, a copy remains in the Clipboard.

Draw a tail for the box kite. Even though many box kites do not have tails, Katie has assured Joe that any box kite worth its salt can support a long tail. She has even asked for a tail with exactly five segments! You make good use of the Copy and Paste commands as you carry out her orders. Your results should look like figure 2.16.

Figure 2.16:

A box kite with a tail.

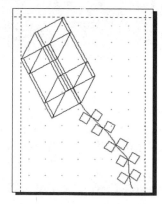

Drawing and Pasting in the Kite's Tail

Click on the Rectangle tool

Draw two squares 0.50" wide

Click on the Pick tool

Click on the first square

Rotate the square 45 degrees

Click on the second square

Rotate the second square 45 degrees

Drag the square so that its leftmost point is touching the rightmost point of its peer. You have drawn the first segment of your kite's tail.

Shift-click on or marquee-select tail segment	The handles encompass both objects, the status line reads 2 objects selected
Click on Arrange	
Click on Group	The status line reads Group of 2 objects
Click on Edit	
Click on Copy	
Click on Edit	
Click on Paste	New group appears on copied group
Drag the new segment into position	The kite tail has two segments
Paste in three more tail segments; drag them into position	
Marquee-select the entire tail	The entire tail is selected
Click on Arrange	
Click on Group	The status line reads Group of 5 objects selected
Drag the tail into position underneath the kite	
Click on Arrange	
Click on Ungroup	
Rotate and place the tail sections as desired	

Now that you have completed the preceding exercises, you should be getting a good feel for using the grid as well as the Rectangle tool. Although the grid is very convenient, it can make things difficult at times. Items drawn without the grid on do not always snap to the grid easily after you enable it.

Shortcut

Press Ctrl-G to group objects. Press Ctrl-U to ungroup objects.

You also can use keyboard shortcuts to group and ungroup objects. To group objects, use Ctrl-G. To ungroup objects, use Ctrl-U.

If, up until now, you have been working with CorelDRAW!'s Wireframe, rather than Full-Color editing mode, turn on the Full-Color mode by pressing Shift-F9.

Working in Wireframe mode speeds up your computer's screen display. It cuts down on the number of computations the processor must perform, and that can make a large difference in the time it takes to display a drawing. On complex projects, work with the wireframes and pop in and out of Full-Color mode only as needed.

Draw also provides a Full-Screen Preview; simply press F9. Chapter 8 gives you a closer look at preview strategies. For now, however, just try switching between Full-Color and Wireframe modes.

Shortcut

Press Shift-F9 to switch between Wireframe and Full-Color editing modes. Press F9 to enable Full-Screen Preview.

Putting Outline and Fill to Work

The Outline and Fill tools affect the way an object appears, rather than its shape. *Outline* refers to the line surrounding an object. You invoke it by clicking on the Outline icon (it looks like an old-fashioned pen nib). *Fill* is just that—a tool for filling, in much the same manner as you might fill a pie crust. Selecting different fills is like choosing different pie fillings. Fill is invoked by clicking on the icon that looks like a paint can.

CorelDRAW! has amazing outline and fill capabilities. The program gives you the power of color, fountain, fractal texture, pattern, and PostScript fills. Although this chapter only touches the surface, later chapters of the book go into depth on the subject. You see the various methods that Draw provides for selecting outlines and fills: fly-out menus, roll-up menus, and the on-screen color palette (at the bottom of the screen). You use only the fly-out menus for the exercises in this chapter.

In the default mode, new objects have an outline of None and a 100-percent black fill, which explains why the box kite in the preview window is black. You can alter the Fill and Outline attributes for objects before you create them by clicking on the Fill or Outline tool while no objects are selected. When you see the New Object Uniform Fill dialog box, shown in figure 2.17, click on OK to change the defaults. Your copy of CorelDRAW! might still be running with the factory defaults, but make sure that you have the same defaults by resetting them now.

Figure 2.17:
Setting new Fill and Outline defaults.

The dialog box offers three options: **G**raphic, **A**rtistic Text, and **P**aragraph Text. In this exercise, you set the default for Graphic.

Setting New Fill and Outline Defaults

With no objects selected, take the following steps:

Click on the Fill tool	The Fill fly-out menu appears
*Click on **B**lack*	A dialog box appears
*Click on **G**raphic*	
Click on OK	The Fill default is reset
Click on the Outline tool	The Outline fly-out menu appears (see fig. 2.18)
*Click on **N**one (X)*	The dialog box appears
*Click on **A**ll Objects*	
Click on OK	The Outline default is reset

You might have noticed that None is denoted by a simple X. The icons can get rather interesting when language is removed! In the next step, you outline every object in your box kite drawing with a hairline. The Hairline icon is unique; it consists of two vertical arrows pointing at a thin rule.

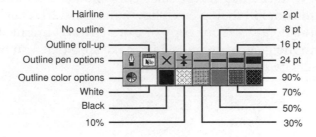

Hairline	2 pt
No outline	8 pt
Outline roll-up	16 pt
Outline pen options	24 pt
Outline color options	90%
White	70%
Black	50%
10%	30%

Changing the Outline

Click on the Pick tool

Click on **E**dit   The Edit menu appears

Click on Select **A**ll   Handles appear around all objects

Click on the Outline tool   The Outline fly-out menu appears

Click on Hairline   All objects have a hairline outline

You probably cannot distinguish the difference (all objects are still black), but the objects now are outlined with a hairline rule. After the next step, you can see the hairline rule. While all objects are still selected, you are going to fill them with white.

After you change the fill to White, the different outline weights become readily visible. Apply the various rule weights to the drawing to get an idea of how they look.

Changing Fills

With all objects still selected, take the following steps:

Click on the Fill tool   The Fill fly-out menu appears
                                             (see fig. 2.19)

Click on White   All objects are filled with white

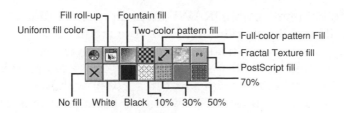

Figure 2.19:
The Fill fly-out menu.

Your full-color screen is starting to look like your wireframe screen—you have a wireframe rendering of a wireframe! Do something about that now.

Deselect the objects by clicking on an empty place. Now you can select individual objects or groups of objects. Then fill the objects with a tint of your choice. The right side of the status line shows each object's fill.

Selectively Changing Fills

Click on a blank area of the screen	Objects are deselected
Marquee-select the top of the box kite	
Click on the Fill tool	The Fill fly-out menu appears
Click on 50% black	The status line shows top of the kite filled with 50-percent gray
Click on the cloud	The cloud is selected
Click on the Fill tool	The Fill fly-out menu appears
Click on 10% black	The status line shows that the cloud is filled with 10-percent gray
Press Ctrl-S	Get in the habit of saving often

Continue with all the individual pieces until you get the kite looking as you like it. Try using lighter or darker fills on the various sides of the box kite. When you are finished, try the different outlines.

As mentioned, CorelDRAW! offers far more outline choices and a wealth of fill possibilities. The fly-out menus take care of your immediate needs. In subsequent chapters, you learn about on-screen palettes, roll-ups, calligraphic pens, fountain fills, pattern fills, and other marvelous features. For now, however, the fly-out menus offer a quick and easy way to build your images.

The kite's frame prints on top of the kite. You can adjust this by arranging the objects in your drawing with the To Front and To Back commands. These commands are located under the Order submenu of the Arrange menu. For more information on arranging your work, refer to the next chapter.

Next, you get a quick preview of the Text tool.

Setting Type with the Text Tool

Typography, the craft of setting type, is made possible through one of CorelDRAW!'s most enabling features, the Text tool. You learn more about typesetting later on. For now, you set up a simple letterhead and incorporate your box kite and cloud drawings. You use Draw's Text tool, which looks like the letter A.

Setting Up a Letterhead

Click on the Text tool	The cursor becomes a +
Click on the top of the page	The Text I bar appears
Type **Katie's Kite Nook**	The type appears
Click on the Pick tool	
Click on Text	The Text menu appears
Click on Text Roll-Up	The Text roll-up menu appears
At the Text Roll-Up menu:	
Click on BernhardFashion BT	
Click on Apply	The text changes to the Bernhard Fashion typeface
Click on the top of the page	The Text I bar appears

Type **14th and the Boulevard, Seaside**	The type appears
Click on the Pick tool	
Click on Text **R**oll-Up	The Text roll-up menu appears
At the Text roll-up menu:	
Select 14 *from the* Size *field*	
Click on BernhardFashion BT	
Click on **A**pply	The text changes to 14 point Bernhard Fashion
Drag Katie's Kite Nook, press + as you drag	To drag duplicate the text
Click on the Text tool	The text I bar appears
Drag over the new Katie's Kite Nook, type **800/555-7777**	
Click on the Pick tool	

You now should have three blocks of text: the words "Katie's Kite Nook" and the phone number, both in 24-point Bernhard Fashion, along with the address in 14-point Bernhard Fashion.

Select and group all objects in the box kite drawing and scale them down proportionally to about a third of their original size. Drag the box kite to the upper left-hand corner of the page.

Use the Pick tool to drag the clouds into position at the top right side of the page. Add guidelines as needed to help you properly align the different design elements, then finish up by dropping the type into position within the clouds. Your finished letterhead should look something like figure 2.20.

Figure 2.20:
The finished letterhead.

If you are not quite happy with the way your clouds look, wait until the next chapter—you refine their shapes soon enough. In any case, reduce the clouds to fit, and give them a hairline outline and a white fill. Congratulations—you have completed your first project! Remember to save your file.

Summary

In this chapter, you learned the basics of CorelDRAW!'s toolbox as you created your first project, a simple letterhead. You used the Pencil tool to draw objects consisting of both straight and curved lines. You saw the difference between an open and a closed path, and you learned how to close an open path. The Ellipse and Rectangle tools were shown to operate in a similar manner. Likewise, the Outline and Fill commands were compared and explained, and Draw's Grid and Guidelines features were explored and implemented. Finally, you finished your first project by adding text and scaling the drawing.

Chapter 3 deals with editing and manipulation. You begin by touching up a few items on your letterhead. The second part of the chapter shows you how to build a set of playing cards to explain the concept of layering and grouping your drawings.

Editing and Manipulating

 his chapter has two basic purposes: to enlighten you on the finer points of nodes and to help you understand the principles of grouping and layering your work. The concepts and practices in this chapter are a bit more complex than what was previously covered, so hang in there. You end up drawing some playing cards, although not as complex as the one shown in figure 3.1.

In Chapter 2, you learned to lay down the lines that you will soon be refining. You might think, "But my drawing is perfect—what do I have to change?" Plenty. If you begin to look at your work with a critical eye (and the Zoom tool), you will soon see the shortcomings of drawing with a mouse. You are going to use CorelDRAW!'s Shape tool to fine-tune your drawing.

As with any creative work, you cannot expect to create excellence in an instant. Inspiration strikes with speed, but true perfection can only be accomplished through diligent attention to detail. Beauty takes time.

Figure 3.1:
The one-eyed jack.

When you were drawing with the Pencil tool, you probably noticed that CorelDRAW! added little boxes to your curved lines. These boxes were positioned at distinct changes in the line's direction. These boxes are what CorelDRAW! refers to as *nodes*, and they are the key to producing high-quality images.

A good portion of this chapter deals with manipulating nodes and their control points. For many people, working with nodes is the most difficult CorelDRAW! function to understand. Although you can create drawings without ever using the Shape tool, its proper use is a clear delineation between the amateur and the expert CorelDRAW! user.

Understanding the concepts behind nodes and control points can help you perform more efficiently and produce work of a higher caliber. You must, therefore, not only sit through this little diatribe but also spend time learning through doing. Consider yourself warned. You might need some practice before you become proficient with the Shape tool.

Just as important as grasping the idea of node manipulation is understanding the concepts behind building your work in a series of logical layers and groups. Building structured pieces is, again, the mark of the journeyman electronic artist. Simply looking good does not cut it; your pieces must be functional.

Again, it is a good idea to remember that you are assembling an electronic collage of shapes. Those shapes are of many different tints, colors, and patterns. They have other shapes—filled with other tints, colors, and patterns—"glued" on their surfaces. Planning the construction of your imagery takes time. The more thought you put into building your collage, the easier it is for you to go back and edit it.

One of the awful truths of commercial art is that the client often asks the artist to alter work that the artist feels is—for all intents and purposes—finished. The artwork could be very difficult, if not impossible, to alter. Conventional artists have been frustrated by this fact for years. Imagine Michelangelo at the Sistine chapel: "It is beautiful, Michelangelo, my son, but maybe the angel should be looking to his left instead of his right, and perhaps you could add a cherub or two in the corner?"

This scenario might have thrown the Old Masters into a fit, but it does illustrate the advantages of creating electronic artwork. Your images are reworkable. You do not have to start a piece over from scratch should your clients decide that they want a different color scheme or an extra angel.

To accommodate changes, however, you must plan for them. You must build your collage in a way that accommodates easy editing. You must be able to edit lines and combine and group objects to make yours a "working" drawing. CorelDRAW! provides the tools. To be effective, you must learn how best to use them.

Drawing with Bézier Curves

CorelDRAW! uses a device called the *Bézier curve* to generate smooth, resolution-independent objects. Bézier curves are produced by a mathematical formula that governs the shape of a line.

Don't worry: you don't have to get out your scientific calculator to complete a drawing—CorelDRAW! does all the math for you.

One Bézier curve requires two nodes, each with its own control point(s), to complete the equation. The node is the hub from which the control points radiate. *Control points* are the mechanisms that govern the trajectory of a line segment. People have described the on-screen appearance of a node and its control points as looking "like a box with two knitting needles sticking out of it," a "bug with antennae," or even "the world's smallest voodoo doll." The last description echoes the way you might feel about nodes and control points after you spend a frustrating session wrestling with them.

Segments are the lines between the nodes. They form the edges of objects and can be curved or straight. A curved segment requires a control point at each end. Straight lines, however, have no control points. A node has a corresponding control point for each curved segment that radiates from it.

If a node is the first node of an open path, it can have only one control point. If it looks as if it has more, you probably have two selected nodes sitting on top of each other.

You can affect the shape of a line segment in four basic ways without adding a node. The first method is to move the node. Repositioning the node affects the position at which the control points do their work. Because a line segment is governed by the nodes at either end, as one node is moved, it affects the relationship between both nodes. When you move a node, the shape of the line segments on both sides of that node is altered.

If you do not want to move the node, you have three alternatives. The second approach is to change the node type. As you soon see, different node types enable you to create curved or straight line segments. You specify the node type by using the Node roll-up menu. CorelDRAW! 4.0 introduced a third way to change a line's shape. You now can use the Shape tool to click and drag on the line itself. This new method feels like you are tugging on a garden hose; the nodes remain anchored, but the line segment moves freely.

The fourth and final method of altering the shape of a line segment is through control-point positioning. This process is the most involved of the three, and it is the one in which you do the heaviest tweaking. When you reposition a node's control points, you change the mathematical equation that defines the corresponding line segment. The power of Bézier curves lies in numbers. One Bézier curve is not much use; linking Bézier curves to form paths fully exploits their potential.

Of course, you always can add a new node to an existing line segment. Adding a new node splits one line segment into two and enables you to make radical changes to that line.

At this point, review the various methods for drawing lines. Chapter 2 covered these techniques in depth, so if you have any questions beyond that which is reviewed here, check back a few pages.

Here are a few basics:

- Click for single straight lines

- Double-click for connected straight lines

- Hold the Ctrl key to constrain straight lines to 15-degree increments (default setting)

- When drawing curved lines, remember to hold down the left mouse button until you are finished drawing the line

- If you want to erase a portion of a curved line (while drawing), hold down the Shift key and "back over" the offending portion of the line

Selecting Node Types

CorelDRAW! supports three types of curved nodes: smooth, symmetrical, and cusp. When you execute a freehand drawing or import a traced object, CorelDRAW! (or CorelTRACE!) takes its best guess at which type of node is needed. On many occasions, the program does not make the right choice. (What do you want, a program that does all the work for you?) Because you are the artist, you should make the ultimate decision. Take the information that the program gives you and alter it as you see fit.

Drawing Some Curves

Before you get into a formal explanation of the different node types, try drawing some curves. Attempt to draw an octopus—an appropriately curved undersea creature. Try working in Wireframe mode to get a better view of the nodes' control points. To switch between Full-Color and Wireframe modes, press Shift-F9.

You do not need a prompted exercise; just click on the Pencil tool and start drawing. It will probably take a few tries to draw an octopus that you are almost happy with. Do not worry about making it perfect the first time out. You can go back in later to alter the curves and improve its appearance.

After you have drawn a nice-looking cephalopod, as shown in figure 3.2, select it with the Shape tool. Notice that your octopus has many nodes spread along the path that outlines its body. These nodes are not suckers or even hooks; they are a means for you to change the shape of your drawing.

Figure 3.2:

An octopus.

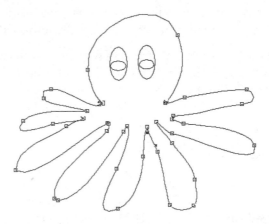

Select a node and try dragging it around. Watch what happens to the curves as you move the node. The node's control points become active after the node is selected. The control points are the squares at the ends of the dashed lines. Try pulling on the different control points and take note of the way the control points alter the shape of the line.

As you select different nodes, you see that they do not all act the same. Also notice that a selected node's type appears in the status line. The next sections discuss CorelDRAW!'s assortment of curved and line nodes.

Smooth Nodes

In a *smooth* node, both of the control points and the node itself are in a straight line (see fig. 3.3). Pull up on one node, and the other goes down. The control points and the node are linearly linked. Think of a spinning propeller on a seaplane. The blades always spin in the same direction, be it clockwise or counterclockwise. Unlike a propeller, however, the control points in a smooth node do not have to be the same distance from the node. The farther away a control point is from the node, the larger the curve.

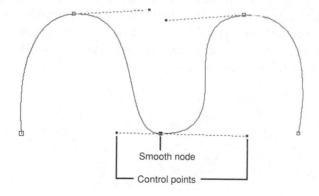

Smooth node

Control points

Figure 3.3:
A smooth node.

Symmetrical Nodes

The *symmetrical* node takes the smooth node's propeller analogy a bit further. Not only are the control points and node linearly linked, the control points are of equal distance from the node. Moving one control point affects the other control point, resulting in exactly the same curve on each side of the node.

Symmetrical nodes are, in effect, smooth nodes with equidistant control points (see fig. 3.4).

Figure 3.4:

A symmetrical node.

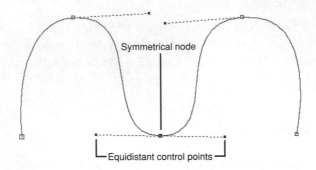

Cusp Nodes

Cusp nodes are very different from smooth and symmetrical nodes. In a *cusp* node, the control points operate independently of each other (see fig. 3.5). One side of the curve can be affected without altering the other side. A cusp node is used where there is a radical change in direction or a severe angle. You can compare cusp-node control points to a set of rabbit-ear antennas on a television set. To pick up different stations, you adjust each antenna individually. To manipulate a curve, you move the control point corresponding to that curve.

Figure 3.5:

A cusp node.

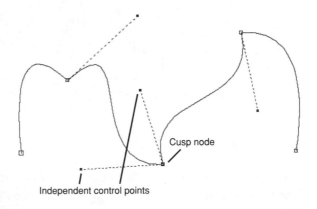

Line Nodes

Line nodes are not as flexible as curve nodes. Where a line meets a line, you must have a cusp node. Two straight lines cannot be connected with a smooth node or a symmetrical node. On the other hand, when a line meets a curve, you can have either a cusp or a smooth node (see fig. 3.6). Because they do not curve, straight line segments do not have control points. Objects often are made up of both curved and straight line segments. A node with a straight line segment on one side and a curved line segment on the other has only one control point.

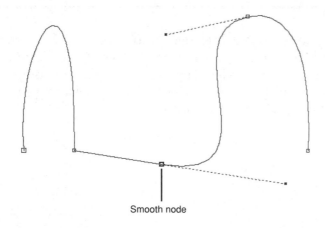

Smooth node

Figure 3.6:

A smooth node where a line meets a curve.

Now it is time to put you to work. Remember the letterhead you completed in the last chapter? You are going to pull out that drawing and clean up the clouds using the Shape tool.

If you have the octopus drawing or another unsaved file on the screen when you attempt to open BOXKITE.CDR, the program asks whether you want to save the file. Respond to this and to the following dialog boxes accordingly. If you prefer, save the file as OCTOPUS.CDR.

Editing Nodes

Click on **F**ile	The File menu appears
Click on **O**pen	The Open File dialog box appears
Click on BOXKITE.CDR	Selects the letterhead file from Chapter 2
Click on OK	The letterhead appears
Click on the Zoom tool	The Zoom fly-out menu appears
Click on the + tool	
Marquee-select the cloud	Zooms in on the cloud
Click on the Shape tool	The cursor becomes the Shape tool
Click on the cloud	The cloud's nodes appear (see fig. 3.7)

According to the status line, the cloud in figure 3.7 has 24 nodes—far more than necessary for this basic object. Your cloud can have many more (or less) nodes. The first thing you are going to do is remove some of the excess nodes by simply selecting each node and deleting it with the Del key.

Figure 3.7:

A cloud with the nodes showing.

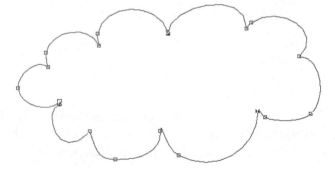

Before you continue, however, save this as a new file by clicking on Save **A**s (from the **F**ile menu). Name the file BOXKITE2. This action prevents you from overwriting the original version.

If you marquee-select your cloud, notice that curved nodes are denoted by small black boxes. Line nodes show as larger outlined boxes. The first node of a closed curve is always a large, black box when selected. Your cloud drawing should consist of mostly curved nodes. Go in and prune a few extra nodes. As you do, watch the status line; it reads Selected node: Curve Cusp, or Smooth or Symmetrical, depending on what type of node is selected.

Removing an Extra Node

Click on File	
Click on Save As	
Type BOXKITE2	
Click on OK	
Click on an extra node	The node turns black
Press Del	The node is deleted

You have two other ways to delete a node. After you select a node, you can click on Delete from the Edit menu or from the Node Edit roll-up menu to accomplish the same thing. You also can add nodes—that is covered in the next section.

CorelDRAW! enables you to work with more than one node at a time. Go back in and remove a pair of nodes by selecting them with a marquee, and then deleting them. Another way to select more than one node at a time is to hold down Shift as you click on the nodes you want to select.

After you finish selecting and deleting nodes and you have grown tired of cloud pruning, move on to working with (rather than simply deleting) the remaining nodes.

Begin by selecting a node. Click and drag that node to a new location. Watch how the node's control point (or points) move with the node. The curves change, governed by the relationship between neighboring nodes.

When you click on a node, the control points for that point—as well as the relevant control points of all related nodes—become active. These "knitting needles" bend and flex their respective curve segments according to the conventions of their node type.

Now change a curve by dragging the curve. This latest editing method is a quick and easy way to reach outline editing nirvana.

TIP

If a line segment goes whacko after you delete a node, fear not; a quick fix is available. Select the wayward line, then click on To **L**ine on the Node Edit roll-up; this changes the whacko curve into a straight line. Click on the (now straight) line again, and click on **T**o Curve. Finally, tweak the control points until the curve is back in shape.

As you drag the line around, watch the control points reposition themselves. Try clicking at different locations on the line. Notice how the selected location affects the way the curve is altered.

Before you get into a prompted exercise, you should begin to get the feel of nodes and control points. Just tweak those nodes until it seems familiar. Push and pull on the different control points. Tug on the curves like you are bringing in the lines.

As you get further and further into tweaking your cloud, you begin to understand the differences between the types of nodes. You see that the control points in a cusp curve operate independently of each other. And you see the similarity and differences between smooth and symmetrical curves.

Adding Nodes to an Object

In this next exercise, you build a cloud from scratch. Start by drawing an ellipse and use Convert To Curves to enable access to the object. Then, use Add (+) from the Node Edit menu to add four extra points.

CorelDRAW! does not enable you to manipulate the nodes in an ellipse, rectangle, or text without first using Convert To Curves. If you try to use the Shape tool on a "normal" ellipse or circle, CorelDRAW! turns the object into an arc or pie wedge (this technique is covered in Chapter 6). Using the Shape tool on a rectangle renders a rounded-corner rectangle (which you learn more about later in this chapter).

After an object has been converted to curves, you can perform some amazing maneuvers. By the time you finish with this exercise, you have more than a hint of what the Convert To Curves command enables you to do.

To get started, set up your grid so that there are six lines per inch. Then use this setup to build some perfectly cartoony clouds. Convert To Curves adds three nodes to the oval (it starts with one). If you click on each node, you find that they are all symmetrical curves.

Turning the Ellipse into a Cloud

Click on **L**ayout

Click on Gr**i**d Setup

Set the **H**orizontal *and* **V**ertical *Grid*
Frequency prompts to 6.00
per inch

Make sure that **Sn**ap *to Grid is selected*

Click on OK

Click on the Ellipse tool

Draw an oval   Make it 1 1/2 inches high by
                                                5 1/2 inches wide

Click on **A**rrange   The Arrange menu appears

Click on Con**v**ert To Curves   Three nodes are added to the
                                                oval (see fig. 3.8)

Click on the Shape tool

Marquee-select all four nodes

Double-click on a node   The Node Edit roll-up menu
                                                appears

Click on +   Four new nodes are added
                                                (see fig. 3.9)

At the Node Edit roll-up menu, click on **C**usp   All nodes are now cusp nodes

Click on the screen   The cloud is deselected

Click on a node   The node is selected

Pull control points from object   Curves grow out from
at a 90-degree angle   the object

Continue pulling out control points   A cloud forms (see fig. 3.10)

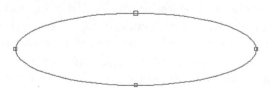

Figure 3.8:

An oval with four
nodes.

Figure 3.9:

An oval with eight nodes.

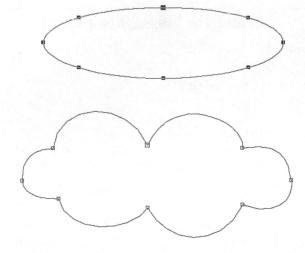

Figure 3.10:

The finished cloud.

The Node Edit roll-up menu provides a simple way to change node types. To initially display the menu, double-click on a selected node (the roll-up remains on the screen until you put it away). In this roll-up menu, you can choose line or curve nodes—the latter in cusp, smooth, or symmetrical variations. The menu also enables you to break or join a path and add or delete a node.

As you have seen, cusp nodes enable the severe change in direction needed to render this object. See what happens when you change all the nodes to smooth or symmetrical curves. Remember, you can immediately undo any wayward actions with Ctrl-Z or Alt-Backspace.

CorelDRAW! 4.0 offers other significantly enhanced node-editing features over previous versions. You now can rotate, skew, scale, and stretch selected curve segments. In addition, you can edit nodes in either Standard or Elastic mode. When you use Elastic mode, you notice a subtle difference in the way that groups of nodes react as you move them around (think of a rubber band). In Standard mode, all the nodes move in locked-in harmony. In Elastic mode, however, the nodes move in springy relation to the node you are dragging.

If the new cloud looks any better than what you already have, save it. Use the Scale function to bring it down to the correct size for your drawing. If the new cloud looks worse than what you already have, go ahead and delete it.

Nodes and Tracing

Generally speaking, you should use as few nodes in your objects as possible. The more nodes in an object, the larger your files. With the increase in file size also comes a loss of speed, both in screen display and in printing time. Less is more. An autotraced or freehand-rendered image often includes far more nodes than necessary to portray the object accurately. If you notice an excessive amount of jaggedness, you probably have a bunch of untweaked cusp nodes. For this reason, use cusp nodes sparingly—only where you must. The time you ultimately save is your own.

CorelDRAW! 4.0 also introduced a fabulous node editing time-saver: Auto-Reduce. Like a diet plan that helps you shed unwanted pounds, Auto-Reduce kills off needless nodes with just one click. To Auto-Reduce, use the Shape tool to select the object (or portion of an object) that you want to lean down. Then press the Auto-Reduce button on the Node Edit roll-up menu. Excess nodes are instantly removed. It's like eating a huge lobster dinner (with gobs of drawn butter, of course) and waking up the next morning to find that you have actually lost five pounds!

Node Pointers

Here are a few other things you should know about nodes.

- When moving a node or control point, you can constrain movement by using the grid. In addition, holding down Ctrl while moving a node or control point restricts the action to either vertical or horizontal movement.

- You easily can add a node at a specific point. With the Shape tool, click at the spot you want to add the new node. At the Node Edit roll-up menu, simply click on +. A node is added at the exact coordinates at which you clicked. To add nodes with pinpoint precision, remember to use Draw's Snap To Guidelines. Drag out a set of horizontal and vertical guidelines, adjust them for dead-on accuracy, and go! Take the time to try this technique on one of your clouds.

- If a control point is hidden beneath a node, you can easily dig it out. First, make sure that the node is deselected. Press and hold Shift, then drag the control point from underneath the node.

Do not worry if you still feel uncomfortable with nodes. It takes time. The best advice is practice, practice, practice. After you are finished with your node tweaking, remember to save your work. In the next section, you start with a clean screen. As you get further along in the book, you see how important it is to create lean, mean objects with a minimum of nodes. An extra node is a wasted node.

Drawing in Bézier Curve Mode

CorelDRAW! enables you to draw directly in Bézier curve mode. This might seem like torture for some, but others welcome the extreme precision and flexibility this feature affords.

Learning to draw in Bézier mode helps you to understand the way the curves function. No substitute for practice exists when it comes to mastering the skill of working with Bézier curves. Practice is essential if you want to be successful with object-oriented graphics programs like CorelDRAW!, Adobe Illustrator, or Aldus Freehand.

To work in Bézier mode rather than in Freehand mode, you select a variant of the Pencil tool. When you click on the Pencil tool, hold down the left mouse button and drag downward and to the right to access the Pencil fly-out menu. Click on the second icon to get into Bézier mode.

When you click on the Pencil tool, the status line reports Drawing in Bézier Mode.... When you draw straight lines in Bézier mode, you might not notice any differences between it and Freehand modes. Drawing curves in Bézier mode, however, is quite different from drawing curves in Freehand mode.

When drawing curves, consider how the curve exits and enters its starting and ending nodes (respectively). Think of threading a line through a series of fish hooks. The line segments form your fishing line and the nodes are the hooks. The direction you pull the line through the hook affects the first half of the arc. Likewise, the direction you thread the line into the next hook (node) affects the second half of the arc. Figure 3.11 shows a variety of Bézier curves.

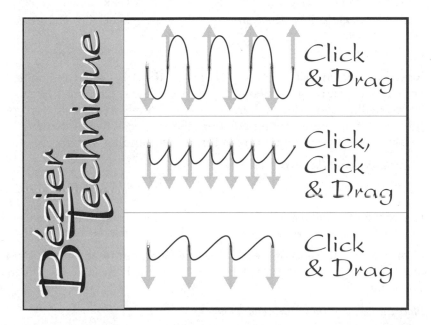

Figure 3.11:
Point and shoot Béziers.

In practice, it goes something like this: if you click-and-drag away from the first node in one direction, then click-and-drag (placing the second node) in the opposite direction, you draw a one-bump curve. However, if you click-and-drag away from the first node in one direction, then click-and-drag (placing the second node) in the same direction, you draw a two-bump curve.

Try working in Bézier mode. Start by laying down a few straight lines to form a triangle. After you have that down, move on to the curves. For the straight lines, you can turn on the grid for precision, but you may want to turn it off when you draw your curves.

Drawing in Bézier Mode

First, draw a triangle with straight lines:

Click on the Pencil tool, drag down and to the right	The Pencil fly-out menu appears
Click on the Bézier icon	The cursor becomes a +
Click on the page	The first node is placed
Click two inches to the right of first node	A two-inch line is drawn
Click one inch to the left and one inch above second node	A one-inch line is drawn
Click on the first node	A triangle is formed

Now try some curves. When you first click, the curve's starting node appears. As you drag, two control points pull away from the node in opposite directions. Remember: the curve is drawn in the direction you pull away from the starting node until the apogee, where it then is drawn in the direction you thread through the ending node.

Place the cursor at the curve's starting point

Click and drag down	Node and control points appear
Release the mouse button	Node and control points remain on-screen

Now, position the end of the curve segment, and draw the curve. Draw a one-bump curve to begin. Watch the way in which the curve is altered as you drag.

Place the cursor at the curve's ending point

Click and drag upward	The end node, control points, and line segment appear
Release the mouse button	A line segment is drawn, and the end node and control points remain on-screen

Draw a few more connected curves. Then try pulling in the same direction for both the starting and ending nodes. You see the curves change into two-bump segments.

To draw cusp nodes, you need a little more patience and a bit more skill. The technique here consists of a double-click on each end node and a control-point position for each segment. Double-click, position; double-click, position; double-click, position—not quite as tough as learning to waltz in junior high! Try drawing a few clouds this way. Give yourself plenty of time—soon you will be laying down Béziers with precision!

At this point, save your drawing and open a new file.

Shortcut

To begin drawing a new object, press the spacebar twice. (This shortcut works in Freehand or Bézier modes.) This deselects any active objects or nodes and reselects the Pencil tool.

Planning a Layering Strategy

Layering and arranging your work is like shuffling a deck of cards. You can stack the deck in your favor by assembling your image so that it can be easily manipulated.

Except for the most rudimentary drawings, all your drawings should contain groups. Only the most quick-and-dirty scribbles, with a minimum of objects, should not be grouped.

Complex work, however, requires careful planning and execution. Thankfully, CorelDRAW! has a sophisticated layering function. In addition to layer control, Draw can arrange the order of objects through the use of five basic commands: To Front, To Back, Forward One, Back One, and Reverse Order. This command set works well, especially when used in conjunction with layer control.

You can extend the versatility of these commands by using two other commands from the <u>A</u>rrange menu: <u>G</u>roup and <u>C</u>ombine.

By building groups of objects, you take the first step toward forming an effective layering strategy. A complex work should not consist of hundreds of individual objects. It should be broken down into as few groups/layers as practical.

If you do not arrange your work properly, you will spend far too much time reworking the composition when the time comes to make changes. And you *will* make changes, like it or not.

Although it can take more time initially, grouping and layering saves time in the long run. Similar objects should be strategically combined to take advantage of like features, such as outline and fill. Likewise, objects or combined objects should be arranged into layer-specific groups.

The spots on a leopard and the stripes on a zebra are excellent examples of objects that might be grouped, if not combined. If they are exactly alike and on the same layer, combine them. If they are all on the same layer, but not necessarily alike, group them. You can group combined objects with other objects. You cannot, however, combine objects and maintain individual attributes.

As you get further on in the book, you delve into the subject of layering and grouping in depth. In the next exercise, you see that with strategic grouping, you can rearrange your drawings at will.

A Lonely Saturday Night at DeLook Design

What is Joe DeLook doing? It is Saturday night, and he is still sitting at his desk, working with CorelDRAW! That is what owning your own business will do for you. Joe would rather be with his buddies in the back room of the Tiki Bar for the regular Saturday night poker game. He would even settle for playing blackjack in Atlantic City and donating his money to Donald Trump. But here he is.

Joe has cards on his mind. He has promised himself that he will only work for an hour or so before he cuts out. Determined though he is, Joe is itching to lose some money to his pals. He cannot stop thinking about cards.

Arranging Objects without Using Layer Control

Building a set of cards and shuffling the deck goes a long way toward illustrating the concept of grouping and layering your work. In this exercise, you create a few playing cards to learn to arrange objects without using layer control.

To make your computer respond faster, make sure that you are in
Wireframe mode. You turn full-color mode back on again at the
end of this chapter for a quick shuffle of the deck.

Drawing a Card

Click on **L**ayout	The Layout menu appears
Click on Gr**i**d Setup	The Grid Parameters menu appears
Set the **H**orizontal *and* **V**ertical *Grid Frequency prompts to 6.00 per inch*	
Make sure that **S**nap *to Grid is checked*	
Click on OK	
Click on the Rectangle tool	The cursor becomes a +
Click and drag a box. Make the box 2 1/2 inches wide by 3 1/2 inches high	The Rectangle tool snaps to the grid
Release the mouse button	A rectangle is drawn
Click on the Fill tool	The Fill fly-out menu appears
Click on White	The rectangle is filled with white
Click on the Outline tool	The Outline fly-out menu appears
Click on 2 point rule	The rectangle is outlined with a two-point rule. You cannot see this change until you print or preview

Rounding Corners

You now have a white rectangle outlined with a two-point rule
that is approximately the same size as a playing card (see fig.
3.12). Although it might be the same size and shape as a playing
card, you still need to make one little adjustment: you must round
the corners.

Figure 3.12:

The square-corner playing card.

This modification is easily accomplished by using the Shape tool. Earlier in the chapter, you manipulated the nodes and control points in your cloud drawings using the same tool. When you use the Shape tool on a rectangle, it behaves quite differently.

Rectangles are constructed in a way that enables you to round corners without altering the overall dimensions. This feature prevents you from radically messing up your original object. Using the following procedure, you cannot pull any of the points off their original positions. When you click on a rectangle using the Shape tool, the only thing that the tool enables you to do is round the corners.

As you begin, notice that the status line reads `Rectangle: corner radius: 0.00` inches. As you drag, the corners become rounded, and the status line reflects the corner radius. Change the corner radius to 0.14 inches.

Cutting the Corners

Click on the Shape tool	The cursor becomes an arrow
Click on the rectangle	The rectangle is selected
Click on the top left node	The top left node is selected
Drag the selected node to the right	The second set of nodes appears
When the radius is 0.14 inches, release the mouse button	The rectangle now has 0.14-inch radius rounded corners (see fig. 3.13)

Figure 3.13:
A rounded-corner playing card.

As you were dragging the corners around, you probably noticed that they work in only one direction. If you pull away from the object, rather than toward the center, the corners of the rectangle return to 90-degree angles.

The Shape tool also works on ellipses. If you need to draw perfect arcs or pie wedges, using the Shape tool on an ellipse is the slickest way to go. This tool can be extremely valuable for building pie charts, as you learn in Chapter 6.

Setting Special Characters

Now that you have drawn the card, you need to place some suits and numbers on it. Corel has conveniently included a number of different fonts filled with special characters in the font load that comes with the program. It also has provided many symbols in the fonts that you will want to use from time to time. These symbols include stars, arrows, boxes, and musical symbols, to name a few.

Right now, you are building playing cards. Consequently, you need symbols for the four different suits: clubs, diamonds, hearts, and spades. You can find these symbols in two of the fonts: Dixieland or Greek/Math. You use the Dixieland characters for this project.

To use these special characters, you must specify Dixieland in the Type dialog box and use a special keyboard sequence to access the character. This procedure is necessary for a simple reason: there are more characters in a font than can be directly accessed from the keyboard's standard keys. Use your Alt key and your keyboard's numeric keypad to access the special character sets, using the sequences shown in table 3.1. Make sure that Num Lock is on. This procedure works only with the numeric keypad; using the top row of number keys yields no result.

Table 3.1
Dixieland Special-Character Entry Sequences

Special Character	Keyboard Sequence
Club	Alt-0168
Diamond	Alt-0169
Heart	Alt-0170
Spade	Alt-0171

Until you select the correct font, the symbol portrayed does not necessarily match the symbol you are requesting. Do not worry. After you select the proper font, the correct symbol appears. Follow the directions in the next exercise carefully and you should have no problems. You begin with an easy card: the Ace of Spades.

Drawing the Ace of Spades

Click on the Text tool	The + appears
Click inside the card	The Text I bar appears
Hold down Alt and type **0171**	The special character appears
Click on Te<u>x</u>t	The Text menu appears
Click on Edit Te<u>x</u>t	The Artistic Text dialog box appears
Scroll down and click on Dixieland	Dixieland is now the specified typeface
In the Point Size window, enter **144**	144-point type is specified (see fig. 3.14)
Click on OK	A 144-point spade is drawn

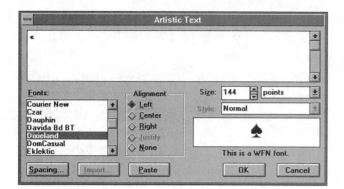

Figure 3.14:
The Artistic Text dialog box.

You might have noticed that the character that originally appeared in the text-editing window was not the spade symbol. After you changed the font to Dixieland, however, the character appeared as it should. And after the character was placed on the page, everything looked fine. If you use many special characters, you will eventually become accustomed to this way of "typing" a character. You also might have noticed the little box to the left of the spade—that is the character's node. As you will see in the next chapter, character nodes are invaluable tools for controlling inter-character spacing (kerning) and baseline alignment.

CorelDRAW! version 4.0 includes an extensive symbol library, apart from the special-character fonts. You use these symbol libraries in a different manner than the special-character fonts, although you access both with the Text tool. The symbol libraries are covered in Chapter 4. The Windows Character Map utility is a great convenience for setting special characters. If you want, flip forward to Appendix A for more information on Character Map.

Using Align

Now that you have a big symbol on your card, center it. Rather than eyeballing it, use the Align command. You find that Align is an invaluable tool for positioning objects relative to each other.

In this instance, you center the big spade, both horizontally and vertically, on the card.

Aligning the Spade

Click on the Pick tool	
Marquee-select the card and the spade	Draws a blue dashed box
Release the mouse button	The status line reads `2 objects selected`
Click on **A**rrange	The Arrange menu appears
Click on **A**lign	The Align dialog box appears (see fig. 3.15)
Click on Horizontally **C**enter	
Click on Vertically C**e**nter	
Click on OK	The spade is horizontally and vertically centered within the card (see fig. 3.16)

Figure 3.15:

The Align dialog box.

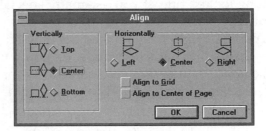

Figure 3.16:

The centered spade.

Shortcut

Press Ctrl-A to get to the Align menu.

The Align command has a few characteristics that you should be aware of. When aligning two or more objects to the left, right, top, or bottom, Draw aligns all objects to the last object selected. The last object selected does not move. When marquee-selecting objects, Draw aligns the selected objects to the first object drawn. These differences can be confusing. You might find it easier to Shift-click on the items you want to align.

The Align dialog box also provides the options of Align to Grid or Align to Center of Page. If you want to use these options, you must select them before you set horizontal or vertical alignment.

Soon, you use the Align command again. The next time, however, you only need to worry about horizontal centering. Before you center anything else, however, you need to place the objects that you will be centering.

Scaling with Leave Original

Instead of using the procedure for inserting special characters again, you are going to repeat a technique you tried briefly in Chapter 1: creating a new, smaller spade while leaving the old one in place. You do this by pressing and releasing the + key on the numeric keypad as you use the scale function. The + tells CorelDRAW! to leave the original alone and to create a new object.

Remember that, alternatively, you can click the right mouse button to leave an original.

As you perform this next maneuver, watch the status line. You want to scale down to approximately 43 percent of original size. When you release the left mouse button, a new shrunken spade is drawn, and the original spade remains unscathed.

Using Scale with Leave Original

Click on the spade	The spade is selected
Position the cursor over the bottom right handle	The cursor becomes a +
Press + and drag toward the spade's upper left corner	Leaves original (see fig. 3.17)

continued

Release the mouse button when status line reads 43%

A new shrunken spade appears

Drag the spade to the upper left corner of the card

Figure 3.17:

The Scale/Leave Original function in action.

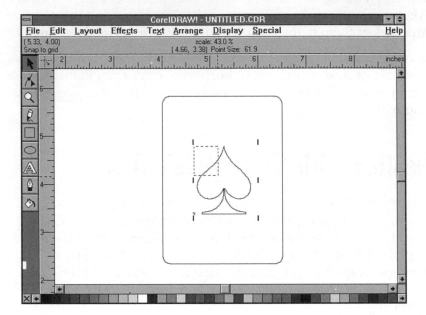

You can use other methods to accomplish the function you just performed. The first way is to duplicate the object and scale the duplicate. This procedure takes two steps and can be a waste of time. But your time is your own, and you can waste it if you want to.

The second method for simultaneous duplicating and scaling is done by using the Effects menu. Although it also can take more time, the Effects menu offers a distinct advantage to eyeballing your scales. The Effects menu enables you to access the Rotate & Skew and Stretch & Mirror dialog boxes (see fig. 3.18). These dialog boxes enable you to leave the original behind while creating a new object. More importantly, through these dialog boxes, you can input precise numbers for your rotations, skews, stretch/ scales, and mirrors. Use the dialog boxes when creating a scale that needs to be "right on the money."

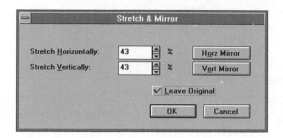

Figure 3.18:
The Stretch & Mirror
dialog box.

Now that you have a little spade, drop in an A for Ace. Then align the two objects horizontally and group them. This procedure is another quick and easy one.

As you work through the following exercise, notice that the Text tool "remembers" its last settings. You go in and alter the type specifications after the character is on the page.

A Is for Ace

Click on the Text tool	The + appears
Click on the card	The Text I bar appear
Type **A**	
Click on Te**x**t	The Text menu appears
Click on Edit Te**x**t	The Artistic Text dialog box appears
Scroll down and click on Davida Bd BT	Davida Bold is now the specified typeface
In the Point Size window, enter **48**	48-point type is specified (refer back to fig. 3.14)
Click on OK	A 48-point A is drawn
Click on the Pick tool	
Drag the A above the small spade	
Shift-click on the small spade	The status line reads `2 objects selected`
Click on **A**rrange	The Arrange menu appears
Click on **A**lign	The Align menu appears
Click on Horizontally **C**enter	

continued

Click on OK	The small spade and the A are horizontally aligned with each other
Drag the A and the small spade into position at the card's upper left corner	
Click on **A**rrange	The **A**rrange menu appears
Click on **G**roup	The status line reads `Group of 2 objects on Layer 1`

The card is really starting to look like the Ace of Spades! With a few more steps, this card will be complete. The next procedure is similar to the Scale/Leave Original that you just completed.

Using Stretch & Mirror

Shortcut

Press Alt-F9 to get to the Stretch & Mirror dialog box.

In the next sequence, you use Stretch & Mirror with Leave Original to create the upside-down version of the symbols for the bottom of the card. To perform this maneuver, you access the Stretch & Mirror dialog box from the Effe**c**ts menu.

Creating an Upside-Down Duplicate

Click on the A and the spade group	The status line reads `Group of 2 objects`
Click on Effe**c**ts	The Effects menu appears
Click on **S**tretch & Mirror	The Stretch & Mirror dialog box appears (refer to fig. 3.18)
Click on H**o**rz Mirror	
Click on V**e**rt Mirror	
Click on **L**eave Original	
Click on OK	A new A and spade are drawn upside-down. The original pair remains (see fig. 3.19)
Drag the new pair to the card's lower right corner	

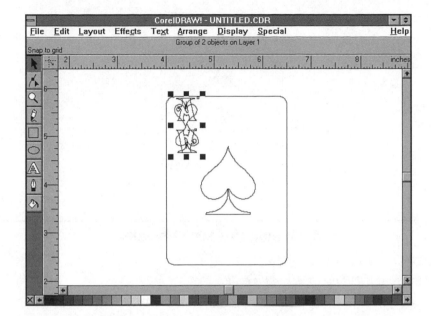

Figure 3.19:
A horizontal/vertical mirrored duplicate.

Because of the magnetic pull of the grid, you might not be able to position this second set of symbols exactly. You can wing it, and turn off the grid. This point is where the good old art of eyeballing comes into play. Press Ctrl-Y, zoom way in on the card, and place the symbols by eye.

On the other hand, you might want to increase the grid frequency if you are more comfortable with the grid on. Start by doubling the grid frequency to 12 units per inch. This setting might help you to line up the symbols with a minimum of hassles. The grid allows up to a maximum of 72 units per inch.

After you have the Ace of Spades looking the way it should, arrange all the symbols into one group. The results should look like figure 3.20.

Figure 3.20

The completed Ace of spaces.

Grouping the Ace of Spades

Click on the Pick tool

Marquee-select all the objects in the card

Release the mouse button　　　　The status line reads
　　　　　　　　　　　　　　　　`4 objects selected`

Click on **A**rrange　　　　　　　The Arrange menu appears

Click on **G**roup　　　　　　　　The status line reads `Group`
　　　　　　　　　　　　　　　　`of 4 objects`

Shortcut

Press Ctrl-G to group selected objects.

The Ace of Spades is now one group. You can move it around, rotate it, duplicate it, and generally perform any function you want. Every item in the group moves in concert.

Setting Up and Using Duplicate

Copy the Ace of Spades and make a second card, the Three of Clubs. Begin by using the Duplicate command. Then you alter the new card after you ungroup the objects. Grouped objects cannot be individually altered, so they have to be ungrouped.

Duplicate works in a similar fashion to Copy and Paste, but it does so in a more direct manner. Instead of being a two-step operation, like Copy and Paste, Duplicate works in one step.

You can use Duplicate to create step-and-repeats. It is great for setting up small labels for gang printing. Unfortunately, the maximum distance you can step is limited to two inches. This makes the feature unusable when stepping larger images, such as business cards; in these cases, you want to use either the Move command or a Drag/Leave Original/Repeat approach.

Before you use Duplicate, check out the Preferences dialog box. Among other things, the Preferences dialog box controls where CorelDRAW! places a duplicate. You can access the Preferences dialog box by using the Special menu.

In the next sequence, set up the Preferences dialog box (see fig. 3.21) to place duplicates 12 picas (2 inches) from the left side of the original objects. This procedure might seem confusing, but it ensures that the duplicated objects are aligned to the grid.

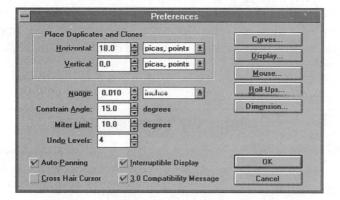

Shortcut

Press Ctrl-D to duplicate objects. Press **+** to place a duplicate on top of a selected object.

Figure 3.21:

The Preferences dialog box.

Note that Duplicate works differently than simply pressing the + key. When you press **+**, a duplicate object (or objects) always is placed directly *on top of* the selected object. By using the Duplicate command, you have control over the placement of the duplicate(s).

Setting Up the Duplicate Preferences

Click on **S**pecial	The Special menu appears
Click on Pr**e**ferences	The Preferences dialog box appears (see fig. 3.21)

continued

Set Place Duplicate **H**orizontal *to* 12,0
picas, points; *set* Place Duplicate **V**ertical
to 0,0 picas, points
Click on OK

Notice that the Preferences dialog box also includes settings for curves, display, and a host of other selections. These settings do not apply in the present exercise, but you now know where to find them.

Shortcut

Press Ctrl-T to call the Edit Text dialog box.

The next step is to duplicate the Ace of spades card and turn it into the Three of Clubs. Use the Text tool to alter the text that has already been set. CorelDRAW! version 3.0 first introduced on-screen text-editing capabilities. In previous versions of Draw, you had to access the Edit Text dialog box to make any text changes. Now, to alter a piece of type already on the screen, all you have to do is click on the Text tool and click and drag over the text you want to edit.

Creating the Three of Clubs

Click on the Ace of Spades	The Ace of Spades is selected
Press Ctrl-D	The Ace of Spades is duplicated and placed to the right of the original
*Click on **A**rrange*	The Arrange menu appears
*Click on **U**ngroup*	The duplicate Ace of Spades is ungrouped
Click on the screen	The card is no longer selected
Click on the big spade	The big spade is selected
Press Del	The big spade is deleted
Click on the upside-down A *and spade*	The status line reads Group of 2 objects
Press Del	The group is deleted
Click on the remaining A *and spade*	The status line reads Group of 2 objects
*Click on **A**rrange*	The Arrange menu appears
*Click on **U**ngroup*	The objects are ungrouped
Click on the screen	The objects are no longer selected

Click on the Text tool	The cursor becomes a +
Click and drag over the A	The A is selected
Type **3**	A 3 replaces the A
Click and drag over the spade	The spade is selected
Hold down Alt and type **0168**	A club replaces the spade
Click on the Pick tool	
Marquee-select or shift-click on the 3 and the club	
Release the mouse button	The status line reads `2 objects selected`
Click on **A**rrange	The Arrange menu appears
Click on **A**lign	The Align dialog box appears
Click on Horizontally **C**enter	
Click on OK	The 3 and the club are horizontally centered
Click on **A**rrange	The Arrange menu appears
Click on **G**roup	The 3 and the club are grouped. The status line reads `Group of 2 objects`

You have just replaced the A and a spade with the 3 and a club. Now use the upside-down duplicate procedure you learned a few pages back to create the second set of objects.

After you have done that, add three smaller clubs to the middle of the card using the Text tool. Then center the three clubs on the card both vertically and horizontally using the Align command. Finally, group the three clubs together by using the Group command.

Adding the Three Clubs

Click on the Text tool	The cursor becomes a +
Click on the center of the card	The Text I bar appears
Hold down Alt, type **0168**, *and press Enter three times*	Three clubs appear
Click on **E**dit	The Edit menu appears
Click on Edit Te**x**t	The Artistic Text dialog box appears

continued

Click on **C**enter	To center the clubs
At Point Size, enter **30**	Creates 30-point type
Scroll down and click on Dixieland	Dixieland is now the specified typeface
Click on **S**pacing	The Spacing dialog box appears
At Line, enter **150**	For 150 percent of point size (45 points) leading
Click on OK	
Click on OK again	Three clubs appear
Shift-click on the three clubs and the card	The status line reads `2 objects selected`
Click on **A**rrange	The Arrange menu appears
Click on **A**lign	The Align menu appears
Click on Horizontally **C**enter *and* Vertically **C**enter	Centers the clubs on the card

Now, go back and make sure that everything is positioned perfectly. You might have to move a few things around. If you have properly grouped everything, this should be no problem. After everything is in position, group the entire card as you did with the Ace of Spades. Congratulations, you have completed your second card!

You need to build one more card before you proceed to the next phase. To make things simple, why not build a Two of Hearts? Use the procedures you have just learned to construct this last card. The keyboard sequence you need for the heart symbol is Alt-0170.

Arranging Grouped Objects (or Shuffling the Deck)

You should have three separate playing cards: the Ace of Spades, the Three of Clubs, and the Two of Hearts. Not a winning hand, but good enough to illustrate your point. Drag the three cards into a horizontal row, with space between them. Go ahead and turn on Full-Color editing (turn off Wireframe mode).

You should see three perfectly complete cards in the preview window (see fig. 3.22). If one of the cards seems to be missing objects from its face, have no fear. The wayward object merely needs to be brought forward. Ungroup the card in question, click off, click on the unruly object(s), and select To **F**ront from the **A**rrange menu. When you are done, group the card again.

Figure 3.22:
The three cards next to each other.

If you had to mess around with anything in the last paragraph, you got a head start on everyone else. The opening of this chapter promised that you were going to shuffle the deck, which is what you are just about to do (in an abbreviated manner), using just three commands.

Start shuffling by dragging all three cards on top of each other. Stack them perfectly by selecting them all, and then using horizontal and vertical align (see fig. 3.23). If you look at them in Full-Color mode, or in a full-screen preview, only the top card should show, as in figure 3.24. Deselect the deck.

Cutting the Cards

Click on the top card	The top card is selected
Click on **A**rrange	The Arrange menu appears
Click on **O**rder	The Order fly-out menu appears
Click on To **B**ack	The top card is sent to back and the next card in the deck appears (see fig. 3.25)

Figure 3.23:

The deck in Wireframe mode.

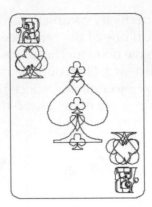

Figure 3.24:

A deck in Full-Color mode.

Figure 3.25:

A new card.

As you learned earlier, Draw has five commands in its object-arranging lingo: To Front, To Back, Forward One, Back One, and Reverse Order. Now that you have seen what To Back does, try To Front.

One More Time

Click on Arrange	The Arrange menu appears
Click on Order	The Order fly-out menu appears
Click on To Front	The original top card reappears

That was easy. Try sending the cards to back and front a few times. By using To Front and To Back, you can place an object on top of everything or underneath everything.

You can handle the in-between layers—those neither at the top nor bottom—by using Forward One and Back One. Reduce your work to as few logical levels as possible. Each level can contain many other levels and sublevels. Try shuffling the deck by using Forward One and Back One. You can cycle through the cards by using Tab or Shift-Tab.

The last object-arranging tool, Reverse Order, is the device that you often use for between-object work. Reverse Order works with two or more selected objects and transposes the sequence between them.

Start this next exercise by sliding the cards out, as if you were fanning them out on a table. On each card, leave a half-inch vertical strip showing. Make sure that the card numbers and suits are visible (see fig. 3.26).

Switching Cards with Reverse Order

Shift-click on the top two cards	The top two cards are selected
Click on Arrange	The Arrange menu appears
Click on Order	The Order fly-out menu appears
Click on Reverse Order	The top two cards swap sequence

Figure 3.26:
The fanned cards.

This simple example demonstrates the way the object-arranging command set works. Obviously, as you get more proficient with CorelDRAW! and your illustrations become more complex, it is increasingly important that you construct and arrange your work logically.

Using Layer Control

Shortcut

Press Ctrl-F3 to access the Layers Roll-Up menu.

In response to many requests from the installed user base, CorelDRAW! version 3.0 introduced a full-blown layering structure. Layer control is handled through the Layers Roll-Up menu, which you can summon by using the keyboard shortcut Ctrl-F3 or by selecting Layers Roll-Up from the Layout menu.

If you are accustomed to working with overlays on conventional mechanical artwork, you should feel right at home with the Layers roll-up. You can think of each layer as residing on its own individual acetate.

Consider the following example—it demonstrates when you might want to use layers in a drawing. Say you wanted to use the cards you just created in another drawing. This new drawing contains a number of elements, including a glass (filled with scotch on the rocks), a stack of chips, a patterned tablecloth, and perhaps an ashtray (can we add any other vices?). To simplify the composition of a complex drawing, you might want to place each object on its own layer. Furthermore, Draw enables you to name the layers as you want using up to 32 characters. You can call the tablecloth layer Tablecloth, and the ashtray layer Ashtray.

As you delve further into more complex projects, you learn to handle layers with authority. After you have completed the project in Chapter 8, "Assembling Complex Images," you should have a thorough understanding of the way Draw's layers work. For now, reflect on the project you just completed, in which you worked on just one layer. You need these skills whether or not your artwork requires the control afforded by the Layers roll-up menu.

Summary

This chapter covered some heavy subjects. You took on the Shape tool and looked into manipulating the various node types. In a rudimentary exercise, you changed your cloud drawing from a rough to a finished object. You learned about Bézier curves, and used a small deck of cards to illustrate some of the simple concepts behind layering and arranging your work.

These skills are important foundations on which subsequent chapters build. The more complex your work gets, the more imperative it is to build working drawings. You might work on a drawing for hours, days, or even weeks. To prevent a lot of wasted time, be mindful of how you are constructing your image. The question is not whether you will change your drawing, it is when.

Perhaps you are working on an illustration for a men's clothing store. You have got the right cut on the suit. The model looks dashing. Everything looks great, except that the store's owner does not like the color of the suit. As the saying goes, "You want a green suit? Turn on the green light." You need to be able to turn only the suit green, not the model's gills, and to do so with a minimum of hassles. By building your illustrations logically, you can effect those changes with just a few clicks.

Part Two

▼ Putting CorelDRAW! To Work

4

Basic Typography

ith the drawing basics out of the way, you can move on to working with type. After the preceding chapters, you should be familiar with the CorelDRAW! interface. You even did a few exercises that briefly involved the Text tool. This chapter and following chapters show you ways in which you can use CorelDRAW!'s Text tool in the real world to produce flyers, T-shirts, advertisements, 35mm slides, and more.

In this chapter, you use the Text tool to produce a simple flyer. It isn't pretty, but it serves its purpose. The flyer is an uncomplicated piece, designed so that you can get the hang of setting type using Draw.

Those of you who bought CorelDRAW! to set fancy type will spend much of your time using the Text tool. You must, therefore, have a thorough understanding of the tool and its features. The Text tool packs a lot of wallop in a simple guise.

Using CorelDRAW!'s Typographic Conventions

Draw's Text tool can operate in one of three modes: Artistic (headline) Text, Paragraph Text, or Symbol. This chapter touches on all three modes. You see that the Text tool operates in a logical manner (like the other implements in Draw's toolbox) and with a consistent look and feel.

The workings of the Artistic Text and Paragraph Text tools are analogous. You use the Artistic Text tool for much of the following exercise, add a bit of embellishment with the Symbol Text tool, and finish up by using the Paragraph Text tool in a two-column layout.

The Text tool's user interface is similar to that of many other drawing packages. Type size and face are specified by using scroll bars and edit boxes. Type weights (normal, bold, italic, and bold italic), where available, are selected by using the text-entry windows buttons. In addition, you can select ragged left, ragged right, centered, unaligned, and fully justified margins.

Implementing CorelDRAW!'s many text options can be perplexing to the novice and the professional alike. Specifically, the superfluous duplication of controls between the Text Roll-Up menu and the Text dialog box is confusing. You can use either method to specify type, but the Text dialog box is a holdover from the earliest versions of the program.

Type Sizes

In Draw, you can freely specify type point sizes. The Text dialog box enables you to indicate point sizes as large as 2,160 points or as small as 0.7 point, in tenth-of-a-point increments. This flexibility is a boon to the typographer whose clients continually ask for type to be set "to fit." After you have set a block of type, you can scale type proportionally or anamorphically just as you can any other object.

Be careful when using a 300 dpi laser printer: the legibility of type smaller than 6 points is severely impaired. On a high-resolution imagesetter such as the Lino L/300, however, you need not worry about this restriction; the L/300 is capable of imaging at 2,540 dpi. Newer, high-end imagesetters from Linotype-Hell, Scitex, and other manufacturers can print at even higher resolutions.

Typefaces

You will never run out of typefaces; CorelDRAW! 4.0 ships with dozens of immediately accessible typefaces in TrueType format. The CD-ROM version of Draw features over 750 fonts (in both PostScript and TrueType formats). If you need a font not supplied with the program, it is no more than a phone call—and a credit-card charge—away. With more than 10,000 fonts available in PostScript format, your design choices are governed only by your financial resources.

If you take a look at Draw's font list, you'll notice some old favorites along with some unfamiliar names. The bizarre names refer to many typefaces with which you are probably already familiar. Corel had to name them with those curious names to avoid stepping on anyone's copyright. For some obscure reason, the laws protect typeface names, but not designs. This unfair practice only serves to punish type designers who spend inordinate amounts of time creating and perfecting new typeface designs. Generally, the (oddly named) CorelDRAW! typefaces are inferior to the original designs. If you are a professional designer or typographer, you might want to purchase the authentic font from its original foundry.

Version 4.0 features a greatly improved font load, in quantity as well as quality. The Bitstream fonts are a quantum leap in caliber over earlier versions. Although the 750 fonts supplied with CorelDRAW! provide an instant type library, it still is possible that your favorite faces might not be included. Check out Chapter 11 for more information on obtaining fonts.

Other Type Specs

Type specifications other than point size, type face, and alignment are easy to set with the Text Spacing dialog box. You can access the Text Spacing dialog box through a button on the bottom of the Text dialog box. Use the Text Spacing dialog box to specify character, word, and line, as well as (in paragraph text) before and after paragraph spacing. Typographers usually refer to these settings as *tracking*, *word spacing*, *leading* (pronounced "ledding"), and *paragraph spacing*, respectively.

CorelDRAW! 4.0 offers a functional improvement over earlier versions. You now can specify line and paragraph spacing in either relative (based on a percentage of point size) or absolute (such as 12-point type on 14-point leading) terms. Absolute settings are the typographer's choice for paragraph text (and in many cases, artistic text), because different typefaces set in distinctly different sizes. Copperplate will set at approximately 80 percent of the height of Galliard, for example.

These text-spacing settings, along with settings available in the Character Attributes dialog box, make setting type with CorelDRAW! a breeze; the clients make the job tough.

PostScript or TrueType?

CorelDRAW! 3.0 and Windows 3.1 introduced a new dilemma for electronic artists and desktop publishers. Earlier versions of Draw used only proprietary WFN fonts; CorelDRAW! 4.0 uses the system fonts, which can be either PostScript or TrueType (although WFN fonts are still used for symbols). Now, you have to decide which font format you want to use.

Although with version 4.0 Corel provides over 750 fonts in both formats, only a small portion of the TrueType fonts are loaded automatically from the distribution floppy disks. The vast majority of the fonts—both TrueType and PostScript—are on CD-ROM. You must use the Adobe Type Manager (ATM) control panel to load the PostScript fonts from the CD-ROM. If you want to load the TrueType faces, you can use either the Windows Fonts control panel or Corel's font installation program.

Managing all those fonts is a chore. The more fonts you have loaded on your system at any one time, the slower Windows will load and run. The best commercial solution to the font dilemma is Ares Software's FontMinder. You find more information on FontMinder in Chapter 10, "The Windows DTP Arsenal."

Which font format should you choose? It all depends on who you are, what you do, and where your images are ultimately printed. Because Windows 3.1 integrates TrueType, many offices will likely use TrueType. If your work is printed on a laser printer and run on an office copier, you'll do just fine with TrueType.

Professional graphic designers, typographers, and publishers should stick with PostScript. If your files are printed on a high-resolution imagesetter, your service bureau will probably want nothing but PostScript files and fonts. The same is true for files handed up to a high-end prepress system at a color trade shop or large printer. If your work goes to a Lino or Scitex system, save yourself some hassle and stick with PostScript.

Why Is Every Job a Rush?

If you have been in the graphic arts field for a while, you know that rush jobs are the norm—as are last-minute changes. With that in mind, and just for fun (?), hang a deadline over your head when you work through the example in this chapter.

Although you are doing this for kicks, the sample flyer you create in this chapter is an excellent example of the way things are. It seems that clients can never stop in to see the typesetter until the job is already a week late. This chapter should give you an idea of how CorelDRAW! can be put to work in the real world.

Speaking of the (almost) real world, stop in at DeLook Design and see what Joe and the crew are up to. Monday morning has arrived. Joe has learned some CorelDRAW! essentials over the weekend, and he is anxious to put them to work.

Freddie Needs a Fast Flyer

DeLook Design has just landed a new client—Fast Freddie, proprietor of a local used-car lot specializing in summertime fun vehicles.

Freddie has come up with the idea of distributing flyers on car windshields. It is not the type of work that DeLook Design likes to take in, but Freddie has that wad of bills out, and he is willing to cover Joe's troubles as long as Joe can whip up something in half an hour. Considering that the rent is due, and Joe is a bit short, he agrees to do some quick-and-dirty flyers—like it or not!

Freddie hands over a napkin from Thurston's combination bait, tackle, and coffee shop next door. On it, Freddie has scrawled his basic information (see fig. 4.1). The flyer is intended to promote the grand opening of Fast Freddie's Speed-O-Rama Service Center. Freddie is offering a lube and oil change for $20 in 20 minutes flat or your money back.

Figure 4.1:

The napkin layout.

With a qualifying, "Think you can handle that in half an hour? I'm going over to Thurston's for an early lunch," Freddie heads out the door.

Joe doesn't even have time to roll up his sleeves. He fires up CorelDRAW! and goes to work! Looking at Freddie's napkin layout, Joe sees he doesn't have time to prepare any intricate graphics. A big, bold, hard-sell approach is called for here.

Building the Flyer

This advertisement has three basic parts. The first is the introduction, which would be effective in a starburst. The starburst is tacky, but Freddie will love it. You need to know your customer and his audience. Second, the offer—$20 oil change—has to hit the reader in the face. The hook is "20 Minutes, Or Your Money Back!" Finally, the logo and address have to be big and bold, but not too large.

In this flyer, limit the number of typefaces. In practice, you find that the fewer typefaces you use, the less likely you will commit typographic hara-kiri. This flyer will not win any awards, but at least it will be readable and do its job. Joe will not have time to do any kerning, but who ever saw a pretty advertisement from a garage anyway?

One of CorelDRAW!'s greatest features is its excellent typographical screen representation. Although not perfect, it is about as good as you are going to get without Display PostScript. The screen quality is good enough that you can specify typefaces on the computer itself, rather than on a layout sheet. If a block of type is too big at 60 points, you can see it immediately and reduce the point size before you run a copy out of the printer.

Without wasting any more time, open a new file and get down to work. In the Page Setup dialog box, specify a portrait letter page. When you choose a letter-sized page (or any other predetermined page size), the horizontal and vertical settings boxes are grayed out. Custom is the only page-size option that enables you to make changes to the horizontal and vertical dimensions.

Opening a New File

Click on **F**ile	The File menu appears
Click on **N**ew	A new page appears
Click on **L**ayout	The Layout menu reappears
Click on Page **S**etup	The Page Setup dialog box appears
Click on L**e**tter	
Click on **P**ortrait	
Click on OK	A new page appears

Using the Text Tool

The preceding two chapters gave you a taste of using the Text tool. Now you really start setting type. In the next exercise, you use all the settings in the Spacing dialog box (see fig. 4.2). Take a moment to learn about the spacing specifications:

Figure 4.2:

The Spacing dialog box.

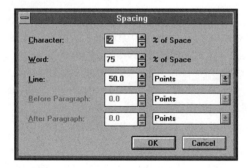

- **Character spacing (or tracking).** This specification controls the space between all characters in a text block. Do not confuse character spacing with kerning, which affects only the space between two specific characters. Tracking influences the overall "color," or density, of the type on the page. You will find that a slightly negative number works best in everything but body copy sizes. You should tighten up headlines to maintain readability, but avoid tightening up body copy.

- **Word spacing.** This specification governs the space between words. The factory default setting (of 100 percent) might be too wide for display-type purposes. At times, you might find yourself adjusting this specification to a value of 70 percent or less.

- **Line spacing.** This specification, more commonly referred to as *leading*, affects the space between lines of type in a text block. Most type is set with a slightly positive leading (more than 100 percent of the size of the typeface). A value slightly larger than 100 leaves white space between the lines of text. Negative leading (less than 100 percent) is used in special cases, such as when type is set in capital letters. Care must be taken when setting uppercase and lowercase type with negative leading to avoid crashing ascenders and descenders. CorelDRAW! 4.0 enables you to specify leading as either a percentage of character height or in absolute points.

- **Paragraph spacing.** This specification affects the space between paragraphs, and is available only when using the Paragraph Text tool. When you use the Artistic Text tool, the Before and After Paragraph options are grayed out. Draw adds paragraph spacing when it encounters a hard return. The first line of each paragraph is given the Before Paragraph spacing value (which defaults to 100 percent). This function can be misleading, however, because a Before Paragraph spacing percentage of less than 100 percent yields negative leading. The After Paragraph spacing, on the other hand, defaults to 0 percent—so much for consistency!

You can control tracking and leading interactively, in addition to entering precise measurements in the Text Spacing or Frame dialog boxes. When you click a text block with the Shape tool, character and line spacing control arrows appear to the left of and below the text block, respectively. Although this method is easy to use with Artistic text, it is difficult to use with paragraph text.

Lay down the first text block in 48-point Geometric Slab Extra Bold, centered in the top third of the page. Take the time to cover all the specs, making sure not to miss any of the dialog boxes.

Shortcut

Press F8 for the Text tool.

This typeface is just about as big, bold, and hard-sell as typefaces come. Fast Freddie will appreciate the impact of this typeface.

Setting the Headline

Click on the Text tool	The cursor becomes a +
Click on the page	The Text I bar appears
Type the following and press Enter after every line except the last one:	

```
Fast Freddie
Announces the Opening
of his Brand New
Speed-O-Rama
Service Center
```

Press Ctrl-T	The Artistic Text dialog box appears
At Si<u>z</u>e, *enter* **48**	
Make sure that you have points selected	
At <u>F</u>onts, *roll down, click on* GeoSlab703 XBd BT	
Click on <u>C</u>enter	
Click on <u>S</u>pacing	The Spacing dialog box appears
At <u>C</u>haracter, *enter* **-2**	
At <u>W</u>ord, *enter* **75**	
At <u>L</u>ine, *select points, then enter* **50**	
Click on OK	
Click on OK again	The type is set according to your specifications

Use the Pick tool to drag the block of type to the top of the page and eyeball it into position (see fig. 4.3).

You should have a 48-point Geometric Slab Extra Bold headline, set centered on 50-point leading. The word and character spacing should be moderately tight, but by no means touching. You might have noticed that you did not need to click on the <u>B</u>old button because GeoSlab703 XBd BT is obviously a heavy hitter.

On second thought, it looks like 48 points is just a bit too large. Bring the size down to 36 points. Although you can attempt to scale down the text by eye, do it with precision. You should go back into the Text dialog box to adjust the point size accurately.

Fast Freddie Announces the Opening of his Brand New Speed-O-Rama Service Center

Figure 4.3:

A size of 48 points is too large.

Adjusting the Point Size

With the text still selected, take the following steps:

Press Ctrl-T	The Artistic Text dialog box appears
At Si̲ze, enter **36**	
Click on S̲pacing	The Spacing dialog box appears
At L̲ine, enter **38**	
Click on OK	
Click on OK again	The type is reset according to your specifications

When you use the Text tool in this next exercise, notice that all previously entered type specs are gone. CorelDRAW! 4.0 (unlike prior versions) requires that you plug in the specs from scratch. Although the program now supports Styles, you will not need them for this simple display advertisement. Styles are, however, covered a bit later.

Shortcut

Press Ctrl-T for the Text dialog box.

Setting the Second Block of Text

Click on the Text tool	The cursor becomes a +
Click on the page	The Text I bar appears
Type the following and press Enter after the first line:	

20 Minute
OIL CHANGE

Press Ctrl-T	The Artistic Text dialog box appears
*At Si*ze*, enter* **60**	
Make sure that you have points selected	
At F*onts, roll down, click on* Geometr231 Hv BT	
Click on C*enter*	
Click on S*pacing*	The Spacing dialog box appears
At C*haracter, enter* **-4**	
At W*ord, enter* **60**	
At L*ine, select points, then enter* **60**	
Click on OK	
Click on OK again	The type is set according to your specifications

Use the Pick tool to drag the block of type to the left side of the page.

Drag this block of type over to the left side and center it vertically on the page. Notice that this last block of type was "set solid"— with no extra leading. You can get away with setting solid when you are setting text in all caps, or when there are no (or very few) descenders. At times, you might even want to use negative leading by setting the line spacing a few points less than the type size.

Using Base-Alignment

The next piece of type you set is the largest type on the page. After you set it, you first base-align it with OIL CHANGE, and then go back and make one of the characters a superscript (or superior) figure.

Bottom vertical alignment is a quick way to pseudo base-align different blocks of text. It might not, however, always provide true base-alignment. The vertical alignment command does not look at character baselines; instead, it looks at the character nodes as the baseline (text characters have only one node, positioned directly to their lower left). If the character nodes are exactly on the baseline, things should be fine.

This next exercise performs base-alignment before creating (and positioning) the superior figure for one simple reason: if you drag a single character node down from the baseline, all bottom alignment will subsequently take place from that lowest node. Bottom alignment always works from the lowest node.

Of course, you do not have to rely on the Alignment command. You can always do it manually. Although it takes a bit of finesse to align the baselines by eye, using snap-to guidelines can reduce your frustration level. As you work through this next exercise, notice that the alignment command does not base-align the two blocks of text. You must align these two blocks of text manually.

Setting and Base-Aligning the $20

Click on the Text tool	The cursor becomes a +
Click on the page	The Text I bar appears
Type **$20**	Enter this string in the text-entry window
Press Ctrl-T	The Artistic Text dialog box appears
At Size, enter **148**	
At Fonts, select Geometr231 Hv BT	
Click on Center	
Click on OK	The type is set according to your specifications
Drag the $20 *to the right side of the* 20 Minute OIL CHANGE *text. Give it even horizontal spacing*	
Click on the Pick tool	

continues

Shift-click 20 Minute OIL CHANGE	The status line reads: `2 objects selected`
Click on **A**rrange	The Arrange menu appears
Click on **A**lign	The Align dialog box appears
Click on Vertical **B**ottom	
Click on OK	The type is base-aligned

Look at the baselines of the two blocks of text. They probably are not in sync. Take a moment to finesse them into position.

Setting Superior Characters

Now that the $20 is in position, it's time to turn the dollar sign into a superior figure with the Character Attributes dialog box. You can make alterations in this handy dialog box that apply only to selected characters in a text string. This feature enables you to use superior and inferior (subscript) characters. It also enables you to change the type face, size, and baseline of individual characters. Additionally, the dialog box provides a precise method for character kerning and rotation.

Remember when you double-clicked on a selected object's node to display the Node Edit roll-up menu? The Character Attributes dialog box is accessed in a similar manner by double-clicking on a selected text character's node. If you are only kerning or shifting baselines, you need not use the dialog box. You can manually kern characters or shift individual baselines by dragging the characters by their nodes. You will see this in the next exercise when you drag a character down.

Creating a Superior Figure

Click on the Shape tool	
Click on $20	Nodes appear for the characters
Double-click on the $ node	The Character Attributes dialog box appears

At **P**lacement, *click on* Superscript

Click on OK

The $ is now a superior figure

Drag the $ node down and to the left

The $ is now properly positioned

Double-click on the $ node

The Character Attributes dialog box appears

Take a look at the **H**orizontal and **V**ertical Shift percentages. They should be set at -6 and -19, respectively.

Click on OK

The superior $ is properly positioned

If you set many advertisements that include price information, the superscript option comes in handy. The steps were necessary to precisely align the superscript $ to the imaginary line at the top of the caps. Your working style will dictate how much precision you need and to what degree you use the mouse or enter exact specifications.

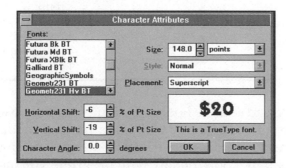

Figure 4.4:

The Character Attributes dialog box.

Condensing Type

The two-objects (the 20 Minute OIL CHANGE and the $20) are slightly too wide for the page. Next, you use the stretch function to anamorphically scale the group to 85 percent of its original width. This action maintains the character heights as it condenses the widths.

The stretch function is a convenient CorelDRAW! feature, but it is often abused. Condensing type beyond a certain percentage reduces the type's legibility. It might fit on the page, but the reader cannot read it.

Be very careful not to squeeze type too much. The same goes for extending (or squashing) type. Use these two tricks with caution. With that warning out of the way, move on to the exercise.

Grouping and Squeezing Text

Click on the Pick tool	
Shift-click on 20 Minute OIL CHANGE	The status line reads: `2 objects selected`
Click on **A**rrange	The Arrange menu appears
Click on **G**roup	The two objects are grouped
Drag the right-side center handle	Drag toward center of group; watch the status line and release the mouse button when the group is squeezed 85 percent

Now you need to add the hook, 20 Minutes, or Your Money Back, to the bottom of this group of text. Use a smaller, condensed sans serif typeface: 36-point Geometric 231. After you set this line of type, center-align it horizontally with the group you just made and group them all together.

Adding the Hook

Click on the Text tool	The cursor becomes a +
Click on the page	The Text dialog box appears
Type `20 Minutes, or Your Money Back`	
Press Ctrl-T	The Artistic Text dialog box appears

At Si<u>z</u>e, *enter* **36**	
Click on Geometr231 BT	
Click on **B**old	
Click on **C**enter	
Click on OK	The type is set according to your specifications
Click on the Pick tool	
Drag 20 Minutes, or Your Money Back	Drag underneath 20 Minute OIL CHANGE $20
Shift-click on 20 Minute OIL CHANGE $20	The status line reads: `2 objects selected`
Click on **A**rrange	The Arrange menu appears
Click on **A**lign	The Align dialog box appears
Click on Horizontal **C**enter	
Click on OK	The type is horizontally centered
Click on **A**rrange	The Arrange menu appears
Click on **G**roup	The two objects are grouped (see fig. 4.5)

This exercise is probably starting to feel like the last chapter, in which you built the playing cards. By now, you are getting the feel of how to build and use groups.

Figure 4.5:

The half-finished flyer.

Changing Face with Character Attributes

You have one more block of type to set before you are done with this grubby little flyer. Although this block has four lines and three different typefaces, you learn how easy it is to use character attributes to alter lines of type.

When you accessed the Character Attributes dialog box a few pages back, you turned the dollar sign into a superior figure. Now you are going to use the dialog box to change typeface and size.

The capacity to have multiple typefaces and sizes in a single block of type is essential for professional typography. It gives the artist the flexibility to move one block of type around, instead of trying to position, align, and group many individual pieces. If you have ever had the displeasure of building big, nasty supermarket advertisements, you are sure to appreciate the power that the Character Attributes dialog box provides.

Setting the Logo with Character Attributes

Click on the Text tool   The cursor becomes a +

Click on the page   The Text I bar appears

Type the following and press Enter after every line but the last. You will have to do a keyboard gyration (Alt-0146) to set the apostrophe in Freddie's. Hold down the Alt key and type **0146** (on the numeric keypad). Also notice that you are setting the logo with slightly negative leading (52-point type on 48-point lead).

```
Fast Freddie<Alt-0146>s
Speed-O-Rama
Service Center
On the Causeway 555-1234
```

Press Ctrl-T   The Artistic Text dialog
                                                            box appears

At Si̲ze, enter **52**

At F̲onts, select GeoSlab703 XBd BT

Click on C̲enter

Click on **S**pacing	The Spacing dialog box appears
At **C**haracter, *enter* **-2**	
At **W**ord, *enter* **65**	
At **L**ine, *enter* **48 Points**	
Click on OK	
Click on OK again	The type is set according to your specifications
Click on the Shape tool	
Click on Fast Freddie's	Nodes appear for the characters
Marquee-select Fast Freddie's	Character nodes are selected
Double-click on any selected character's node	The Character Attributes dialog box appears
Change typeface to Lydian Csv BT	
At Si**z**e, *enter* **60**	
Click on OK	
Marquee-select On the Causeway 555-1234	Character nodes are selected
Double-click on the O node	The Character Attributes dialog box appears
Change face to Geometr231 BT	
Click on **B**old	
At Si**z**e, *enter* **42**	
Click on OK	

Try to select the middle block of text with the Shape tool; you can't do it! That is because it is part of a group of objects and cannot be manipulated with the Shape tool until it first is ungrouped.

As you have seen, the Shape tool is a valuable instrument for adding typographic versatility. In the next chapter, you use the Shape tool to do some kerning. And you get into setting some aesthetic and tricky type.

Centering Objects to the Page

You are almost done. You need to use a nifty little option to horizontally center all the items on the page (see fig. 4.6). Normally, when you use the Align command to center objects, they center against each other, not the page. To center objects to the page, you must click on Align to Center of Page in the Align dialog box. This option—introduced in Draw version 2.0—is a great convenience. After clicking on Align to Center of Page, you click on Vertical Center to deselect that option. If you do not deselect Vertical Center, all three selected objects are placed on top of each other—in the center of the page, of course!

Figure 4.6:

The flyer text, unaligned.

Centering Objects to the Page

Click on **E**dit	The Edit menu appears
Click on Select **A**ll	Three objects are selected
Click on **A**rrange	The Arrange menu appears
Click on **A**lign	The Align dialog box appears
Click on Align to Center of **P**age	
Click on Vertical C**e**nter	Deselects the option
Click on OK	All items are centered horizontally on the page (see fig. 4.7)

Figure 4.7:
The flyer text,
aligned.

Quick Changes with the Text Roll-Up Menu

CorelDRAW! 3.0 introduced a great device known as the roll-up
menu. This little time-saver is a wonderful convenience. To access
the Text roll-up menu, select the Text **R**oll-Up option from the
Te**x**t menu, or use the Ctrl-F2 keyboard shortcut. When a roll-up
menu is on your screen, you can move it around at will (see fig.
4.8). Why is it called a *roll-up* menu? Simply because a click on its
up arrow makes the menu spring up and close like a roller shade.
Another click drops the menu down again.

Figure 4.8:
The Text roll-up
menu.

The Text roll-up menu offers instant access to a number of text
attributes, including typeface, size, and justification. You can set
type in bold or italic with one click. You can summon the Character Placement dialog box and set the character(s) as superscript or
subscript. You also can make changes to horizontal or vertical
shift and character angle. Clicking on the Frame button displays

the Frame dialog box, which offers complete control over paragraph text. Although you cannot access the Frame dialog box from the Text roll-up menu when you are using Artistic Text, you can always select Frame from the "normal" Text menu.

You can use the Text roll-up menu in two ways to make changes to text already on the screen. The first is to select a block of text with the Pick tool, and then use the Text roll-up menu to make changes to the entire block. The second method is to use the Text tool to click and drag over a range of text, and then make changes in much the same way that you make changes with the Character Attributes dialog box, affecting only a selected range. Remember that you can access selected character kerning only if text has been selected with the Text tool rather than the Pick tool.

Use the Text roll-up menu to set the flyer text in a variety of typefaces. It is easy to select a block of type, choose a typeface, and click on Apply to make the changes. When you are done, set the type back to its original specs.

Choosing between the Text dialog box and the Text roll-up menu can be a tough decision. Again, it depends on your personal preferences. It is hard to say if Corel eventually will choose to do away with the Character Attributes dialog box, in favor of the roll-up menu.

Starburst Effects

Now you have all the flyer text, but something is still missing. Remembering the scribbled starburst on Freddie's napkin, Joe whacks himself in the head for inspiration.

Try building your own starburst instead of searching for one in Draw's Balloon symbol font or your electronic or conventional clip-art files. You do not have time to look (you have a deadline, remember?) and certainly no time to scan and trace. By drawing straight lines, connected with double-clicks, you can weave a custom starburst into the page in under two minutes (with luck).

After the starburst is drawn and selected, choose a fill of 20 percent and a two-point outline rule from the fly-out menus. You do not have time to mess with all the dialog boxes. The defaults are good enough for this job. When you are done, send the starburst to the back.

Building a Starburst

Click on the Pencil tool

Double-click around the headline   Draw lines to form a
                                                      starburst

When you are done drawing the starburst, you can go back in and tweak the individual nodes to make the starburst look just right.

Click on the Shape tool

Tweak the nodes

Click on the Pick tool

Click on the Fill tool   The Fill fly-out menu
                                                      appears

Click on the 10% Fill *icon*

Click on the Outline tool   The Outline fly out menu
                                                      appears

Click on the 2 Point *icon*

*Click on **A**rrange*   The Arrange menu
                                                      appears

*Click on **O**rder*

*Click on To **B**ack*

Switch your display to full-color mode (it has been in Wireframe mode) with Shift-F9. Looks like this baby is done (see fig. 4.9)!

Figure 4.9:
A starburst.

Freddie Wants More

Joe sends the file to the PostScript printer with little time to spare. Phew! Five minutes to go, and here comes Freddie through the door. Just as he reaches the desk, the page emerges from the laser printer. Good thing this flyer has no time-consuming fills or intricate graphics! Freddie is wide-eyed as he takes the camera-ready laser print in hand. "Hey, this is pretty good!" he says. "Yeah," he continues, "this is exactly what I wanted, except..." Freddie pauses as he thinks. "Maybe I could add something else. Just look at all that space at the bottom of the page."

Bringing in Clip Art

Realizing that Freddie has no appreciation for the aesthetic use of white space, Joe immediately reaches for CorelDRAW!'s clip-art book. "Freddie," Joe says with confidence, "I know exactly what you want."

CorelDRAW! 4.0 comes with an abundance of clip art: thousands upon thousands of pieces of clip art come on the CD-ROMs, where you can find the checkered flag that should finish off the flyer. If you do not have a CD-ROM drive yet, consider getting one in the near future. Prices have been dropping, and CD-ROM currently is the best method for distributing large programs, clip art, and typeface collections.

Do not fret if you do not have access to a CD-ROM drive. You can easily create your own flags with the Rectangle tool and the snap-to-grid!

Adding Clip Art to the Flyer

Click on File	The File menu appears
Click on Import	The Import window appears
Click on CorelDRAW! CDR	The Import window configures for CDR import

Maneuver to your CD drive	
At **D**irectories, *double-click on* Clipart	The Clipart Directory is selected
Roll down, double-click on Flag	The Flag Directory is selected
Double-click on Totem	The Totem directory file names appear
Roll down, double-click on WAVING.CDR	The WAVING.CDR file is imported

The checkered flag clip art is too big to fit on the flyer, so you have to size, rotate, and finally, mirror-duplicate it. To do this with precision, use the dialog boxes.

Scaling, Rotating, and Mirroring the Flag

With the flag selected, take the following steps:

Click on E**ffe**cts	The Effects menu appears
Click on **S**tretch & Mirror	The Stretch & Mirror dialog box appears
At Stretch **H**orizontally, *enter* **25**	
At Stretch **V**ertically, *enter* **25**	
Click on OK	The flag is scaled 25 percent
Click on Effe**c**ts	The Effects menu appears
Click on **R**otate & Skew	The Rotate & Skew dialog box appears
At Rotation **A**ngle, *enter* **-15**	
Click on OK	The flag is rotated –15 degrees
Click on Effe**c**ts	The Effects menu appears
Click on **S**tretch & Mirror	The Stretch & Mirror dialog box appears
Click on H**or**z Mirror	

continues

Click on Leave Original

Click on OK

The flag is horizontally mirrored, and the original is left alone

Drag the flags, one to either side of the Speed-O-Rama Service Center text at the bottom of the page. Align and group the flags and text. Be sure to save your page with the file name FREDSAD.

Uh-oh. Fast Freddie has taken a look at the flyer and he is still not satisfied with it. "Too much wasted space," he says with a sigh. Joe is rapidly losing what little respect he had for this client, but he knows exactly what to do.

Using Symbols

As mentioned in the beginning of this chapter, Draw's Text tool does triple-duty. Until now, you have set all the flyer type using only the Artistic Text tool. Now, finish it off by adding a pair of symbols with the Symbol Text tool.

The Symbol Text tool is a fast way to place rudimentary art—objects that are more icon-like than life-like—into a file. Amazingly, CorelDRAW! comes with thousands of black-and-white symbols at no additional cost. The program also enables you to export images and create your own personal symbol library. You soon see the advantages of using and creating symbols.

The Symbol Text tool is easy to access: click on the Text tool, drag down and to the right, and the Text tool fly-out menu appears. The Symbol Text tool is denoted by a star. Select it and the Symbols roll-up menu appears. You now have dozens of symbol libraries from which to choose. To scroll through an individual symbol library, click on the up and down arrows at the bottom of the roll-up menu.

The Symbols roll-up menu asks you to make three choices. First, you must select the library you want to use. Then, you select the size of the symbol you are placing. Finally, you select and place a symbol by clicking on it and dragging it onto the page. This is known as drag-and-drop symbol placement. When you click on a symbol, notice that the symbol number appears at the # entry window; alternatively, you can type the symbol number directly into the entry window.

After the symbol is on the page, you can scale, stretch, rotate, skew, or mutate it as you would any other object. Symbols can be assigned different fills and can be extruded, blended, and enveloped—or manipulated in whatever other manner you can dream up. The libraries that come with CorelDRAW! 4.0 are listed in table 4.1.

Table 4.1
Corel's Symbol Library

Animals	Czar
Arrows1	Electronics
Arrows2	Festive
Awards	Food
Balloons	Furniture
Borders1	GeographicSymbols
Borders2	HomePlanning
Boxes	HomePlanning2
Buildings	Household
Bullets1	Hygiene
Bullets2	Kidnap
Bullets3	Landscaping
Business&Government	Landmarks
Charting	Medicine
Clocks	Military
CommonBullets	MilitaryID
Computers	MorseCode
Music	Sports&Hobbies

continues

Table 4.1
continued

MusicalSymbols	SportsFigures
NauticalFlags	Stars1
OfficePlanning	Stars2
People	Symbol
Plants	SymbolProp BT
Science	Technology
Semaphore	Tools
Shapes1	Tracks
Shapes2	Transportation
Sign	Weather
SignLanguage	Wingdings
Space	ZapfDingbats BT

Placing Symbols

Click on the Text tool, drag down to the right	The Text tool fly-out menu appears
Select the Symbol Text tool (denoted by a star)	The Symbols roll-up menu appears
Roll down, click on Transportation	The transportation symbols appear

Remember, you can select a symbol in one of two ways: click on the symbol in the sample window, or type the symbol number directly into the text box.

At #, type **82**	The ragtop sports car is highlighted in the sample window
At Size, *type* **2.0**	

Drag-and-drop the sports car onto the page

A 2.0-inch ragtop sports car is drawn

Now you are going to add another ragtop, this one a 4x4 sport utility vehicle. Its symbol number is 90. Use the preceding steps to place it on the page (see fig. 4.10).

Figure 4.10:

The Symbols roll-up menu.

When you have the symbols on the page, position them below the starburst. Put the sports car on the right side, and the 4x4 on the left side. Use the mirror tool to make the 4x4 face into the middle of the page. Finish up by giving both a 50-percent tint.

Fast Freddie grins. Joe's stomach is churning, but the page looks pretty good (considering). Now Joe runs out a print (see fig. 4.11).

"That's it!" exclaims Freddie, as the page rolls out of the laser printer. "Just in time to get it to the Seaside Print Shop before they close for lunch!" A big grin washes over his face as he reaches for his wad of bills. "Say, we're gonna do right well together, if you keep up that kind of work!"

Joe grins back sheepishly, shakes his hand, takes his money, and laughs like hell as soon as Freddie is up the block and out of earshot. The rent is paid. It is time to take a break before tackling the next section on importing text.

Figure 4.11:
The final flyer.

Importing Text

Luckily for Joe, Freddie's flyer had only a small amount of text on it. Joe is a two-finger typist; he could never have made Freddie's half-hour deadline if he had to type a lot of characters. You can, however, import big blocks of text into Draw in a couple of ways.

Why import text? Two simple reasons: to save time and trouble. By importing text, you eliminate the need to retype text that might already exist electronically. Unless you really enjoy typing, it makes good sense to import text, especially large amounts of text. If you type, rewrite, and proofread large blocks of text before bringing them into Draw, you save time in the long run.

With your word processor, you can check your text's spelling and run it through a thesaurus. (Even though CorelDRAW! now contains both a spelling checker and thesaurus, they are not tools for wordsmiths.) Alternatively, you can scan in text or capture it from electronic mail—even from PC-Fax. You can bring in files from across the office network or across the world. Importing text enables you to concentrate on design, not keyboard skills. You might even do yourself a favor and let your clients do the typing on larger jobs.

This method encourages workgroup computing: the designer designs, the writer writes, the proofreader proofreads. This is the way it should be.

If you have been using desktop publishing for a while, you have probably had the occasion to import text from a word processing program into a desktop publishing program like PageMaker. PageMaker has a large variety of text (and graphics) import filters that are similar in purpose to CorelDRAW!'s selection of graphics import filters.

Although CorelDRAW! 4.0 finally contains text import filters, you do not get into that just yet. You still can import unformatted ASCII text using one of two methods. The first method, which works for either headline or paragraph text, makes use of the Clipboard and those old friends, the Cut, Copy, and Paste commands. The second method, which can be used only with paragraph text, enables you to import ASCII files with the TXT extension. The Clipboard method is presented first.

The Clipboard

A functional feature of the Windows environment is the capability to move items between two concurrently running programs by using the Clipboard. Never heard of the Clipboard? Whether you are aware of it or not, you have been using the Clipboard since you first booted up CorelDRAW!—or any other Windows program for that matter.

Each time you use the Cut, Copy, or Paste commands, you access the Clipboard. When you cut or copy an object, it is placed onto the Clipboard. When you paste an object, it is pasted from the Clipboard.

The Clipboard is like a shallow bucket; it can hold only one object or group of objects at a time. If you copy something to the Clipboard, it dumps itself out before allowing a new item (or group of items) to be poured in. Although the Clipboard can only be full or empty—whether with a block of text or a graphic—you can store Clipboard files. Check out your copy of the Windows documentation for more information on saving CLP files.

Text Importation and the Clipboard

Windows comes with its own word processor, Windows Write, which is a bit limited in function. Write has no built-in spelling checker or thesaurus, although you can always use Draw's built-in spelling checker and thesaurus. It does, however, provide a couple of ways to key text ultimately intended for inclusion in a CorelDRAW! file.

For best results, use a Windows-based word processing program such as Microsoft Word for Windows, Lotus Ami Professional, or WordPerfect for Windows. These programs allow a direct link to the Clipboard. Simply copy the block of text you need, switch to Draw, open the Text dialog box, and paste the block.

In addition, CorelDRAW! 4.0's text filters enable you to import text files—from a variety of word processors and spreadsheets—into paragraph text blocks. Table 4.2 lists Draw's bevy of text import filters.

Table 4.2
CorelDRAW!'s Text Import Filters

Program	Versions	File Extension
Ami Professional	2.0, 3.0	SAM
Excel for Windows	3.0, 4.0	XLS
Lotus 123	1A, 2.0, 3.0	WK?
Lotus 123 for Windows	3.0	WK?
MacWrite II	1.0, 1.1	
Microsoft Rich Text Format RTF		RTF
Microsoft Word	5.0, 5.5	DOC
Microsoft Word for Windows	1.0, 2.0	DOC
Microsoft Word for Macintosh	4.0, 5.0	
Text		TXT
WordPerfect	5.0, 5.1	
WordPerfect for Windows		

For the following exercise, assume that Windows Write is your only word processing program. First, you type the text into Windows Write (which you should have), copy it to the Clipboard, and paste it into Draw. Then you try saving a Write file as a text-only file and naming it with the TXT file extension.

If Draw is already running, minimize it by clicking on the down arrow in the upper right corner of the screen. You must bring up the Program Manager to start Windows Write. For the sake of an uncluttered screen, minimize the Program Manager after bringing up Write.

Running Write and Draw Next to Each Other

Click on the minimize arrow	CorelDRAW! is minimized

In the Windows Program Manager, take the following steps:

Double-click on the Accessories *icon*	The Accessories folder opens
Double-click on the Write *icon*	Windows Write launches
Drag the Write window's left side to the middle of the screen	Write is in a half-screen window

Type the following. (Press Enter after each line except the last, and add an extra line after the fourth.)

```
USE THE CLIPBOARD!
You can save time and trouble
by using the Windows Clipboard
to import text into CorelDRAW!

Simply use the Copy and Paste
commands to capture text that
has already been keyboarded.
```

Double-click on the CorelDRAW! *icon*	CorelDRAW! is maximized
Drag the Draw window's right side to the middle of the screen	Draw is in a half-sceen window

Shortcut

Press Ctrl-Esc to summon the Windows Task Manager.

Shortcut

Press Alt-Tab to switch between running programs.

You should now have Draw running on the left side of the screen and Write running on the right side. The text you typed into Write is waiting for you to do something wonderful with it.

If you like to work with full-screen windows, you can switch between programs in a couple of easy ways. By pressing Ctrl-Esc, you summon the Windows Task Manager. You can then pop between programs by selecting the one you want from a dialog box. It is even easier to use Alt-Tab to move between programs. Each time you press the Tab key, you have instant access to another (already running) program.

Importing Text from Windows Write

Copy the text from Write and paste it into Draw. A simple click and drag in Write, followed by pressing Ctrl-Ins or selecting a couple of menu options, copies the text to the Clipboard. Then switch over to Draw, select the Text tool, click on the page, and paste the copied text.

Copying and Pasting Text

In the Write window, drag the cursor over the text	The text is reversed, white on black
Click on **E**dit	The Edit menu appears
Click on **C**opy	The text is copied to the Clipboard
In the CorelDRAW! window, click on the Text tool	The cursor becomes a +
Click on the page	The Text I bar appears
Press Shift-Ins	The text is pasted onto the page (see fig. 4.12); change any type settings you want

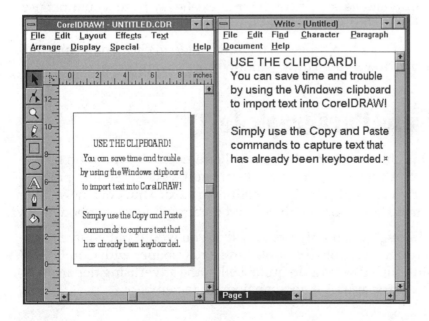

Figure 4.12:
CorelDRAW! and Write running simultaneously.

Pretty slick. You can use the Copy-and-Paste method to import text from almost any word processor. The stipulation is that the text might first need to be saved in ASCII format for it to be opened by Write. The only file formats that Write can open are WRI, DOC, and TXT. The upcoming section, "Using Paragraph Text," teaches you to import text files directly into CorelDRAW!

Some Provisos

Did you get a warning box or two? According to Corel's specifications, the program enables you to paste a maximum of approximately 256 characters into its artistic text-entry window. However, this might not add up in the manner you expect. Each carriage return counts as two characters: the carriage return and the line feed. This limitation is imposed by Draw, not by the Clipboard itself.

This character-limit handicap is not specific to imported text. It applies only to any artistic text entry. CorelDRAW! treats all artistic text as objects, whether the text has been converted to curves or not. Although the "per object" character count can be restrictive, it does not limit the number of characters on a page. It simply means that if you have a text-heavy page, you must use either multiple text entries or paragraph text.

To get back to a full-screen Draw window, click on the maximize (up) arrow in the Draw window's upper right corner.

Using Paragraph Text

This chapter has made repeated references to paragraph text. "Exactly what is paragraph text?" you wonder. Simply put, paragraph text is body (or columnar) text. Think of a newspaper; artistic text is for headlines, and paragraph text is for body copy.

Although it is highly unlikely that you would put yourself through the agony of publishing a newspaper with CorelDRAW! (although it would do quite well in the advertising department), the newspaper is a good analogy to remember.

The Paragraph Text tool adds a new dimension to CorelDRAW! If you produce brochures and other similar documents, you will welcome the flexibility that the paragraph tool offers.

The Paragraph Text tool builds on the basics of the Artistic Text tool, embellishing it with the additional capabilities of columnar text, full justification, and (from within the text edit dialog box) ASCII-text import capabilities up to a maximum of 4,000 characters per text block. If you want to import an ASCII text file with more than 4,000 characters (or a formatted text file, for that matter) you have to import the file with the Import command.

Even though you can fully justify paragraph text, the results might be disappointing with narrow columns. If you have narrow columns, you will be much happier with the flush left/ragged right setting. Wider column measures allow the program more room for inter-word spacing.

You can use the Paragraph Text feature for many projects. Although Draw might seem slow to process paragraph text, it might still be faster than shuttling between two separate programs. If your job contains one or two simple colors and is more text-based than design-based, you probably are better off using PageMaker or QuarkXpress for the text-heavy pages.

But if your project involves multiple colors, it might be better to do the whole job in Draw. PageMaker 4.0, for example, cannot fully color-separate the placed graphics, which can lead to increased prepress charges for film stripping. The idea behind CorelDRAW! is to generate plate-ready film, complete with traps. Although this is a lofty goal, it can save the experienced graphic artist money. For more information on trapping, see Chapter 11.

Thankfully, QuarkXpress and PageMaker 5.0 now can color separate placed graphics. These two programs are far better (and faster) tools for producing text-heavy documents, such as magazines and catalogs. Ultimately, the decision—on which program to use and when to use it—is yours.

The Paragraph Text Tool

The Paragraph Text tool is just as easy to use as most other Draw tools. If you understand how the Artistic Text tool works, then you have all the basics. The only important extras you need to know are how to access the tool, how to set up columns, and how to import text files.

Over at DeLook Design, Fast Freddie has shown up again. This time, he needs a disclaimer for the flyer that Joe just finished. The addition is an easy job, and one that is well suited for the Paragraph Text tool.

Freddie has the text on a disk—his secretary typed it on their old XT clone—and he claims that it is in ASCII format (as if he knew what that meant).

The text reads something like this:

DISCLAIMER

We are not responsible for anything. If your oil is not changed within 20 minutes, you do not have to pay. However, if there is no oil in your car at the time, you'll have to pay a $50 towing charge to get your car out of our garage. This may seem harsh, but what do we care? We own the tow truck anyway.

If we actually get your oil changed in 20 minutes, please note that the oil we use isn't fit for a greasy pizza parlor, much less your car's crankcase. If you want real oil, you have to pay for it, at an additional charge, of course. Nor will we replace your oil filter, so all that new cheap oil will just get dirty, real fast. What do you expect for $20? If you want a new filter, that'll be an extra $15.

If our grubby mechanics smear sludge over your beautiful velour upholstery, you're out of luck. We're not covered (and neither were your seats). If you happen to drop your car off for a few hours while you're shopping, don't be surprised if one of the mechanics takes your car for a test drive (using up all your gas). Hey, at least we didn't charge you for that.

If all this seems rather frightening, so what? There's no other garage for 15 miles, and besides, you're on vacation. What do you care?

Of course, only Joe DeLook can use Freddie's floppy disk—you have to type the disclaimer text using Windows Write. Then save the file as a text-only file, and give it a file name with a TXT extension. You should be familiar with Write after the last exercise, so get to work.

Before you start this next exercise, be sure to store the most recent version of FREDSAD.CDR. Then you can open a brand new Draw file, and (if it is not already open) open Windows Write as you did in the last exercise. Type in the paragraphs of the disclaimer. When you are finished, proceed with the following exercise.

Saving an ASCII TXT File in Windows Write

Click on **F**ile	The File menu appears
Click on Save **A**s	The File Save As dialog box appears

At Save File As Type, *Click on* **T**ext files (*.TXT)

Take note of where the file is to be stored. Most likely, it is in the Windows directory.

At Filename, *type* `FREDDIE.TXT`

Click on OK	The file is stored in the Windows directory as FREDDIE.TXT

The file is now stored as an ASCII text file.

The Paragraph Text Dialog Box

Now you must bring the ASCII text file into the Paragraph Text dialog box. The Paragraph Text tool works in the same click-and-drag fashion as the Rectangle tool (see fig. 4.13). Used in conjunction with snap-to-grid or guidelines, the Paragraph Text tool can lay down a text box of exact proportions. The status line reports the size of the paragraph text box as you draw it. But beware: after paragraph text is on the page, the status line does not report any dimensions.

You can resize a paragraph text box after it is on the page; it can be stretched or scaled to fit. The concept of paragraph text boxes will be very familiar to QuarkXPress users. You "pour" your text into the box after it is drawn. Unlike XPress or PageMaker, however, if a box is too small for the text file you have imported, Draw will not tell you that there is more text. You have to figure it out for yourself.

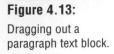

Figure 4.13:

Dragging out a
paragraph text block.

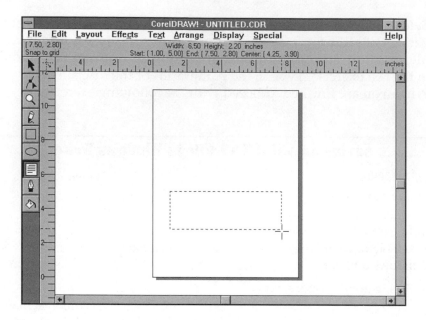

The Paragraph Text dialog box looks almost exactly like the
Artistic Text dialog box. Take note of the Import button at the
bottom of the dialog box. You soon see what this button does,
because you use it in the next exercise to import the text you just
typed in Windows Write.

CorelDRAW! 4.0 enables you to draw a paragraph text box and
immediately access the Paragraph Text dialog box (unlike version
3.0, which requires that you first have a character in the text box
before you can open the dialog box). In the next exercise, you will
draw a text box, access the Paragraph Text dialog box, and import
your text file. It sounds more confusing than it really is.

After you import your text into the Paragraph Text dialog box,
pay close attention. At the top right of the dialog box, you will
notice a number entry box and corresponding up and down arrow
buttons. These relate to a paragraph's sequence in the text block.
You must use this strange contraption to move from paragraph to
paragraph while in the Paragraph Text dialog box.

To make matters more confusing, you set type specifications while
in the Paragraph Text dialog box on a paragraph-by-paragraph
basis. Although this might have made sense to those who thought
up the scheme, it runs contrary to normal DTP conventions.

To avoid having to set the specifications for each individual paragraph, you will plug in the point size, typeface, and spacing information before you import the text file. By using this method, the specs apply to all the paragraphs in the text block. Remember to always try to set the type specs first! After you click on the import button, it's too late.

Laying Down a Paragraph Text Box with Imported Text

Click on the Text tool

Click and drag a text box on the Draw screen; make it 6.5 inches wide and 2.2 inches high

Release the mouse button   The paragraph-box outline appears (see fig. 4.13)

Press Ctrl-T   The Paragraph Text dialog box appears

*At Si*ze*, enter* **11**

Click on Geometr231 BT

Click on J*ustify*

Click on S*pacing*

At C*haracter, enter* **0**

At W*ord, enter* **70**

At L*ine, enter* **12 Points**

At B*efore Paragraph, enter* **0 Points**

At A*fter Paragraph, enter* **20 Points**

Click on OK

Click on I*mport*   The Import Text dialog box appears

Change to the Windows directory in preparation for bringing in the FREDDIE.TXT file you just created.

Double-click on FREDDIE.TXT   FREDDIE.TXT is imported (see fig. 4.14)

Click on OK

Figure 4.14:

The Paragraph Text dialog box with imported disclaimer text.

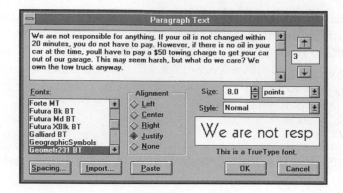

After you have the text on the page, the best way to change the specs is through the Text roll-up menu. It enables you to access the full paragraph specifications, with tabs, indents, bullets, and automatic hyphenation. You learn more about these advanced functions in the next chapter.

The Frame Attributes Dialog Box

CorelDRAW! splits paragraph text specifications over a number of different dialog boxes. You just used the first of the them—the Paragraph Text dialog box. The second is the Frame Attributes dialog box. In this second dialog box, you can alter the number of columns and the space between columns. The Frame Attributes dialog box is accessed from either the Text menu or the Text Roll-Up menu.

Now you are going to set up two columns for Freddie's disclaimer with the Frame Attributes dialog box.

Setting Up Columns with the Frame Attributes Dialog Box

Click on Te**x**t *from the menu bar*	The Text menu appears
Click on **F**rame	The Frame Attributes dialog box appears
At **N**umber, *enter* **2**	
At **G**utter Width, *enter* **2 picas**	

Click on OK

The settings specified in the Frame Attributes dialog box are accepted (see fig. 4.15)

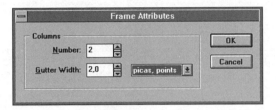

Figure 4.15:

The Frame Attributes dialog box.

As you have seen, the Paragraph Text tool enables you to import your text—a powerful, time-saving feature. Of course, you can always type your text directly into CorelDRAW!. All text within a paragraph text block does not have to be of the same typeface and size; CorelDRAW! 4.0 enables you to alter individual characters within a paragraph. This enables you to boldface or italicize certain words (although it takes more work to do it in Draw than to do it in a word processor or page layout program).

Unfortunately, CorelDRAW!'s text import filters do not convert inch- and foot-marks into *sexed* (right and left) quotes. Nor do they convert two hyphens into an em dash. Veteran DTPers have long come to expect both of these features from their page layout programs. If you import text that contains apostrophes, quotation marks, and em dashes, you have to manually replace them with the correct characters. Of course, you can always use Draw's handy new search-and-replace feature!

Now that you have a block of paragraph text on your page, you can start fooling around with it. Try different numbers of columns, gutter widths, point sizes, and so on (see fig. 4.16). You can change the size and shape of the text box as you would any other object in CorelDRAW!. Like objects, the text block can be scaled, stretched, skewed, and rotated.

PARAGRAPH TEXT CONVENTIONS

Figure 4.16:

The paragraph text conventions.

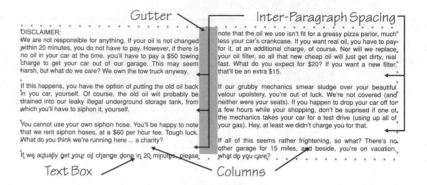

Experienced typographers know the difference between display type and body type. Fancy typefaces (*display type*) are fun for headlines, but they can make lousy body type. For *body type*, stick with faces that are legible at smaller sizes, like GillSans. Do not use faces like Shelly Allegro. These two examples are rather extreme—and you should not limit yourself. Just try to keep it within the realm of good taste!

Print Time with Paragraph Text

When you use paragraph text, it soon becomes apparent that Draw's font-description scheme has drawbacks relative to print file sizes and printing times. A simple solution to the problem is to either use resident fonts or download your fonts beforehand, and then click All Fonts Resident in the Print dialog box when you are ready to print.

When Draw sends a file to a PostScript output device, it assumes that the fonts are not printer-resident unless the fonts came with the printer. Consequently, print files can grow in alarming pro-portions as the program downloads font-outline information for every character in your file.

Once again, the way to get around this problem is to download the needed fonts before sending the file to the printer. By using this trick, print files shrink and print times are reduced. If you revise your proofs repeatedly along the way, downloading fonts to the printer can save hours a day in print time alone. Of course, if you enjoy waiting for your printer, keep doing what you are doing—you do not have to become more productive!

For more information on printing, refer to Chapter 11.

Editing Using Spelling Checker, Thesaurus, and Hyphenation

CorelDRAW! includes three powerful text-editing functions: a spelling checker, a thesaurus, and an automatic hyphenation option. This trio of features helps you do an even better job creating text-intensive artwork. Although you might have used a spelling checker and thesaurus in a word processing program, automatic hyphenation might be new to you. Even if you have never used any of these features, you have little to fear. They are all easy to use, and you should be power-editing with the pros in no time flat.

Get It Right with the Spelling Checker

The CorelDRAW! Spelling Checker is easy to use. Simply highlight a word or range of text with the Text tool or select a block of text with the Pick tool. Then select Spell Checker from the Text menu. Click on Check Text to begin checking. If no errors are in the selected text, a dialog box pops up and notifies you that everything checks out. If Spelling Checker finds a questionable word, a dialog box shows you the first unknown or misspelled word. Click on the Suggest button to display alternative spellings. Double-click on the desired word in the Alternative box (or select the desired word and click on Replace) to replace the misspelled word with the alternative. The Spelling Checker then moves on to the next anomaly.

If you click the Always Suggest button, alternative spellings automatically pop up. If you repeatedly spell the same word incorrectly in a selected range of text, click on the Replace All button to immediately change all instances. Conversely, you can click on the Ignore All button to leave all instances of an unknown word alone (see fig. 4.17).

Figure 4.17:

The Spelling Checker dialog box.

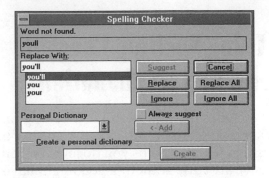

The use of a spelling checker should be an adjunct to, and not a replacement for, good proofreading. In many cases, however, you might not have the luxury of a real proofreader. Considering that many people find it difficult to proof their own work, Draw's Spelling Checker can be a great help. Use it, but do not rely on it. A spelling checker cannot pick up a number of typographical errors, including outsets (missed sections), transposed words, the wrong (although correctly spelled) word, and bad grammar.

Make the effort to get someone else to take a look at your files before you send them out to print. You can save yourself untold grief (and reprints).

Want to try out Spelling Checker? If you would like, select Fast Freddie's disclaimer text with the Text tool, and let Spelling Checker go to work!

Try the Thesaurus When You Can't Think of a Word

Perhaps you have needed a synonym for a word, but have not had a thesaurus at hand. With CorelDRAW!, you easily can use the built-in Thesaurus to change a word with a few clicks. Just use the

Text tool to highlight the word you want to replace, and select the Thesaurus from the Text menu. The Thesaurus dialog box pops up with the selected word in the Synonym for field. Depending on whether the selected word is in the computer's dictionary, its definition and any synonyms (and their definitions) might or might not appear (see fig. 4.18).

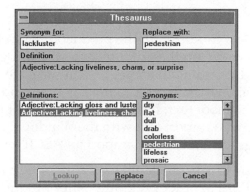

Figure 4.18:
The Thesaurus dialog box.

If no definition or synonyms appear, enter a new word in the Synonym for field and click Lookup. When you find a synonym that fits your needs, double-click on the synonym (or select the synonym and click on Replace), and the synonym replaces the word you originally selected in your text.

Cut Yourself a Break with Hyphenation

Have you ever had to consult a dictionary to decide where to hyphenate (break) a word? Those days might be over! Now you can set your hyphenation options in CorelDRAW! without leaving your seat for the bookshelf. The Automatic Hyphenation option has Draw do all the work. All you need to do is select the text block, click on the Paragraph button (on the Text Roll-Up menu), and turn on Automatic Hyphenation (which you will find at the bottom of the Paragraph specifications dialog box).

Automatic Hyphenation is adjustable via the Hot Zone setting. The *hot zone* is an imaginary band that runs down the right side of a text block where hyphenation is allowed to take place.

Typographers and designers refer to unjustified text as *ragged* (or simply, rag)—hence the terms ragged right and ragged left. A larger Hot Zone setting yields a more radical rag; a smaller Hot Zone setting gives you a tighter rag.

Summary

This chapter took you through the production of DeLook Design's first "real" job with CorelDRAW!. It covered placing, aligning, modifying, and grouping blocks of text on the page. You used the Character Attributes dialog box to modify type, and you delved into the use of symbol text. In the second section of the chapter, you learned how to import text with the Windows Clipboard, and used the Paragraph Text tool to import an ASCII text file.

As you continue to see, much of Draw's strength is in its text handling and links to other programs. After producing that first simple flyer, the program's typographical power should begin to become apparent. The exercise on importing text gives you an idea of how the program can be used in a workgroup environment.

Building an effective system composed of both computer and human factors is the key to success in electronic arts. For more information on putting together a selection of software and hardware, refer to Chapter 10.

In contrast to the preceding chapters in which Joe uncovered the basic functions of the program, the following chapters include more advanced hands-on projects. First up is a project in the next chapter that delves into some complex typographical maneuvers.

5

Advanced Typography

ith the previous chapters, you have already learned
many of the basics of setting type. Next, you continue to explore the many typographical possibilities
that CorelDRAW! offers the designer. This chapter
discusses some of Draw's more advanced typographical, special effect, outline, and fill features,
as well as CorelDRAW! 4.0's new features, such as
multipage documents (with prerequisite linked paragraph text
boxes), style tags, tabs, bullets, and indent settings.

You begin by setting some text and proceed to kerning that text
while it is still in its native state. Then, using Convert To Curves,
you gain access to the text's character outlines. This feature gives
you an incredible amount of control over character shapes. Even
more amazing are Draw's Envelope and Extrude effects. The
exercise you begin here is finished up in Chapter 11 with a study
of CorelDRAW!'s trapping capabilities.

The chapter includes a survey of the new text features, but goes
lightly on creating multipage documents. CorelDRAW! is not a
mature multipage document tool. If your workload includes
magazines, large newsletters, newspapers, or the like, you are
better off with a page-layout program such as Aldus PageMaker,

QuarkXpress, or Ventura Publisher. The time you save by using one of these packages far outweighs whatever financial outlay you might have to make (assuming you do not already own a copy of one of these programs).

This book does not attempt to teach the art of typography. Teaching typography is not an easy task; becoming a master of typography takes years of study and practice. This book can, however, show you how to use the tools of typography incorporated within CorelDRAW!; what you do with these tools is your decision.

The purpose of this chapter is to show you how to use Corel-DRAW! to produce type with various effects. Like kids on the beach with pails and shovels, one builds a beautiful sand castle while another digs a hole. Yet both begin with the same tools and foundation. Remember, it is important to establish a solid foundation—by learning to use your tools properly—before laying the bricks of good design.

Using the Right Tool for the Job

To be most efficient, an electronic artist must know each program's limitations. CorelDRAW! offers superb control, but it does have its restrictions.

Although things have greatly improved with version 4.0, CorelDRAW! is at its best when it does not have huge amounts of type to set. Some examples of typographical projects for which Draw has been best suited include advertisements with tightly kerned headlines, company logos, newsletter mastheads, and standing heads. But you don't have to stop there any more! The new features ensure that you now can use Draw for more text-heavy projects such as formatted columns of text, lengthy brochures, or tabular column work. You wouldn't want to typeset a book in Draw, but a brochure or newsletter is fine.

Due to the overall restrictions of the program's text-editing features and the Artisting Tool's 256-character text string limit, be sure to think a project through before you decide to use CorelDRAW! or before you get too heavily involved in production. If you are going to use Draw, you need to decide whether to use the Artistic or Paragraph Text tool.

While the Paragraph Text tool now includes real formatting features such as tabs, indents, and bullets, implementing these features feels slow and clunky compared to the established page-layout packages. For a seriously text-heavy project, consider looking for the PageMaker or QuarkXpress icon. In other words, do yourself a favor: use the right tool for the job.

In the imaginary town of Seaside, it is lunch time at DeLook Design. Joe and the crew have taken their lunch break at Thurston's Bait and Tackle (and coffee shop). Sam Thurston, the proprietor and namesake, appears eager to see Joe DeLook. It seems that Fast Freddie dropped in on his way to the printer to show off his new flyer.

Sam wants DeLook Design to create a T-shirt that would convey some of the history and ambiance of Seaside's oldest bait-and-tackle shop. After a few thumbnail sketches, Joe decides that the shirts emblem should look similar to the sign that hangs over Thurston's front door (see fig. 5.1). The sign is rendered in classic sign painter's style and has hung there for over six decades.

Joe knows what he wants. Now he has to figure out how to use CorelDRAW! to create what he needs.

Treating Text as an Object

The last chapter mentioned that Draw treats all text as objects. It does this in two ways. The first is to treat text as normal, editable text. The second is to convert text to curves.

While text is in its "native"—or unconverted—state, you can use CorelDRAW!'s tools to perform any number of transformations. Text can be filled, outlined, rotated, stretched, mirrored, and fit to a path. In addition, individual characters can be kerned, rotated, pulled above or below the baseline, and sized. Most of the time, you apply these modifications to text that is still in its original, non-converted state.

Figure 5.1:

Thurston's sign.

One basic reason to convert text to curves is to alter individual character shapes. After text has been converted to curves, you can make some amazing modifications. You can bend, pull, stretch, twist, and mutate individual character outlines at will. Strong stuff, but exactly the things that make CorelDRAW! so powerful.

After a block of text has been converted to curves, there is no going back. Text that has been converted is no longer editable in the normal sense. It becomes pure object and cannot be reconverted to text. While it might still look like text, it does not act like text. You cannot access it from the Text dialog box or the Text roll-up menu. In the next exercise, however, you see the control afforded by text that has been converted to curves. As you stretch out the letters in the design, the advantages (and disadvantages) of manipulating a character's individual nodes become obvious. This is a time-consuming, though superb, feature.

Text in a "converted-to-curves" state can be a challenge to work with. Get in the habit of saving multiple versions of your files. If a foul-up occurs, simply recall the last version you stored.

Using Special Effects on Text

CorelDRAW! version 2.0 introduced a trio of effects that greatly enhance your ability to produce customized type in a tight time frame. Designs that previously took hours to accomplish now can be done in a fraction of the time by using the following effects:

- **Envelope.** This effect enables you to place a boundary around a piece of text (or other object), and apply different arcing styles with a few click ons and drags. The Thurston's sign that you create in this chapter is a prime example of such an effect. Corel has refined the Envelope effect in version 4.0.

- **Extrude.** This effect applies depth to text or other objects. Using extrude, you easily can create block type with a three-dimensional effect. The direction and amount of depth, as well as the percentage of perspective, is unrestricted.

- **Perspective.** This effect is a snazzy tool for altering the line of sight by varying degrees. You can make a line of text appear to run down the side of a building or package. This can be a fabulous instrument for package design and conceptualization. Chapter 9 covers this effect.

When you use these effects, text remains in an editable state. However, you might find that to fine-tune things, you need to convert the text to curves. It all depends on your professional perspective. High-end advertising typography, for example, has far different standards from a relatively unsophisticated in-house newsletter.

You use the good old manual method to begin this next project. Along the way, you save a copy of the file so that you can go back in and try a more automated method later. You will be amazed at the possibilities after you have gained an understanding of what can be accomplished using these powerful tools.

Tackling the Bait-and-Tackle T-Shirt Project

This group of exercises begins with setting the type for the Thurston's Bait-and-Tackle T-shirt project. After the type is set, you kern the characters to optimize spacing. After converting the text to curves, you stretch out the letters to form the arcing sign painter's style of the original design.

You begin this exercise with two identically sized blocks of text. By the end of the exercise, though, those blocks will be radically different in appearance. Through Convert To Curves, you achieve dramatic results that would be difficult to produce with other drawing programs.

This design fits on a landscape 8 ½-by-11-inch page, so take care of the Page Setup dialog box first. Make sure that the grid is turned on and set to six per inch. You turn the grid off once the type has been converted to curves.

Using Nonprinting Guidelines to Lay Out Designs

CorelDRAW! version 3.0 first introduced the Layers roll-up menu. This feature enables you to assign objects to specific drawing layers. In the following exercises, you create a number of objects on the non-printing guide layer. You lay out your design on a guide rectangle 9.17 inches wide by 7.17 inches deep. This rectangle is your design boundary line. You easily can scale and align objects using this boundary line.

You also can use Draw's snap-to guidelines for many such situations. Unlike most other programs, however, Draw supports more than just vertical or horizontal guidelines. For those times when you need an arc or diagonal guideline, Draw has you covered!

Anyone who has spent time at an old-fashioned drawing board is familiar with the idea of using guidelines. In Draw, non-printing rectangles, ellipses, and lines are invaluable drawing aids. Use them the same way you would draw blue lines on a board. Although PageMaker users will be quite familiar with the concept of snap-tos, these "do-it-yourself" guides are a bit different in theory and practice.

Shortcut

Ctrl-F3 brings up the Layers roll-up menu.

Set up your page and design boundaries, then set the type. If something on the screen should be saved, make sure that you save it now.

Setting Up the Page

Click on **F**ile	The File menu appears
Click on **N**ew	A blank page appears
Click on **L**ayout	The Layout menu appears
Click on Pa**ge** Setup	The Page Setup dialog box appears
Click on **L**andscape	
Click on L**e**tter	
Click on OK	Page changes to landscape orientation
Click on **L**ayout	The Layout menu appears
Click on G**ri**d Setup	The Grid Setup dialog box appears
Change the grid frequency to six *per* inch	
Make sure that **S**nap-to-Grid *is selected*	
Click on OK	
Click on **L**ayout	The Layout menu appears
Click on Layers roll-up	The Layers roll-up menu appears
At Layers roll-up, *click on* Guides	Guide-layer is selected
Click on right arrow	Layers fly-out menu appears
Make sure that Multilayer *is selected*	
Click on the Rectangle tool	
Drag a rectangle	Make the rectangle 9.17 inches wide by 7.17 inches tall. Center it on the page
Release the mouse button	A guideline rectangle is drawn

Now the preparation is out of the way. A clean piece of paper is on the board, and the first guidelines are drawn. You can begin setting type for this design.

Setting Type

Corel includes approximately 50 typefaces on Draw version 4.0's distribution floppies, and more than 750 on the CD-ROMs. This collection provides an amazing variety of faces, and, as you see later on in the book, you easily can add more faces to your personal collection.

Each typeface has its own distinctive features, and each sets differently from other faces. In figure 5.2, you can see the differences in height and width between four of the sans serif typefaces supplied with Draw. The figure also gives a visual representation of some common typographical conventions.

Figure 5.2:

Typeface sizes and conventions.

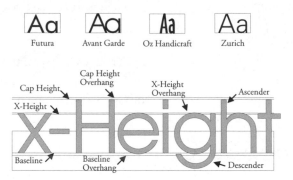

For the first block of text, you use 144-point Bookman, a fairly popular typeface included as one of the 35 standard PostScript fonts in many laser printers. Set the spacing at a moderately tight –5 percent.

Setting THURSTONS

Click on **L**ayout	The Layout menu appears
At Layers roll-up, *click on* Layer 1	Layer 1 is selected

Click on the text tool	The cursor becomes a +
Click on the page	The Text I bar appears
Type **THURSTONS**	
Press Ctrl-T	The Artistic Text dialog box appears
Click on **Center**	
Enter **144** *in the point size window*	
Click on Bookman ITC Lt Bt	
Click on **Spacing**	The Text Spacing dialog box appears
At Character, enter **–5**	
At Word, enter **65**	
Click on OK	
Click on OK *again*	The type is set according to your specifications
Click on the Pick tool	
Drag THURSTONS *to the center of the page*	

Do not worry if the text runs over the edges of the page; you will condense it in a few moments. Next, you are going to set the bottom line, BAIT & TACKLE. There will be a few differences.

In previous versions of CorelDRAW!, the type entry dialog box remembers the last typeface and size specified. You will not enter any type specifications. Instead, you will use the Copy Attributes From command. Consequently you did not have to reenter similar type specs each time you created a new block of type. Alas, for whatever reason, this time-saving feature is no more.

Setting **BAIT & TACKLE**

Click on the Text tool	The cursor becomes a +
Click on the page	The Text I bar appears
Type **BAIT & TACKLE**	
Click on the Pick tool	
Drag BAIT & TACKLE *to the center of the page*	

Rather than using the Text roll-up menu or Edit Text dialog box to re-enter the type specifications, use a shortcut to quickly assign the specs.

Borrowing Attributes

Copy Attributes From is a shortcut that you can use for a wide range of purposes on various objects, not just type. This command is a great time-saver, because you can use it to copy object details from one item to the next.

In this case, you copy type specifications from one block to the next. When you use this shortcut, you can avoid the Edit Text and Spacing dialog boxes altogether and ensure that the typographical attributes are consistent from line to line.

Copying Attributes

With BAIT & TACKLE still selected, take the following steps:

Click on **E**dit	The Edit menu appears
Click on Copy **A**ttributes **F**rom	The Copy **A**ttributes From menu appears
Click on **T**ext Attributes	
Click on OK	The From? arrow appears
Click on THURSTONS	The type specifications are copied

That was quick and easy, wasn't it? The Copy Attributes From command comes in handy on many occasions. Later in this exercise, you use the command to copy fill and outline information from one object to the next.

Condensing Type

The next step is to squeeze the two text blocks to fit into your design boundary. Looking at the screen (see fig. 5.3), you can see that although the height of the characters is correct, both lines of type are too large for the design. In order to make the two lines of type fit, you must stretch them to size horizontally.

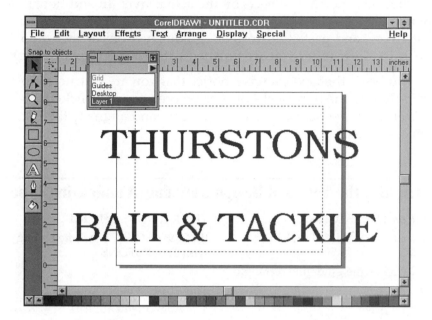

Stretching was covered way back in Chapter 1, and you even condensed some type in Chapter 4, so these next few steps should be familiar by now. Begin by aligning the left side of the two text lines to your nonprinting design boundary by using Align/ Horizontal/Left. You then vertically align the text to the boundary. Finish by horizontally scaling the text to fit and grouping all the objects.

Notice all the arranging, grouping, and ungrouping going on. To align multiple objects, you often need to work in this fashion. When aligning an assortment of objects with different orientations, grouping enables you to maintain the relationship between two objects while you align them with other objects. As an example, two objects can be horizontally left-aligned with each other and grouped; then, the group may be horizontally right-aligned with a third object, and so on. For more information about grouping and aligning, refer to Chapter 3.

A note of caution: if you group objects with guide-layer objects, the guide-layer objects are pulled forward from the guide layer and become "normal" objects on the active layer. In addition, they then are assigned the default outline and fill. In these cases, you need to cut and paste the "former" guide-layer object back onto the guide layer (after you are finished with your group-aligning)!

As you begin the next exercise, notice that you are instructed to shift-click on the two blocks of type before you shift-click on the guideline. Remember that the Align command aligns to the last object selected!

Aligning the Text and Design Boundary/Condensing Type

Click on THURSTONS	THURSTONS is selected
Shift-click on BAIT & TACKLE	BAIT & TACKLE is selected along with THURSTONS
Shift-click on the guideline rectangle	
Click on **A**rrange	The Arrange menu appears
Click on **A**lign	The Align menu appears
Click on Horizontal **L**eft	
Click on OK	The objects are horizontally left-aligned

At this point, all three of the objects (the rectangle, THURSTONS, and BAIT & TACKLE) should be horizontally left-aligned and should still be selected. By shift-clicking on BAIT & TACKLE, it will be deselected.

Shift-click on BAIT & TACKLE	The words are deselected
Click on **A**rrange	The Arrange menu appears
Click on **A**lign	The Align menu appears
Click on Vertical **T**op	
Click on OK	The two objects are almost vertically top-aligned
Click on **A**rrange	The Arrange menu appears
Click on **G**roup	The objects are grouped
Click on page	The objects are deselected
Click on BAIT & TACKLE	The words are selected
Shift-click on the guideline rectangle	

Click on **A**rrange	The Arrange menu appears
Click on **A**lign	The Align menu appears
Click on Vertical **B**ottom	
Click on OK	The objects are almost vertically bottom-aligned
Shift-click on BAIT & TACKLE	The words are deselected
Click on **A**rrange	The Arrange menu appears
Click on **U**ngroup	The objects are ungrouped
Shift-click on the rectangle	The rectangle is deselected
Drag THURSTONS *right-center handle to the left*	The handles are replaced by a blue dashed box
Release the mouse button	When the status line reads (approx.) `73 percent`
Click on BAIT & TACKLE	The words are selected
Drag the right-center handle to the left	The handles are replaced by a blue dashed box
Release the mouse button	When the status line reads (approx.) `61 percent`

Notice that the type blocks might not vertically align with the rectangle. Use zoom to get a better view of the objects. You need to turn the grid off to achieve proper alignment. Drag (or nudge) the text blocks into position. Turn the grid back on when you are finished.

Click on **E**dit	The Edit menu appears
Click on Select **A**ll	All objects are selected
Click on **A**rrange	The Arrange menu appears
Click on **G**roup	The objects are grouped (see fig. 5.4)

If necessary, use Align to **C**enter of Page (in the Align dialog box).

Click on **A**rrange	The Arrange menu appears
Click on **U**ngroup	The objects are ungrouped
Click on the page *to deselect objects*	
Click on the rectangle	The rectangle is selected
Press Shift-Del	The rectangle is cut
At Layers *roll-up, Click on* Guides	Guide-layer is selected
Press Shift-Ins	The rectangle is pasted onto the guide-layer

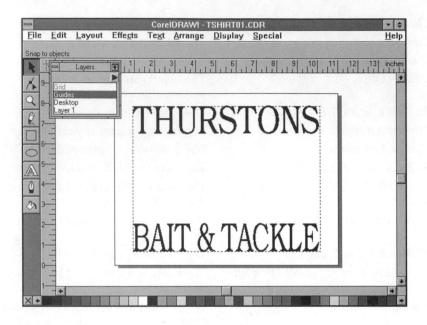

A wise typographer is careful as to which typefaces she scales anamorphically and the percentages she uses. It is easy to create an unreadable mess by scaling the wrong face or by scaling too much. However, this project calls for a certain look, and Bookman seems to hold up fairly well. It will not win any awards, but it will do for this example.

Before you go any further, take the time to save your file!

Saving Progressive Files

You will save your page under the file name TSHIRT. As a complex drawing progresses, it is wise to name the file in such a way that you can create multiple copies. Use a short prefix (up to five or six characters) followed by a numeric extension.

Each time a difficult maneuver is performed, use Save As to renumber the file. Name your first save TSHIRT01, and proceed on to TSHIRT02, TSHIRT03, TSHIRT04, and so on. By using this routine, you have a file to fall back on if the current file gets ruined.

Saving the File

Click on **F**ile	The File menu appears
Click on **S**ave	The Save File dialog box appears
At File, *type* **TSHIRT01**	
Click on **S**ave	The file is saved as TSHIRT01.CDR

The next step is to add another nonprinting guideline. This guide is the imaginary line around which you stretch characters.

Adding an Arc Guideline

Next, you add another object to the guide layer. This time, you draw an ellipse, around which your type arcs. The ellipse starts out as 9.17 inches wide by 1.50 inches high, which is approximately the width and height of the word THURSTONS. You then use a constrained vertical stretch to scale the ellipse anamorphically to approximately 300 percent of its original height, and finish by centering the ellipse.

Drawing, Stretching, and Positioning the Ellipse

At Layers *roll-up, click on* Guides	Guide layer is selected
Click on the Ellipse tool	The cursor becomes a + sign
Align the cursor with top left corner of the rectangle	
Drag down and to the right	The cursor snaps to the grid as it is moved
Release the mouse button	When the status line reads `9.17"` by `1.50"`, an ellipse is drawn
Click on the Pick tool	The ellipse is selected
Position the cursor over the ellipse's bottom-center handle	The cursor becomes a +
Drag the bottom-center handle down	
Release the mouse button, then Ctrl	When the status line reads `y scale 300%` (vertical stretch)

continues

Click on **A**rrange	The Arrange menu appears
Click on **A**lign	The Align menu appears
Click on Align to **C**enter of Page	
Click on OK	The ellipse is centered
Press Ctrl-Y	Turns off the grid

The top of the ellipse should approximately touch the baseline of the upper block of text, and the bottom of the ellipse should approximately reach the lower text block's cap height (see fig. 5.5).

Figure 5.5:

Using an ellipse as the guideline.

You are done using the grid—you turned it off with Ctrl-Y at the end of the exercise. You see why after you convert the text to curves and begin manipulating the individual outlines.

Kerning Text

After the type is in position, you need to kern the text. *Kerning* is the art of reducing or increasing the space between character pairs to achieve an even visual appearance. Certain character combinations, such as LT, VA, To, and Wo are commonly tightened to give an aesthetic character fit. Figure 5.6 shows many of these commonly kerned combinations.

AT AV AW AY Av Aw Ay

Figure 5.6:
The kern pair chart.

FA LT LY PA TA Ta Te

To Tr Tu Tw Ty VA Vo

WA Wa We Wo Ye Ya Yo

Typeface: Berthold City Light (Adobe)

Few skills in the graphic arts are quite so esoteric as kerning. The amount of time spent kerning is entirely up to the kerner. Some people can spend hours on a single headline, while others have no qualms about setting unkerned type. If you fall in love with the craft of finely-kerned type, it's likely that your spouse (or significant other) will look at you with dismay when the conversation turns to kerning. Some—no, make that most—folks just do not understand, nor will they ever.

Is kerning an acquired skill or an innate ability? Quite possibly, it is more than a little of both. Those people who do not comprehend the concept of kerning are not alone. Thousands of people out there who call themselves typesetters, or even typographers, could not kern themselves out of a loose (as opposed to a tight) spot.

If you have the ability and the desire, you can learn to kern. But, you must *want* to learn. Developing an "eye" takes time and effort. It is all too possible to lose half a day kerning a headline. One key is to make consistent changes and do so in small steps.

CorelDRAW! makes kerning easy for professional typographers. In addition to its excellent screen representations (from both TrueType and PostScript/ATM fonts), the program offers a number of kerning methods to select from. It offers the user a chance to make a precise numeric entry via the Character Attributes dialog box, or use the visual click-and-drag approaches. Nudge is an additional way to finesse type in fine, measured increments. You can set up your Nudge preferences and massage letters into position. As you will see, each method has its advantage, and the different methods can be used in combination.

Drag-kerning text by eye is the fastest way to bridge a large space. Results are immediate—you can see exactly what is happening; this is the method you use most often. But not always. Nudge-kerning also is very visual and direct.

Kerning Using Character Attributes

The Character Attributes dialog box can move text in increments as fine as one percent of a character's point size. You use this device when you need to squeeze just a hair between characters, or to move a measured amount in one shot. At larger point sizes, however, you might want to use Nudge (with a fine setting) to finesse character fit. Character Attribute kerning is specified in a percentage relative to point size; nudge kerning is denoted by absolute distances.

In the last chapter, you used the Character Attributes dialog box to make the superior dollar sign for the Fast Freddie flyer. The dialog box offers a variety of text manipulation tools in one easily accessible place.

In addition to typeface, point size, superior, and inferior typographic controls, the Character Attributes dialog box offers control over other important character specifications. These specs include horizontal shift (kerning), vertical (or baseline) shift, and character angle (rotation). This section covers the horizontal shift controls. The rest comes shortly.

By specifying –5 percent character spacing, you asked for a relatively tight track. There should not be much individual letter-pair kerning to do here, but after you learn how, you can take the practice as far as you want.

Begin by kerning the word THURSTONS. Remember to hold down Ctrl to constrain your movement to the baseline. Use the Zoom tool to get a better look at the area in which you are working. You can move one or more characters at a time. Be sure to pay attention to the status line. If the Layers roll-up menu gets in your way, roll the menu up by clicking on the menu's up-arrow button. You can roll it back down by clicking on the same button.

Kerning THURSTONS

At Layers roll-up menu: Click on Layer 1	Layer 1 is selected
Click on the Layers up-arrow button	The Layers roll-up menu rolls up!
Click on the Zoom tool	
Click on the +	
Marquee-select THURSTONS	
Release the mouse button	The screen zooms up on THURSTONS
Click on the Shape tool	
Click on THURSTONS	
Marquee-select the NS *nodes*	The nodes are selected
Ctrl-drag the NS *nodes to the left*	Move the nodes to (approximately) dx: -0.09
Shift-click on the N *node*	The N node is deselected
Ctrl-drag the S *node to the left*	Move the node to dx: -0.05
Double-click on the S *node*	The Character Attributes dialog box appears
At the horizontal shift, type **-12**	
Click on OK	

Notice that when you used the Character Attributes dialog box, the <u>H</u>orizontal Shift entry listed the approximate total distance from both moves (see fig. 5.7). This amount is the total cumulative distance from the original position. This information can be a bit confusing, because the status bar reports on absolute distances, while the dialog box reports on a change in distance as a percentage of point size.

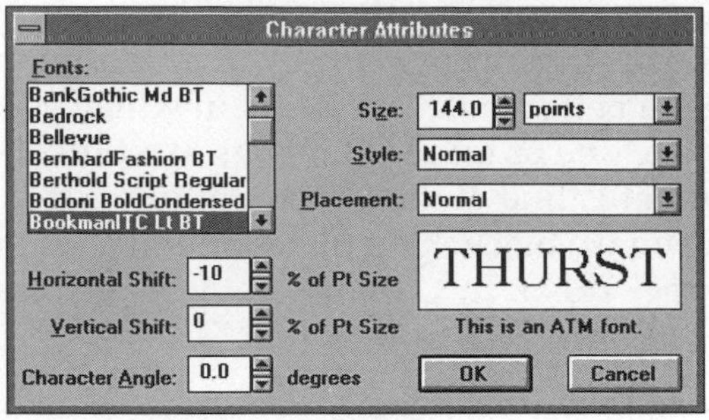

Figure 5.7:

The Character Attributes dialog box.

It is much easier and far more precise to handle the last tweaks with Nudge or the dialog box rather than by drag-kerning. Make your big moves with the mouse and fine-tune using Nudge and then the dialog box (if necessary).

Shortcut

Double-click on a selected character node to get to the Character Attributes dialog box.

The Character Attributes dialog box can be accessed in one of two ways. The first (and more roundabout) way is to select a node and click on Text and Character. The second (and easiest) way is to simply double-click on a selected node.

As you have seen, drag-kerning can be used on more than one character at a time. In the next exercise, you move large blocks in one fell swoop.

Now that you have kerned the word THURSTONS, you move on to the second block of text, BAIT AND TACKLE. Since this block of text was "squeezed" a bit tighter, it provides plenty of kerning opportunities.

Kerning goes both ways. Although most people think of kerning as something that is only done to tighten up text, this is hardly the case. Certain character combinations, in certain fonts, can cause a "too tight" situation to appear. Look at the AI, IT, and KL character combinations; they all should be "opened up."

Give It a Nudge!

Nudge was one of the most convenient features introduced in CorelDRAW Version 2.0. It enables you to move an object or objects (including type) by a pre-specified distance.

Using your keyboard's cursor keys, you can move objects up, down, to the left, or to the right in increments as fine as one tenth (0.1) of a point or as large as 12 picas. The amount of Nudge is specified in the Preferences dialog box. You will find many opportunities to use this wonderful feature; kerning is but one of them.

To kern individual (or groups of) letters, click on the Shape tool, select the nodes of the letters you want to move, and bang away at the appropriate cursor key. The characters instantly pop into place. Another advantage of using nudge-kerning, as opposed to drag-kerning, is that baseline alignment is easily maintained.

As a typographer's tool, Corel does have limitations. Although the Preferences dialog box enables you to set the Nudge increment to as fine as one tenth (0.1), of a point, settings less than .3 are disregarded. If you need to nudge things in finer increments, use the following work-around. While .3 points is the smallest effective Nudge setting, remember that you can initially set your type in a larger size and then scale it down after you are finished tweaking. Using this method, you can kern effectively in minuscule increments. Just make sure that your type is not too tight after you reduce it!

Figure 5.8 shows what the word "BAIT" looks like on screen before you do anything to it. Figure 5.9 shows the results of the following exercise.

BAIT

Figure 5.8:
Before kerning.

The BAIT & TACKLE Kernfest

Before you begin this exercise, call up the Preferences dialog box and set Nudge to 1 point.

Click on the Shape tool	
Click on BAIT & TACKLE	The words are selected
Marquee-select the AIT & TACKLE *nodes*	The nodes are selected
Ctrl-drag the AIT & TACKLE *nodes to the left*	Move the nodes to dx: -0.06
Release the mouse button	The text is kerned
Shift-click on the A *node*	The A node is deselected
Drag the IT & TACKLE *nodes to right*	Move the nodes to dx: 0.05
Release the mouse button	The text is kerned
Shift-click on the IT & T nodes	The IT & T nodes are deselected
Ctrl-drag the ACKLE *nodes to the left*	Move the nodes to dx: -0.05
Release the mouse button	The text is kerned
Shift-click on the A *node*	The A node is deselected
Ctrl-drag the CKLE *nodes to the left*	Move the nodes to dx: -0.8
Release the mouse button	The text is kerned
Shift-click on the C *node*	The C node is deselected
Ctrl-drag the KLE *nodes to the left*	Move the nodes to dx: -0.05
Release the mouse button	The text is kerned
Shift-click on the K *node*	The K node is deselected

Now, nudge-kern the last two nodes:

Press the right-arrow key four times	The characters are kerned four points to the right
Shift-click on the L *node*	The L node is deselected
Press the left-arrow key twice	The character is kerned two points to the left

NOTE

The type may need "more" or "less" kerning, depending on your personal preferences. Use either the drag- or nudge-kerning technique.

That seems like a lot of work for one line of text. Get ready, because it gets worse. After you begin moving individual character nodes around, kerning seems like a vacation at the beach!

BAIT

Figure 5.9:
After kerning.

Realigning Text to the Baseline

When you kern characters, you might accidentally pull them off their baseline. Perhaps you forgot to hold down Ctrl while you were drag-kerning. This problem is just as easily corrected by using the Align To Baseline command.

Align To Baseline can be used on a block of text while it is selected with either the Pick or the Shape tool. The command returns all text to its original horizontal baseline.

Shortcut

Press Ctrl-Z to align text to baseline.

Using Align To Baseline

Click on the Pick tool	
Click on THURSTONS	The word is selected
Click on Te<u>x</u>t	The Text menu appears
Click on Align to Base<u>l</u>ine	The text is aligned to the baseline
Click on BAIT & TACKLE	The words are selected
Click on Te<u>x</u>t	The Text menu appears
Click on Align to Base<u>l</u>ine	The text is aligned to the baseline

Now that you have finished kerning and aligning the second block of text to the baseline, it is a good idea to align the text horizontally. When you kerned the text, you changed the line lengths; consequently, the objects are no longer centered to the design boundary. You use a variation of Align to Center of Page to restrain alignment to the horizontal plane.

Realigning the Text

Click on THURSTONS	The word is selected
Shift-click on BAIT & TACKLE	Both pieces of text are selected
Click on **A**rrange	The Arrange menu appears
Click on **A**lign	The Align menu appears
Click on Align to Center of **P**age	
Click on Vertical C**e**nter	Vertical Center is deselected
Click on OK	The objects are horizontally centered
Click on **F**ile	
Click on Save **A**s	Save the file as TSHIRT02.CDR

Okay, all the easy work is out of the way. Now things start to get more complicated. It is almost time to convert your two lines of type to curves. After you do that, there is no going back. You cannot unconvert to curves. Make sure that you have saved your file before you continue!

Editing and Manipulating Character Outlines

Converting text to curves enables you to modify individual character shapes. This feature can be extremely useful for custom logos and hand-lettering techniques. Figure 5.10 shows some samples of effects created using type that has been converted to curves. In the following exercise, you pull text around the ellipse to give the look of a traditional freehand-rendered sign.

After you convert a block of text to curves, you cannot edit the text using the Text dialog box. It becomes just another curved object. This reason is why it is important to make sure that no typographical errors are present before you convert text to curves!

Figure 5.10:
Type that has been
converted to curves.

Converting Text to Curves

Converting to curves is quite simple. The work you perform afterwards, however, is quite complex.

Converting THURSTONS BAIT & TACKLE to Curves

Click on the Pick tool	
Click on THURSTONS	The word is selected
Click on **A**rrange	The Arrange menu appears
Click on Con**v**ert To Curves	Notice the nodes: the word THURSTONS is now curves
Click on BAIT & TACKLE	The words are selected
Click on **A**rrange	The Arrange menu appears
Click on Con**v**ert To Curves	BAIT & TACKLE is converted to curves

Shortcut

Press Ctrl-Q to convert to curves.

Notice that individual nodes have appeared on the characters. As far as CorelDRAW! is concerned, the characters are now objects, not letters. You are about to see exactly what that means.

Remember fooling around with the clouds back in Chapter 3? You pushed and pulled on the clouds' nodes and control points to alter their sizes and shapes. You can now do the same thing to your letters.

You begin the next exercise by zooming in on the first part of THURSTONS. Using the Zoom tool, you drag a marquee around the letters THUR. With the screen zoomed in, the individual character nodes are apparent.

As you drag the characters out, watch the status line. To avoid an overabundance of node tweaking, try to maintain an x: 0.00 coordinate as you drag. Nonetheless, you will have to align the nodes anyway. Using the status line helps, but it does not circumvent all imperfections.

Shortcut

Use Ctrl-drag to constrain movement to horizontal and vertical.

To keep from pulling the characters out of vertical sync, a keyboard drag modifier helps ease your pain. Hold down Ctrl as you drag a node (or group of nodes) to constrain movement to a horizontal or vertical plane.

Using Node Edit To Alter Character Shapes

Click on the Zoom tool	The Zoom fly-out menu appears
Click on the +	The cursor becomes a magnifying glass
Marquee-select THUR	
Release the mouse button	The screen zooms in on THUR
Click on the Shape tool	
Click on THURSTONS	The word is selected. Nodes appear
Marquee-select the six nodes of the T's bottom serif	The letter's nodes are selected
Hold down Ctrl and drag the nodes straight down to meet the ellipse	
Release the mouse button	The T is stretched

*Marquee-select the six nodes of the H's
bottom left serif*

*Hold down Ctrl and drag the nodes
straight down to meet the ellipse*

Release the mouse button   The H's left leg is
                                               stretched

*Marquee-select the six nodes of the H's
bottom right serif*

*Hold down Ctrl and drag the nodes
straight down to meet the ellipse*

Release the mouse button   The H's right leg is
                                               stretched

Marquee-select the U's six lower nodes

*Hold down Ctrl and drag the nodes
straight down to meet the ellipse*

Release the mouse button   The U is stretched

The R appears to be almost resting on the ellipse. Move the vertical foot
(touching the ellipse) just slightly. The diagonal foot that extends below
the ellipse can be altered later. Use the scroll bar to move over to fit
STONS on the screen.

*Shift-click on the eleven lowest nodes
on the S*

*Hold down Ctrl and drag the nodes
up about 0.04 inch*

Release the mouse button   The S is shortened

Notice that the S has lost a bit of its smoothness. You need to use the
Shape tool later to tweak the control points for the nodes involved. The
next character, T, might already be resting on the ellipse. If it is, move on
to the N.

Marquee-select the six nodes of the T's bottom serif

*Hold down Ctrl and drag the nodes straight down
to meet the ellipse*

Release the mouse button   The T is stretched

Stretch the N before you do anything to the O. The N is a two-part
stretch, like the H.

Marquee-select the N's six lower left nodes

*Hold down Ctrl and drag the nodes
straight down to meet the ellipse*

Release the mouse button   The left side of the N is
                                               stretched

continues

Marquee-select the N's three lower right nodes

Hold down Ctrl and drag the nodes straight down to meet the ellipse

Release the mouse button   The right side of the N is stretched

Figure 5.11 shows the results of this exercise.

Figure 5.11:

Some stretched characters.

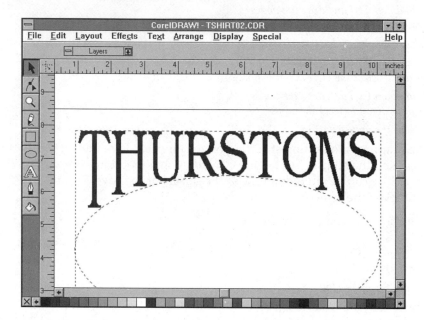

You have reached an impasse. You were supposed to rotate the O. Unfortunately, it cannot be rotated with the Node Edit tool. If you had remembered to rotate the character before converting to curves—while the text was still text—it would have been no big deal. Now, the best way to accomplish the task is with Break Apart.

Break Apart

Break Apart is used for breaking up combined objects, such as text that has been converted to curves, so that individual objects can be altered without affecting the other objects.

You duplicate the word THURSTONS and perform your mutations upon the duplicated copy. After you have duplicated the word, save your work using Save As. Name the new file TSHIRT03.

One small stipulation should be considered when using Break Apart on text objects. When you break apart a text object, characters such as the uppercase A, B, D, O, P, Q, and R lose their counters. The counters (or holes) fill in with whatever color or tint the character is filled with (see figs. 5.12 and 5.13). This quirk can be quite disconcerting at first, but you soon get accustomed to dealing with it.

Figure 5.12:

Filled counters.

Figure 5.13:
Unfilled counters.

Figure 5.13:
Unfilled counters.

Using Combine To Reassemble Multiple-Path Characters

Shortcut

Press Ctrl-C to combine objects.

There is a simple way to return a character with a filled-in counter to its proper state. In the next exercise, you combine two paths into one object. The character is returned to its proper appearance. This maneuver must be performed for every multiple-path character. Recombining is a necessary step.

Using Break Apart and Combine

Click on the Zoom tool

Click on the ×   Reduces the artwork's
                                                size to show more
                                                surrounding space

Click on the Pick tool

Click on THURSTONS   The word is selected

Click on **E**dit   The Edit menu appears

Click on **D**uplicate   The word THURSTONS
                                                is duplicated

Drag the new THURSTONS *off the page*

Click on **A**rrange	The Arrange menu appears
Click on Brea**k** Apart	The word THURSTONS is broken apart (see fig. 5.12)
Click on the page	The new THURSTONS is deselected
Shift-click on THURST N	
Press Del	The THURST N characters are deleted
Marquee-select the O *and the* S	
Drag the O *and the* S	Positions the letters above their counterparts

Look at the O. It does not look good! The counter is filled with black because the O is two separate objects. The next step solves the problem. Use Combine to fuse the two separate objects into one object.

Shift-click on the S	The S is deselected
Click on **A**rrange	The Arrange menu appears
Click on **C**ombine	The two parts of the O are combined

You now have your transplant letters. The time has come to dig out the original characters and replace them with the new models. You select the old characters by shift-clicking on all their nodes. A simple delete removes the characters.

Removing the Originals and Transplanting the New Letters

Click on the Zoom tool	
Click on the +	
Marquee-select THURSTONS O S	To zoom in
Click on the Shape tool	
Click on THURSTONS	
Shift-click on all the old O *and* S *nodes*	All old O and S nodes are selected

continues

Press Del	The old O and S are deleted
Click on the Pick tool	
Click on the new O	The new O is selected
Drag the new O *into position*	
Click on the new S	The new S is selected
Drag the new S *into position*	

Now that the transplanted characters are in position, you can do something special with one of them. You rotate the O –28 degrees. Then you add a second nonprinting ellipse to your design. This ellipse is based on the first ellipse and scaled 105 percent proportionally. You need it when you arc out the bottom serifs of the word THURSTONS.

Begin this next exercise by creating the second nonprinting ellipse and a fourth nonprinting guideline—a skinny, horizontal rectangle.

Adding More Guidelines

At Layers *roll-up, click on* Guides	Guide layer is selected
Click on the Pick tool	
Click on the ellipse guideline	The ellipse is selected
Click on Effects	The Effects menu appears
Click on Stretch & Mirror	The Stretch & Mirror dialog box appears
At stretch horizontally, enter **105**	
At stretch vertically, enter **105**	
Click on Leave Original	
Click on OK	A new ellipse is drawn, 105 percent of original size
Click on the Rectangle tool	

Drag a rectangle	Begin at the left side of the design boundary, at the same level as the top of the bottom serif in the first T in THURSTONS; make it 9.17 inches wide by 0.57 inches high
Release the mouse button	A rectangle is drawn

With the new nonprinting guidelines inserted, you rotate the O and stretch the S to fit. After it is rotated, the O looks a bit small, so you also stretch it a little. At this time, you also pull out the diagonal leg of the R.

Rotating the O and Stretching the S

Click on the Pick tool	
At Layers *roll-up, click on* Layer 1	Layer 1 is selected
Double-click on the O	The O is selected in Rotate/Skew mode
Drag the top right rotate arrow down and -28 degrees to the right	
Release the mouse button	The O is rotated–28 degrees
Drag the O *into position*	
Click on the O	The O is selected in Stretch/Scale mode
Stretch the O *horizontally to fit*	You can do this by eyeballing the letter
Release the mouse button	The O is horizontally stretched
Click on the S	The S is selected
Drag the S's *lower center handle down*	Adjust the amount of stretch to figure 5.14's specification
Release the mouse button	
Drag the S *into position*	

Pay careful attention to the status line in this next maneuver.

Zoom in on the R

continues

Click on the Shape tool

Click on **R**   THURST N is selected

Shift-click on the lower four nodes of the R's right leg

Drag the nodes down and to the right

Release the mouse button when the   The R's diagonal stem is
status line reads   stretched
dx:09 dy:-07 distance:
0.11 angle: -37

Oops! You forgot the apostrophe in the word "THURSTONS." Was it a planned mistake, or was that a mistake in the plan? Whichever it was, you have to remedy the situation and add the missing apostrophe.

Since you have already converted the text to curves, you do not have the option of inserting the apostrophe into the text stream. You have to drag it into place. Even though the apostrophe is added at this stage, the people who look at the sign will not know the difference!

Figure 5.14:

Work in progress!

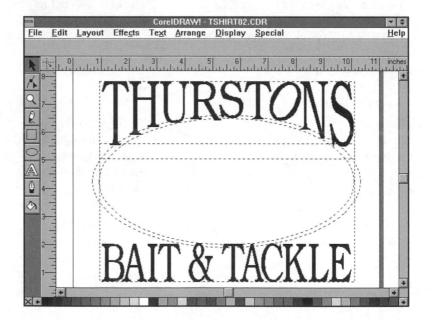

To add an apostrophe to the word THURSTONS, you have to create a new piece of text. Use the text tool to set a 144-point Bookman apostrophe, and horizontally scale it approximately 76 percent. Zoom in on the NS and drag the apostrophe into position. The tighter you zoom in, the more control you have in placing the character. An exercise is not necessary for this little blunder. By now, you should be able to handle this task without assistance.

Use Snap to Objects for Precision!

What do you do if you want to move or stretch an object to a specific point? The solution is simple: use Draw's magnet-like Snap to Objects! Among the precision tools that were introduced in CorelDRAW! 3.0, Snap to Objects is your weapon-of-choice for accurate alignment. You can have any object snap to any other object at a predetermined point. This yields far more flexibility than using Snap to Guidelines or Snap to Grid, alone.

Every object, from a block of paragraph text to an open line path, has a number of snap to points. Where do Snap Points occur? In general, you find a Snap Point at every node along an object's path. Each object (except an open line path) also has a Snap Point at its centerpoint.

If you want to snap to a point on an object other than an existing point use the Shape tool to add a node at the exact point you want to snap to. To add a Snap Point to a rectangle or ellipse, you need to convert the rectangle or ellipse to curves before you add the node.

For more accuracy, zoom in on the objects that you want to snap. The magnetic effect is measured in absolute screen distances. Consequently, this means that the magnetism is relative to the distance you are zoomed in or out. No preference settings control snap distance.

Using Snap to Objects is easy. First, make sure that the function is checked in the **D**isplay menu. Then, using the Pick tool, click on (at the exact point you want to align) and drag the object you want to snap towards the (stationary) object to which you want to snap it. When you get close enough, the magnetic effect pulls the object to the nearest snap point. You can maneuver the object from snap point to snap point.

Guide-layer objects have full snap point functionality with an added bonus—they work even if the Snap to Objects function is turned off (as long as Snap to Guidelines is turned on)! In addition, when you use Snap to Objects with the function off, you are not hampered by the magnetic effect when you select the snap point on the moving object. In other words, you are free to select any point along an object rather than just its own snap to points.

Try using snap points when you complete the next phase of the exercise.

Arcing the Serifs

This design is developing a distinctive style, which is one of the basic reasons for converting text to curves. The availability of convert to curves is why CorelDRAW! is so much more than either a typesetting or drawing program. It is really a synthesis of both media.

To take this design to the next step, you are going to arc the serifs. Use the two ellipses as guidelines for the top and bottom of the serifs. This approach gives you the hand-lettered look of Thurston's original sign.

Arcing the serifs is a time-consuming task. The results, if properly rendered, make it time well spent, however. This feature is one of the factors that sets this design apart.

Rather than go all the way through this next exercise one step at a time, you learn the principles, modify a couple of serifs, and are invited to finish the exercise on your own. Because the work is getting rather complex, save your file frequently. By the end of the book, this will be drilled into your head. Save your files frequently!

The mechanics behind arcing serifs are rather straightforward. In practice, they can sometimes be difficult to attain. They consist of pulling the affected nodes down (or up) to meet the nonprinting guidelines. The smaller ellipse is the guide for the bottoms of the serifs. The larger ellipse is the guide for the tops of the serifs.

Begin by shift-clicking on (or marquee-selecting) groups of involved nodes and dragging them down to meet the smaller ellipse. Proceed by dragging individual upper and lower nodes to intersect the outer and inner ellipses respectively. Remember that you can use Ctrl-drag to keep your movements horizontal or vertical.

The curves that connect the serif to the character stems become distorted. To clean them up, use the control points for the affected nodes. Use the ellipse as a guide to align the "knitting needles." Try to be as consistent as possible. The far ends of the ellipse will give you the most trouble. The best advice is to tweak and tweak some more.

Begin with the serif at the base of the first T in THURSTON'S. Create a new term for your purposes—call it *peer node*. A peer node is the node on the opposite side of a symmetrical character, relatively perpendicular to the node with which you are working (see fig. 5.15). The peer node controls the parallel function of a selected node, but it does so on the opposite side of the character. The relationship between the two controls how "even" the serif curves appear.

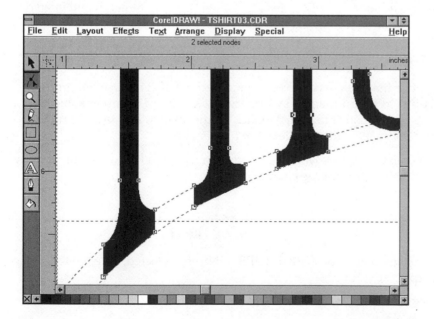

Figure 5.15:
Peer nodes on.

Arcing the First Serif

Click on the Shape tool	
Click on THURSTON'S	The word is selected
Marquee-select the four left nodes of the T's base serif	
Ctrl-drag the selected nodes down to the inner ellipse	
Release the mouse button	The nodes are moved
Shift-click on the lowest selected node	The node is deselected
Ctrl-drag the selected nodes up to the upper ellipse	The lowest node (of the three) should intersect the ellipse
Release the mouse button	The nodes are moved
Shift-click on the lowest selected node	The node is deselected
Ctrl-drag the selected node up	Align it on same horizontal plane as its peer node
Release the mouse button	The node is moved
Marquee-select the three upper right nodes of the T's base serif	
Ctrl-drag the selected nodes up to meet the outer ellipse	The lowest node (of the three) should intersect the ellipse
Release the mouse button	The nodes are moved

Notice that the curves have been pulled out of sync. Use the control points to return them to symmetry. This step can be rather subjective, so use your artistic judgement. Click on the involved node and pull the control points out to achieve the proper curve.

The next exercise covers one more character, the H. You are on your own to finish the rest of the characters.

Arcing the H

In Shape mode and with THURSTONS still selected, take the following steps:

Marquee-select the four left nodes of the H's right base serif

Ctrl-drag the selected nodes down to meet the inner ellipse	
Release the mouse button	The nodes are moved
Shift-click on the lowest selected node	The node is deselected
Ctrl-drag the selected nodes up to meet the upper ellipse	The lowest node (of the three) should intersect the ellipse
Release the mouse button	The nodes are moved
Shift-click on the lowest selected node	The node is deselected
Ctrl-drag the selected node up	Align it on same horizontal plane as its peer node
Release the mouse button	The node is moved
Marquee-select the two upper right nodes of the H's left base serif	
Ctrl-drag the selected nodes up to meet the outer ellipse	The lower node (of the two) should intersect the ellipse
Release the mouse button	The nodes are moved

That takes care of the left base serif. Now finish the character by doing the right base serif.

Marquee-select the three left nodes of the H's right base serif	
Ctrl-drag the selected nodes down to meet the inner ellipse	
Release the mouse button	The nodes are moved
Shift-click on the lowest selected node	The node is deselected
Ctrl-drag the selected nodes up to meet the upper ellipse	The lowest node (of the two) should intersect the ellipse
Release the mouse button	The nodes are moved
Shift-click on the lowest selected node	The node is deselected
Ctrl-drag the selected node up	Align it on same horizontal plane as its peer node
Release the mouse button	The node is moved
Marquee-select the two upper right nodes of the H's right base serif	
Ctrl-drag the selected nodes up to meet the outer ellipse	The lower node (of the two) should intersect the ellipse
Release the mouse button	The nodes are moved (see figs. 5.16 and 5.17)

Figure 5.16:

The arced letters
THUR.

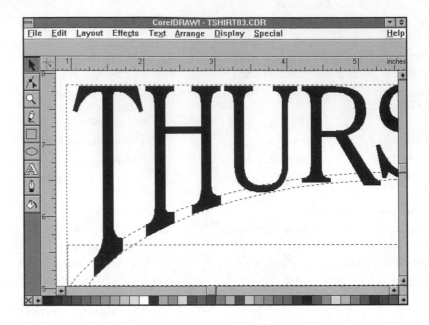

Figure 5.17:

Almost done.

No more examples are needed at this point. Use the techniques covered if you want to complete the design on your own.

Pushing the Envelope

Without a doubt, the Envelope effect is one of Draw's engaging features. This fabulous implement makes designing type that looks hand-lettered a simple task. You are about to see how the time and effort you spent on the last exercise can be substantially reduced. Though envelopes are less exact, you can use them to get similar results in a much shorter time frame.

Remember the Silly Putty you had as a kid? You could press it onto the Sunday comics for an image of your favorite cartoon character, then stretch and tug the likeness into bizarre shapes. A CorelDRAW! envelope works in a similar manner. After you apply an envelope to an object, you can control the overall shape of that object. Applying an envelope gives you eight handles around the selected object that you can drag until you are silly.

Enveloped text is still text. You can still make changes to typeface, size, and spacing. This capability affords incredible flexibility. You can even access the text with Print Merge (which a later chapter will cover).

Envelope Basics

The four basic styles of envelope are Straight Line, Single Arc, Two Curves, and Not Constrained, as shown in figure 5.18. The icons that designate each style do a good job of explaining how each works, but the best way to gain an understanding is to try them out.

The Straight Line, Single Arc, and Two Curves choices enable you to apply those shapes *once* to each of the envelope's four sides (top, bottom, left, and right).

After you select Not Constrained, you are given control points at all eight handles. These work just like the control points on a curve. The side handles are smooth nodes and the corners are cusp nodes. Using this method, you can bend and twist objects (including type) into amazing shapes.

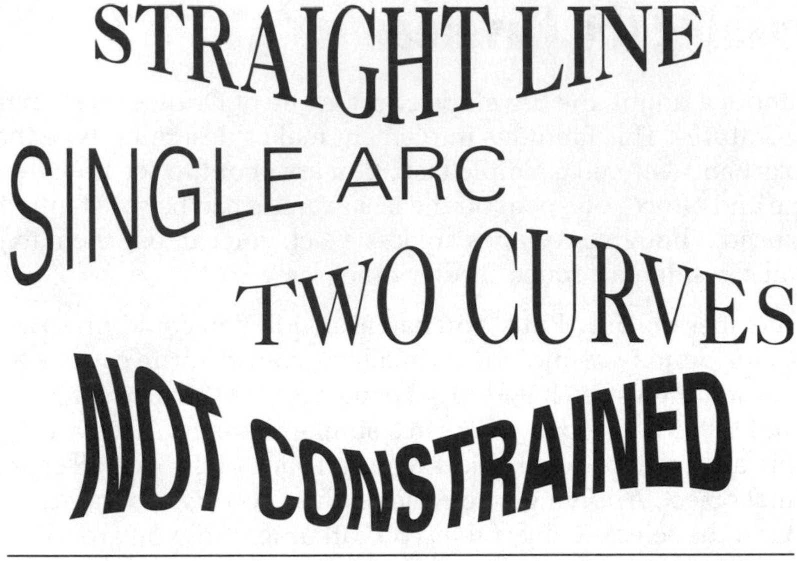

Figure 5.18:
Envelope styles.

STRAIGHT LINE

SINGLE ARC

TWO CURVES

NOT CONSTRAINED

You can use Copy An Envelope between two objects, which works just like Copy Style From, but you cannot copy multiple envelopes at once.

If you want to use one envelope around a number of objects, group or—if applicable—combine the objects. You cannot add a new envelope to a number of selected objects unless they are grouped (although you can copy an envelope to them). If, for example, you select three objects and copy an existing envelope to them, an envelope will be applied to each object rather than to the three objects as a whole. If you copy an envelope from an existing (enveloped) object onto those three (ungrouped) objects, you get some wild effects.

An object can have multiple envelopes, although it might be easier to get the desired effect by using the Not Constrained mode. Look at figure 5.19. On the left, not constrained was used to get a straight line on the baseline, and a double curve on the cap line. On the right, a straight line envelope was used on the baseline. Then, Add New Envelope was used to add a second (two curves) envelope, and then the cap line was pulled out. Notice that the baseline is no longer straight.

Figure 5.19:
Unconstrained and multiple envelopes.

When you are using envelopes, things often can get out of control. But there is an easy way to get your objects back to normal. You can remove an envelope by using Clear Envelope. To remove all envelopes at once, use Clear Transformations.

The keyboard modifiers, Ctrl and Shift, have special functions when used with the envelope effect. If you hold down Ctrl and drag a handle, that handle and the handle opposite it move in unison. If you hold down Shift and drag a handle, that handle and the handle opposite it move in opposite directions. If you hold down Ctrl and Shift together and drag a handle, all four sides (or corners) also move in opposite directions.

Before you get going on this next exercise, store your current file. You need to bring back TSHIRT02.CDR, or the version of the THURSTON'S sign that you saved just before converting the text to curves.

Shortcut

Ctrl-F7 summons the Envelope roll-up menu.

Giving THURSTON'S an Envelope

Now you can try the envelope effect. Instead of doing something rigid at this point, just have some fun!

Click on THURSTON'S	The word is selected
Click on Effects	The Effects menu appears
Click on **E**nvelope Roll-Up	The Envelope roll-up menu appears (see fig. 5.20)
Click on Add New	
Click on Single Arc	

continues

Click on Apply

TIIURSTON'S is
assigned a single-
envelope

*Click on and drag the lower left
handle down to meet ellipse*
Release the mouse button
Click on Apply

THURSTON'S is re-
drawn with a one-sided
baseline arc

*Click on and drag the lower right
handle down to meet ellipse*
Release the mouse button
Click on Apply

THURSTON'S is re-
drawn with two-sided
baseline arc

*Click on and drag the lower center
handle up to meet ellipse*
Release the mouse button
Click on Apply

THURSTON'S is re-
drawn with a big two-
sided baseline arc

Now that you have the idea, go ahead and try arcing BAIT & TACKLE
upward (see fig 5.21). If your envelope goes wildly astray, clear it by
using the following procedure.

Click on Effe**c**ts

The Effects menu
appears

Click on **C**lear Envelope

The envelope is cleared

Next, try assigning the different envelope styles to the THURSTON'S
design. You will find this tool easy to use, but it still takes some effort to
master!

Figure 5.20:

Envelope roll-up
menu.

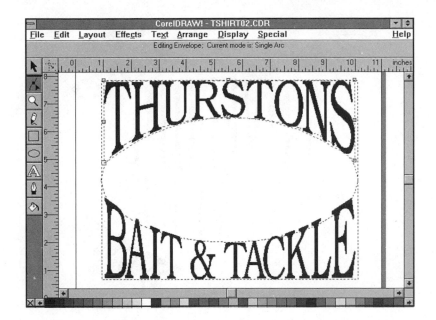

Figure 5.21:
THURSTON'S
envelope.

If you get your design almost to the point you want with the
exception of few tweaks, you must use Convert To Curves to
access the individual nodes and control points.

CorelDRAW! 4.0's Envelope Enhancements

Once again, Corel's engineers have been busy refining features!
As you have seen, envelopes have been awarded their own roll-up
menu. In addition, CorelDRAW! version 4.0's Envelope effect
includes some preset envelope shapes (see fig. 5.22). In addition,
you can create an enveloped shape from any single-path object.
And they didn't stop there! You also can assign a mapping option
(Original, Putty, Vertical, or Horizontal) for each object, and you
can use the Keep Lines mode to prevent straight lines from becoming curved lines.

Figure 5.22:

Envelope presets.

The most wonderful enhancement to the Envelope effect, however, is the capability to assign an envelope to paragraph text.
When you envelope paragraph text, the overall shape of the text
block is affected, not the shape of the individual characters. This
feature enables you to design a Valentine's Day card that sets your
poem in the shape of a heart, or a Christmas card that sets your
greeting in the shape of a tree (see fig. 5.23).

Figure 5.23:

Enveloped paragraph
text.

Happy   Valen-
tine's   Day!   · Happy Valentine's
Day! · Happy Valentine's Day! · Happy
Valentine's Day! · Happy Valentine's Day! ·
Happy Valentine's Day! · Happy Valentine's
Day! · Happy Valentine's Day! · Happy
Valentine's Day! · Happy Valentine's
Day! · Happy Valentine's Day! ·
Happy   Valentine's Day! ·
Happy   Valentine's
Day! · Happy
Valen-

PageMaker and Xpress users have come to regard text runarounds (typeset around a picture or pull quote) as an everyday occurrence. Unfortunately, prior versions of CorelDRAW! did not include the capability to create automated runarounds. But take heart! If you need to create a text runaround in CorelDRAW! 4.0, the Envelope effect now gives you the means to do so. Plan your artwork carefully, however; paragraph text frames have only one envelope.

Did Envelope dazzle you? Just wait—the next effect you try, Extrude, is going to pull you overboard!

Extrude Is Heavy Stuff

The next time you look through your local newspaper, take a gander at the automobile section. Among the many screaming headlines, you are bound to find an example of extruded type. This effect gives new meaning to the word "weight" when used to describe a piece of type. Extruded type looks as if it has been carved from stone.

The Extrude effect was completely overhauled in CorelDRAW! version 3.0 (and altered ever-so-slightly in version 4.0). When it was first introduced in version 2.0, it offered revolutionary power, but was difficult to master. The latest incarnations have exponentially increased both power and ease-of-use. This is not to say that the Extrude effect is child's play (even though it is fun to use on a fast machine!). In fact, you can expect a considerable learning curve.

To create an extrusion, you must use the Extrude roll-up menu, which is accessed by means of either the Effects menu or the Ctrl-E keyboard shortcut. The illustration in figure 5.24 shows the Extrude roll-up menu's six different modes, which cover four different extrusion characteristics: Shape and Position (which have two menus), Lighting, and Color. Buttons for these four modes line the left side of the menu. To switch to a different mode, click on the button that corresponds to the mode you wish to switch to.

Shortcut

Ctrl-E summons the Extrude roll-up menu.

Shape

When you first access the Extrude roll-up menu, it opens in Shape mode. This mode has been improved in version 4.0 to help make it more understandable. The Shape mode is where you assign the depth (from 1-99) and the extrusion type (Small Back, Small Front, Big Back, Big Front, Back Parallel, and Front Paralell). The *extrusion type* controls the overall look of the extrusion. In contrast, *depth* controls how deep the extrusion is; setting it to a maximum value of 99 extends the extrusion all the way to the vanishing point.

Clicking on the little button at the bottom right of the Extrude menu switches you to the second Shape mode, where you can assign an *extrusion direction* that corresponds to the menu's horizontal and vertical Vanishing Point settings. You can measure the vanishing point from the Page Origin or the Object's Center. You can reset the vanishing point using a number of different methods. You can alter the ruler's 0/0 setting, or you can numerically change the horizontal and vertical settings. The third method, and probably the most fun, is to interactively drag the vanishing point around the page. After you have a vanishing point on a page, subsequent extrusions on that page follow to the same vanishing point.

Position

Click on the Position button to summon a globe-like object surrounded by arrow buttons. The Position mode controls an object's rotation in three dimensions. Each click on of an arrow button yields a five-degree move in that direction of rotation. The arrow buttons on the perimeter of the circle control clockwise and counter-clockwise rotation. The horizontal-arrow buttons control left and right rotation; the vertical-arrow buttons control over-the-top and under-the-bottom rotation. The best way to understand this one is try it out!

After you click on the page icon button in the lower right hand corner of the menu, the Extrude Position menu changes to a far more precise but far less graphical description of object rotation. Here, you can enter specific degrees of rotation. Although each click of an up or down arrow gets you another five degrees, you can always type in a specific amount of rotation in one degree increments.

Lighting

Click on the button that looks like a child's drawing of the sun to open the Lighting menu. This menu gives you three choices. The first is an on/off toggle switch, which determines whether or not the Lighting effect is used. Flipping the light switch to the on position enables you to set the *lighting angle* and *intensity.* After you turn the feature on, you see a globe appear inside the wireframe box. The X on the wireframe box determines the location of an imaginary light source. As you move it around, watch the globe's highlight change. The light source can only be set to one of the wireframe intersection points. The intensity setting controls the amount of light shining on the object.

Lighting affects all types of extrusion fills, adding shadows to the backsides of each object. Lighting is not a full-blown 3-D lighting implementation, and no cast shadows are available. Each object is independent of the next.

Color

The last of the four Extrude buttons summons the Color menu. Here you are given three more choices, this time relating to the extrusion's color. Use Object Fill does exactly what you would expect. Solid Color enables you to assign a specific process color. Shade performs a fountain-fill-like gradation, that follows the contours of the extrusion.

Care must be taken when you assign shades or lighting to an extrusion. What looks really cool on the screen might take ages to run on the printer or imagesetter. Shades and lighting are complex functions. Try not to overdo them, or you will pay the price (literally, if you are sending work to a service bureau) for the time that it takes to image the file!

Extrude does have its limitations. You can extrude only one object at a time. You cannot extrude a group of objects, nor can you extrude a number of selected objects. You can extrude combined objects, however. After you have executed an extrusion, the original object becomes tied to the extrusion. You can break them up by clicking on **S**eparate from the **A**rrange menu.

After Draw extrudes your object, the extrusion itself becomes a group of objects with the same outline and fill as the original object by default. As you have seen, the roll-up menus offer plenty of extrude fill options. You also can change the extrusion's outline and fill in its entirety or by separating, ungrouping, and making changes object by object. Remember to regroup and/or group with the original object so that the complete, extruded object can be scaled or moved without falling apart.

The math involved in creating the Extrude effect makes you glad that the Draw program handles the computations. You can worry about the structure of your design, not the equations necessary to complete it!

In the next short exercise, you take the finished Thurston's sign and use Extrude to give it some depth. Save your current file, if need be, and call up your most recent (and complete) version of the Thurston's sign.

Extrusion, like Envelope, is a workout for your computer's processor. Depending on the speed of your computer, you might have to wait a while. The end result is well worth it, however.

Extruding THURSTON'S

To make the screen less cluttered, go ahead and delete all those nonprinting guidelines. Ungroup the sign if necessary. Combine the word THURSTON'S into one object.

Click on THURSTON'S	The word is selected
Click on Effects	The Effects menu appears
Click on Extrude Roll Up	The Extrude roll-up menu appears
Click on Apply	THURSTON'S is extruded

Now that you have extruded the word THURSTON'S downward, extrude BAIT & TACKLE upward. Notice that Draw remembers your last dialog box entries.

Click on Bait & Tackle	The words are selected.
At the Extrude roll-up menu, click on Apply	BAIT & TACKLE is extruded (see fig. 5.24)

Now, go ahead and try different extrusion depths, positions, lighting, and fills! Drag the vanishing point icon around to see how different angles affect the extrusion. Notice how the Pick tool changes to a + when you are interactively adjusting the vanishing point. Use Snap To Guidelines to position the vanishing point in a specific spot.

Extrusions look good when they have a hard edge. You can use a thin outline rule to make the surface pop out. Depending on the size of the extruded object, this edge can be anything from a hairline to a two-point rule, relative to the size of the objects you extrude.

Advanced Paragraph Text Settings

CorelDRAW! version 4.0 features full-blown paragraph text controls, including spacing, tabs, indents, and bullets. To access these advanced specifications, select Paragraph from the Text menu or the Text roll-up menu. The Paragraph dialog box switches between the four different modes by clicking on the appropriate button below the Category heading at the left of the dialog box.

Figure 5.24:

Adjusting the vanishing point.

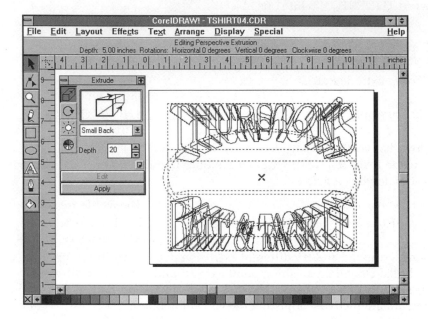

The Spacing specifications dialog box (see fig. 5.25) include controls for Charact**e**r, **W**ord, **L**ine, **B**efore Paragraph, and **A**fter Paragraph spacing. It also enables you to set the alignment to **L**eft, **C**enter, **R**ight, **J**ustify, or N**o**ne. In addition, you can turn on or off Automatic Hy**p**henation and set the hyphenation Hot **Z**one.

The Tab specifications dialog box shown in figure 5.26 enables you to set up tabular columns using a point-and-shoot interface. You can set tabs interactively or automatically by applying tabs at specified intervals. A **D**ecimal alignment option is included to help with those pesky financial tables.

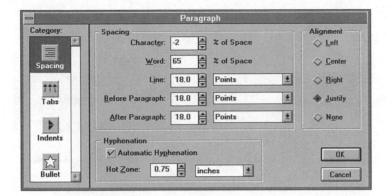

Figure 5.25:
Paragraph Spacing controls.

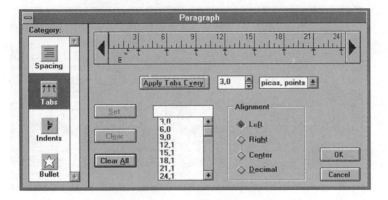

Figure 5.26:
Paragraph Tab controls.

The Indents specification dialog box looks suspiciously like the Tab specifications dialog box (see fig. 5.27). You can add or edit tabs while in this mode as well. This dialog box, however, provides settings for the four different indents, First Line, Rest of Lines, Bullet Indent, and Right Margin, in your choice of inches, millimeters, picas and points, or just plain old points.

The Bullet specifications dialog box shown in figure 5.28 might remind you of the Symbols roll-up menu, because it features all those same funky symbols. CorelDRAW! 4.0 enables you to use any symbol as an automatic bullet. The dialog box comes to life when you select the Bullet On checkbox. You can choose from more bullets than you will ever need, in sizes up to 2160 points.

Figure 5.27:
Paragraph Indent controls.

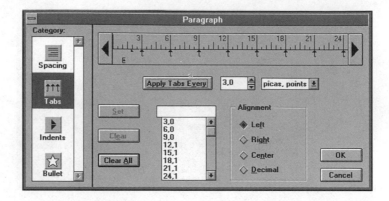

Figure 5.28:
Paragraph Bullet controls.

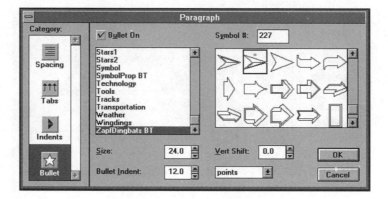

Styles

Power DTPers should be quite familiar with style tagging, because Aldus PageMaker, Quark Xpress, and Ventura Publisher have used style tags for years. Styles are not as common in illustration packages—but then again, CorelDRAW! is going through a bit of an identity crisis. In any case, CorelDRAW! version 4.0 has incorporated a Styles roll-up menu (see fig. 5.29) to give you point-and-shoot text tagging. After you have created a set of type specifications, you can use those specs to create a style. The Styles roll-up menu is accessed from the Layout menu.

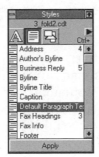

Figure 5.29:
The Styles roll-up menu.

Multiple Pages

CorelDRAW! version 4.0 now features multiple-page documents.
You can have anywhere from 1 to 999 pages per file. Although the
program is no competition for the real DTP packages, it does set a
precedent for what was previously considered an illustration
package. CorelDRAW! has become the Wal-Mart of graphics
software—everything in one place!

Adding pages is easy. If you are starting with a one-page file, all
you need to do is select Insert Page from the Layout menu. This
action summons the Insert Page dialog box, which enables you to
add one or more pages before or after a specified page. After a
document contains more than one page, you see a pair of buttons
appear at the left side of the horizontal scroll bar along with a
legend that informs you of the current page. You also can call up
the Insert Page dialog box by clicking on the + button.

Moving from page to page is equally simple. You can choose Go
To Page from the Layout menu, click on the left or right button on
the left of the horizontal scroll bar, or use the PgUp and PgDown
keys. PgUp moves you forward (1,2,3...) through the document;
PgDown moves you backwards (3,2,1). When you are on the first
or last page of a document, pressing PgDown or PgUp, respectively, summons the Insert Page Dialog box.

Shortcut

Type Alt-L, then G,
to reach the Go To
Page dialog box
from the keyboard.

Summary

This chapter introduced a fairly advanced project that carries over into a later chapter (covering advanced fill and outline trapping techniques). You have tried out a variety of commands and techniques. Among them, Convert To Curves, Break Apart, and Combine played major roles. After fiddling with Draw's Envelope and Extrude effects, a new appreciation for Corel Corporation's programmers is in order! You have seen that Draw is a program that builds upon its simplicity to provide design solutions.

As mentioned earlier, typography is perhaps CorelDRAW!'s strongest area. The program offers designers a world of fonts with editable outlines. And remember, you are not limited to the range of fonts that came with CorelDRAW! Literally tens of thousands of PostScript fonts are available today from a host of foundries. Comparatively, as of this writing, relatively few TrueType fonts are on the market. Chapter 11 covers the subject of fonts and font conversion. One additional text effect has not yet been discussed: Fit Text to Path. This powerful command is examined in Chapter 8.

Outline, Fill, and Color

 well-designed page can work in black and white or in color. Structure is what makes the difference. Of course, a poor choice of colors can ruin a design from a chromatic standpoint, but the mere inclusion of color cannot make up for poor design. A flashy paint job on a leaky hull does not keep the boat from sinking.

Because color printing can be expensive, the place to experiment with color is certainly not on the printing press. Mistakes can be more than expensive; they can cost you your job or an account. Take precautions at every step and keep an eye on the meter. When you are working with color, the meter is always running. See Chapter 11 for more information on avoiding the pitfalls of color printing.

This chapter is rather ambitious. It covers the color basics for both spot and process colors. In addition to color, the chapter also explains the many properties of the Outline and Fill tools, including full- and two-color patterns. To illustrate some practical applications of color, the chapter touches on the subject of charts and 35mm slides. CorelDRAW! version 3.0 introduced CorelCHART!, a powerful charting program; this module was substantially revamped in version 4.0. Slides, one of Draw's least-exploited output options, can be a relatively inexpensive way to experiment with color.

The only way to gain real experience with color is through trial and error. Like most subjects in the art world, learning through experience is mandatory. Understand the theory, then practice, practice, practice!

Using CorelDRAW! and Color

Color is described in one of two ways depending on the medium. Printed color involves layering partially transparent inks onto opaque paper. The subsequent printed piece is an example of *subtractive color*, which subtracts wavelengths (colored inks) from white light (paper). When you are working with video screens or producing 35mm slides, projected color entails *additive color*. Draw treats all color as subtractive, however, even when composing an image that ultimately is used as a 35mm slide.

When you create artwork destined for the printing press, CorelDRAW! has two different methods for specifying color: spot and process. These terms refer to the two basic methods of reproducing color images on a printing press. *Spot color* is used when two or more specific colors are required for a print job. *Process color* is used to give the printed illusion of full color.

For those just entering the world of printed color, the first place to start is with spot color, rather than process. Remember, you should wade into uncharted waters, not dive in head first.

PANTONE Color

In most print shops, a scheme known as the *PANTONE Matching System* (PMS)—commonly referred to simply as PANTONE color—ensures that the final printed color correctly corresponds to the color specified by the designer. Quite simply, PANTONE is a recipe book for mixing printing inks. The pressperson follows a predefined recipe to cook up the correct color, the same way a cook prepares clam chowder. A dash of this and a spot of that; three parts blue to two parts red.

When specifying a color using the PANTONE system, an exact color is requested. The printed color should match the one chosen from the PANTONE color swatch book. A few colors come straight from the can, but most colors must be mixed from combinations of other colors.

This process should eliminate inconsistencies, but the system relies on the pressperson to accurately mix the specified ink. If the ink is not meticulously mixed, the printed color will not match the requested color. If color printing is important to you, find a competent printer and stay with them.

Although CorelDRAW! does a laudable job with PANTONE color screen representations, do not, under any circumstances, trust the screen colors to be true. Buy a PANTONE book and use it to accurately specify your colors. Most graphic arts supply houses carry them. They are not cheap, but they are worth the investment.

Process Color

As opposed to PANTONE or spot color, process color mixes ink on the printed page, not before it is put on the press. Process color is commonly referred to as *four-color printing*, alluding to the four colors of ink used: cyan, magenta, yellow, and black (CMYK). Each color has a separate printing plate and, when printed, the four colors are combined in different ratios to give the illusion of a full-color photograph. When you specify a color using the process color model, you can enter specific percentages of each of the four process colors, blending them to create a full spectrum of color.

CorelDRAW! does an excellent job of creating either spot or process color separations. The power of the PostScript language enables you to send Draw files to a high-resolution imagesetter, where negatives can be produced. These negatives are then used to *burn* or make the printing plates. By imaging directly onto negative film, you are assured the highest-quality image possible.

Much of the manual (and costly) preparation that you might have formerly encountered with color printing is eliminated.

You also can proof images on a color PostScript output device prior to sending the files out for separations. The best of these printers can print using either process or PANTONE color-simulating capabilities. Although (in most cases) they should not be used for final output, color printers can be helpful in the design process, enabling comps to be made in a short time frame. The Fiery/Canon Color Laser Copier is an exception. This device is perhaps the most significant advance in short-run color printing to occur in the past few years. It enables you to print your full-color CorelDRAW! (and other DTP) files directly, without going to film, plate, or printing press. Although the Fiery's quality cannot match that of a real four-color (or more) press and a good pressperson, you can achieve wonderful results at previously unheard-of prices. More on this later!

Later in this chapter, you specify both spot and process colors, and ultimately image them as 35mm slides. Preparing artwork for color printing—whether spot or process—is not something to be taken lightly. Fooling around with slides first gives you some slack. For more in-depth information on preparing your work for color printing, refer to Chapter 11.

For now, this chapter moves on to the extended functions of the Outline tool, where it covers the fundamentals of specifying color.

Using the Outline Tool

Draw offers a wide range of outline colors, widths, and shapes. Until now, you have worked with only the most immediate choices—those present on the Outline fly-out menu (see fig. 6.1). Although this menu offers enough options to render uncompli-cated black-and-white drawings, you must delve farther into the menu structure to make use of color outlines.

As your drawings become more complex and your familiarity with Draw increases, you learn that new possibilities are continu-ally unfolding. The Outline tool provides versatility without being cumbersome. Its options are there if you need them, but are not a hindrance if not needed for the task at hand.

Outline fly-out menu ——

Pen roll-up menu ——

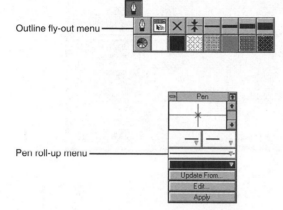

You can access the Outline dialog boxes from the Outline fly-out menu (or the Pen roll-up menu shown in figure 6.1). Notice the two icons at the far left of the fly-out menu in addition to the default line width and color choices. The upper icon, a pen nib, is a duplicate of the icon that opens the Outline fly-out menu; click on this icon to access the Outline Pen dialog box. The lower icon, which represents a color wheel, gives you access to the Outline Color dialog box. The icon next to the Outline Pen accesses the Pen roll-up menu.

Customizing the Outline Pen

The Outline tool is as versatile as a slew of real calligraphic pens. Much can be explored here, so experiment with some different combinations.

Through the Outline Pen dialog box, you can control pen type and shape, color, corners, line caps, dashing, and arrowheads (see fig. 6.2). Options also are provided for placing the outline behind the fill, and for scaling the outline with the image. Take a look at some of the choices.

Figure 6.2:

The Outline Pen
dialog box.

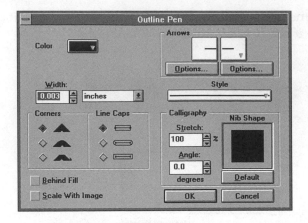

Style

Draw offers great flexibility with regard to dashed and dotted line
styles. Right out of the box, you get 15 predefined line styles (in
addition to solid lines) with the option of adding up to 25 more.
To access dashed and dotted lines, click on the line under Style
(which brings up the Dashed and Dotted Line Styles pop-up
menu, shown in fig. 6.3). Use the scroll bars to browse through the
available line styles. To change a dashed line style into a dotted
line style, select a short dash and click on the round Line Caps
selection.

Figure 6.3:

The Dashed and
Dotted Line Styles
menu.

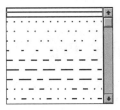

The dash sizes are scaled in direct proportion to the weight of the
line specified. Hence, the thicker the line, the larger the dash
pattern. The predefined line styles probably will not meet all your
needs. To add your own custom variations of dashed lines, you
must edit CORELDRW.DOT, a text file that describes line styles
(see fig. 6.4). You can find CORELDRW.DOT in your
CORELDRW\CUSTOM directory.

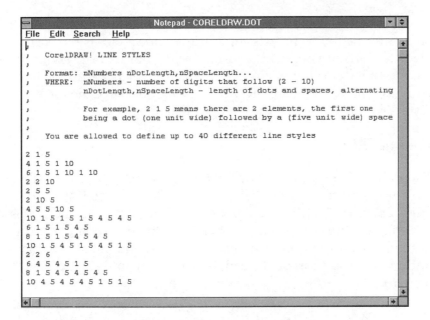

Figure 6.4:
CORELDRW.DOT.

Editing the CORELDRW.DOT file might sound difficult, but is really quite easy. You need to use an ASCII text editor, such as Notepad, to do the job. Just remember to make a duplicate copy of CORELDRW.DOT before you edit the original.

Take a look at figure 6.4. Each line style is defined by a row of text, which includes the number of elements (maximum of ten), length of the dash, and space between dashes. Dashed lines run in a continuous loop from left to right. One of the effects you can create with dashed lines is shown in figure 6.5.

Figure 6.5:
A dashed coupon border.

To create a line style, type the specifications for the new line style on a new line (after the existing group of line styles is the best place to start). If you want, you can bring your favorite styles to the top of the chart by using the cut-and-paste procedure. After you have altered CORELDRW.DOT, you must save the file and restart CorelDRAW! for the changes to take effect.

Behind Fill

The **B**ehind Fill option is useful when working with text. Outlines are always centered upon the perimeter of an object. If **B**ehind Fill is enabled, the fill prints to the midpoint of the outline. If it is not enabled, the outline encroaches upon the fill. The thicker the outline, the more important this option is. If you fail to use this option, the result can be unreadable or just plain ugly text (see fig. 6.6).

Figure 6.6:

Use caution (and **B**ehind Fill) when outlining text.

In other words, when **B**ehind Fill is enabled, the outline prints at half its weight because the outline's width is centered on an object's outline. The **B**ehind Fill option proves to be of definite interest when you attempt some rudimentary trapping in Chapter 11.

Scale With Image

The **S**cale With Image option is extremely important when creating artwork to be scaled or rotated. For instance, say you create a logo at full-page size, then you scale the logo for use on letterheads and business cards. If **S**cale With Image is not used, the outline weight remains constant. The too-thick outline fills in the logo. The logo that looked good at full-page size turns into mud when reduced (see fig. 6.7).

Figure 6.7:
Scale With Image logo.

Scale With Image
NOT Selected

Scale With Image
Selected

In addition to affecting line weight, **S**cale With Image also plays an important role when scaling or rotating objects that have been drawn with a calligraphic pen shape. Enabling this option ensures that the pen shape rotates along with the image. If **S**cale With Image is not checked, the object rotates, but the pen stroke does not.

Corners

You have three options for line corners: miter, round, and bevel. The options are rather self-explanatory (see fig. 6.8). Miter extends the outer edges of the two meeting lines. To avoid corners in small angles that overshoot, you might need to adjust the miter limit upward. The miter limit setting is accessed from the Preferences dialog box.

Figure 6.8:

Mitered, rounded, and beveled corners.

Mitered   Rounded   Beveled
Corners   Corners   Corners

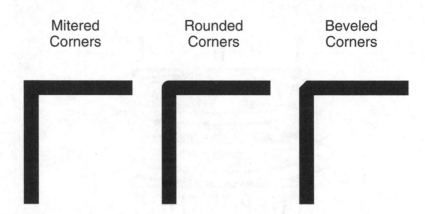

For an example of what happens when the miter limit is improperly set, look at the word "Summer" in the "Seaside Aquarium" color plate. The Ms show the spiky results.

Arrows

Draw comes with an array of arrowheads and other symbols necessary for technical illustrations. The program also enables you to create your own arrows and doodads. The Arrowhead pop-up menus are accessed by clicking on the starting (left) or ending (right) arrow buttons in the Outline Pen dialog box (shown in fig. 6.9). Use the scroll bars to browse through the arrowhead styles.

When you find the arrowhead that you want, assign it by clicking the left mouse button. Choose an arrowhead from the left menu to place it at the start of the line; choose an arrowhead from the right menu to place it at the end of the line. To return a line to non-arrowhead form, click on the flat line. To switch starting and ending arrowheads, click on Options and swap!

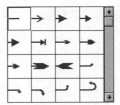

Designing a new arrowhead for the Arrowhead pop-up menu is an easy task. You simply select any object (including combined objects) and use the Create **A**rrow command (found on the **S**pecial menu). Draw asks if you really want to create a new arrowhead before it stores the arrowhead. Note that the outline and fill attributes do not carry over (for example, you cannot have a fountain-filled arrowhead); instead, these settings are governed by the outline color and weight. If you want an arrowhead with no fill, draw a combined doughnut object or break a closed path object by using Node Edit roll-up menu.

The Arrowhead pop-up menu also enables you to delete or edit existing arrowheads. You can delete an arrowhead from the list simply by clicking on the arrowhead that you want to remove, and then clicking on Delete.

To edit an existing arrowhead, click on Option, and then click on Edit. This summons the Arrowhead Editor (see fig. 6.10). The Arrowhead Editor enables you to stretch/scale, reorient, and position the arrowhead in relation to the line. Stretching and scaling an arrowhead works the same as stretching and scaling other objects in Draw, although the keyboard modifiers (such as Ctrl and Shift) have no effect. Side handles stretch; corner handles scale. Unfortunately, the editor has no Undo command within it (except for Cancel)!

You cannot edit individual arrowhead nodes, but you can use them as snap-to points. By clicking and dragging on a node, that point becomes magnetic and will be attracted to the guidelines. **R**eflect in X and R**e**flect in Y flip the arrowhead on the vertical or (middle) horizontal guideline, respectively.

Center in **X** and Center in **Y** center the arrowhead to those same guidelines (also respectively). **4**X zoom zooms up by a factor of four.

Figure 6.10:

The Arrowhead
Editor dialog box.

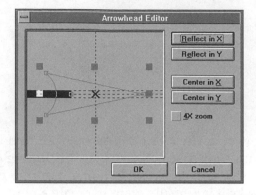

Line Caps

In addition to arrowheads, line caps have three options: butt, round, and square (see fig. 6.11). Line caps apply to both ends of a line. Line caps apply to both ends of a line—unless, of course, you use an arrowhead on one or both ends of the line.

Figure 6.11:

Line caps.

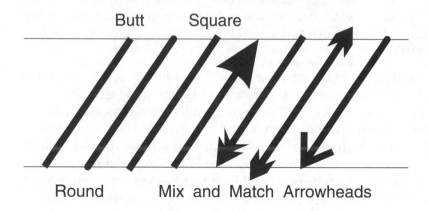

Pen Shape (Calligraphic Pens)

The Pen Shape option gives flexibility to the pen width, shape, and angle. This feature is like being able to snap in a completely different pen nib with only a few clicks (see fig. 6.12). Show this feature to a calligrapher, and watch him salivate!

Figure 6.12:
The calligraphic jellyfish.

Specifications are entered in typical Corellian fashion. Width defines the size of the pen nib, and can be specified in inches, centimeters, points and picas, or fractional points. Stretch alters the actual shape of the pen, and Angle rotates the pen upon its axis.

A standard 300 dpi laser printer outputs a line 1/300 inch in width; an imagesetter might be able to print lines 1/1270 or 1/2540 in width (possibly even thinner, depending on the model).

A subtle feature introduced in CorelDRAW! 3.0 was the interactive capability to define a calligraphic pen shape. Place your cursor in the Nib Shape window, and click and drag around the window; the cursor becomes a plus sign (+). You can freely adjust both the stretch and angle of the pen nib without ever touching the keyboard or size buttons!

To get the feel of using different calligraphic pens, try signing your name, duplicating the signature, and assigning different outline pen attributes to the duplicates.

Signing Your Name with Different Pens

Click on the Pencil tool
Sign your name at the top of the page

Your signature probably looks pretty bad, especially if you used a mouse to do it. The creator of the illustration was lucky and had a cordless pen and graphics tablet (see fig. 6.13). In any case, feel free to tweak your signature by using the Shape tool. Try to get the signature to look at least vaguely as it should. You are going to duplicate the signature twice, to end up with a total of three.

Duplicating the Signature

Click on the Shape tool	
Tweak the nodes until you are content	
Click on the Pick tool	
Shift-click all the paths in the signature	
*Click on **A**rrange*	The Arrange menu appears
*Click on **G**roup*	The signature is grouped
*Click on **E**dit*	The Edit menu appears
*Click on **D**uplicate*	The signature is duplicated
Drag the signature to the bottom of the page	
*Click on **E**dit*	
*Click on **D**uplicate*	The signature is duplicated again
Drag the new signature to the middle of the page	

You should have three signatures on the page. Now assign a different calligraphic pen type to each signature so that you can see the differences between the various pen nib shapes. At this point, make sure that the full-color editing is turned on (press Shift-F9 to switch it on or off).

Assigning a Pen Type

Click on the Pick tool	
Click on the uppermost signature	The signature is selected
Click on the Outline tool	The Outline fly-out menu appears
Click on the Outline Pen *icon*	The Outline Pen dialog box appears
Click on the round corners	The corners are selected
Change the pen width to **0.02** *inches*	
Change Angle to **0** *degrees*	
Change Stretch to **100** *percent*	
Click on OK	
Click on the middle signature	The signature is selected
Click on the Outline tool	The Outline fly-out menu appears
Click on the Outline Pen *icon*	The Outline Pen dialog box appears
Click on the square corners	The corners are selected
Change the pen width to **0.03** *inches*	
Change Angle to **40** *degrees*	
Change Stretch to **50** *percent*	
Click on OK	
Click on the lower signature	The signature is selected
Click on the Outline tool	The Outline fly-out menu appears
Click on the Outline Pen *icon*	The Outline Pen dialog box appears
Click on the round corners	The corners are selected
Change the pen width to **0.04** *inches*	
Change Angle to **60** *degrees*	
Change Stretch to **20** *percent*	
Click on OK	

If you have a printer available, try printing the file to see the distinction between pen shapes (see fig. 6.13). The differences in pen shape might be less than obvious. In general, the larger the pen nib and the more extreme the stretch, the more apparent the pen shape becomes. The rectangular pen nib yields a harder, sharper edge, while the rounded pen nib is softer and more flowing.

Figure 6.13:

The signature of John Q. Public.

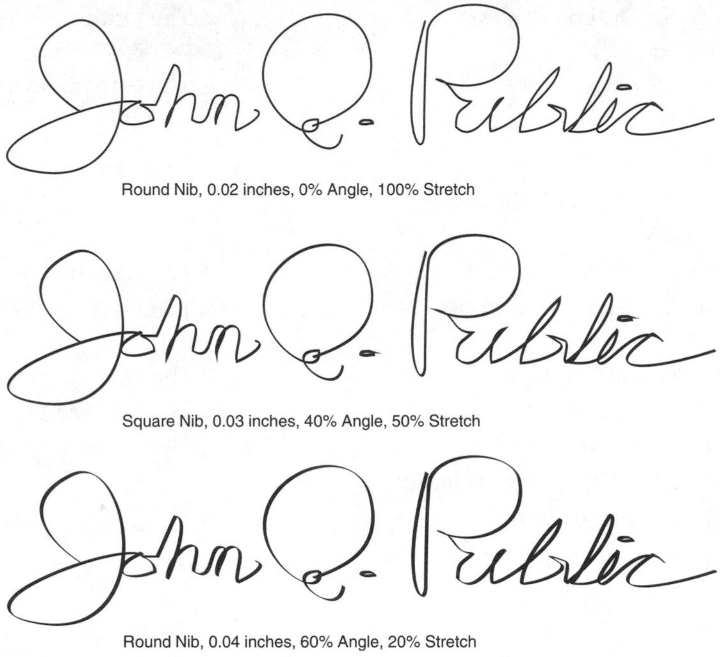

Round Nib, 0.02 inches, 0% Angle, 100% Stretch

Square Nib, 0.03 inches, 40% Angle, 50% Stretch

Round Nib, 0.04 inches, 60% Angle, 20% Stretch

The Outline Pen Roll-Up Menu

Yet another of Draw's time-saving menus is the Outline Pen (see fig. 6.14) roll-up menu. This menu offers point-and-shoot convenience for line characteristics, including line width, arrows, line style, and outline pen color. In addition, the menu enables you to use Update From (which is the same as Copy Attributes From) to copy the characteristics of any other line, and it provides easy access to the Outline Pen dialog box (from the Edit button). Like other roll-up menus, you must remember to click on Apply to assign any changes!

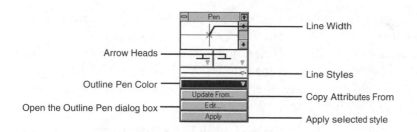

Arrow Heads

Outline Pen Color

Open the Outline Pen dialog box

Line Width

Line Styles

Copy Attributes From

Apply selected style

Figure 6.14:
The Outline Pen roll-up menu.

Understanding Draw's Color Selection Methods

Specifying color with CorelDRAW! might seem, at first, like a mystifying procedure. The color selection choices are vast and the methods might not be instantly comprehensible. The secret lies in using the proper palette (which depends on the printing method you will be using). The first choice is to specify either spot or process color. If you specify spot, your choices are simple; you are allowed to choose spot PANTONE colors either visually or by name.

If you are working with process color, your choices are far more varied. Draw enables you to specify process color from a number of color models. Choosing each method determines the layout of the Outline Color or Uniform Fill dialog boxes. For the purposes of the exercises, you deal with spot PANTONE and process CMYK color exclusively. CorelDRAW! 4.0's color models include the following:

>CMYK (Cyan/Magenta/Yellow/Black)
>
>RGB (Red/Green/Blue)
>
>HSB (Hue/Saturation/Brightness)
>
>Custom Palette
>
>PANTONE Spot Colors
>
>PANTONE Process Colors
>
>TRUMATCH Process Colors

The Outline Color and Uniform Fill dialog boxes have plenty of smarts. You can specify a color with one color model (perhaps

RGB), switch to another (say, CMYK), and retain a semblance of color integrity. With a quick click, the program converts any color into a CMYK, RGB, or HSB color. Draw does not, however, automatically convert any color into a PANTONE or TRUMATCH color. In addition, only one type of process color model can be active at any one time.

Each time you specify colors, CorelDRAW! remembers the mode in which you left the color selector. If, for example, you used process colors the last time you specified a color (either for an outline or a fill) in CMYK, the dialog box pops back up in the same mode the next time you access it. Like other portions of the program, CorelDRAW! configures itself around the way you work. The color specification methods might seem odd at first, but you become accustomed to them quickly.

Outline Colors

A full range of colors is available for outline use. These include spot as well as process color choices. To access the Outline Color Palette, click on the color palette icon on the Outline menu. When you get into color fills later in this chapter, you see that this dialog box is similar to the Uniform Fill dialog box (see fig. 6.15).

Figure 6.15:

The Uniform Fill dialog box.

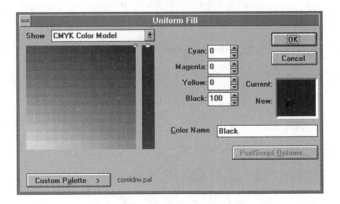

The first option in the Outline Color dialog box is the choice of color specification method: spot or (various flavors of) process color. Choose a graphics color method according to the type of printing press that the project ultimately will be printed on.

To select a color, just click on it. As you scroll through the different color choices, you will notice that Draw shows a color swatch and name for each selected color. Once again, use the on-screen color sample as a loose guide only; the sample is not accurate. To specify colors precisely, you must use an actual printed process (be it PANTONE or TRUMATCH) or spot PANTONE color guide. If you want to view a more traditional color list with a name next to the color swatch, select Show color names. This enables you to use the Search String box to quickly assign a color.

Spot Color Outlines

If the graphic is to be reproduced using spot colors, click on PANTONE Spot Colors. Draw enables you to choose PANTONE colors, either visually from the palette or by name using the Search String.

If you use the palette method, notice that, as you click on each color, its PANTONE number appears in the Color Name box. You cannot specify directly by number in this box, but all inks are in sequential order. Need a PANTONE 288 blue? Scroll to the blues, and start clicking while looking for 288 in the Color Name box. This is not the most direct method, however.

If you want to be dead sure about what you are selecting, you can specify by name. Here, you can scroll through the ink colors numerically rather than visually. The fastest way to specify a PANTONE color is to use the Search String option. Type the number into the field, and violá!

With spot colors, you easily can specify tint percentages, which can greatly extend the color range of a printed piece. Reds can yield pinks, dark blues can spawn lighter blues, and so on. When the file is output as color separations, each color's separation will include all the tints of a color, along with the color at full strength. To specify a Spot Color tint percentage, click on the up/down arrows at the % tint box, or type in the tint percentage directly.

You also can render a depth-filled black-and-white graphic by using the full range of grays made available on the Outline Color

Shortcut

If you are working with a traditional printed swatch book, you can speed up your color specifications by selecting Show color names and by using the Search String option.

dialog box. Simply leave the color at Black and specify the percentage of tint. This can lead to a far more realistic effect than you would get by simply specifying the default fills from the fly-out menu or on-screen color palette.

PostScript Options

Draw enables those with PostScript printers to specify the PostScript screen type of any spot color outline. The subject of PostScript halftone screens is covered in the Fill tool section. In addition, you can overprint colors using this dialog box (more in Chapter 11).

Process-Color Outlines

If the graphic is to be printed on a four-color press, you have a number of choices. Outline colors can be specified directly; in percentages of cyan, magenta, yellow, and black (CMYK); or by one of the other process color models.

Try using the custom palette. As you select different colors, you will notice that a descriptive name might pop up in the Color Name box. This is a nice touch that proves useful when you begin building your own colors. For instance, say you are illustrating a woman's face. You can mix specific colors for each tone, calling them by descriptive names like ruby lips, ear lobe, nostril, rosy blush, and so on.

Process Color can be chosen by using one of a number of methods: CMYK (Cyan/Magenta/Yellow/Black), RGB (Red/Green/Blue), HSB (Hue/Saturation/Brightness), PANTONE Process Colors, or TRUMATCH. This diversity can be confusing. You should try to use either PANTONE Process Color or TRUMATCH for four-color print work (along with a swatch book). RGB and HSB are common in the computer video world but not for print graphics. If you specify colors using either RGB or HSB, the colors are converted to CMYK values when the file is printed (although the conversion might not be exact).

If you choose to work in CMYK directly, you can go about mixing colors by one of two methods. The first method is to specify the exact amount of cyan, magenta, yellow, and black ink using the elevator buttons or numeric entry. As you change the ink values, you get an on-screen representation. The second method is to use the Visual Selector.

The Visual Selector

The Visual Selector is a snazzy way to choose colors. It consists of two separate but linked color boxes. As you click and drag the cursor around, the CMYK values are calculated; when you release the mouse button, they pop into place.

The Visual Selector uses a process known as *Gray Component Replacement* (GCR) to reduce the amount of ink used. The concept behind GCR is that you can remove equal amounts of cyan, magenta, and yellow, and replace them with black while rendering the same color. The black makes colors snap by adding contrast.

TRUMATCH Process Color or PANTONE Process Color?

TRUMATCH process color was a significant addition to CorelDRAW! 3.0. In this method for specifying process colors, hues are described in exact terms. For example, picking TRUMATCH 18-a from the color palette specifies a shade of green that is built from 100-percent yellow, 0-percent magenta, 85-percent cyan, and 0-percent black. By specifying exact colors, TRUMATCH provides a common ground for designers, service bureaus, color trade shops, and, most important, printers.

CorelDRAW! 4.0 adds PANTONE process color to the list of color specification methods. This scheme, which works in the same manner as TRUMATCH, is a precise way to specify process color. As with spot PANTONE colors, you should use a swatch book to choose accurate TRUMATCH or PANTONE process colors. Once again, these swatch books require an additional investment, but is well worth the few dollars you will spend. Do not be foolish and rely on your screen to pick colors to be used on a printing press—

even if you have a very expensive 24-bit display system! Of course, the better the display is, the closer the color will be.

Printing with process colors is a costly business best left to the professionals. You cannot expect that the mere ownership of a program like Draw gives you the experience and wisdom to work with process color. This is not to say that it should not be attempted, but it should be approached with extreme caution (and deep pockets).

Using the Fill Tool

Tapping into the Fill tool's capabilities is a little like sneaking into Grandma's jelly cupboard: you can pick from so many delicious choices that it can be tough to decide on which one to use. Draw gives you enough choices so that you will not become bored with the same old flavors. Each one is a treat!

The Fill fly-out menu offers the default fills of black, white, 10-, 30-, 50-, 70-, and 90-percent tints, along with no fill. In addition, the menu gives you access to the Fill roll-up menu, Uniform Fill, Full- and Two-Color Pattern Fill, Fountain Fill, Fractal Texture Fill, and PostScript Texture Fill dialog boxes. Figure 6.16 illustrates this menu. Figure 2.19 in Chapter 2 identifies each icon in the Fill fly-out menu.

Figure 6.16:

The Fill fly-out and roll-up menus.

Uniform Fills

At the far left of the Fill fly-out menu, you see Uniform Fill, which is accessed through a color wheel icon. A click on the color wheel summons the Uniform Fill dialog box.

This dialog box looks and functions exactly like the Outline Color dialog box. You are once again offered the choice of spot or process color, as well as access to the PostScript Halftone Screen dialog box.

PostScript Screens

An interesting feature of the Uniform Fill and Outline Color dialog boxes is the opportunity to specify different PostScript halftones and to set screen frequencies and angles (see fig. 6.17). This flexibility enables you to design artwork that uses a wide range of fill patterns.

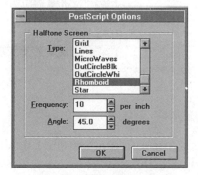

Figure 6.17:

The PostScript Options dialog box.

Screen Types

The PostScript halftone screens are most enticing when used with screen frequencies of 30 per inch or less. With low frequencies, the different screen types become prominent, and can be used to their best advantage. At higher screen frequencies, the eye loses focus on the patterns, resulting in the visual interpretation of gray rather than black-and-white lines.

PostScript Halftone Screen types include Default, Dot, Line, Diamond, Diamond2, Dot2, Elliptical, Euclidean, Grid, Lines, MicroWaves, OutCircleBlk, OutCircleWhi, Rhomboid, and Star (see fig. 6.18). As with the Outline color choices, you cannot specify the PostScript Halftone Screen when using process color.

Figure 6.18:

Examples of PostScript halftone screens.

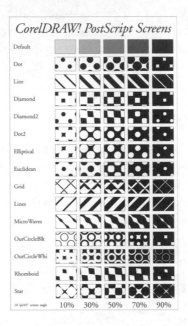

Screen Frequency and Angle

Every halftone screen has a frequency and angle. The rule of thumb is that the higher the quality of printing, the higher you should go with screen frequency. The finer the screen, the less noticeable it is to the naked eye. Newspapers customarily use halftone screens of 85 lines per inch while magazines use 110, 133, or even higher.

If you are outputting to a desktop laser printer, try not to specify more than 60 lines per inch. High-resolution imagesetters can commonly handle screens of 150 lines per inch. Screen angle becomes readily apparent at low-screen frequencies and also is a very important part of process color separations.

Overprint

If you are preparing spot colors for printing, your printer (the person, not the machine) might need overprints or traps. Chapter 11 deals with this subject.

Fountain Fills

Fountain fill is one of Draw's most seductive features. Everyone has been (or will be) attracted to the smoothness this tool provides in blending one color to the next. This appealing characteristic can be used with either spot or process color.

CorelDRAW! version 4.0 features greatly enhanced fountain fill capabilities. The program now provides three types of fountain fills—linear, radial, and conical—which you can specify by means of the Fountain Fill dialog box (see fig. 6.19). *Linear* fountain fills start at one side of an object and migrate to the facing side (see fig. 6.20) *Radial* fountain fills start at the outside edges of an object and radiate inward to the object's center point. *Conical* fountain fills sweep around an object and are anchored by the object's center point.

You can now specify (and create) fountain fill presets. This gives you point-and-shoot control over fountains and ensures that you can assign accurate and consistent fills. Two of the color plates in this book illustrate CorelDRAW! 4.0's fountain fill presets.

Linear Fountain Fills

Linear is the most common form of fountain fill. You have seen these fills plenty of times and have probably wondered how they were created. With CorelDRAW! 4.0, creating linear fountain fills is simple. In the next exercise, you set up a simple one-color linear fountain fill and try setting different fill angles. Full-color editing should be on for this exercise. If it is not, press Shift-F9 now to turn it on.

Figure 6.19:

The Fountain Fill
dialog box.

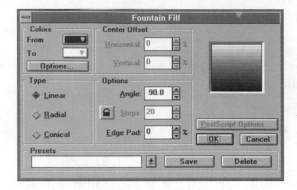

Figure 6.20:

Linear fountain fills.

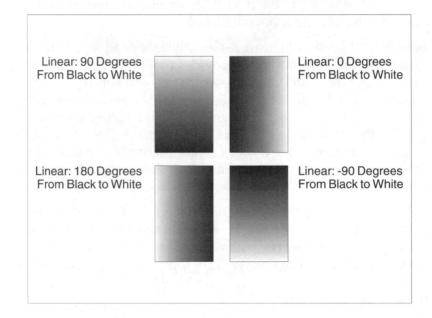

Experimenting with Linear Fountain Fills

Click on the Rectangle tool

Hold down Ctrl *and draw a three-inch square*

Click on the Fill tool   The Fill fly-out menu
                                                       appears

Click on Fountain Fill   The Fountain Fill icon
                                                       looks like a vertical
                                                       gradient

The default fill should appear as follows: Linear; 90 degrees; From Black; To White. If these are not your settings, change them for the purposes of this exercise.

Click on OK	The square is fountain-filled

At 90 degrees, the square is filled from the bottom up. Change the direction of the fill.

Click on the Fill tool	The Fill fly-out menu appears
Click on Fountain Fill	The Fountain Fill dialog box appears
Change the angle to **-90** *degrees*	
Click on OK	The square is fountain-filled

If you want, try setting the fill to 180 or 0 degrees.

The Fountain Fill dialog box offers you a choice of Draw's full complement of colors and PostScript options. Colors can be freely specified using any color model. Clicking on More (accessed by clicking on a color to show a mini-palette) brings up a dialog box that looks remarkably like the Uniform Fill or Outline Color dialog boxes, which provides access to any possible color fountain fill (see fig. 6.21). Click on **P**ostScript Options while in Spot Color mode to access to PostScript halftone screens, which can add dramatic effects to fountain fills.

Edge Pad enables you to increase the fountain fill starting and ending color bands by up to 45 percent. Because fountain fills follow an objects bounding box, irregularly shaped objects can be persnickety; **E**dge Pad ensures that the starting/ending fountain fill colors hit the edges of the object, rather than fall outside. You also can alter the specific number of steps (or bands) in a fountain fill by changing the **S**teps setting. To access **S**teps, you must first unlock it by clicking on the lock/unlock button.

CorelDRAW! version 3.0 introduced the capability to interactively alter linear fountain fill angles. Remember the way you changed the Calligraphic pen shape earlier in the chapter? You can change angles just as easily! Just click and drag in the fountain fill display window. Your cursor turns into a + sign, and a line appears, drawing itself from the middle of the window through the cursor to the edge of the window. As you drag around the window, notice the angle percentage changing. When you release the mouse button, the display window is redrawn with the angle you have specified. The easiest way to understand the way this procedure works is to click near the edge to which you want the fountain fill to go.

Figure 6.21:

Centered and Offset Radial fountain fill.

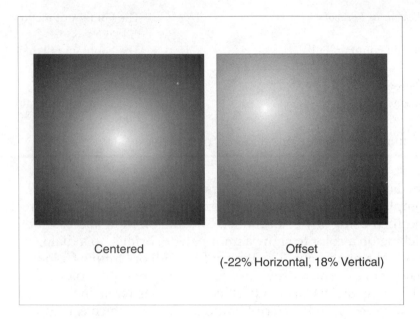

Centered

Offset
(-22% Horizontal, 18% Vertical)

Radial Fountain Fills

Now that you have seen the way a linear fountain fill works, try a radial fill. The Fountain Fill dialog box enables radial fountain fills that flow to the center of an object. The From color spec refers to the outside of the object. The To color spec refers to the inside of the object. No angles are involved. What if you want to have the radial fill flow to the top left corner? Don't worry; you can achieve this effect in a few simple steps.

The easiest method of changing the lighting angle is to use the interactive click-and-drag technique. When you click in the radial fountain fill display window, crosshairs appear, enabling you to drag to any position you want. Alternatively, you can specify Center Offset in horizontal and vertical percentages. Positive values push the light source upward and to the right. Negative values push the light source downward and to the left. The Fountain Fill dialog box also enables you to use Edge Pad.

Fill the square you just drew with a radial fountain fill and try different center offsets.

Altering the Lighting Angle of a Radial Fill

Click on the square

Click on the Fill tool — The Fill fly-out menu appears

Click on Fountain Fill — The Fountain Fill dialog box appears

Click on Radial

Set Colors as From Black *and* To White

Click on OK

Click on Edit — The Edit menu appears

Click on Duplicate — The square is duplicated

Drag the duplicate square below the original

Now that you have set the fill and made a duplicate, use Center Offset to change the lighting angle.

Click on the Fill tool — The Fill fly-out menu appears

Click on Fountain Fill — The Fountain Fill dialog box appears

At Horizontal: type -25

At Vertical: type 25

Click on OK — The fountain fill is offset

The center of the radial fill should now be in the upper left corner of the square. You can alter the lighting angle with this method fairly easily, once you get the hang of it. Figure 6.22 shows samples of the effects you can achieve. Go ahead and alter the center offset by using the interactive method.

Conical Fountain Fills

This spinning fountain fill was added to CorelDRAW! in version 4.0. Conical fountain fills are great for creating everything from a hubcap to a desert road at sunset. In a conical fill, the gradient spirals around a center point, which you are free to move at will, either by entering precise Center Offset percentages, or by clicking and dragging around in the preview window. Take a look at the color pages elsewhere in this book. The Baby and Gold Plated fountain fill presets are two good examples of a conical fountain fill. Try using a few conical fountain fills on your own.

Figure 6.22:

Conical fountain fill options.

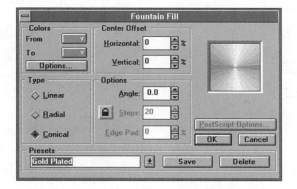

Fountain Fill Options

Draw enables you to set a wide variety of fountain fill color options in addition to those already discussed. Click on Options to access the Fountain Fill Color Options dialog box. This button enables you to control the type of blend: **D**irect, **R**ainbow, or **C**ustom. All the exercises thus far have been direct blends—from one specific color directly to another specific color. The **R**ainbow blend works differently. It enables you to spin around the color wheel—in a clockwise or counterclockwise direction—to yield a rainbow-like effect.

Perhaps most interesting is Draw's new **C**ustom fountain fill option. With **D**irect blends, you can only go from one color to another color (or shade). The custom fountain fill feature gives you the capability to "ping-pong" a fountain fill between different colors or shades. In other words, you now can go from blue to red to blue, all in one fountain fill. If you look at the color plates, you see that the Gold Plated, Green Metallic, Orca, and Pink Neon Presets are all good examples of this effect.

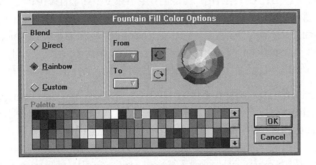

Figure 6.23:

Rainbow fountain fill color options.

To add more colors to a custom fountain fill, click on one of the little black squares at either end of the preview window, and a black triangle appears (see fig. 6.24). You then can drag it into position and assign a color to it by clicking on a color in the palette. Just remember that the black triangle is the active triangle. You can assign a new color to an existing blend point by selecting its triangle and clicking on a new color.

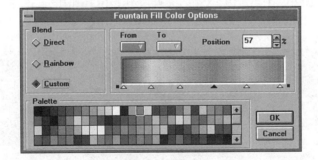

Figure 6.24:

Custom fountain fill color options.

As you have read, CorelDRAW! enables you to create fountain fills with either spot or process colors. You cannot, however, have a fill that changes from a spot color to a process color. If you specify the first color as spot and the second as process, the first color is converted to process automatically.

Fountain fills can give a dimensional look to an illustration. Take care, however, to limit the use of this feature. Fountain fills are quite demanding on the printer, and the use of too many fountain fills, or fountain-filling objects with many nodes, will slow down your printer. Sometimes, using too many fountain fills or fountain-filling an object with too many nodes will actually prevent a file from printing. The time for your preview screen to redraw also increases dramatically. Fountain-filling a rectangle is safe, but doing the same to an object with dozens of curved nodes is just asking for a long run on your printers RIP. Of course, you could go out to lunch while you are waiting!

If a fountain-fill–laden file refuses to print, try replacing some of the fountain fills with solid color fills. Avoid rotating fountain-filled objects. Also try to minimize the number of nodes in any fountain-filled object. The trick is to construct the leanest file possible. The subject of building intricate illustrations is covered in Chapter 8.

PostScript Texture Fills

The PostScript texture fills are located under the letters PS on the Fill fly-out menu. They are available only when printing on a PostScript output device. The 42 different characteristic fills can be individually altered to yield a seemingly limitless number of possibilities. Figure 6.25 shows some sample effects.

Figure 6.25:

PostScript texture fills.

Draw's documentation contains a comprehensive section that displays the many texture fills, along with sample settings for each. To specify a PostScript texture fill, click on PS on the Fill fly-out menu. The PostScript Texture dialog box (see fig. 6.26) enables you to specify the type of fill and its parameters, which include Frequency, Linewidth, ForegroundGray, and BackgroundGray. Parameters depend on the fill being used. These parameters differentiate the many possibilities within each fill type.

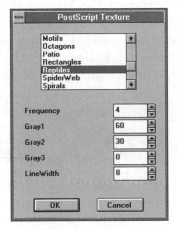

Figure 6.26:

The PostScript Texture dialog box.

The warning given on fountain fills holds doubly true for PostScript texture fills. They might look real neat, but they can take a long time to print. These little critters (one is even called Reptiles) are an extreme drain on output device resources. If plans include using texture fills, be sure to allow plenty of time for the printer to image the file.

Hopefully, advances in PostScript technology and increases in printer speed will make these warnings a thing of the past. Only PostScript printers can print PostScript fills—yet another reason to recommend using one!

Two-Color Pattern Fills

Although CorelDRAW! is basically a vector-based illustration package, the program ships with a number of two-color bit-map patterns, and additional patterns are available from a variety of sources. Bit maps can be imported from scanned images or created in CorelPHOTO-PAINT!, Windows Paintbrush, and other paint programs. Draw's Two-Color Pattern Editor can create new patterns or edit existing ones. The **S**pecial menu even has a **C**reate Pattern option for creating bit-map (as well as vector) pattern fills from existing CorelDRAW! objects.

The Two-Color Pattern Fill icon (located on the Fill fly-out menu) looks like a tiny checkerboard. Clicking on it summons up the Two-Color Pattern dialog box (see fig. 6.27). Here, you can click on the preview pattern to access the pop-up menu, and use the scroll bars to select a bit-map pattern visually. If you cannot find a pattern that you like, you can import or create a new one.

Figure 6.27:

The Two-Color Pattern dialog box with pop-up menu.

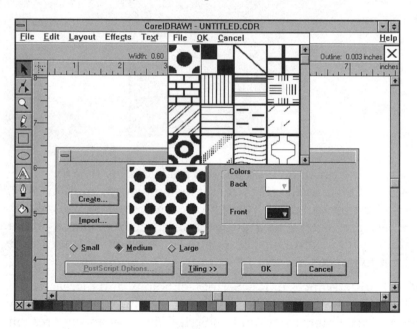

As its name implies, each two-color pattern fill can have only two colors: a foreground and a background. They are initially black and white (respectively), but they do not have to stay that way! You can use spot or process methods to colorize patterns; you cannot, however, mix process and spot colors in a pattern. Plan your color scheme carefully; you can use only two process or two spot colors. The dialog box includes a handy preview feature so that you can try applying different foreground and background colors without leaving the box. PostScript options provide over-printing capabilities and control over PostScript screens (in spot-color mode only).

Pattern fills are based on the tile concept. Click on Tiling to expand the dialog box and show tiling options (see fig. 6.28). The dialog box provides three default tile sizes: Small, Medium, and Large. You are free to resize tile width and height to suit your needs. Be careful not to stretch out or squish tiles too far. Remember, these are bit maps; they become jagged or blurred when removed from their original size and scale.

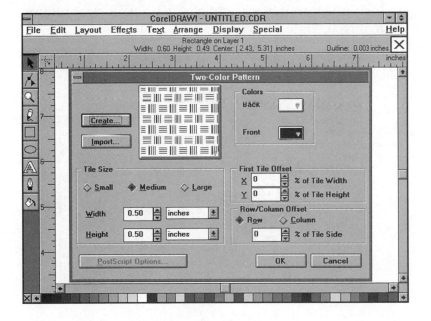

Figure 6.28:

Two-Color Pattern tiling options.

Patterns can be offset to compensate for discrepancies in object size the same way a tile man sets floor tile. If a pattern does not fit an object cleanly, you can use X and/or Y offsets to lay down the pattern precisely. You also have the option of using Row/Column Offset to stagger the pattern.

Working with matrix patterns takes some thought, but sometimes the best stuff happens by chance. Once again, the time spent here is worth the effort you put in. You will learn more about how patterns work by experimentation.

Two-color pattern fills are print-time consumers. The more times a pattern is reproduced, the larger your print file becomes and the longer it takes to print. For this reason, patterns should be used with caution. The caveats that apply to fountain fills also apply here.

The Two-Color Pattern Editor works in three bit-map sizes and four pen sizes (see fig. 6.29). The Two-Color Pattern Editor is summoned by clicking on the Create button in the Two-Color Pattern dialog box. The Editor might remind you of Windows Paintbrush in its Zoom Up mode. Click on a square with your left mouse button to turn it black, and click with your right mouse button to turn it white.

Figure 6.29:

The Two-Color Pattern Editor.

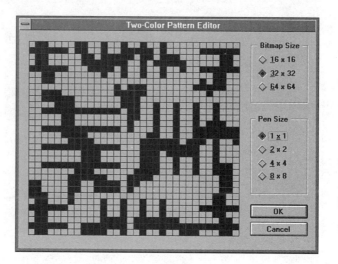

Full-Color Pattern Fills

Somewhere in between two-color patterns and PostScript textures lies full-color (or vector) patterns. Drawing from a little of both, full-color pattern fills can offer more flexibility than either of the aforementioned fills. Full-color pattern fills, however, fall to the same print-time malady as do all other fancy fills. If you want to use them, be prepared to wait for the output.

Like two-color patterns, full-color pattern fills can be created from existing CorelDRAW! objects with the Create Pattern option on the Special menu. Unlike two-color patterns, however, you can use more than two colors or tints.

Full-color patterns are stored as files. When you choose a full-color pattern, you select a file from the Load Full-Color Pattern dialog box. Thankfully, a preview window enables you to check out the different patterns one by one.

Like two-color patterns, you can control the tile size and offsets of full-color patterns. You cannot, however, alter the color of a full-color pattern through the Full-Color Pattern dialog box. To do so, you must edit the objects that the full-color pattern was based upon and re-create the pattern.

Editing an existing full-color pattern fill is no more difficult than editing any other Draw file. To edit an existing full-color pattern fill, you open it, edit it, and then use Create Pattern (on the Special menu) to save it (see figs. 6.30 and 6.31). The trick is to use the PAT file extension in the Open Drawing dialog box in place of the CDR extension.

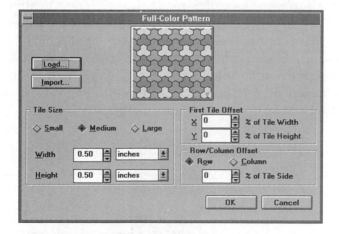

Figure 6.30:
Loading a full-color pattern.

Unlike two-color patterns, full-color patterns can be resized without losing image quality. But once again, full-color patterns are tough on the printer. The more patterns you use, the longer you can expect to wait!

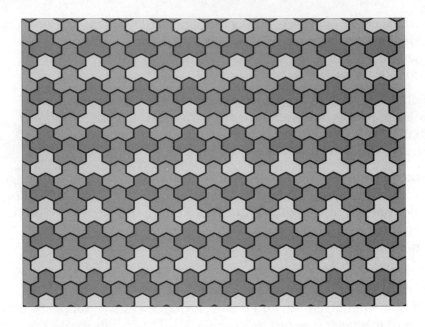

The Fill Roll-Up Menu

The Fill roll-up enables quick-picking, easy access to almost all of Draw's fills: uniform, fountain, two-, and full-color patterns (see fig. 6.32). In addition, it enables you to Update From (which is the same as Copy Style From) any other fill, and it also can whisk you to the supporting fill dialog boxes (via the Edit button) to make more involved fill decisions. The Fill roll-up menu lacks one thing: you cannot access PostScript Pattern Fills.

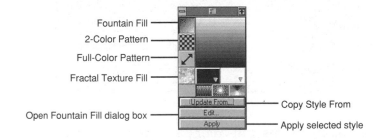

You can save plenty of time with the Fill roll-up menu. Assigning existing two- or full-color pattern fills (from their respective pop-up menus) is a breeze, as is altering fountain-fill characteristics.

You have just covered a lot of ground, including learning how to specify color outlines, fills, and patterns. In the next section, you are going to put that theory to work as you build an opening slide.

Creating Charts and Slides

Producing charts and slides is important to many corporate electronic artists. Preparing business presentations makes up a large portion of many a corporate shop's workload. Many computer programs enable users to prepare colorful charts, graphs, and text for use in 35mm slide presentations. CorelDRAW! is but one of them.

Prior to version 3.0, CorelDRAW! had no built-in automatic charting capabilities. To produce charts with the program, you had to either import the chart or build it from scratch. CorelCHART! was introduced with Draw version 3.0. This program filled a gap by providing advanced 3D charting in the Corel environment. You can quickly and easily create stunning charts and incorporate them into your other artwork. With spreadsheet import capabilities and other powerful features, Chart literally adds a new dimension to CorelDRAW!.

As you progress through the rest of the exercises, you put Draw's fountain- and color-fill capabilities to use. Why cover color and slides in the same chapter? At the present time, color printers are too expensive to be commonplace. Proofing in color is important, but most people have only black-and-white printers hooked up to their computers.

When you proof an image intended to be black and white, you get black-and-white prints. No problem. But when you proof an image intended to be color, you still only get black-and-white prints. Currently, 35mm slides are among the least expensive ways to produce color output from Draw.

Producing Charts and Graphs

Before the advent of personal computers, charts and graphs were produced in one of two ways. The first method was the old-fashioned way, on a drawing board with skilled designers wielding technical pens, T-squares, and triangles. The second method was accomplished by using programmers, mainframe computers, and plotters. If you worked either way in the past, you are sure to appreciate the changes the past decade has brought.

Of these two methods, the drawing board was capable of yielding much more distinctive results. Artists are capable of making aesthetic decisions; computers are not.

Thankfully, today's dedicated PC graphing software programs offer far more flexibility than their mainframe ancestors did. With a trained operator, excellent results are possible in real time. With an untrained operator, however, you do not get what you do not pay for.

CorelDRAW! and CorelCHART! bring together the methods employed by designers and computer users. These two applications should form a cornerstone of your slide and chart-building repertoire. You also should have a spreadsheet program to round out the set.

Building Your Own Pie Charts

If necessary, you can build your own pie charts by using the Shape tool to modify a circle into a pie slice (see fig. 6.33). This method is not automated, but it can be useful in a pinch. Simply click on an ellipse's node with the Shape tool and drag it around. Dragging inside the ellipse yields a pie slice; dragging outside the ellipse creates an arc.

You need a separate circle for each slice. If you were planning six slices, for example, you would copy five more circles on top of the first circle.

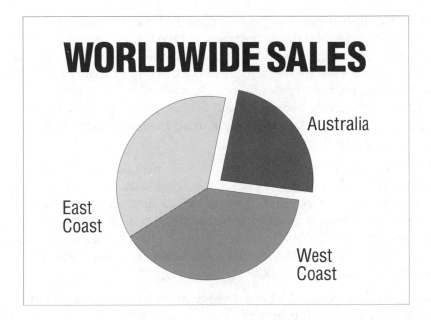

Figure 6.33:
A pie slice made with the Shape tool.

The status line shows the angles of the pie slice/arc. Using Ctrl constrains the pie slice to 15-degree (default setting) increments. To facilitate the alignment of pie wedges, the highlight box is the same size as the original ellipse. If you Shift-click or marquee-select all the pie wedges and use horizontal/vertical center to align, things fall a bit short. Enabling Snap To **O**bjects works well here.

Making Your Presentation Count

Presentations that consist of slide after boring slide will surely put the audience to sleep. On the other hand, arrays of flashy charts can leave the audience dazed and confused.

Cut presentations down to the minimum. Use only the charts that are absolutely necessary. This limitation helps to prevent the audience from suffering from information overload. Remember, information can easily get lost in the delivery. The message is the important thing; do not let the medium get in the way.

You also should provide printed copies of the important information in your presentations; but do not take the visuals, print them out full size, and staple them together. That is just sloppy. Given the time, incorporate the visuals into a document that consists of a written recap of the presentation. Do not make it a rehash of the voice-over; include background information too lengthy for the presentation itself. And do not just read from the slides; rather, elaborate upon them.

The value of a presentation is not determined solely by its charts and graphs. The complete package is what sells. Make sure that it is comprehensive. Artists should strive to eliminate cookie-cutter charts. Do not use a chart program's preset defaults for background and text colors if you have time to find something better. Above all, do not put style above substance; strive for style with substance. Use what works.

Right now, stop in at DeLook Design and see what kind of colorful work Joe is getting into.

DeLook Design Lands Rippin' Surfboards, Inc.

The crew at DeLook Design is elated. They have just hooked their first corporate client, Rippin' Surfboards, Inc. It was not too difficult, because the president and founder of the company is Joe DeLook's old surfing buddy, Rip Raster.

Rip wants a presentation he can give to the local bank as part of his request for a loan. Rippin' Surfboards is thriving and has outgrown its present location (which is Rip's garage, of course). Rip has just found the perfect spot for his new production facility. The owner is eager to sell and Rip is ready to buy. Unfortunately, all of Rippin' Surfboards' capital is tied up in its inventory. Rip is counting on this presentation to save his business.

Joe DeLook has promised Rip that he can put a slide presentation together in just a couple of days. The presentation will consist of an introductory slide, a text slide, and a chart. In the following exercise, you make the introductory slide for Rippin' Surfboards, Inc. (see fig. 6.34).

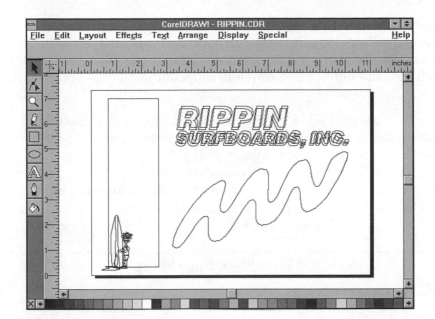

Figure 6.34:
The introductory slide.

Building Slides

When building images that will ultimately become slides, you should first change the page setup to match the aspect ratio of a 35mm slide. Because the size of a 35mm slide is approximately 24 by 36 millimeters, the aspect ratio is 2:3.

Do not worry about making any difficult calculations; once again, Draw makes things a snap. Just click on Slide in the Page Setup dialog box, and your page size is instantly configured for the correct aspect ratio. Because this translates to 7.33 inches by 11 inches, you can even proof your work on any Windows-supported printer.

If you do not use the proper page setup, the slide image probably will be clipped or incomplete. Right now, take the time to open a new page and properly set it up for 35mm slides. While you are in Page Setup, you can use **A**dd Page Frame to place a rectangle that you will fill with the background color. When a page frame is initially placed, it will have the default object fill.

By using a page frame, you ensure that the background color reaches to the edge of the image area and no farther. If the background color rectangle does not reach the page edge, your slide will be outlined in black or white (depending on how you export your slide).

Do not confuse Page Frame with Paper Color. A *page frame* is an object that you can fill with any color or pattern, while *paper color* is a device for on-screen print proofing. Paper color assigns a paper shade of your choice to emulate printing on colored paper. The color exists only in the preview window; it does not appear on the copy that rolls out of your output device.

35mm Slide Page Setup

Click on **L**ayout	The Layout menu appears
Click on Page **S**etup	The Page Setup dialog box appears
At Paper Size, roll down, click on **S**lide	
Click on **A**dd Page Frame	A page frame is added
Click on OK	The page is set up in the proper aspect ratio
Click on **L**ayout	The Layout menu appears
Click on Gr**i**d Setup	The Grid Setup dialog box appears
Change the grid frequency to **3** *per inch*	
Click on S**n**ap to Grid	
Click on OK	

The slide presentation you are about to construct consists of a group of repetitive elements. Chief among them is the slide structure itself, which is of a rather standard design, incorporating a solid color background with a fountain-filled bar running vertically along the left side.

Along with the overall design are three more repetitive elements: the logo and two motifs, a surfer and a wave. Remember, you are at the beach! You will build the slide structure first and then move on to setting the logotype. You will finish by creating the wave pattern and importing and coloring the surfer clip art.

Because you used a page frame, the background will reach the page edge. Fill the page frame with a solid color from the Uniform Fill dialog box.

As you have seen, the Uniform Fill dialog box offers a choice between spot and process colors. You are going to address the spot colors first. After you have clicked PANTONE spot color, the dialog box enables you to choose color as well as tint percentage.

Setting up the Background with a PANTONE Fill

Click on Page Frame	
Click on the Fill tool	The Fill fly-out menu appears
Click on the Uniform Fill *icon*	The Uniform Fill dialog box appears
At Show, *click on* PANTONE Spot Colors	The dialog box is configured for spot (PMS) color

You need to scroll down a bit to get down to the color you want. Remember that when you select a color, the PANTONE number appears in the Color Name box.

Scroll through the PMS colors	
Select PANTONE 255	
Click on OK	The rectangle is filled with the selected color

With the solid filled background in place, draw and fill a vertical rectangle along the left side of your slide layout.

Drawing and Fountain-Filling the Rectangle

Click on **D**isplay
Click on Show **R**ulers (*if they are not on*)

continued

Click on the Rectangle tool	
Position the cursor .67 inches from the left side and .33 inches from the top of the page	
Draw a rectangle 2.00 inches wide by 6.67 inches tall, as shown in figure 6.35	
Click on the Fill tool	The Fill fly-out menu appears
Click on the Fountain Fill *icon*	The Fountain Fill dialog box appears
Click on **L**inear	
At From, *click on the arrow, click on* More	The Fountain Fill Color Options dialog box appears
At Show, *click on* PANTONE Spot Colors	The dialog box is configured for spot (PMS) color
Select PANTONE Process Blue	
Click on OK	
At To, *click on button, click on* More	The Fountain Fill Color Options dialog box reappears
Select PANTONE 255	
Click on OK	
At Presets, *Type* `Slide Fade`	
Click on Save	
Click on OK again	The rectangle is fountain-filled

The rectangle should be 100-percent process blue at the bottom, fading to the background's PMS 255 at the top—an interesting twist to a standard layout. You saved the fountain fill as a preset, so you have the option of assigning it to a new object with a couple of clicks.

Now, set the logotype. You are going to use another fountain fill on the word RIPPIN and a solid color fill on SURFBOARDS, INC. Be careful not to overdo it with fountain-filled text—large blocks of text or complex letter forms can lead to trouble.

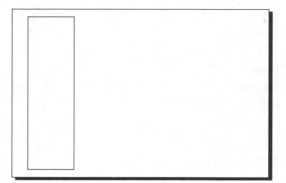

Figure 6.35:
Rectangle for fountain-filling.

Setting the RIPPIN Logotype

Click on the Text tool
Click on the center of the page
At the text I bar, type **RIPPIN**
Press Ctrl-T

The Artistic Text dialog
box appears

Scroll down and click on Swis721 Blk BT
At Style, *click on* Italic
At Point Size, *enter* **84**
Click on **S**pacing

The Spacing dialog box
appears

At **C**haracter, *enter* **-1**
Click on OK
Click on OK again
Click on the page below RIPPIN
At the text I bar, type **SURFBOARDS, INC.**
Press Ctrl-T

The Artistic Text dialog
box appears

Scroll down to and click on Swis721 Blk BT
At Style, *click on* Italic
At Si**z**e, *enter* **48**
Click on **S**pacing

The Spacing dialog box
appears

continued

At Character, *enter* **-1**	
At Word, *enter* **60**	
Click on OK	
Click on OK again	
Click on the Pick tool	
Click on RIPPIN	
Click on the Fill tool	The Fill fly-out menu appears
Click on the Fountain Fill *icon*	The Fountain Fill dialog box appears
At From, *click on button, click on* More	The Fountain Fill Color Options dialog box appears
At Show, *click on* PANTONE Spot Colors	The dialog box is configured for spot (PMS) color
Select PANTONE 354	
Click on OK	
At To, *click on button, click on* More	The Fountain Fill Color Options dialog box appears
Select PANTONE YELLOW	
Click on OK	
At Presets, *type* **Rippin Logo Fade**	
Click on Save	
Click on OK	The type is fountain-filled
Click on SURFBOARDS, INC.	
Click on the Fill tool	The Fill fly-out menu appears
Click on the Uniform Fill *icon*	The Uniform Fill dialog box appears
At Show, *click on* PANTONE Spot Color	
At Color, *select* PANTONE 354	
Click on OK	The type is uniformly filled

Now, drag the type so that the words are in position with each other. Use the horizontal left align command if necessary.

Shift-click or marquee-select **RIPPIN** *and* **SURFBOARDS, INC.**	
Press Ctrl-G	The logotype is grouped

Now that the logotype is positioned and grouped, add a drop shadow behind the type to make the logo stand out. With the logotype still selected, take the following steps:

Press Ctrl-D

The logotype is duplicated

Drag the duplicate logotype a few points below and to the left of the original, use the Nudge (cursor) keys to fine-tune things

Click on the Fill tool

The Fill fly-out menu appears

Click on Black

The drop shadow is filled with black

Shift-click on the original logotype

The shadow logotype should still be selected

Click on Arrange

Click on Order

The Order menu appears

Click on Reverse Order

The drop shadow is behind the original logotype

Press Ctrl-G

The logotype is grouped (see fig. 6.36)

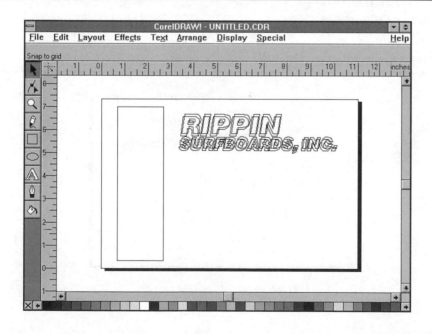

Figure 6.36:

The logotype in place.

Now draw the squiggly wave symbol and fill it with a graduated fill. Remember the warning about fountain fills? Keep the number of nodes to a minimum to avoid trouble. Use AutoReduce (on the Node Edit roll-up menu) to painlessly remove extra nodes.

You are going to be assigning the exact same fill as the first RIPPIN. Although you can use Update From (on the Fill roll-up menu) or Copy Attributes From (on the Edit menu) instead of manually assigning the fountain fill, a much easier way is available. Because you saved Rippin Logo Fade as a fountain fill preset, it will be a snap!

Drawing and Filling the Wave

Click on the Pencil tool
Draw the wave symbol, as shown in figure 6.37
Click on the Fill tool   The Fill fly-out menu
                                                  appears

Click on the Fountain Fill *icon*   The Fountain Fill dialog
                                                  box appears

At Presets, *click on* Rippin Logo Fade
Click on OK   The wave is fountain-
                                                  filled

Save the file with the name RIPPIN

Figure 6.37:
The wave.

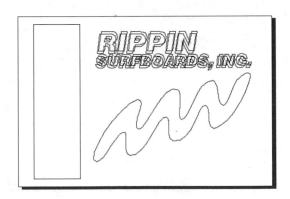

The last element is the surfer. Thankfully, you do not have to draw him, just import him. You can find the surfer on the CD-ROM that comes with CorelDRAW! version 4.0. He is located in the CLIPART\MAN\IMAGECLU\SPORTS library.

Bringing In the Surfer from the Sports Library

Click on File	The File menu appears
Click on Import	The Import dialog box appears
At List Files of Type, *select* CorelDRAW! *.CDR	
Maneuver to your CD-ROM drive	
Double-click on CLIPART	
Scroll down, double-click on MAN	
Double-click on IMAGECLU	
Double-click on SPORTS	
Roll down, double-click on SURFERI	The surfer appears (see fig. 6.38)
Click on OK	

Figure 6.38:
The surfer.

On the slide, the surfer is a black-and-white dude in a multicolored world. You do not want a boring-looking surfer, so pick him apart and fill him with whatever colors you like.

Because you want to produce a full-color slide, you need to ungroup the surfer and fill the individual objects with some surfer-like colors. To do this with the largest possible number of colors, use process fills to colorize the image.

Usually, mixing PANTONE and process colors together is an expensive situation. But because these compositions are to be imaged as 35mm slides, you can mix colors as you see fit. Just don't expect to do this with a normal print job unless you have an unlimited budget and absolutely no conscience!

The CMYK process color uniform fill option works in a manner similar to the spot color option. The difference is that if you click on CMYK rather than Spot, you can specify uniform fills by entering exact percentages of any combination of the four process colors in addition to selecting prespecified, named colors.

To reiterate: don't get lulled into specifying color based on what you see on the screen. Use a PANTONE or TRUMATCH swatch book. If you are specifying color for a certain printing press, you should have an absolute reference. Your printer might be able to supply a comprehensive process color guide run from his own press.

Ungroup the surfer and individually color his parts. Color just his limbs, chest, head, and shorts. You can finish him up and regroup him later.

Coloring the Surfer

Click on the Zoom tool	The Zoom fly-out menu appears
Click on the +	
Marquee-select the surfer	The screen zooms up
Click on the Pick tool	
Click on the surfer	
Press Ctrl-U	The surfer is ungrouped

Now that you have 34 separate objects, try to colorize them in a logical manner. Start by shift-clicking the surfer's legs, arms, and head.

You are going to start out by creating a named color that you will call *Surfer's Tan*, making the color easy to identify in the Fill dialog boxes and on the status line. Notice that as you repeatedly go back into the Uniform Fill dialog box, the dialog box remembers which mode you left it in. The dialog box will be in the most recently used Color Model.

Creating a Named Color

Shift-click on the surfer's legs, arms, and head

Click on the Fill tool   The Fill fly-out menu appears

Click on Uniform Fill   The Uniform Fill dialog box appears

Click on CYMK Color Model   The dialog box configures for process color

At Cyan, *enter* **0**
At Magenta, *enter* **25**
At Yellow, *enter* **30**
At Black, *enter* **10**
At Color Name, type **Surfer's Tan**

Click on OK   The surfer gets a slight tan

Marquee-select the nose and mouth

Click on the Fill tool   The Fill fly-out menu appears

Click on Uniform Fill   The Uniform Fill dialog box appears

At Cyan, *enter* **0**
At Magenta, *enter* **40**
At Yellow, *enter* **30**
At Black, *enter* **10**
At Color Name, type **Surfer's Nose**

Click on OK   The surfer's nose gets a burn

continued

Click on the surfer's shorts	
Click on the Fill tool	The Fill fly-out menu appears
Click on Uniform Fill	The Uniform Fill dialog box appears
At Cyan, *enter* **0**	
At Magenta, *enter* **77**	
At Yellow, *enter* **27**	
At Black, *enter* **23**	
At Color Name, type **Surfer's Shorts**	
Click on OK	The surfer puts on some bright shorts
Click on the surfer's hairdo	
Click on the Fill tool	The Fill fly-out menu appears
Click on Uniform Fill	The Uniform Fill dialog box appears
At Cyan, *enter* **0**	
At Magenta, *enter* **0**	
At Yellow, *enter* **100**	
At Black, *enter* **5**	
At Color Name, type: **Surfer's Do**	
Click on OK	The surfer's hair gets bleached

That should give you the general idea of how the process (no pun intended) works. Remember, the only time you would be able to affordably mix this many PANTONE and process colors together would be when printing to a slidemaker or color proof printer.

Continue filling the surfboard and puddle with whatever colors you like. Stick with a somewhat limited palette; pick up colors that have been used elsewhere. This helps to tie the slide together.

When you are finished, scale the surfer down to 30 percent of original size, group the surfer, and drag him to just above the bottom of the vertical bar. You have created Rip's introductory slide!

Using Palettes to Your Advantage

Specifying colors in CorelDRAW! can be simplified through intelligent use of the on-screen color palette. You might have noticed it on the bottom of the Draw window and wondered why you are not using that. Well, you should use the on-screen palette whenever possible, in the same manner a painter loads paint onto his palette. The palette is a great time-saver, but you must understand how to specify and mix the colors before you can start saving the time.

The on-screen color palette saves you time by allowing you to specify an object's fill or outline color with one mouse click. With an object selected, position your cursor over the chosen color. Click with the left mouse button to fill; click with the right mouse button to outline. Instant colors! See the X button at the far left of the palette? Select an object and click on the X with your left mouse button to assign a fill of None, and click with your right mouse button to assign an outline of None.

The palette can be switched on or off from the Display menu (which enables you to choose from PANTONE Spot Colors, PANTONE Process Colors, TRUMATCH Process Colors, or the Custom palette). To move through the on-screen color palette, use a pair of scroll buttons. But, if you have to use them, you are overlooking the advantage of having the most frequently used colors loaded at the top of the palette.

When you start working on a piece of artwork, consider the color scheme. First, decide whether the image will be constructed with spot or process colors. As the artwork evolves into the production stage, decide which colors you want to load onto your palette, then arrange them to fit your working style.

In the preceding exercise, you created custom colors that were loaded to the custom palette (even though you never asked that they be loaded there). When you create custom colors, they are added to the end of the custom palette. Fortunately, they don't have to stay at the end of the list!

You can make the most of the palette by reordering the colors so that those you use often are at the top of the list. To shuffle the colors around, go to the Uniform Fill dialog box and select the Custom Palette. Then click and drag colors, positioning them to set up your palette in the order that best suits the artwork at hand. The order of the Uniform Fill dialog box Custom Palette matches the order of the on-screen custom palette.

As you have seen, you must first switch to CMYK to create a new color and add it to the custom palette. After you are in CMYK mode, you can mix up a color to your liking and assign it a descriptive name of your choice. When you click on OK, the color is automatically added to the custom palette. It is easy to both add and delete individual colors from the Custom Palette button. And, you have the option of naming and saving completely new custom palettes. In all, proper use of CorelDRAW!'s palettes will add to your enjoyment of the program and help you be more productive to boot!

Fractal Texture Fills

The addition of fractal texture fills is the most radical enhancement to CorelDRAW! version 4.0. These awesome, chaotic beauties have got to be the coolest thing to come out of Ottawa in ages! What's a fractal texture fill? Just take a look at the color signature. You will find 11 pages of incredible textures—just 44 (default) textures out of millions of possibilities.

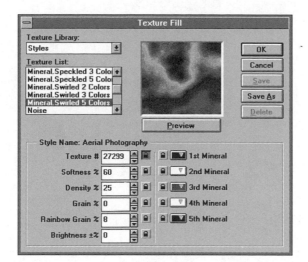

Figure 6.39:
The Fractal Texture
Fill dialog box.

Summary

Draw provides a full range of outline and fill capabilities. This chapter covered the advanced features of both, while using a real-world example of 35mm slidemaking as a vehicle for displaying Draw's utility as a powerful communications tool. Although Draw itself is not a charting or graphing program, CorelCHART! is a powerful addition to the Corel Graphics Toolkit.

Your role as an electronic artist is to help your clients get their messages across. Whether the medium is print, slides, or even three-dimensional objects, Draw enables you to do it right. The program's control over color, in both PANTONE and process permutations, makes it an essential instrument in your quest for artistic success.

As you move through the rest of this book, Draw's potential should become increasingly obvious. It is up to you to harness that power, whether your field is commercial art or somewhere within the fine arts.

7

Bit Maps and Draw

raw is a vector-based drawing program rather than a bit-mapped paint program. Still, Draw does a nice job of importing bit-mapped images from other sources, and Draw can even be used to export bit maps of its own. This chapter discusses the different types of bit maps you can use within the Draw environment. CorelDRAW! version 3.0 introduced CorelPHOTO-PAINT!, a powerful bit-mapped paint program. Although Photo-Paint is touched on here, you can find it covered in depth in Chapter 12.

Unlike object-oriented images, a bit-mapped image is rasterized—that is, imaged dot by dot. Each pixel on the screen corresponds to a single dot on the output image. A bit-mapped image can be considered a grid of pixels or a matrix of dots. As you can see in figure 7.1, the individual dots in a bit-map matrix can be either on (in black, or in a variety of colors or grays) or off (white).

Figure 7.1:
The bit map
blown up.

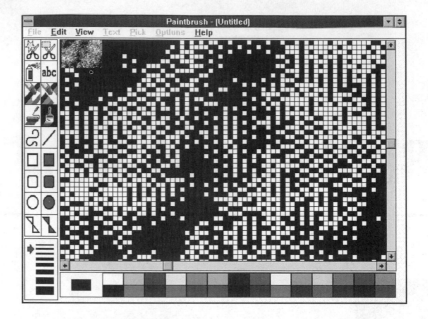

Figure 7.1:
The bit map blown up.

Finding Bit Maps

Bit-mapped images can come from a variety of sources. These sources include scanned images, original paint-type graphics (such as those you create and export from Photo-Paint), and electronic clip art. You can, in fact, import a limitless variety of images into Draw, whether they begin as electronic files or printed originals.

In addition, you can incorporate "screen shots" or screen dumps into Draw images. In fact, many of the graphics in this book were reproduced in this way. Screen shots are especially useful for producing software documentation or promotional materials. Although New Riders Publishing uses a dedicated screen capture program, for light duty you can use the Corel screen capture utility, CCapture, supplied with CorelDRAW! version 4.0.

Scanners

A *scanner* makes it possible to bring a printed image or piece of artwork into a computer program. Scanners transform analog artwork into digital data through a process known as *digitizing*. These devices now are commonplace, but just a few years ago they were playthings reserved for those with deep pockets, long vision, and a taste for the exotic.

Scanners are available in a variety of sizes and styles, from hand-held scanners at the low end to serious "heavy-metal" drum scanners at the high end. In the past, very few shops combined six-figure scanners with CorelDRAW!, but times are changing. Now that Photo-Paint is bundled in the Draw package, Corel users have the ability to alter 24-bit images.

Today, many people buy scanners in the $200 to $2,000 range. Some of these scanners are limited in image quality, but they have come a long way in a short time. Line art and grayscale scanning is commonplace. As computers grow faster, more powerful, and less expensive, expect to see a corresponding increase in scanning accuracy and resolution.

One of the most interesting developments in scanner technology is the advent of drum scanners in the $30,000 to $40,000 range. Entries from DS America Scanview and Howtek are changing the way people work with color. Instead of relying on outside suppliers, designers can create high-caliber scans at their desktops. Quality four-color work, however, has never been a poor (or an unskilled) person's game. It takes serious commitment, skill, and expertise to create realistic full-color scans. It might be subjective, but there is no replacement for having an "eye."

A Scanning Caveat

You must be careful, however, about the images you scan. It is too easy to break the law by using images that belong to another person or organization. While the "copyright police" might not come knocking on the door, a little professional courtesy goes a long way.

If a client should ask to include an image of, say, a popular cartoon character, *do not* do this without obtaining the proper authorization from the copyright owner. In many cases, you can easily contact the licensee, pay a fee, and avoid the legal ramifications.

Because Draw has no internal provisions for working with graphics on a bit-by-bit basis—other than bit-map fill patterns—a paint program, such as Photo-Paint, is necessary for dealing with bit-mapped graphics. Many other PC programs are available to accomplish this task, and one of them, Windows Paintbrush, is included in the Windows program.

Windows Paintbrush

Anyone who has spent some time in the Windows environment knows that Microsoft was kind enough to include a program known as Windows Paintbrush along with the package. The latest version, included with Windows 3.1, is an improvement over its predecessor, Windows Paint.

Windows Paintbrush's obvious advantage over any other paint package is that it is basically free, because it comes with the Windows package. Price aside, the powerful but diminutive program has enough horsepower to take care of many bit-mapped graphic needs.

The program can produce images that appear to have been rendered with charcoal or pen and ink, as shown in figure 7.2. When coupled with a graphics tablet, Windows Paintbrush is capable of surprising results.

Paintbrush's toolbox might seem abbreviated, but it contains enough versatility to get many a job done. And for the price, you should have no complaints. In a few moments, you create some artwork with Paintbrush; later in the chapter, you import the file into Draw.

If Windows Paintbrush or CorelPHOTO-PAINT! does not have enough horsepower for you, a number of alternatives are available. A capsule review of a few of the most popular bit-map paint programs available is included in Chapter 10.

Figure 7.2:
Paintbrush imagery.

Take a few moments to play around with Windows Paintbrush. You have to minimize Draw to an icon and bring up the Windows Program Manager to launch Paintbrush (see fig. 7.3). This chapter does not cover Paintbrush in depth, but you will see that the program is easy to grasp.

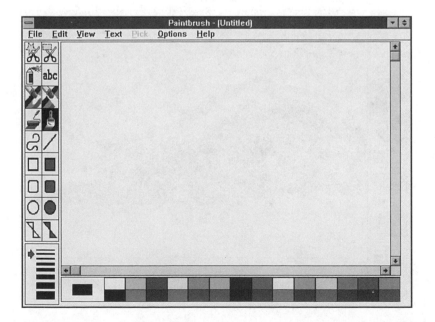

Figure 7.3:
The Windows Paintbrush screen.

Launching Windows Paintbrush

Click on the minimize arrow in the upper right corner of the screen	Draw becomes an icon

At the Windows Program Manager Accessories window:

Double-click on the Paintbrush icon	Windows Paintbrush launches

Now that you have Paintbrush up and running on the screen, go ahead and try out the various tools. Many are self-explanatory, but here are the basics.

Along the left side of the Paintbrush window is the toolbox, with its many easily identified painting implements. Beneath the toolbox is the line size box, where line width is chosen. Along the bottom of the window, the palette offers a choice of 28 colors or shades.

You are going to create a drawing of a wave, like the one shown in figure 7.4. Later, you import this file into Draw using black, white, and shades of gray. After importing into Draw, you colorize the bit map using the Outline and Fill tools.

Figure 7.4:

The wave pattern.

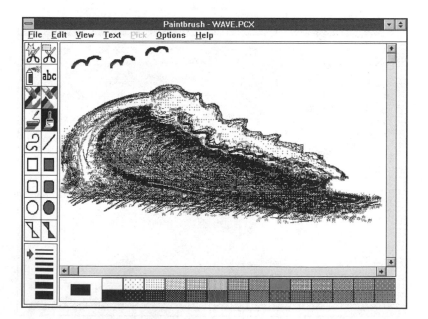

At this point, you should get comfortable with Paintbrush's various painting tools. Pay particular attention to the Airbrush tool (it looks like a spray can)—you are going to create a bit-mapped image using it. If additional material is required at this time, in-depth information on Windows Paintbrush can be found in the Microsoft Windows *User's Guide*.

DeLook Designs for Island Sports

The DeLook Design studio has become one hopping place! Word of the studio's new capabilities is spreading through Seaside like a red tide. Island Sports has just asked Joe and the gang to design the graphics elements and a logo for its next marketing campaign.

Ready to get to work? Okay, here is the first assignment. You need to draw a wave pattern for Island Sports' newspaper ad. It should be easy to crank out the image in a short time using the Airbrush tool. If you use the smaller line widths, the airbrush has less propensity to "spit." It's amazing that the software designers have also included this frustrating aberration. A little less realism would have sufficed!

Remember, Paintbrush maintains the standard Windows Undo function. If needed, it is readily available on the <u>E</u>dit menu. In addition to Undo, the Eraser tool comes in handy for touching up mistakes.

Drawing a Wave Graphic with the Airbrush Tool

This should be a fun and easy exercise. Don't worry about getting everything exactly perfect. Just have a good time with it!

Click on the Airbrush tool	The cursor turns into a plus sign (+)
Draw a wave graphic using only black, white, and grays	
Click on the paintbrush tool	
Draw a few sea gulls at the top of the screen	

Before you leave the Paintbrush program, you need to save your image (see fig. 7.5). Paintbrush offers five different formats for saving files, as shown in table 7.1. The program defaults to the Windows bit-map file (BMP). Draw is capable of importing any of these file formats—but make it easy on yourself and save the wave as a PCX file.

Table 7.1
Paintbrush File Formats

PCX
Monochrome bit map
16-color bit map
256-color bit map
24-bit bit map

Figure 7.5:

Windows Paintbrush Save screen.

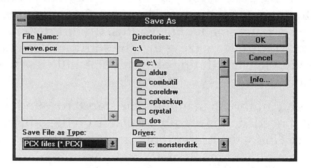

Saving the Wave as a PCX File

Click on **F**ile	The File menu appears
Click on **S**ave	The Save dialog box appears
At Save File as **T**ype, *click on* PCX files (*.PCX)	Saves the file as WAVE.PCX
Type **WAVE** *in file name box*	
Click on OK	
Click on the minimize arrow	Paintbrush is minimized
Bring Draw up	

Electronic Clip Art

You might have worked with object-oriented electronic clip art in CDR, EPS, and CGM formats, but these vector-based formats are certainly not the only formats in town. Many electronic clip-art libraries also are available in the ever-popular PCX and grayscale information-laden TIFF formats. You need not limit yourself to object-oriented libraries alone. Using bit-mapped art expands the depth and breadth of your clip-art choices.

Working with bit-mapped clip art can be more difficult than working with vector-based art. It requires extra steps, which might (as you will see) include converting the raster image into vector format. This process is referred to as *tracing*, and can be handled in variety of ways.

A wide range of bit-mapped formats exists on the PC platform, and Draw supports most of the major players: BMP, GIF, PCX, JPEG, TGA (Targa), and TIFF. Bit-map file-format support was greatly enhanced in version 3.0 with the addition of color bit map export along with support for GIF and TGA. Corel bolstered its bit-map support again in version 4.0, with the addition of JPEG and TIFF 6.0 (four-color bit-map) formats. Confusingly, Corel refers to its TIFF 6.0 files as SEP files.

Draw's bit-map file export filters enable selectable image resolution and image sizing control. Bitmap support does exclude one important format. As of CorelDRAW! version 4.0a5, the Desktop Color Separation (DCS) format is not supported. Hopefully, Corel's engineers will add this format—crucial to high-end graphic arts work—to Draw's burgeoning bit-map list.

BMP

The summer of 1990 saw the introduction of the BMP Windows bit-map format. A few months later, with the release of version 2.0, CorelDRAW! had the capability to import these files. As you might recall from the Paintbrush Save As dialog box, Windows BMP files come in four flavors: monochrome, 16-color, 256-color, and 24-bit.

Take caution: as with other bit-map formats, the more colors in a BMP file, the larger the file. Hence, you should save BMP files using the file format with the smallest number of colors. You have no reason to save a 16-color image as a 24-bit file. BMP file compression is optional, although it is not available for 24-bit files.

GIF

In 1992, CorelDRAW! added support for the popular GIF (Graphic Interchange file) file format, originally created for CompuServe. This format is supported by a number of programs, including Autodesk Animator. Draw can import and export black-and-white, grayscale, and 16- and 256-color GIF files. File compression is standard.

JPEG

CorelDRAW! version 4.0 now features import and export filters for the JPEG (Joint Photographers Experts Group) bit-map format. The chief advantage of using JPEG files is the high level of image compression they allow. CorelDRAW! uses technology developed by LEAD Technologies to import and export both standard JPEG or LEAD's proprietary CMP bit-map file formats.

PCX

As the most common denominator in PC bit-map formats, PCX originally was developed by the Z-Soft Corporation for PC Paintbrush (the forerunner of Windows paint programs). Because the PCX format is so popular, most paint packages provide the option of saving files in PCX format.

Draw provides extensive support for the many flavors of PCX: black-and-white, 16-level grayscale, 256-level grayscale, 16-color, 256-color, and 16-million-color, with file compression standard. One of the distinct advantages of PCX images is that most PC printers can print them.

TGA

CorelDRAW! version 3.0 added support for the Truevision Targa (TGA) bit-map files. This format is immensely popular in the 3D modeling, video, and animation worlds. While *Targa* (so named for the video board for which it was designed) files once lived only in those realms, they have now been brought to the PC graphics mainstream. You can save files in 16- or 256-level grayscales, and in 256 or 16 million colors as well. File compression is optional.

TIFF

TIFF is the acronym for *Tag Image File Format*. This type of image often contains more information than its PCX counterpart. Draw can import and export a range of TIFF images. You have your choice of black-and-white, 16-level grayscale, 256-level grayscale, 16-color, 256-color, and 16-million-color TIFF files. File compression is optional.

While Draw can import color and grayscale TIFF images, these images can be correctly printed only on a PostScript output device. Grayscale TIFFs are typically used to generate halftone reproductions of continuous-tone originals. Draw now supports both the TIFF 5.0 and 6.0 file format standards.

Dealing with Bit Maps through Draw

Draw treats bit-mapped images in one of two ways, regardless of whether the file format is BMP, GIF, JPEG, PCX, TGA, or TIFF. In the first method, Draw treats bit maps as bit maps. This method is the one you use to incorporate color and grayscale images or line art that needs no tweaking. The second method involves tracing the outline of a bit-mapped file. Tracing converts bit-mapped artwork into object-oriented artwork. Tracing can be automatic, using CorelTRACE! or AutoTrace, or you can do it manually. CorelTRACE! also has the capability to trace color or grayscale bit maps. Automatic tracing almost always requires some degree of manual clean-up.

To trace or not to trace is the question to ask yourself when importing a bit-map file. It is a far better thing to bring in a clean bit map than to spend hours cleaning up traced outlines in Draw.

Think of a pasteboard. When you bring in a bit map to be used "as is," it is as if you are pasting up a line art or halftone stat. Aside from cropping and scaling, you do not plan to mess with the image.

Now think of a light table. When you import a bit map for tracing, it is as if you are pasting the original to the light table and overlaying it with frosted acetate or tracing paper. If the original is choppy and uneven, you compensate for that as you trace, whether on the light table or on the computer monitor.

Import bit-mapped images that are as clean as possible. Draw has absolutely no provision for cleaning up bit maps being used as originally drawn. A messy original yields an equally messy trace. Do not throw away your technical pens just yet!

Soon, you import the wave graphic you drew in Windows Paintbrush and use it as a bit map (not for tracing). You then use the bit-map image as a background for a text mask, an interesting effect that has many uses. After that, you try tracing a bit map.

Using Bit Maps as Bit Maps

Most paint-type graphics are available as PCX files, whereas most high-quality grayscale images are in the TIFF format. You saved the wave file as a PCX image. Whether a bit map begins life as a paint file or as a scanned image, the technique that you use here can be applied to either file type.

Incorporating Bit-Map Images

Next, you import the WAVE.PCX file you painted in Windows Paintbrush. Importing a file into Draw should be a familiar procedure—strictly point-and-click!

Importing the Bit-Mapped Wave

This exercise assumes that the WAVE.PCX is stored in the C:\WINDOWS directory. If it isn't, substitute the appropriate drive and directory.

Click on **F**ile	The File menu appears
Click on **I**mport	The Import dialog box appears
At List Files of **T**ype, *click on the down-arrow button*	The pull-down file type menu appears

Click on CorelPHOTO-PAINT!,*.PCX

Maneuver to the directory in which the WAVE.PCX file is stored.

Double-click on WINDOWS

Click on WAVE.PCX

Click on OK	The wave is imported

Drag the wave to the center of the page (click on the bounding box)

The bit map appears to be quite small, but it works for your purposes. Now that you have imported the wave, you are going to perform some interesting maneuvers with it. Bit-mapped images can be cropped, scaled, stretched, skewed, and rotated. You won't do all these operations on this particular bit map, but feel free to experiment on your own after you are done here.

Cropping Bit Maps

You easily can remove unwanted image area by *cropping* the image Shape tool. This procedure will be quite familiar to those who have done either conventional paste-up or desktop publishing. The advantage of cropping in Draw, as opposed to doing so on a "real" pasteboard, is that you can undo an errant crop. If your electronic razor blade wavers, you do not need to go back to the camera room for a redo!

NOTE

If you are working in Wireframe mode and the bit map does not appear on the screen (all you see is a bounding box), the bit-map display is turned off. It can be switched on and off through the **D**isplay menu.

Bit-map cropping is controlled by the four cropping handles: left, right, bottom, and top. These handles are active only when the bit map is selected with the Shape tool. After the bit map is selected, the status line reflects the crop percentage for the four sides. When the cursor is properly positioned over a cropping handle, it turns into a + sign.

Cropping the Wave Bit Map

The sea gulls might seem just a bit too trite for this graphic. Remove the birds by cropping them with the top cropping handle.

Click on the Shape tool	
Click on the wave bit map	The bit map is selected; cropping handles appear
Position the cursor over the top cropping handle	The cursor becomes a +
Pull the top cropping handle down	To remove the unwanted sea gulls
Click on the Pick tool	To exit from cropping mode

Draw enables you to crop bit maps, but it makes more sense to crop while in a paint program. Importing large bit maps and cropping them in Draw leads to needlessly large file sizes. Smaller bit maps, obviously, make smaller files. These files can be loaded, displayed, and handled at much faster rates. In addition, the screen representations should be of a higher quality.

Scaling Bit Maps

Scaling bit maps within Draw can sometimes be disappointing. Anyone who has ever enlarged a minuscule piece of artwork—whether on an office copier or a litho camera—knows what happens when it is blown up too much. The artwork turns into mud. The same thing occurs on a computer when you enlarge (scaling up) a bit-mapped graphic.

The results can best be appreciated by actually going through the motions. Try increasing the size of a bit-map graphic. Print it out and see what happens. It is possible that the resulting image may be useful for a special effect, but as a realistic rendering, forget it.

Always try to bring in a bit map that is the same size or larger than the final printed size will be. Bit maps reduce (scale down) more acceptably than they enlarge. Scaling up always results in a loss in image resolution.

Stretching, Skewing, and Rotating Bit Maps

Three bit-map manipulations that should be approached with caution are stretching, skewing, and rotating. This is not to say that these operations should not be performed, but they should be done with care. The same caveat that applies to scaling up bit maps applies here as well.

When a bit map is rotated or skewed, it displays as a rectangle in Wireframe mode (see fig. 7.6). A white triangle in the top left corner of the rectangle denotes the bit map's orientation. Thankfully, CorelDRAW! 4.0 has improved its treatment of rotated or skewed bit maps over earlier versions of the program. Rotated and skewed bit maps now display in full-screen preview mode and can be printed on both PostScript and non-PostScript output devices. When working in editable preview mode, however, rotated or skewed bit maps are displayed in low resolution (128×128 pixels) for the sake of sanity. With full resolution, there are too many pixels to push around!

Scaling, stretching, skewing, or rotating bit maps in Draw does not always give pleasing results. If you really need to perform any of these functions to a bit map, do so in a paint-type program before you import the file into Draw.

In addition to eating up memory, imported bit maps can slow printing times to an insufferable pace. This reason alone makes one seriously consider using a real stat rather than a scanned grayscale image.

Figure 7.6:

Rotated bit map in Wireframe mode.

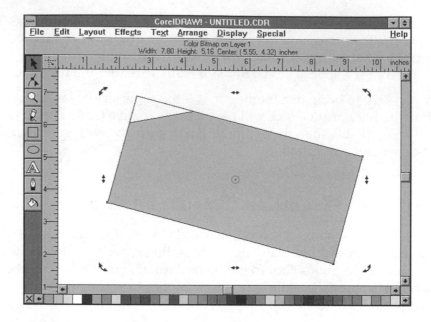

Changing Bit Map Color and Fill

The bit maps imported into Draw may be either black-and-white or color. After a monochrome (black-and-white) bit-mapped image has been imported, you can colorize it. Nevertheless, you are not able to change the hues of imported color bit maps from within Draw (these can be altered in Photo-Paint). The program's capability to deal with bit maps on a bicolor basis can lead to some interesting effects. For example, black-and-white bit maps can be changed to purple and pink or to different shades of gray. Although changing the color of a bit map is a simple process, picking the right color can take time.

The black portion of the bit map is colorized by selecting the bit map and using the Outline tool. Color choices can be spot or process. If a spot color is chosen, the tool also enables you to render different halftone screen patterns on the bit map itself.

The white portion (or background rectangle) of the bit map can be colorized by using the Fill tool. The same color/screen flexibility is provided as above.

In short, the Outline tool affects the bit map, while the Fill tool affects the background rectangle. In the following exercise, you change the colors of the WAVE bit map that you previously imported.

Masking Bit Maps

Although you can alter the size of a bit-mapped image, color it, and even change the image's focal point with cropping, one of the most powerful modifications you can perform on a bit map is to mask it. A mask is similar to a stencil—only the open areas show through. The term is adapted from its corresponding function in conventional printmaking and airbrush work.

In the next exercise, you use a mask as if you are a sign painter employing a conventional airbrush. Remember using the Airbrush tool in Windows Paintbrush? You are about to see why you did what you did.

You perform the electronic equivalent of cutting a stencil. After you build the stencil and position it over the bit-mapped image, only those areas that are open show through. You use this method to fill a word (WAVE) with a bit-mapped pattern consisting of two different tints of blue (see fig. 7.7).

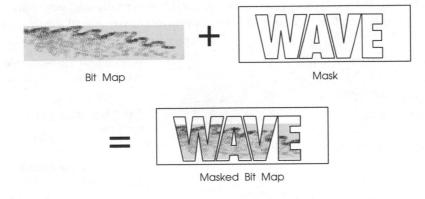

Bit Map   Mask

Masked Bit Map

Figure 7.7:
The mask equation.

Masking and Coloring the Wave

You start out by drawing a rectangular mask outline larger than and centered around the bit map. Then you will add the word WAVE. The results are shown in figures 7.8 and 7.9.

Click on the Rectangle tool

Draw a rectangle slightly larger than the WAVE bit map, and center it on the wave

Click on the Text tool

Click on the left side of the bit map

Type **WAVE**

Press Ctrl-T   The Artistic Text dialog
                                                 box appears

*Set type in Futura XBlk BT,
72 point, centered*

Click on **S**pacing

At **C**haracter, *enter* **-6**

Click on OK

Click on OK again

You might want to scale the type up to fit. After you enlarge it, use the Shape tool to interactively kern the letters:

Click on the Shape tool

Tighten up the kerning between WAV

Now that WAVE looks pretty tight, center it horizontally and vertically, combine it with the rectangle to form a mask, and take care of the outline and fill:

Shift-click on the rectangle   WAVE and the rectangle
                                                 are selected

Click on **A**rrange

Click on **A**lign   The Align dialog box
                                                 appears

Click on Horizontal Center/Vertical C**e**nter

Click on OK   WAVE and the rectangle
                                                 are aligned

Click on **A**rrange

Click on **C**ombine   WAVE and the rectangle
                                                 are combined

Click on the Fill tool   The Fill fly-out menu

	appears
Click on White	
Click on the Outline tool	The Outline fly-out menu appears
Click on Hairline	

You have just built a white mask with a hairline outline. Finish up by coloring the bit map:

Click on the Pick tool	
Click on the bit map	Bit map is selected
Click on the Outline tool	The Outline fly-out menu appears
Click on Outline Color	The Outline Color dialog box appears
Click on CYMK Color Model	The dialog box configures for process color
At Cyan, *enter* **60**	
At Magenta, *enter* **0**	
At Yellow, *enter* **20**	
At Black, *enter* **05**	
Click on OK	The bit map is colored
Click on the Fill tool	
Click on Fill Color	The Fill color dialog box appears
At Cyan, *enter* **60**	
At Magenta, *enter* **0**	
At Yellow, *enter* **0**	
At Black, *enter* **25**	
Click on OK	The bit map's background is colored

If you want, try some other color combinations. Remember, you can use the on-screen color palette to save time. Clicking the left mouse button changes the bit map's background (fill), while clicking the right mouse button changes the bit map's foreground (outline).

NOTE

You cannot change the color of an imported color bit map from within CorelDRAW! If you need to make changes, you have to go back to a paint program that can work with the file.

Figure 7.8:

WAVE in Wireframe mode.

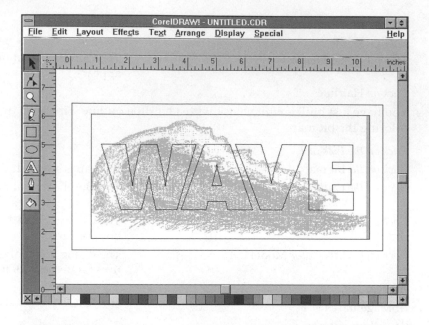

Figure 7.9:

WAVE in Preview mode.

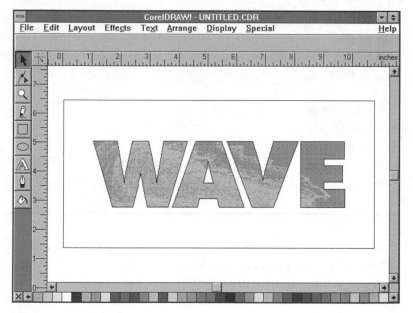

This effect can be extremely useful for filling objects with halftones and intricate patterns not available from Draw's menus. These patterns can be built in Windows Paintbrush,

CorelPHOTO-PAINT!, or another paint program. But be careful as to the number and size of the bit maps imported into a single file. System and printer speed are sure to suffer from an overabundance of bit maps.

If everything looks good with the WAVE image, take the time to save it now with the file name CATCHA. When you are finished, open a new file; you are going to move on to composing your next graphics element.

Using Bit Maps for Tracing

In the first part of this chapter, you used bit maps as bit maps. Now, you are going to use bit maps as tracing patterns. Tracing a bit map gives you the capability to scale an image without fear of distortion and the freedom to output that image to a variety of printers.

For example, what happens if you need to incorporate an existing logo or other artwork—which must maintain high resolution— into your design? Forget the idea of simply importing a scanned image unless you have access to a high-resolution scanner, a screamingly fast computer, and a huge disk drive. If scanned at the more pedestrian 300 dpi, art can be fuzzy, and more often than not, conspicuously jagged. Images scanned at high resolutions (1200 dpi) yield huge files. If at all possible, logos and other similar line art (which are to be used repeatedly) should be converted into vector format.

One way to digitize artwork is to trace the design with a digitizing tablet. The common mouse cannot compare to a high-quality tablet; the rodent does not offer the same precision and intuitive drawing capabilities. Tablets are available from a variety of manufacturers, with a wide range of features and prices.

Digitizing tablets require that you trace artwork as if you were using tracing paper. Simply tape the original to the surface of the digitizing tablet and trace around the outlines with a specialized pen or puck. Although this method is not perfect, it is vastly superior to attempting the same with a mouse. For more information on digitizing tablets, check out Appendix B.

The second choice for digitizing artwork is to scan an image and convert it to vector format with one of three on-screen tracing methods. The first of these three methods is like tracing with a tablet. Bring in the bit-mapped image and trace it on-screen using the Pencil tool. This method is rather time-consuming, but it definitely includes the human element and requires a certain level of hand-eye coordination. The operator, not the computer, draws the outline.

Corel also has provided two automated methods of on-screen tracing. The first of these methods is known as Autotrace. This feature is accessed from within the Draw environment by selecting a bit map and clicking on the pencil tool. This feature is wonderful, but it has been overshadowed by CorelTRACE!, the flagship of Draw's tracing fleet.

CorelTRACE! is a stand-alone Windows program provided with every copy of Draw. CorelTRACE! is a highly automated method of tracing bit-mapped files, and can—if run on a fast 80486- or Pentium-equipped computer—even be run in the background while you are using Draw or another program in the foreground (although this can tax your system). Pretty slick stuff.

Joe's next piece for the Island Sports account is built from a file (SIZZLE.PCX) you can find on the *Inside CorelDRAW!* disk. The file depicts a high-contrast image of a woman riding a personal watercraft (the Sizzler!). Joe scanned the image from a ratty piece of artwork that his client has supplied (see fig. 7.10).

Figure 7.10:

The Sizzler before clean-up.

You begin with the artwork as a bit-map image. Thus so, you can alter it pixel by pixel. The file is cleaned up using Paintbrush, saved under a new name, and imported into Draw. Finally, you trace the artwork.

This method can be faster than attempting to do all the clean-up from within Draw. Take note of the horizontal lines that run behind the image; Joe wants to remove those lines. It is easier to do so prior to tracing in Paintbrush or Photo-Paint than it is to try to remove them after the file has been traced.

In this instance, you use CorelPHOTO-PAINT! to clean up the image. Although you might be using Photo-Paint for the first time, it is fairly easy to use, and you can refer to the on-line help if you get stuck. Remember, Photo-Paint is covered in depth in Chapter 12.

Cleaning Up a Bit Map

At the Windows Program Manager:

Double-click on Photo-Paint	Photo-Paint is launched
Click on **F**ile	The File menu appears
Click on **O**pen	The Open File dialog box appears

Maneuver to the directory where you installed the *Inside CorelDRAW!* files.

Click on SIZZLE.PCX	
Click on OK	The file opens

Now clean up the image by using Photo-Paint. Remove the horizontal background lines, paying close attention to where they attach to the woman and her watercraft. Take out the logotype, and darken any lines that appear too thin for your liking. Use the Eraser tool or the paintbrush (with white ink). To alter the size of the brush, you should have the Width and Shape workbox on the screen. For pixel-by-pixel editing, you want to zoom in very close.

Feel free to alter the image. Pay particular attention to the woman's sunglasses and lips—they both need to be touched up. Straighten out jagged lines as you see fit.

When you are finished cleaning things up and your image looks like figure 7.11, save the file as SIZZLER.PCX. You are going to import the cleaned-up file into CorelDRAW! and explore the tracing options.

Figure 7.11:

The cleaned-up hydrosport.

Importing a File for Tracing

There really is not too much to this one, folks. You import the file the same way you import any other file. If you are not happy with the clean-up work you performed, you can cheat a little and bring in SIZZLE2.PCX instead. That file has been cleaned up for you!

Importing Sizzler

Click on **F**ile
Click on **I**mport

At List Files of **T**ype, *click on the down-arrow button* Pull-down menu
                                                              appears

Click on CorelPHOTO-PAINT!,*.PCX

Maneuver to the directory in which the SIZZLER.PCX file is stored.

Double-click on SIZZLER.PCX

Click on OK   The Sizzler is imported

Now that you have the Sizzler on your system, do a little comparison between manual tracing and autotracing. As you have probably noticed, bit maps are selected by clicking on the *bounding box*
or outline, rather than on the image itself.

Manual Tracing Versus Autotracing

Manual tracing is not a load of fun, but by going through the
process you will gain an appreciation of autotracing, and ultimately, CorelTRACE!. Without the aid of a prompted exercise, try
to trace the outline of the rower using the Pencil tool. Make sure
that the bit map is not selected before you click on the Pencil tool.
If you click on the Pencil tool while the bit map *is* selected, you get
the Autotrace tool rather than the Pencil tool.

You might want to zoom in on the bit map as much as possible.
You also might want to work in Wireframe mode rather than
Full-Color Preview. If you begin to get frustrated, don't fret.
Manual tracing is not fun, nor is it an effective use of your time.
After trying to trace the outlines by eye, you are really going to
enjoy using Autotrace. Instead of grinding teeth and splitting
hairs, all you have to do is point and shoot!

Now, try tracing the Sizzler using the Autotrace tool.

Giving Autotrace a Try

Click on the Pick tool
Click on the bit map's bounding box   Bit map is selected
Click on the Pencil tool   The cursor turns into the

continues

Autotrace tool

*Position the right side of the Autotrace tool
on the edge of the Sizzler*

Click the mouse   The Sizzler is autotraced
(see fig. 7.12).

This last step takes a few moments. After it is finished, the cursor once
again becomes the Autotrace tool.

Figure 7.12:

The Autotrace tool in
action.

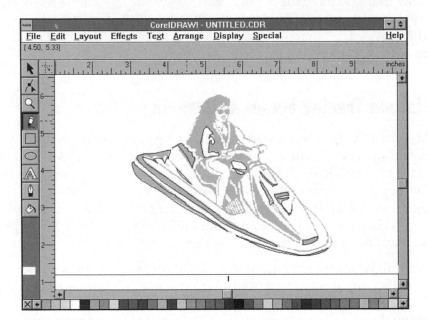

That was far easier than manual tracing. Unfortunately, Autotrace
only traces exterior edges. The image you are working on consists
of many individual objects. Each object within the image must be
traced and assigned a fill or combined with other objects. This
task, too, can be quite time-consuming. It helps to set the autotrace
preferences for the type of image being traced before you begin.

Autotrace Preferences

Properly setting up the Autotrace preferences can alleviate many autotracing woes. There is no single correct setting for Autotrace; the setting depends upon the image being traced. You are going to visit the Preferences dialog box once again, this time to take a look at Autotrace tracking, corner threshold, and straight-line threshold—the three adjustments that affect autotracing. You can find these settings by clicking on the Curves button.

Autotrace Tracking affects the feature's affinity for detail. Low values render complicated tracings that follow each and every variance in the bit map's outline. High values yield smooth, breezy outlines.

The second setting, Corner Threshold, determines the point at which a node is smooth or cusp. High settings render smooth corners, while low settings deliver cusps. This setting also applies to freehand drawing.

Finally, Straight Line Threshold makes the decision between using straight or curved line segments. A high setting biases in favor of straight lines, while a low setting gives favor to curved lines. Use a high setting when dealing with very straight, angular originals.

Again, setting the preferences correctly is application-dependent. The settings hinge entirely upon the material being autotraced. Like Corner Threshold, this setting applies to freehand drawing as well.

Tracing on Auto Pilot with CorelTRACE!

Now that you have done it the hard way, get ready to sit back and let the computer do all the work. CorelTRACE! is a blessing for those of you who do any amount of tracing.

Try tracing a file to see just how wonderful the CorelTRACE! program really is. In this next exercise, you see how Trace converts bit-mapped files (BMP, DIB, GIF, JPEG, PCD (Photo CD), PCX, TGA, or TIFF) into EPS—files you then can import into CorelDRAW!.

CorelTRACE! has been totally revamped in version 4.0. The interface has been changed, and a number of new features have been added. To trace a file, you only need open the file and click on the appropriate button. The program now can trace illustrations in Outline, Centerline, Woodcut, or Silhouette modes. In addition, you can perform optical character recognition (OCR), which enables you to turn scanned text pages into ASCII text files. And even more incredibly, you can convert scanned forms into editable files!

The printed documentation for Trace is rather lean. Instead, Corel has decided to rely on on-line Help files. Furthermore, the program is self-explanatory by means of a *smart cursor*. This handy device explains the function each button performs. As you move the cursor around the CorelTRACE! window, watch the bottom right corner of the your screen.

Using CorelTRACE!

You use Trace to convert the same bit map that you previously imported into Draw. If something on the screen needs to be saved, do it now, because you must exit the Draw environment for a little while.

Click on **F**ile	The File menu appears
Click on E**x**it	If an unsaved file is open, a dialog box asks if you want to save it

At the Windows Program Manager:

Double-click on the CorelTRACE! *icon*	Trace launches; the program's main dialog box appears
Click on **F**ile	The File menu appears
Click on **O**pen	The Open Files dialog box appears (see fig. 7.13)

At List Files of **T**ype, *click on the down-arrow button*	A pull-down menu appears

Click on CorelPHOTO-PAINT (*.PCX)

Maneuver to the directory in which the WAVE.PCX file is stored.

Click on C:

Double-click on ICD4

Click on SIZZLER.PCX	SIZZLER.PCX is selected
Click on Options	The dialog box expands
Click on OK	The bit map is loaded
Click on the Outline Trace *button*	The Sizzler is traced

Tracing takes time. Obviously, the faster the computer, the faster the trace takes place.

The Sizzler image appears as Trace converts the file into EPS format. When Trace is finished, the hourglass once again becomes a cursor (see fig. 7.14).

Click on **F**ile	The File menu appears
Click on **S**ave Trace	The file is saved as SIZZLER.EPS

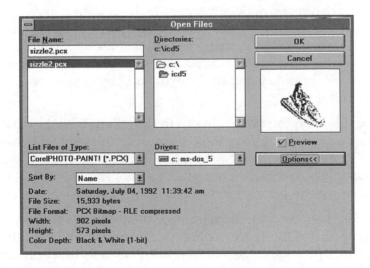

Figure 7.13:

The CorelTRACE! Open Files dialog box.

Figure 7.14:

Traced image in
window.

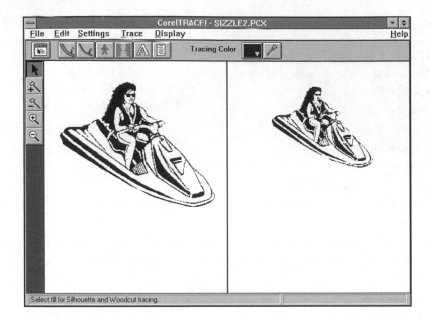

Pretty neat trick! Just wait until you import the file into Draw—
that's when it gets really impressive. CorelTRACE! provides a
high degree of control over tracings, including the capability to
trace just a section of an image. Although you can crop images by
dragging out a marquee, many images include superfluous stuff
that you cannot crop out in a rectangular manner. For this reason,
you always should clean out the extra junk by using a paint
program.

Thankfully, you can pop right out to CorelPHOTO-PAINT! by
clicking on **E**dit Image (on the **E**dit menu). This step launches
Photo-Paint and enables you to make last-minute tweaks to the
bit-map image before you trace it. You must, however, make sure
that your machine has plenty of memory to handle the task!

In the last exercise, you did a point-and-shoot trace without
changing any of the Trace settings or fiddling with any of the
tools. Trace provides a pair of Magic Wand tools that you can use
to add or remove areas to the trace. It also includes Zoom tools.

Take a look at the traced image on the right of your screen. Is there anything missing from the girl's face? Zoom in on the original bit map (you can't zoom in on the traced image). Click on the Magic Wand + tool and click on the girl's cheek. In a moment or two, you see the "marching ants" that signify her face and neck are selected. Now change the Tracing Color to White and click on the Outline Trace button again. CorelTRACE! adds this area to your trace.

Setting Up CorelTRACE!

In the last exercise, you merely ran Trace with its factory defaults. Trace's two common tracing methods, Outline and Centerline, indicate the type of object that should be traced.

Outline

Outline traces the edges of a bit map and fills the resulting objects with black or white. If an area is black on the original, it will be black in the trace. The same goes for white. Outline works best on solid, heavy, filled originals. You even can trace grayscale images using this method, resulting in a high-contrast vector image. Figure 7.15 shows an example of a good outline trace.

Centerline

This option is best used for thinly drawn illustrations. This method assigns a thickness to the resulting lines, but it does not assign a fill unless a definitely filled object is found. Images traced using this method can only be black lines on a white background. Figure 7.16 shows an example of a good centerline trace.

CorelTRACE! performs acceptably with the Outline or Centerline default settings, but for those of you who are terminal tweakers, plenty of things can be fiddled with. The Settings menu enables

Figure 7.15:

An example of an outline trace.

you to modify the settings for Image Filtering, Color Matching, Line Attributes, Centerline Method, Woodcut Style, OCR Method, and Batch Output.

The numerous dialog boxes provide complete control over the way Trace performs its function. All these settings can take some fiddling; sometimes it might be better to go with the defaults and clean up the resulting file. If you have time to tweak, however, by all means do so. After you've developed the ultimate custom settings, Trace enables you to save them by typing a name in the Save Settings As dialog box.

Figure 7.16:
An example of a centerline trace.

Image Filtering

This method provides a number of controls over the way an image is traced, including the following:

- **Smooth Dithering** evens out an image
- **Invert Colors** turns black into white, purple into green, and so on
- **Convert to Monochrome** is set through a threshold level and changes the image into a one-bit (black-and-white) file
- **Reduce Colors To** reduces the number of colors in the trace to a specified number

Color Matching

Color Matching sets the color tolerance levels. The higher the setting, the more play you have.

Line Attributes

This tracing option handles the way lines and curves are created. The settings can be modified in the following ways:

- **Curve and Line Precision** regulates the extent to which the trace is true to the original image's curves and lines.

- **Target Curve Length** defines the span of individual curves. To be effective, this setting must be used in conjunction with Curve Precision and Sample Rate. Shorter curve lengths result in larger numbers of nodes and bigger files; hence, only use this option when you need a maximum of detail.

- **Sample Rate** enables you to rough up or smooth out a trace. With a Sample Rate set to Fine and Target Curve Length set to Very Short, Trace yields the highest image integrity at the expense of file size (not to mention roughness). Set Target Curve Length and Sample Rate to the other extremes to smooth out a rough bit map.

- **Minimum Object Size** governs the size below which bit-map noise is discarded.

Centerline Method

Centerline Method enables you to modify the settings in the following ways:

- **Max Line Width** controls the number of pixels Trace removes; the higher the setting, the more pixels, resulting in smooth, consistent lines at the expense of image integrity. Lower settings follow the original image more closely, resulting in a coarser line (although truer to the original image).

- **Create Lines of Uniform Width** enables you to stipulate an exact line weight.

- **Horizontal and Vertical Line Recognition** allows Trace to automatically rotate crooked images.

Woodcut Style

This trace method controls the way CorelTRACE! creates woodcut tracings, and includes the following options:

- Continuous Cut
- Tapered Ends
- Sample Width
- Angle of Cut

OCR Method

When working with text, OCR (Optical Character Recognition) Method enables you to do the following:

- **Check Spelling** (or not)
- **Select Source** from Normal, Dot Matrix, or Fax Fine

Batch Output

This setting provides you with the ability to select a default output directory for your Trace files as well as to make the file read-only, replace old versions, or save the text as a TXT file.

Needless to say, there is plenty of experimenting to be done here. To become a Tracemaster, expect to spend plenty of time and be sure to set aside loads of disk space.

No Matter How You Trace...

Regardless of the method used to trace an object, you always have a certain amount of tweaking to do to clean things up. CorelTRACE! has a propensity for node-overkill. As mentioned before, pare down objects to a minimum of nodes. Reducing the number of nodes in a trace can be done while tracing (by adjusting the settings) and after the trace has been brought into Draw. Remember to use CorelDRAW! 4.0's new Auto-Reduce function; it is a great time-saver! A strategy of node minimalization saves in a multitude of ways. You can reduce file size, lessen screen redraw time, and slash print time all by eliminating needless nodes. If a node is not needed, remove it; the lines will be smoother, and you will reap all the previously mentioned benefits.

Should you exit Draw before you run Trace? In a word, yes. Running Trace and Draw at the same time can be very demanding for computers without enough system resources. If you have such a system, it makes good sense to shut one program down before you open up the other. If the system you are working on is very fast and has plenty of RAM, you might be able to run the two programs concurrently. Running Trace along with another program, however, can slow tracing speed dramatically.

To speed things up, remember to load the bit-map file to your computer's hard disk before you trace. Floppy disk drives have a slow input/output (I/O) rate, and tracing a file stored on a floppy disk can take an interminably long time.

You can set Trace to batch trace a group of files. This method is a very handy way to convert files while the computer is unattended and works well for images that do not need to be cropped. Select the files you want to trace, and let the computer do all the work! If you choose this option, be sure to scan all images at the same resolution. Also, make sure that you want to trace the image in its entirety; otherwise, someone has to baby-sit the computer as it traces.

The Island Sports Logo

Joe plans to use the Sizzler in the Island Sports logo. You finish your tracing and tweaking phase now, then use Fit Text to Path to finish the logo in Chapter 8. While you have Draw up and running, import the cleaned-up and traced SIZZLER file.

Importing the Trace

Click on File	The File menu appears
Click on Import	The Import dialog box appears
At List Files of Type, *click on the down-arrow button*	Pull-down menu appears
Click on CorelTRACE!,*.EPS	
Maneuver to the directory that the SIZZLER.EPS file is stored in.	
Click on C:	
Double-click on ICD4	
Click on SIZZLER.EPS	SIZZLER.EPS is selected
Click on OK	The cleaned-up Sizzler appears

The power of CorelTRACE! becomes apparent just as soon as you click on Preview (if Full-Color editing is not already on). The program does an amazing job of converting bit-map files to object-oriented drawings.

You should take the time to clean up some of those excess nodes. This procedure can get a little hairy, but you have a little trick that makes tweaking tracings just a bit easier.

A Tracing Tweaking Tip

Whenever you trace something, be it electronically or conventionally, it helps to have some guidelines to follow. This next exercise demonstrates an easy way to align your lines as you remove needless nodes and fine-tune your drawing.

You are going to duplicate the tracing. Then you center the two tracings horizontally and vertically. You ungroup the top tracing and click on the Shape tool. When you do that, the bottom grouped tracing cannot be modified by the Shape tool. You can use these lines to guide you as you remove the excess nodes. Remember, the fewer the nodes, the smoother the drawing, and the faster it loads, redraws, previews, and prints.

As you work through the drawing, removing excess nodes, you find that the Snap to Nodes feature can be a mixed blessing. You end up switching the feature on and off, as needed. In addition, you might need to redraw the screen frequently. This feat can be accomplished in a number of ways: you can click on the scroll bar thumbs, choose Refresh Window (from the Display menu), or press Ctrl-W.

Following Outlines While Tweaking

With the Sizzler selected, take the following steps:

Click on **E**dit	The Edit menu appears
Click on **D**uplicate	The Sizzler is duplicated
Marquee-select both watercraft	
Click on **A**rrange	The Arrange menu appears
Click on **A**lign	The Align dialog box appears
Click on Horizontal Center/Vertical C**e**nter	
Click on OK	The Sizzlers are horizontally and vertically centered on each other
Click on any blank area on the page	Deselects the Sizzlers
Click on the top Sizzler	Selects the top Sizzler
Click on **A**rrange	The Arrange menu appears
Click on **U**ngroup	The top Sizzler is ungrouped
Click on the Shape tool	The bottom cannot be edited

Now comes the challenge of removing the excess nodes while retaining the integrity of the drawing. Start by removing one node at a time, and move on to marquee- or shift-deleting groups of nodes after you feel comfortable with the process. Figures 7.17 and 7.18 show before and after views. Remember, you always can use Undo if you remove the wrong node. Before you get too far along, remember to save the file as SIZZLER2. Now go for it!

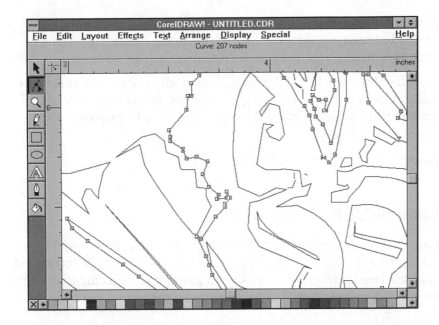

Figure 7.17:
Before tweaking.

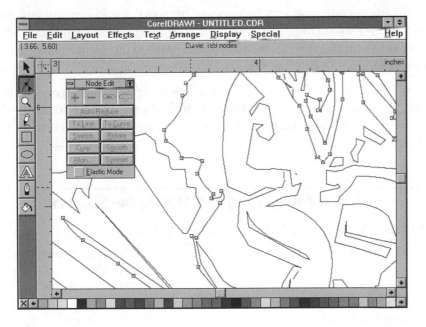

Figure 7.18:
After tweaking.

After you have removed the excess nodes, remove the background Sizzler. Otherwise, all of your node-tweaking will have been in vain.

To select the background group, repeatedly press Tab. When the status line reports that it is a group of objects, you have found the background group. Delete it by pressing Del. Group the remaining Sizzler's parts.

Finish by triplicating the Sizzler.

Duplicating by Using Move

Rather than drag-duplicating, you can use the convenient Move dialog box to create your duplicate Sizzler. This handy command enables you to drop the dupes with precision. You can access the Move dialog box from the **A**rrange menu or with a keyboard shortcut, Alt-F7.

The Move command can be especially useful for executing precise step-and-repeat procedures. As you see in this next exercise, after you perform the first step-and-repeat, subsequent moves can be performed by using the Repeat command (Ctrl-R).

You perform two step-and-repeats. The first uses the Move command, while the second makes use of the Repeat command. Finally, you assign different tints to the watercraft. The results should look like figure 7.19.

Step-and-Repeating and Tinting the Sizzlers

With the Sizzler selected, take the following steps:

Click on **A**rrange	The Arrange menu appears
Click on **M**ove	The Move dialog box appears
At Horizontal, *type* **.25**	
At Vertical, *type* **.25**	
Click on **L**eave Original	

Click on OK	The Sizzler is stepped and repeated
Click on Edit	The Edit menu appears
Click on Repeat	The Sizzler is step-and-repeated again
Click on the left Sizzler	The left Sizzler is selected
Click on the Fill tool	The Fill fly-out menu appears
Click on 10% Black fill	The left Sizzler is assigned a 10-percent black fill
Click on the center Sizzler	The center Sizzler is selected
Click on the Fill tool	The Fill fly-out menu appears
Click on 50% Black	The center Sizzler is assigned a 50-percent black fill

Figure 7.19:
The Sizzler gets triplicated.

One slight problem has cropped up. Because the Sizzler is not a solid object, it is transparent! You have to create a white object with no outline and place it underneath the top Sizzler to knock out the other images. Go ahead and whip one out by using the Pencil tool. Try to keep the number of nodes to a minimum. Use the Move command to move the different elements precisely.

You are done for now. And guess what? You do not have to clean up your drawing pens, pencils, or charcoal! Just make sure that you save this file under the name SIZZLERS.CDR before you forget. You need the file to complete the logo in the next chapter.

Summary

Although Draw is strictly a vector-based drawing program, its bit maps are treated with care. You cannot do any bit-map editing, but you are free to crop, scale, rotate, and stretch bit maps beyond the realm of good taste. As shown in the first series of exercises, Draw enables you to use bit maps as a background to a mask, whether text or otherwise.

Draw offers a wide range of choices for converting bit-mapped originals into vector-based artwork. Through its various methods—manual tracing, autotracing, and the formidable CorelTRACE! utility—Draw gives the user great power to quickly and confidently transform bit maps into objects.

The wise bit-map tracer knows that what the computer gives is not what should be ultimately used. You always have more tweaking to do, and fine-tuning tracings is a tweak's redemption. CorelPHOTO-PAINT! (covered in Chapter 12) provides a power tool for prescan bit-map editing.

If you find that you need a bit-map paint program with more power than CorelPHOTO-PAINT! or Windows Paintbrush, check out the mini reviews of Image-In-Color, Aldus PhotoStyler, Adobe Photoshop, and Fractal Design Painter in Chapter 10.

8

Assembling Complex Images

So far, this book has covered most of the fundamentals of creating electronic artwork with CorelDRAW!. Along the way, it has stressed the proper way to assemble modular images so that you easily can alter and print them with confidence.

Those with an art background who use CorelDRAW! might have a distinct advantage, although such experience does not ensure success. An artist might make wondrous achievements with oil colors but fail to grasp Draw's theory. The vector-based, object-oriented environment might be daunting to those without the vision to use it to their benefit.

An artist whose training includes print-making, whether artistic or commercial, will be comfortable with Draw. Many of Draw's core principles also are found in the arts of serigraphy (screen printing) and lithography.

Success with Draw entails more than just drawing a pretty picture. The intent is to build working drawings—illustrations that have the flexibility to change at a moment's notice. To accomplish this goal, a drawing must not only be designed and rendered, it must be engineered.

Building Images That Work

No matter what the application, solid design is the key to success. A well-engineered building stands the test of time. A precisely crafted automobile handles impeccably. A well-thought-out computer program runs flawlessly. This last example is the key here because when you create an image with Draw, you are writing a computer program.

DRAW (CDR) files are source code. Windows' print drivers could be considered compilers. The files that Draw sends to the printer are object code. If a Draw file is not properly drawn, the resulting program will not run.

There is a right way and a wrong way to solve a problem, write a computer program, and execute a drawing. If a computer program functions, but is slow and difficult to use, it is a flop. If a Draw file fails to print or takes half a day to do so, it too is a failure.

What good is a drawing that you cannot print? A pretty picture on the screen does nothing for you at deadline time. Who do you blame for nonprinting images—the manufacturers of the program, the operating system, the description language, or the artist/operator responsible for using them?

No one should take the blame, but the artist should take the ultimate responsibility. Through in-depth working knowledge, the experienced Draw artist knows the program's limitations. He or she knows what the program can and cannot do. Pushing the design envelope should not be done at deadline time, or at least should be done only with extreme prudence.

A variety of concepts can help you build working images. The following pages cover many of the basic points necessary to achieve success with Draw.

Getting the Most from Combine and Group

The Combine and Group commands are significant players at Draw's cutting edge. While the inexperienced Draw user might see little use for these two commands, you must understand the difference between them. Combine is a function of systematic design, whereas Group is a function of composition convenience. Combine makes a huge difference in screen redraw and printing. Group is of great assistance in image construction. These two commands are similar, but far from the same.

Combine is one of the most important, yet least used, of Draw's command sets. It enables you to fuse objects so that they act as one. Although they are not physically connected, combined objects share the same outline and fill characteristics. Thoughtful use of Draw's Combine command can make it possible to print drawings that would regularly choke a printer. To effectively challenge Draw's frontiers, you first must become practiced in the proper use of Combine.

The following are some general guidelines for using the Combine command effectively:

- **Combine like objects.** For maximum efficiency, try not to combine more than 20 to 25 objects at a clip. Larger combinations can cause problems at print time. Also, avoid combining complex, multinode objects.

- **Use Combine to reduce file size.** Combined files are well-designed files. They take up less space, because file size is kept to a minimum. This consideration is important for conserving disk space, whether it is fixed or removable.

- **Use Combine to reduce screen redraw time dramatically.** Upon preview redraw, you easily can tell if a group of objects has been combined. Uncombined objects pop in, one by one. Combined objects pour down the screen—from top to bottom—in a fraction of the time.

Unlike Combine, Group does not affect screen redraws, file size, or print times. Group simply collects objects, acting mainly as an item of convenience. In the playing card exercise from Chapter 3, you grouped clusters to make assembly easier.

In this chapter's exercises, you see how Group and Combine can simplify image manipulation, speed up screen preview, reduce file size, and help complex images to print with ease.

Keeping Things in Control with Layers

When your drawings start to get complex, CorelDRAW!'s Layer controls are essential to maintain order—not to mention your sanity. The Layers Roll-Up menu (which is accessed through the **L**ayers menu or by the keyboard shortcut Ctrl-F3) is a powerful device, helping you create artwork that would otherwise be impossibly complicated, if not beyond the realm of sense entirely.

Layers are easy to work with after you understand the basics. You can have an endless number of layers, each with a distinctive name (of up to 32 alphanumeric characters). You can make individual layers invisible or nonprinting for the sake of clarity while working, previewing, or manipulating your drawing. Draw also provides the option to assign a color override that designates a specific color outline to all objects on a layer (in addition to making them transparent). Color override affects only the on-screen appearance; it has no effect on output. You can lock layers so that you do not disturb them as you work with other layers.

Artists who render technical drawings will find using layers invaluable. In most basic drawings, you can do your artwork on one layer and the annotation on another. Corel might have taken a number of releases to include layer control, but now that it is here, make use of it!

Using Fountain Fills Properly

Using too many fountain fills is a sure way to choke an output device. If you are imaging a file with fountain fills and the file refuses to print, you have only one realistic option: get rid of some or all of those fountain fills. Of course, you can always increase curve flatness when printing, but that is another story (covered in Chapter 11).

Complexity for complexity's sake is pointless. Slapping layer upon layer of over-noded fountain-filled objects is an exercise in futility. If you really want to waste your (or your employer's) time, you can slap on as many as you want, but the ultimate result seldom is printable. If you have the latent desire to work your imagery to death, you should buy a canvas, a few brushes, and some oil paints.

The intent here is not to discourage the use of fountain fills. You must realize, however, that they can exceed the capabilities of the output device. Use them with great discretion. Additionally, try to avoid fountain-filling objects with a large number of nodes, such as strings of intricate type. This task can be extremely processor-intensive, and, at the very least, the output device can take hours to print the file.

Eliminating Excess Nodes

Like too many fountain fills, excessive nodes can choke a printer quickly. When executing a freehand drawing or tracing a bit-mapped file, Draw invariably lays down far too many nodes. The artist is responsibe for stripping out the unnecessary nodes.

Tracing an image might yield a hundred nodes where two might suffice. This number of nodes created depends on the quality of the original and the user settings. Once again, the artist must rectify the situation. CorelDRAW! 4.0's Node Edit roll-up menu includes a marvelous Auto-Reduce function; using it saves you time and effort.

The fewer the nodes in a file, the smaller that file is and the faster it can be produced, both on the screen and at the output device. In short, file sizes, screen redraw, and print times improve if you eliminate excess nodes.

Some file types (such as CGM and WPG) are vector formats even though they contain line segments instead of Bézier curves. Any time a file is imported in either of these formats, it contains far more line segments than are necessary in CDR format. In addition, the object does not scale with the smoothness that one would expect from a Bézier-based object. When using imported CGM images, select and delete excess nodes before sending the images to a high-resolution output device.

Joe DeLook Takes an Early Lunch

A hungry Joe DeLook has cut out for an early lunch and some fishing. With his lunch bag and fishing gear in hand, he is ready for a few hours of relaxation. He reaches his favorite spot, throws in a line, and opens up his lunch pail.

Although nothing seems to be biting today (save the mosquitoes), Joe welcomes the time out of the office. The quiet bay-front setting is a calming relief from the pandemonium back in the studio. Joe's eyes briefly focus on a monarch butterfly, flitting from flower to flower, before he slips into a peaceful snooze.

Building a Working Drawing

You are going to use an exercise that greatly relies upon your creativity as well as your discipline. This next segment demonstrates the advantages of using Combine and Group in building a working drawing. You draw a butterfly to illustrate some of the principles of complex work.

Because drawing a butterfly is a rather subjective thing, feel free to take off in a different direction from the monarch that is assembled here. If, after completing this exercise, you want to try another critter, do so by all means.

A butterfly is used for this exercise because no hard and fast right or wrong exists. Who is going to know if the butterfly is not exact? Above all, have fun!

The butterfly exercise is broken down into eight separate steps. For clarity's sake, you work in Wireframe mode. You proceed in a methodical fashion, grouping each set of objects as you go along. Grouping makes it easy to move sections around the drawing, whereas Combine makes a big difference in preview speed. You finish one wing before you start combining objects. Draw does not enable you to combine grouped objects. Hence, you select each group, ungroup, and combine.

Before you actually draw your first object, set up the Outline Pen New Object default for a one-point outline. This step is a great time-saver, and it beats going back to the outline menu every time you need the same weight rule.

The first step consists of drawing the silhouette of the butterfly's left inner and outer wings. Figure 8.1 uses only four nodes; you might need a few more. The wings are filled with black and outlined with a one-point black rule.

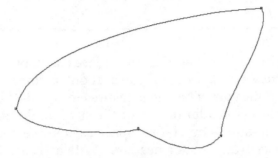

Figure 8.1:

The wing's silhouette.

If you have problems creating closed path curves, check the AutoJoin setting in the Preferences dialog box. Set Autojoin to 10 to zap curves closed. You might want to experiment with different settings. Remember: 1 is the least likely to close, whereas 10 is most likely.

Drawing the Silhouette

Set up the page for letter size, portrait orientation:

Click on the Pick tool	
Click on the Outline tool	The Outline fly-out menu appears
Click on Outline Pen	The Outline Pen for New Object dialog box appears
Click on Graphic	
Click on OK	The Outline Pen dialog box appears
*Set **W**idth to* 1.0 points	
*Click on **S**cale With Image*	
Click on OK	The new object's default outline is set

continues

Click on the Pencil tool
Draw the wing
Click on Fill   The Fill fly-out menu appears
Click on Black   The silhouette is filled with black
Click on the Shape tool
Click on and delete the extra nodes
Tweak the control points to achieve the proper shape.
Save the file as BUT1

Beginning with the next section, you place colors on top of
the silhouette. At this point, the file is about as compact as
CorelDRAW! files get. This file measures in at 11,984 bytes, with
an 8K color image header (but your file sizes might differ slightly).
If you want to save as much disk space as possible, save your files
with 1K monochrome image headers. (With a 1K header, the file is
only 4792 bytes.)

The second step entails drawing nine large orange segments on
the wing. All segments are filled with a uniform fill of 40-percent
magenta and 100-percent yellow, and outlined with a one-point
rule of 60-percent magenta, and 100-percent yellow. The segments
are then grouped (see fig. 8.2).

Figure 8.2:

The wing begins to
develop.

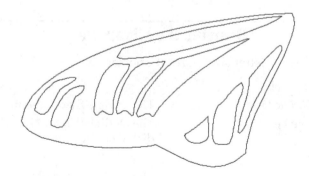

After you open the Uniform Fill and Outline Color dialog boxes
and configure them for Process Color CMYK mode, they stay that
way. Each time you call one of these dialog boxes, it appears in the
same mode as you last left it.

▼

Adding the Nine Orange Segments

Take a look at the preceding illustration for an example of how the nine orange segments should look.

Click on the Pencil tool

Draw nine segments

Click on the Shape tool

Delete the extra nodes. Don't forget to use AutoReduce, too! Tweak the control points to achieve the desired shapes:

Shift-click or marquee-select all nine segments	
Click on **A**rrange	The Arrange menu appears
Click on **G**roup	The segments are grouped
Click on the Fill tool	The Fill fly-out menu appears
Click on Uniform Fill	The Uniform Fill dialog box appears
Select CMYK Color Model	The dialog box configures for process color

If the dialog box is in CMYK mode, leave it that way. If not, change it.

At Magenta, enter **40**	
At Yellow, *enter* **100**	
At Black, *enter* **0**	
Click on OK	The nine segments are filled
Click on the Outline tool	The Outline fly-out menu appears
Click on the Outline Color *icon*	The Outline Color dialog box appears
Select CMYK Color Model	The dialog box configures for process color

If the dialog box is in CMYK mode, leave it that way. If not, change it.

At Magenta, *enter* **60**	
At Yellow, *enter* **100**	
At Black, *enter* **0**	
Click on OK	The nine segments are outlined in orange-red

Save the file as BUT2.CDR

The wing is starting to develop, and the file size is growing: 14,756 bytes (with an 8K color image header).

Step three places 11 oval shapes near the leftmost section of the wing (see fig. 8.3). The ovals are grouped and then filled with 10-percent magenta and 100-percent yellow. They are outlined with a one-point rule of 40-percent yellow.

Figure 8.3:

The wing gets some spots.

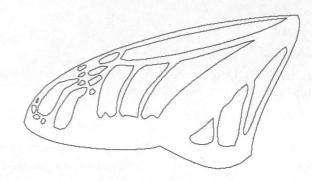

Placing the Oval Shapes

Click on the Pencil tool

Draw 11 oval shapes

Click on the Shape tool

Delete the extra nodes

Tweak the control points to achieve the proper shape:

Shift-click or marquee-select all 11 ovals	
Click on **A**rrange	The Arrange menu appears
Click on **G**roup	The ovals are grouped
Click on the Fill tool	The Fill fly-out menu appears
Click on the Uniform Fill *icon*	The Uniform Fill dialog box appears
At Magenta, *enter* **10**	
At Black, *enter* **0**	
At Yellow, *enter* **100**	
Click on OK	The 11 ovals are filled
Click on the Outline tool	The Outline fly-out menu appears
At Yellow, *enter* **40**	
At Black, *enter* **0**	
Click on OK	The 11 ovals are outlined in light yellow
Save the file as BUT3.CDR	

Figure 8.3 shows how the 11 oval shapes should look.

As the file grows in complexity, so do screen redraw times and file size. At this point, the file weighs in at 16,524 bytes. (Again, your file size might differ slightly.)

Step four adds 66 spots to the bottom of the wing (see fig. 8.4). These spots are filled with 20-percent yellow, and outlined with a one-point rule of 40-percent yellow. The spots are broken into three groups of 20, 23, and 23 items. The slickest way to accomplish this feat is to build one group and duplicate it. Then add or delete spots as needed.

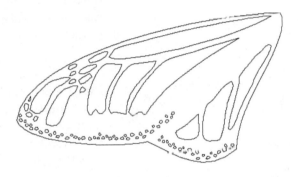

Figure 8.4:
The wing gets some more spots.

Get Your Kicks with 66 (Spots)

Click on the Ellipse tool
Draw approximately six ellipses

Instead of drawing a zillion spots, you use these six as a base. Use Rotate or Mirror with Leave Original to make each spot seem almost unique.

Click on the Pick tool
Double-click on a spot   Displays Rotate/Skew handles

Use a corner handle to rotate the spot
Press and release the + on the numeric keypad   The original remains in place
Release the mouse button
Click on another spot

continues

*Drag a side handle to the opposite side to
mirror the spot*

Press and release +   Leaves the original in place

Release the mouse button

You should now have 8 spots. Repeat the two techniques you just used
to create 15 more. When you're done, you then group, fill, and outline
the spots.

Shift-click or marquee-select all 23 spots

*Click on **A**rrange*   The Arrange menu appears

*Click on **G**roup*   The spots are grouped

Click on the Fill tool   The Fill fly-out menu appears

Click on the Uniform Fill *icon*   The Uniform Fill dialog box
                                                         appears

At Yellow, *enter* **20**

At Black, *enter* **0**

Click on OK   The 23 spots are filled

Click on the Outline tool   The Outline fly-out menu
                                                         appears

Click on the Outline Color *icon*   The Outline color dialog box
                                                         appears

At Yellow, *enter* **40**

At Black, *enter* **0**

Click on OK   The 23 spots are outlined in
                                                         light yellow

Now, you need to duplicate the group of spots two times and drag the
groups into position:

Press Ctrl-D   The group of spots is dupli-
                                                         cated

Drag the new group into position

Press Ctrl-D   The duplicate group of spots
                                                         is duplicated

Drag the second new group into position

You might need to ungroup one of the groups if you can fit 69 spots
rather than the 66 you originally specified.

Save the file as BUT4.CDR

Figure 8.4 shows the 66 spots.

The file is getting larger, and screen redraw should be taking longer and longer. At this point, the file size is 35,872 bytes.

In the fifth step, you combine your first objects—a large number of orange-red one-point rules. Outline them with 80-percent magenta and 100-percent yellow. These are open-path objects and can have no fill. After you're done, check your screen redraw time.

Adding and Combining Lines

Now you can combine the lines in two clusters:

Click on the Pencil tool	
Draw three or four straight lines in each of the orange segments	
Draw a freehand line at the bottom of both the inner and outer wings	
Click on the Shape tool	
Delete the extra nodes on the freehand lines	
Shift-click on half of the lines	
Click on **A***rrange*	The Arrange menu appears
Click on **C***ombine*	The lines are combined
Click on the page	Deselects the lines
Shift-click the remaining lines	
Click on **A***rrange*	The Arrange menu appears
Click on **C***ombine*	The lines are combined
Click on the first set of lines	
Click on the Outline tool	The Outline fly-out menu appears
Click on the Outline Color *icon*	The Outline color dialog box appears
At Magenta, *enter* **100**	
At Yellow, *enter* **40**	
Click on OK	The lines are drawn in deep orange-red

continues

Click on the second set of lines	
Click on **E**dit	The Edit menu appears
Click on Copy Attributes **F**rom	The Copy Attributes From dialog box appears
Click on Outline **C**olor	
Click on OK	The From? arrow appears
Click on the first set of lines	Outline color is copied

If you want, go in and change the straight line segments to curves. Tweak the control points to have the lines follow the dimensions of the orange segments.

Save the file as BUT5.CDR

With the addition of the combined lines, the file size has hardly grown. It is now 37,280 bytes. Figure 8.5 shows the on-screen results of this exercise.

Figure 8.5:

The wing gets lines.

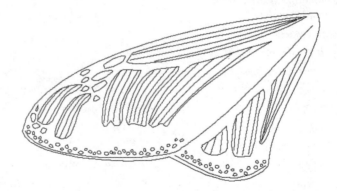

In the sixth step, you combine everything of like fill and outline into assemblies of no more than 25 objects. This procedure considerably speeds up screen redraw time.

Combining the Wing

The time has come to combine each cluster of objects. This procedure is made easier because you have grouped them along the way. The procedure in this case goes like this: select, ungroup, and combine—simple, clean, and effective.

Click on the Pick tool	
Click on an orange segment	
Click on **A**rrange	The Arrange menu appears
Click on **U**ngroup	The segments are ungrouped
Click on **A**rrange	The Arrange menu appears
Click on **C**ombine	The segments are combined; notice that their fill color now appears on the status line
Click on a yellow oval	
Click on **A**rrange	The Arrange menu appears
Click on **U**ngroup	The ovals are ungrouped
Click on **A**rrange	The Arrange menu appears
Click on **C**ombine	The ovals are combined
Click on a group of spots	
Click on **A**rrange	The Arrange menu appears
Click on **U**ngroup	The spots are ungrouped
Click on **A**rrange	The Arrange menu appears
Click on **C**ombine	The spots are combined

Repeat the procedure for the last two groups of spots

Save the file as BUT6.CDR

Now you are seeing the fruits of your labor. Notice the speed at which the wing appears in Full-Color editing mode or in full-screen preview. The wireframe might look identical, but the redraw time tells the story. If you take a look at the file size, you see that it has dropped dramatically: from 37,280 to 17,754 bytes since you last checked. Saving the file with a 1K image header drops the file size to a modest 10,562 bytes.

The seventh step merely involves grouping and mirror/duplicating the first wing, and then dragging it into position and rotating it, if necessary. Next, you group the two wings together so that you can move the pair as one unit.

Duplicating and Positioning the Second Wing

Marquee-select the wing

*Click on **A**rrange*	The Arrange menu appears
*Click on **G**roup*	The wing is grouped
*Click on Effe**c**ts*	The Effects menu appears
*Click on **S**tretch & Mirror*	The Stretch & Mirror dialog box appears
*Click on H**o**riz Mirror, **L**eave Original*	
Click on OK	The wing is mirrored and duplicated

Drag the new wing into position and rotate if necessary (see fig. 8.6).

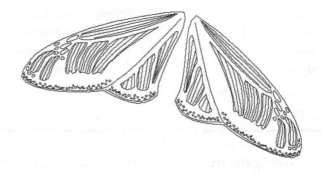

Figure 8.6:

The wing gets mirrored and rotated.

Now to build the butterfly's body. You draw a silhouette body (in black) and use the contour effect to fill the body with a variety of tones. Contouring the original outline into a skinny highlight gives the body a more three-dimensional look. The different tones provide the illusion of lighting.

Before you build the body, construct the head, eyes, and antennae. Use the Pencil and Ellipse tools to build these, and remember to combine like objects.

Contour

The contour effect—introduced in version 4.0—provides a way to create a number of distinctive fills. The contour effect uses an algorithm to create concentric duplicates of an object. You can create these duplicates in one of three ways: to the center, to the inside, or to the outside. At its simplest, a contour resembles a blend. When taken to the extreme, however, a contour can yield stunning results. This concept is difficult to picture without a picture to refer to! Take a moment to look at figure 8.7 before you proceed; it illustrates the difference between the three different types of contour.

To Center Outside Inside

Figure 8.7:

Choose your contour: to center, outside, and inside.

For both inside and outside contours, the Contour roll-up menu gives you control over the number of steps in the contour and the distance between the steps. The To Center Contour, on the other hand, contours directly to the center of the object and uses only the distance setting. (You cannot set the number of steps.) The three contouriffic sea horses (in figure 8.7) were set with identical contour distance settings and outline widths. As you can see, both the inside and outside examples have seven concentric contours.

Like blends, you have the option of changing outline and fill colors of your contours. Similarly, contours are dynamically linked to the original object. If you make a change to the original object, the contour restructures itself to reflect the change.

Shortcut

Press Ctrl-R to repeat the last function.

Contour is a processor-intensive operation. It might take a few minutes for your computer to complete the calculations—even on a fast computer! In the next exercise, you make the butterfly's body pop off the screen when you apply a contour (to center). Watch when you click to center—the Steps setting becomes inactive (grayed out).

Using Contour To Build the Butterfly's Body

TIP

Perhaps you want to shrink (or enlarge) an object, but are not sure what the object's final size should be. Scale the object down (or up) by a small percentage, say 2 percent. Then, use the Ctrl-R shortcut to repeatedly scale the object down (or up) to the exact size. You also can use this technique to rotate objects.

Click on the Pencil tool

Draw the silhouette of the body

Click on the Fill tool — The Fill fly-out menu appears

Click on Black — The silhouette is filled with black

Draw a body section

Click on the Shape tool

Reduce the number of nodes in the body section to about 11

Tweak the nodes as needed (see fig. 8.8)

Click on the Fill tool — The Fill fly-out menu appears

Click on the Uniform Fill *icon* — The Uniform Fill dialog box appears

At Cyan, *enter* **90**

At Magenta, *enter* **40**

At Yellow, *enter* **0**

At Black, *enter* **70**

At the on-screen color palette, click on No Outline

Click on Effects — The Effects menu appears

Click on Contour — The Contour roll-up menu appears

Click on To Center — Steps grays out

At Offset, *enter* **0.01** *inches*

Click on the Contour Fill Color *button* — The Contour Fill Color fly-out menu appears

Click on Light Blue

Click on Apply (see fig. 8.9)

Press F9 to preview	The bútterfly's body looks almost three-dimensional!
Marquee-select the butterfly body, head, and antennae	
Drag the body into position between the wings (see fig. 8.10)	
Marquee-select the entire butterfly	
Press Ctrl-G	The entire butterfly is grouped
Save the file as BUT9.CDR	

Contour does have some restrictions. You cannot contour groups of objects, nor can you use the blend effect to blend contours into other objects, or fill them with bit maps. Although the application of contours might not be initially apparent, after a while you can come up with some really cool effects!

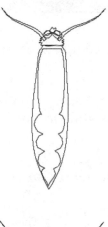

Figure 8.8:
Ready to contour!

Figure 8.9:
The contoured butterfly body.

Figure 8.10:

The finished
butterfly.

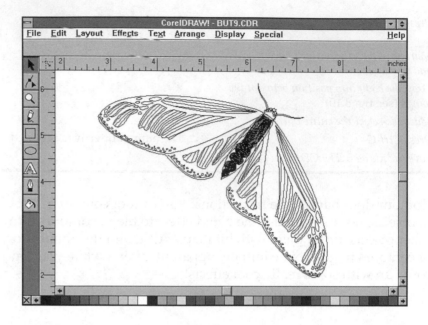

Now that the butterfly is complete, press F9 to view your handi-
work in glorious full color. Watch how quickly the combined
spots pour in, and see how the butterfly's body seems to pop right
off the screen. In the next exercise, you put the butterfly on its
own layer, then create a setting for the butterfly to fly around in.

Put the Butterfly on Its Own Layer

Click on Layout	The Layout menu appears
Click on Layers Roll-Up	The Layers roll-up menu appears
Double-click on Layer 1	The Layer Options dialog box appears
Type **Foreground**	Changes the name of the layer
Click on OK	
Click on the Layer fly-out arrow	The Layers fly-out menu appears
Click on New	The Layer Options dialog box appears
Type **Background**	Changes the name of the layer
Click on OK	
Click on the Layer fly-out arrow	The Layers fly-out menu appears
Deselect MultiLayer	

Before moving on to the next subject, take the time to print your butterfly. If you encounter any problems with printing, check out Chapter 11. Although the butterfly is not a hopelessly complex piece of art, it might tie up your printer for a while.

It's time to draw a world for the butterfly to live in! In the next section, you create some ferns by using both the blend effect and the weld function.

Blender Drinks for Everyone!

Joe DeLook is in the midst of a delirious dream, involving coconuts, blender drinks, and a giant talking beach ball named Olaf. Perhaps he is obsessed with the animation that Rip Raster had asked about (which you create in Chapter 13), or maybe he's just really thirsty in his unconscious state. Whatever the case, now is a good time to dive into the blend effect! Although it's not as refreshing as a frosty blender drink, it's a cool thing in its own right.

The blend effect, which debuted in CorelDRAW! version 2.0, is a powerful drawing tool (see fig. 8.11). Using blend, you can interpolate between two different objects. The outline color and width, fill, and object shape are melded. Blend has a wide variety of uses. You can, for instance, turn apples into oranges, dogs into cats, and purples into reds. In the last case, notice the functional overlap between the blend effect, fountain fills, and contours.

CorelDRAW! version 3.0 featured great improvements of the blend effect. Most importantly, blends were changed so that they became dynamic. Thus, after you have created a blend, you can make changes to the starting or ending objects, and the blend recreates itself. The blend effect was improved again in version 4.0 with the ability to fuse objects in a compound blend.

Blend is accessed through its roll-up menu, which offers incredible control over a number of blend characteristics. In the following exercise, you use only a fraction of blend's capabilities. The engineers put their efforts to good use on this one! Blend is one of Draw's nicest features.

Figure 8.11:
Examples of blend effects.

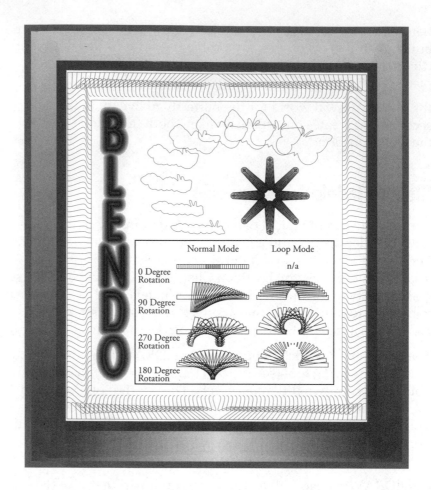

In this next exercise, you create the basic parts of a fern—pinnules. You create one large pinnule and one small pinnule, and then use the blend effect to create a number of intermediate pinnules, which forms the pinna.

Using Blend To Create a Fern's Pinna

Click on the Pencil tool

Draw a kidney-shaped object (a pinnule). Make sure it is a lean and mean object with only 4 nodes, then duplicate the pinnule while stretching it down to 30 percent of its original width (refer to figure 8.12).

Drag the smaller pinnule 3 inches from the original

Tweak it so that it is almost round

Marquee-select both pinnules

Click on Effects	The Effects menu appears
Click on **B**lend Roll-Up	The Blend roll-up menu appears (see fig. 8.12)
At Steps, *type* **12**	
Click on Apply	The pinnules are blended (see fig. 8.13)

Figure 8.12:
The **B**lend roll-up menu.

Figure 8.13:
The pinna after blending.

Notice that the blended segments are grouped together; you easily can delete them if they do not come out looking quite right. Of course, you can ungroup the blend and work with the individual objects, tweaking nodes and colors as you see fit.

Blend works on object shapes, fills, and outlines, but with some restrictions. You can blend between only two entities at a time, but these groups can include objects or multiple-path objects (see figure 8.11). Blending between objects of different fills or outline colors has certain constraints, as outlined in table 8.1.

Table 8.1
Blend Characteristics

Starting/Ending Object Fill	*Blend Objects Fill*
No Fill/Any Fill	No Fill
Uniform/Linear Fountain	Uniform to Linear Fountain
Uniform/Radial Fountain	Radial Fountain
Radial Fountain/Linear Fountain	Radial Fountain
Two Fountains of Same Type	Similar Fountain
Uniform/Pattern	Uniform
Pattern/Any Fill	Other Fill
Two Patterns	Top Object's Pattern
Spot Color/Process Color	Process Color
Two Different Spot Colors	Process Color
Two Tints of the Same Spot Color	Spot Color Tints

In addition to the blend fills mentioned earlier, you can set specific blend color attributes. By clicking on the Blend roll-up's color wheel, you are able to access an HSB color wheel. Clicking on Rainbow enables you to apply a rainbow effect—in a clockwise or counterclockwise direction—to your blend.

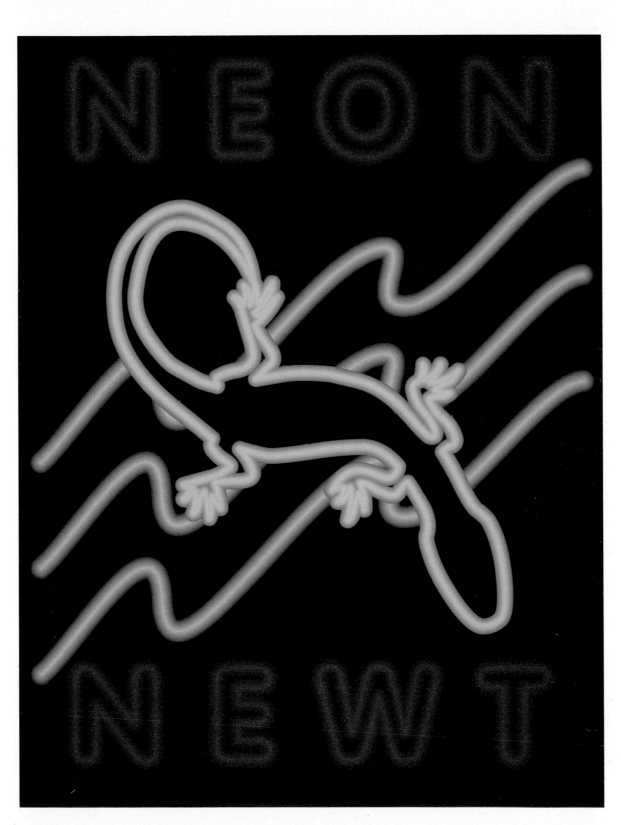

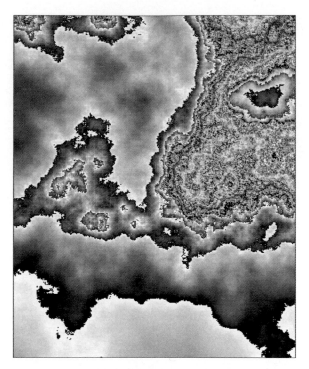

Aerial Photography

Blend Corners

Blend Edges

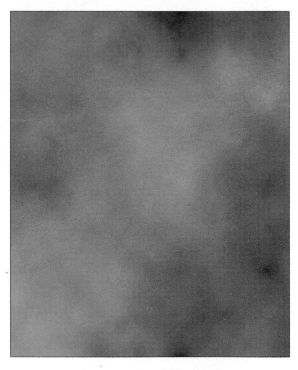

Cosmic Clouds

Cosmic Energy

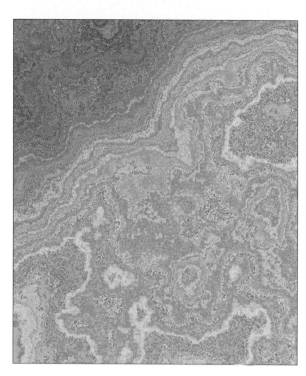

Cosmic Minerals

Drapes

Fiber

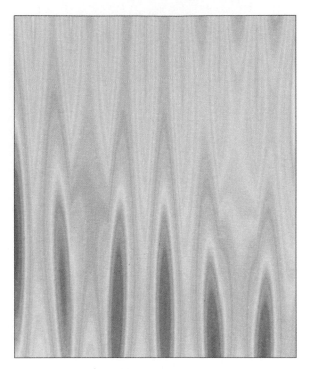

Flames

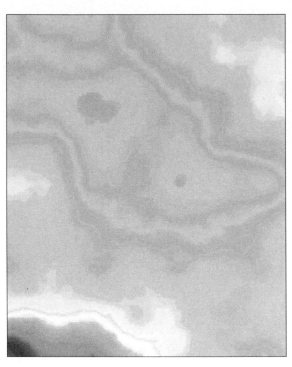

Mineral.Cloudy 2 Colors

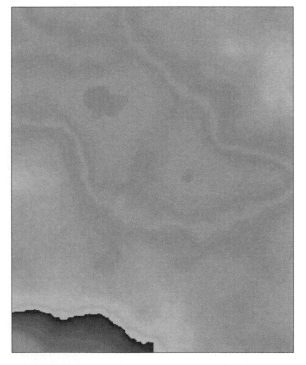

Mineral.Cloudy 3 Colors

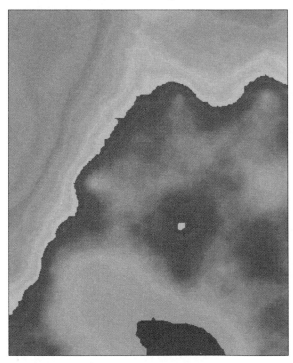

Mineral.Cloudy 5 Colors

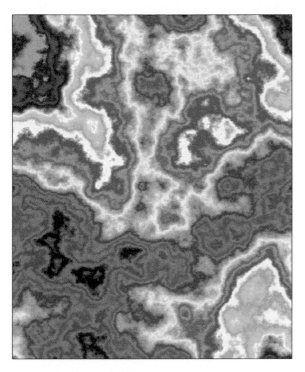

Mineral.Fractal 2 Colors

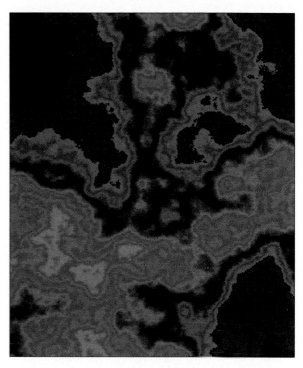

Mineral.Fractal 3 Colors

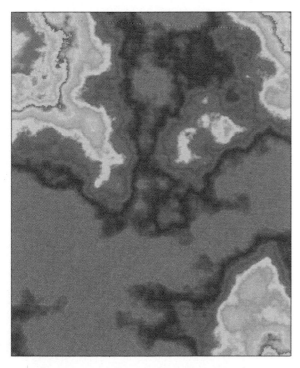

Mineral.Fractal 5 Colors

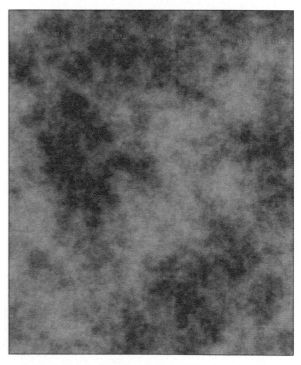

Mineral.Speckled 2 Colors

Mineral.Speckled 3 Colors

Mineral.Speckled 5 Colors

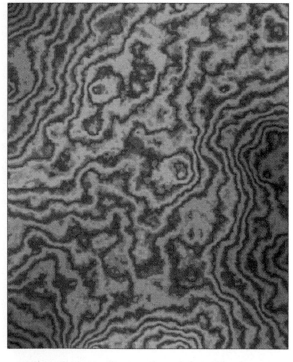

Mineral.Swirled 2 Colors

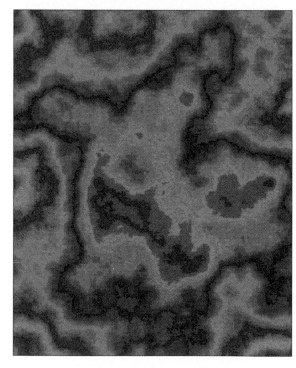

Mineral.Swirled 3 Colors

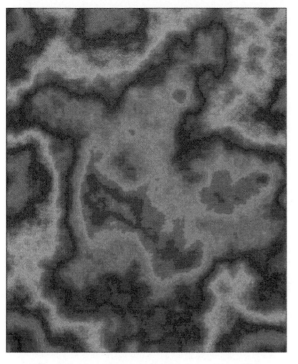

Mineral.Swirled 5 Colors

Noise

Noise.Blended

Noise.Rainbow Blended

Recycled Paper

Recycled Paper2

Satellite Photography

Scribbles

Sky 2 Colors

Sky 3 Colors

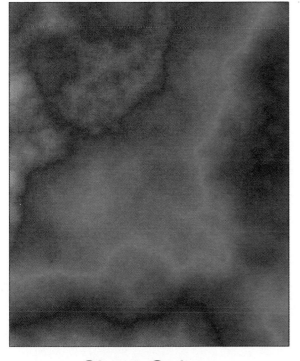

Sky 5 Colors

Sky Solarized 2 Colors

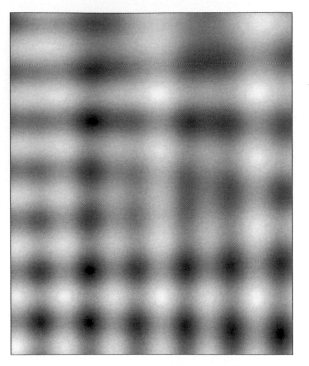

Smooth Weave

Surfaces

Swirls

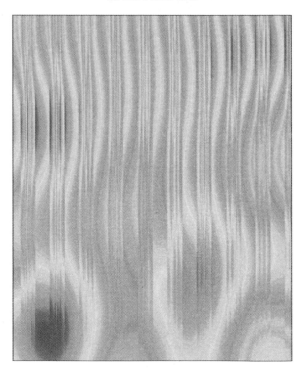

Swirls2

Texture Blend Horizontal

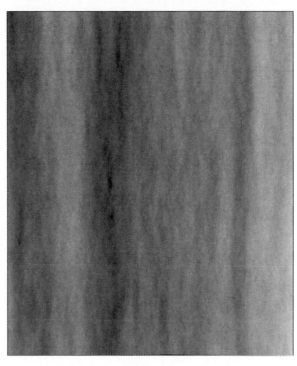

Texture Blend Vertical

Threads

Threads Color

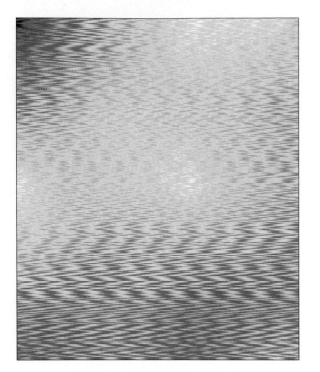

Water 2 Colors

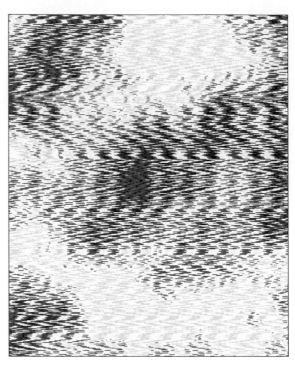

Water 3 Colors

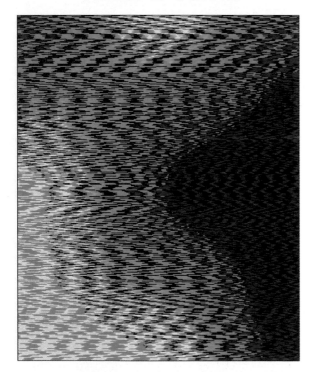

Water 5 Colors

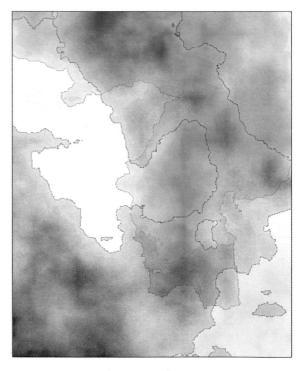

Water Color

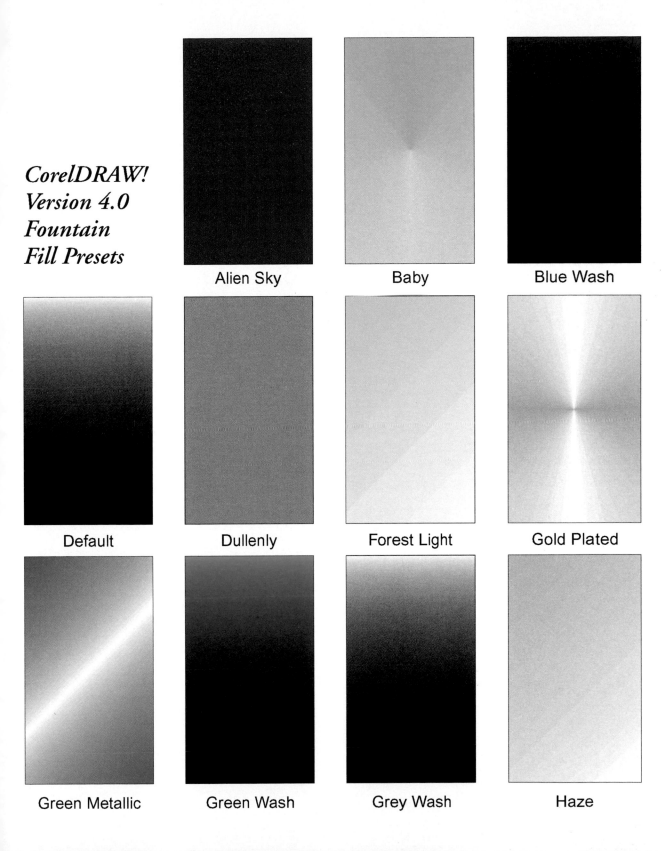

CorelDRAW!
Version 4.0
Fountain
Fill Presets

Alien Sky

Baby

Blue Wash

Default

Dullenly

Forest Light

Gold Plated

Green Metallic

Green Wash

Grey Wash

Haze

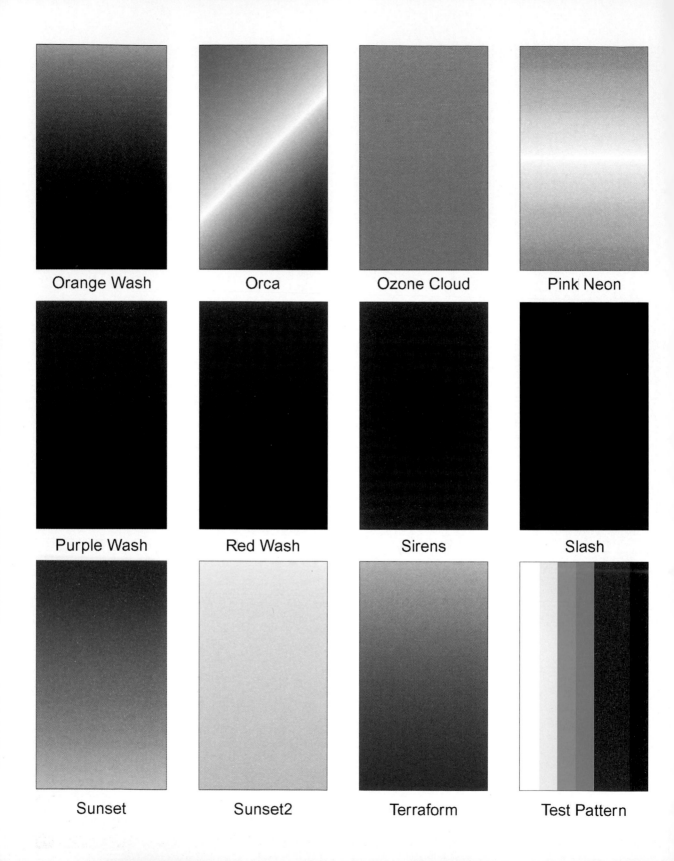

Orange Wash

Orca

Ozone Cloud

Pink Neon

Purple Wash

Red Wash

Sirens

Slash

Sunset

Sunset2

Terraform

Test Pattern

SEASIDE

SUMMER
HOURS
9 - 7
DAILY

AQUARIUM

The Blend dialog box offers a variety of different effects. The first value you might enter is the number of blend steps. This value (from 1 to 999) governs the number of interpolating objects created between the starting and ending objects. Remember that the more objects you use, the smoother the blend; but file size (and print time) grows proportionately.

You can use rotation for some interesting arcing effects. Figure 8.11 shows settings for 270-, 180-, 90-, and 0-degree (clockwise) rotation. Using negative values rotates the objects in the opposite direction. In addition, you can pull out an object's center of rotation before blending to give the blend a twisting path.

Editing intermediate blend objects can yield some interesting results. Ctrl-double-click on any intermediate blend object, and you can alter that object's position, outline, fill, size, and shape. You can even get into some heavy node editing!

The position and number of nodes in each object affect the blend. By default, blends act upon the starting nodes of both objects. You can alter this setting by selecting Map Nodes. This option enables you to choose the nodes—in effect, temporarily reassigning the starting nodes—to achieve different blends.

Blending along a path became a reality in CorelDRAW! 3.0. You now can have a blend follow a specific, editable trail. When blending along a path, you have the option to use predefined spacing or a number of steps. A blend can follow the full path, or just a portion of it, with magnetic accuracy. You also can rotate the blend objects to follow the curve of a path.

Now that blending is interactive, you can move or otherwise alter a starting or ending blend object, and then watch the blend redraw. You even have the ability to reshape the blend path interactively. The blend objects instantly and precisely align themselves to the path.

Blend has many uses. The more you work with the effect, the more you find. In figure 8.11, a caterpillar was turned into a butterfly with seven intermediate steps. The butterfly came from Draw's symbols. It was duplicated and rearranged into a caterpillar shape with the Node Edit tool. By blending two objects with the same number of nodes, some of the bizarre effects that happen when blending two wildly different objects were avoided. Notice that the blend steps are always equally spaced; however, you can separate and ungroup the blend after its completion and space the interpolated objects as you see fit.

The neon effect on the word "Blendo" was easy to create. First, the word was set with a fat 10-percent outline. Then, the word was duplicated and centered on the original. The duplicate was given a 100-percent hairline outline. Eight blend steps were used between the two. Presto! Instant neon. For a step-by-step exercise in creating neon type, check out Chapter 9.

Welding without Safety Glasses

The weld function was introduced in CorelDRAW! 4.0. It works in a manner similar to Combine, with one important difference: it was designed to create one object from a number of overlapping objects. Does that sound confusing? After you work through the next little exercise, you will understand.

Weld works only on ungrouped objects. Because the blend you just created is attached twice—once to the starting and ending control objects, and once to itself—you first must go through the hassle of separating, and then ungrouping before you can proceed with your weld.

Welding the Pinna

Click on the Pick tool	
Click on one of the blend pinnules	The blend group is selected
*Click on **A**rrange*	The Arrange menu appears
*Click on **S**eparate*	The blend is separated
Deselect the group of pinnules	
Click on an intermediate pinnule	The group of 12 blended pinnules is selected
Press Ctrl-U	The group is ungrouped
Marquee-select the complete pinna (all 14 objects)	

Click on **A**rrange	The Arrange menu appears
Click on **W**eld	The pinna is welded (see fig. 8.14)

Figure 8.14:
The welded pinna.

Welding is essential if you want to create your own typefaces and symbol fonts with CorelDRAW!, because neither TrueType nor PostScript type format enables you to overlap objects. Weld takes the drudgery out of combining and node editing combined-path objects.

Now that you have one pinna, you can quickly and easily create the fern's frond, by duplicating, scaling, stretching, and mirroring a number of pinnas. Use the Envelope effect for more realism. You are on your own with this one (refer to figure 8.15).

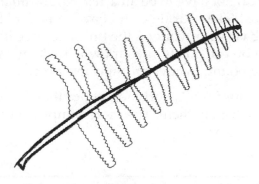

Figure 8.15:
The fern frond.

To really finish off this drawing, you use PowerLines—another one of CorelDRAW! 4.0's amazing new features.

Be a Trendy Artist (or Just Draw Like One) by Using PowerLines!

Have you ever wanted to create electronic artwork that looked as if it were the computerized equivalent of a woodcut or linocut? Draw's new PowerLine feature gives you the tools you need to render illustrations with a real electro-retro feel. CorelDRAW! 4.0 ships with 24 different PowerLines and gives you the option of creating your own personal PowerLines to boot! In addition to creating electronic illustrations that mimic traditional artwork, the PowerLine tool also is great for building design elements for distinctive logos.

PowerLines work with all pointing devices. But when coupled with a pressure-sensitive drawing tablet, such as the Wacom SD-420 (reviewed in Appendix B), PowerLines gain a new dimension. With a pressure-sensitive pen, Draw uses the pressure input to build lines of variable thickness—the harder you press, the thicker the line.

In the following exercise, you add some more vegetation to your butterfly illustration, complementing the fern created in the last exercise. You do not have to be an artist extraordinaire to finish this one off. Just take your time and have some fun! If you would like, you can base your work on the finished piece in the color signature, or you can go off in your own direction. Whatever you choose, you're bound to have an enjoyable time.

As you draw your first PowerLines, notice that the computer can take its time to display them. The more complex a PowerLine, the longer it takes to appear.

Drawing Clover with the Teardrop2 PowerLine

Click on Effects	The Effects menu appears
Click on PowerLine Roll-Up	The PowerLine roll-up menu appears

At the PowerLine roll-up, *roll down,*
click on Teardrop2

Set Max. Width *to* .75 inches

Click on Apply *when drawing lines*

Click on the Pencil tool

Draw a line one inch long   A clover leaf is created

Draw two more leaves, but do not connect them to the first leaf.
Drag them into position after they have been drawn. Use Snap to
Objects so that the leaves touch each other. Go ahead and plant a
whole field of clover (see fig. 8.16)!

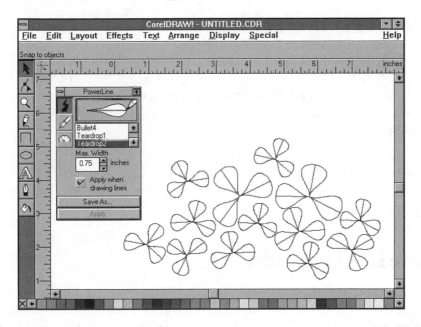

Figure 8.16:

Rolling in clover
with Teardrop2
PowerLines.

You can change a PowerLine's style or attributes after it has been
drawn. And, you can change a line that was not drawn as a
PowerLine into a PowerLine. If you are obsessed with tweaking
things, you'll have plenty to tweak! You can fiddle with a plethora
of settings, in addition to the outline color and fill choices. Figure
8.17 illustrates the four faces of the PowerLine roll-up menu.

Now that you've got a nice collection of clover, try using the
Woodcut3 and Bullet3 PowerLines to create even more vegetation.

Don't forget to save your file frequently. In the next section, you learn more about the pragmatic approach to electronic artwork.

Figure 8.17:
The four faces of the PowerLine roll-up menu.

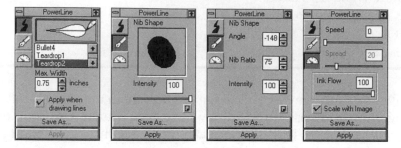

Preventing Problems

It would be tough to find an electronic artist, or any computer user, who has never lost a file—or at least a few hours of work—because of lackadaisical file management practices. Most people learn the hard way. For this reason, you must learn to follow proper file management techniques.

A few basic details should be kept in mind. Nothing earth-shattering here, just commonsense stuff. In fact, you have been using these techniques throughout this book and have done so rather extensively in this chapter.

Save Files Frequently!

Once again, use the Save command to write working files to the hard disk at regular intervals. This procedure prevents file loss in the event of a power outage (barring a disk crash). It also provides a "super undo," for those occasions when the file gets really trashed through a series of unfortunate choices. With a saved file on hand, you merely reopen the file, relax, and get back to work.

Even though CorelDRAW! provides some protection in the form of the backup file, get into the habit of saving the file each time an intricate maneuver is performed. This step helps to thwart the gremlins.

In addition to simply saving files, you also can make multiple copies of intricate files (as you did with the butterfly). This step provides extra insurance in case a version gets trashed along the way. Number these files sequentially to make it easy to go back in and rework the file at any stage of completion.

CorelDRAW! version 2.0 introduced Timed AutoBackup. This feature is yet another mechanism for safeguarding work. Appendix A explains how to alter the backup timing.

Use Undo Immediately!

This next point also might seem obvious, but run through it one more time. Use Undo immediately after fouling up. Do not try to "fix" what has gone wrong. Do not touch anything else, be it an object or a tool.

The second that you say "Oops," stop everything. Then, without delay, select Undo, or use the keyboard shortcut Alt-Backspace. This step ensures that Undo performs its function. Although CorelDRAW! 4.0 now features multiple levels of Undo, failure to use Undo immediately might jeopardize the drawing. With the Undo level's default setting of 4, your drawings can quickly enter the land of no return. If your computer has plenty of RAM, consider devoting some of it to a higher number of Undo levels. You can set the Undo levels in the Preferences dialog box.

Always Back Up Important Files!

The final preventive measure to mention is file backup. Most users have a tremendous amount of information stored on their systems' hard disks, and are unaware of the potential disaster that could befall them. Hard disks are like bank vaults—a great place for storing things, but if the disk should crash, it would be akin to throwing away the key to the vault. Salvaging data from a trashed hard disk can be tougher than breaking into a bank (or trying to resuscitate a failed savings and loan).

Fortunately (or is that luckily?), the author followed strict backup procedures while working on a previous edition of this book.

Deep into the production process, one of the computers had a hard disk failure. Although it was a setback, it was not monumental. All important files had been backed up to floppies. A spare hard disk was slapped into the computer and all the software and data files were reloaded. In half a day, everything was once again running at full speed.

Which files should be backed up? All important CDR files, for starters. Imagine putting days, weeks, or even months into building a library of images, only to have them lost to a disk crash. There are disk utilities on the market that might enable the user to salvage files that would otherwise be lost. One of the most popular is the Norton Utilities. But keep in mind the words *"might enable the user to salvage files."*

Backing up important CDR files to floppy disks is an inexpensive way to safeguard against loss. Use the Windows File Manager on a regular basis to copy all pertinent files from the hard disk to floppies. If you can afford a tape backup, buy one (and use it). Tape drives are cheap insurance against disaster.

Preview Strategies

A lot of the material discussed in this chapter concerns operating efficiency. The time it takes to get things done is vital. Most people have grown up in a world that refuses to wait for anything, including the time it takes for computers to process information.

When building complex drawings, the screen redraw times can become quite substantial. It helps to keep in mind a few strategies that can cut down the waiting time. Of course, you could go out and get the fastest computer available and outfit it with a speedy hard disk and powerful graphics card, but no matter what, you will eventually find yourself (broke and) seeking something a little faster. The concepts you are about to learn work with any PC running CorelDRAW!.

Shortcut

Press Shift-F9 to switch between Wireframe and Full-Color editing.

The simplest advice is to work in Wireframe mode most of the time. This mode obviously cuts down on screen redraw time. You must determine what works best for you. When speed is the prime consideration, work with wireframes. When it is imperative to do full-color editing, press Shift-F9 and go for it!

If you like the biggest preview screen possible, then you should use true full-screen preview. By pressing F9, you instantly summon up a nice big preview, unencumbered by windows, toolboxes, and the like. The disadvantage is that you must return to editing mode to make any changes to the image.

Shortcut

Press F9 to invoke full-screen preview.

Interruptible Display

When you are working on a large file, screen redraws can get to be quite time-consuming. One way to speed things up is to use Interruptible Display. This feature enables you to perform a function before the screen has been completely redrawn. You can switch on and off this time-saving feature at the Preferences dialog box (in the Special menu).

Auto-Panning

Auto-panning was introduced in CorelDRAW! version 3.0, but PageMaker users should be quite familiar with the concept. With this feature enabled, the screen scrolls automatically when you drag an object past the Draw window's border. You can switch auto-panning on or off by means of the Preferences dialog box.

Getting the Most from Layers

Among the Layer Options, you might decide to make a layer invisible, or apply a color override. By hiding a complex layer, your screen redraws faster and your drawing is easier to work with. Assigning a color override can yield much the same result, without losing sight of those layers.

TIP

Click the right mouse button while dragging to leave an original. This procedure has no effect on any of the programmable mouse functions.

Preview Selected Only

This strategy involves using the Preview Selected <u>O</u>nly option, which is found on the <u>D</u>isplay menu. It is useful when composing very complex drawings with a multitude of objects. Using this function speeds up redraw times enormously because the program displays only selected objects rather than the entire drawing.

This option also is useful for isolating objects. If an image contains a heap of objects, each indiscernible from the next, Preview Selected <u>O</u>nly often is instrumental in sorting things out. With this option on, merely click on, or Tab through the objects until the correct one is located, and press F9 to preview.

Save Time by Programming Your Mouse

One last way to speed things up is to set up your mouse button to perform a frequent task. The Preferences dialog box provides the means to instantly pop into four different modes. You can set your right mouse button to summon 2×Zoom, Edit Text, Full Screen Preview, or Node Edit. These shortcuts can save a great amount of time. Future versions of CorelDRAW! might provide additional choices.

It is obvious that Corel Systems truly listens to its user base. Many of the features that were incorporated into the latest incarnations of Draw were requested by users. If you have a feature request, be sure to let Corel know about it.

Joe Wakes Up

When you last left Joe DeLook, he was asleep at his favorite fishing spot. A sharp tug on the line has brought Joe back into the waking world, but, alas, the fish took the bait and swam off. Belatedly, Joe remembers the Island Watersports project that he was working on.

With only a few hours to deadline, Joe hustles back to the studio. The work is not too far from being finished, but he still must do one important thing—fit the company name around the logo.

Fitting Text to Path

One of CorelDRAW!'s most engaging features, Fit Text to Path, enables you to take a string of text and set it around a circle, an oval, a square, or another object (see fig. 8.18). This feature is a valuable asset to the artist who is thrown a curve, and then asked to set type to it.

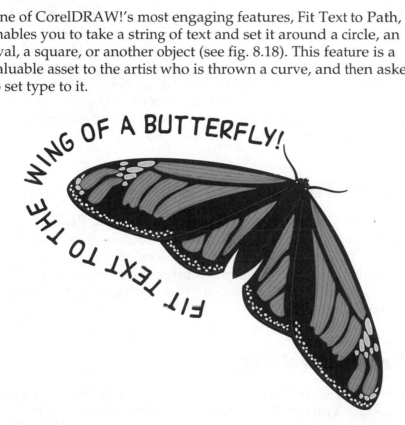

Figure 8.18:

Text made to fit almost anything.

To fit text to a path, you need two obvious things: the text and the path. The mere implementation of the command is easy: select both the text and the path, summon the Fit **T**ext to Path roll-up menu from the Te**x**t menu, make your choices, and click on Apply. Achieving perfection is time-consuming, however; it is not just a point, shoot, and print procedure. You always have plenty of room for tweaking.

After type is aligned to a path, you still can move it. You can reposition individual characters with the Shape tool, and adjust character and word spacing. The Shape tool also enables you to access the Character Attributes dialog box to change the size, typeface, and rotation of individual characters. This last capability is quite important because characters tend to require a touch of rotation to achieve a smooth look.

Unfortunately, text is not directly editable while on a path. You must use the Edit Text command to make changes (like correcting typos). Furthermore, type usually is not perfectly set to a path at first shot. It usually takes at least a few tries to achieve the proper combination of text alignment, character spacing, and rotation. Don't feel too bad if it takes a while to get the hang of it. After you understand the principles, things begin to make sense, and soon you'll be able to fit text to a path like a pro.

Fit Text to Path Roll-Up Menu

Corel's engineers totally overhauled the Fit Text to Path effect in CorelDRAW! version 3.0, and with great success. By using a roll-up menu, they were able to create a full-featured implementation of what was once just a frustrating and underpowered tool. The Fit Text to Path roll-up menu gives you total control of the command.

Character Orientation

The look and set of fit-to-path text is governed by the text orientation setting. You can choose one of four orientations: Rotate Letters, Vertical Skew, Horizontal Skew, or Upright Letters. The accompanying Path-O-Logic figures (figs. 8.19 and 8.20) illustrate how each setting affects text.

It is safe to say that for most designers, the traditional Rotate Letters setting gets the most use. In the following exercise, you use that setting to complete the logo for Island Watersports (begun in Chapter 7). You most likely save the other three settings for special effects, or for more abstract work. Setting the wrong piece of type with Vertical or Horizontal Skew could send your clients into convulsions. It might make them crazy, but, by all means, experiment (as in fig. 8.21)!

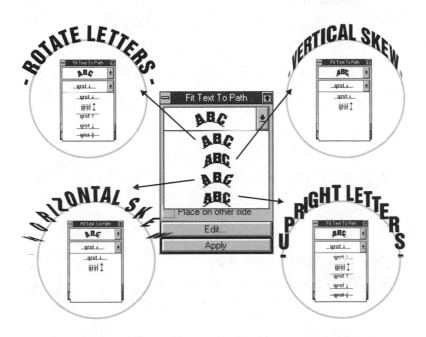

Figure 8.19:
The Path-O-Logic
Chart, part 1.

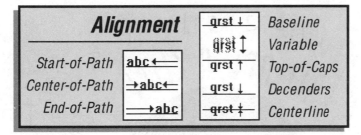

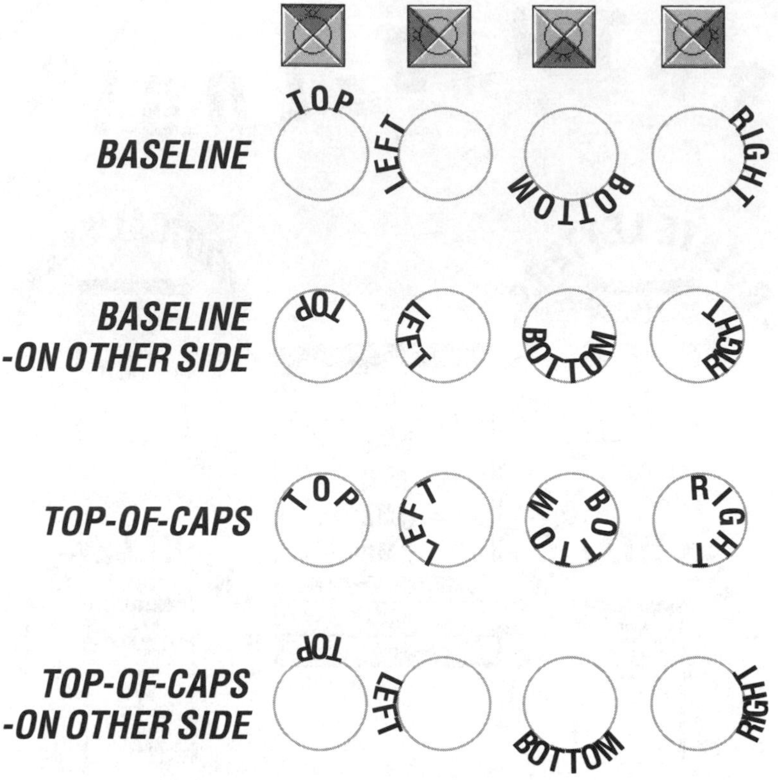

Figure 8.20:

The Path-O-Logic Chart, part 2.

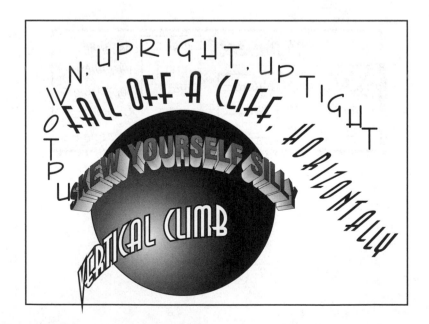

Figure 8.21:

Skew yourself silly!

Character/Path Alignment

Draw gives you plenty of flexibility with respect to character/path alignment. You can choose between five alignment settings: baseline, variable, top-of-caps, descenders, and centerline. All except for the top-of-caps alignment are variations of the same theme—in essence, variations upon character baseline alignment.

As shown by the ever-handy Path-O-Logic, your character/path alignment choices are controlled by the Character Orientation setting. Whereas you are limited to baseline or variable alignments when using either of the skewed settings, both the Rotate and Upright Letters settings provide access to the full range of character/path alignment.

If you decide that you want to change the text's distance from the path (regardless of the original alignment setting), simply click on the text and drag it inward or outward. The Vertical Offset marker appears, and the status line reports the text's distance from the path. When you release the mouse button, notice that the alignment setting has changed to variable. You also might make similar changes (or fine-tuning tweaks) by clicking on the Fit Text to Path roll-up menu's Edit button. This summons the Fit Text To Path Offsets dialog box, in which you can alter the Distance From Path and Horizontal Offset settings.

TIP

Finding it tough to select the text to make edits? Here are two hints. Use Tab to cycle between objects. Or, click on the text with the Shape tool, select the Pick tool, and voilà! You now can press Ctrl-T to access the Artistic Text dialog box.

Influence of Fit To Path Text Justification

The Fit Text To Path roll-up menu configures its text justification settings differently for rectangles and ellipses than it does for other objects. This difference provides a satisfactory interface for both situations.

Rectangles and Ellipses

When you work with a rectangle or ellipse as your path, the Fit Text To Path roll-up menu provides an instant visual clue as to the way your text sets on the path. A four-cornered button controls how you center your text: on the top side, left side, bottom side, or right side of the path. Simply choose the side you want to center your text on and click on the corresponding side of the button.

If you want your text to run on the other side of the path, click on Place On Other Side. This action flips the text over to the inside or outside of the path, depending on whether you are aligning by character baselines or top-of-caps, respectively. Take another look at the Path-O-Logic chart (figs. 8.19 and 8.20).

Other Objects

Text is always fit to a path based on the path's starting and ending nodes. Open path objects (or lines) have obvious starting and ending points. Closed path objects start and end at the same point. If you are drawing an object that you will ultimately use as a path to which text will be fit, you need to take this into consideration.

All text justification is governed by the Fit Text To Path roll-up menu because any other alignment settings are overruled. Left Alignment forces the text string to be set from the path's starting node. Center Aligned forces the text string to be centered between the starting and ending nodes. Right Aligned forces the text string to end at the path's ending node.

How can you tell where a closed path starts? No problem. When an object is selected with the Shape tool, the start/end node appears larger than the other nodes. If you select an object using the Pick tool, look closely and you can see the starting node. (This step works best when you are zoomed out.) Want to move a starting node? It's a hassle, so you should try not to! Objects can always be mirrored or rotated, but the best strategy is to try to draw the object with text alignment in mind. Start the drawing in the place that you plan to align from. Luckily, you have one possible cheap out. If you click on Place On Other Side, the text starts from the ending node and on the opposite side of the path (180 degrees).

Separate/Align to Baseline/Straighten Text/Undo

As you go through the process of fitting text to a path, you invariably need to return the text to its original state as you alter character spacing information or correct a typo. In short, the best way to accomplish this task is immediately to Undo the fit. If you have made too many moves (and made Undo unavailable), you still have a couple of options.

In these cases, you must break the text from the path, by clicking on **S**eparate (from the **A**rrange menu). Then, deselect the text by clicking on the page. After you have reselected the text, both Align to Baseline and Straighten Text reset text strings to a straight baseline. You probably want to use Straighten Text, however. Thankfully (unlike earlier versions of the program), Straighten Text does not remove Character Attributes such as typeface and size.

Align to Baseline does not erase the horizontal shift or character angle values, and holds all kerning and rotation information. Unfortunately, the text lands in a nasty-looking lump if it has been rotated.

How do you get around this dilemma? Usually, the best choice is simply to undo the maneuver. If you make Character Attribute changes, make a duplicate of the block of type for safekeeping.

Right now, you are going to use Fit Text to Path to finish off the Island Watersports logo. Start by opening up the file SIZZLER.CDR that you saved at the end of the last chapter. You add four ovals (see fig. 8.22). Later, you use two of them as non-printing guidelines for fitting the text. The other two ovals are part of the design and outline the logo.

TIP

Always make a duplicate of a block of type before performing drastic character attribute alterations. Drag the duplicate off to the side for safekeeping.

Figure 8.22:

Beginning the Island Watersports logo.

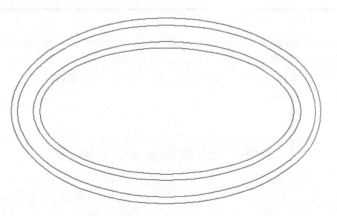

Creating a Text Path for the Island Watersports Logo

Click on File	The File menu appears
Click on Open	
Double-click on SIZZLER.CDR	The SIZZLER file opens

You are going to need four ovals. The first oval is for the inner outline, and the second is for the inner text path. The third is for the outer text path; the final oval is for the perimeter outline. It might sound like overkill, but you use all four ovals. To begin, set the grid to 1 per inch. You turn it off again almost immediately.

Drawing the Inner Oval

Click on Layout	The Layout menu appears
Click on Grid Setup	The Grid Setup dialog box appears
Set Frequency *to* 1 per inch	
Click on Snap To Grid *if the grid is not already on*	
Click on OK	
Click on the Ellipse tool	
Draw an oval 6 inches wide by 3 inches tall	This object is the inner oval
Press Ctrl-Y	Turns off grid

You have created the inner oval. Scale up three more ovals, each from the preceding duplicate. Notice that you are using percentages that are proportional to the horizontal and vertical dimensions of the oval.

Drawing the Rest of the Ovals

Click on the inner oval	The inner oval is selected
Click on Effects	The Effects menu appears
Click on Stretch & Mirror	The Stretch & Mirror dialog box appears

At Horizontal, *enter* **105**	
At Vertical, *enter* **110**	
Click on **L**eave Original	
Click on OK	The oval is scaled up to create the inner text path
Click on the inner text path oval	Selects the inner text path oval
Click on Effe**c**ts	The Effects menu appears
Click on **S**tretch & Mirror	The Stretch & Mirror dialog box appears
At Horizontal, *enter* **112**	
At Vertical, *enter* **124**	
Click on **L**eave Original	
Click on OK	The oval is scaled up to create the outer text path
Click on the outer text path oval	Selects the outer text path oval
Click on Effe**c**ts	The Effects menu appears
Click on **S**tretch & Mirror	The Stretch & Mirror dialog box appears
At Horizontal, *enter* **104**	
At Vertical, *enter* **108**	
Click on **L**eave Original	
Click on OK	The oval is scaled up to create the outer perimeter

Next, you set the text using the default settings, baseline, and top of object when you fit the first piece of text to the path. Consequently, all you need to do at the roll-up menu is click on the Apply button.

The typefaces used in this exercise—Zurich Black and Zurich Light—can be found on the CD-ROM. You can use other typefaces if you wish.

Setting Text to a Path

Click on the Text tool	The cursor becomes a +
Click on the page	The text I bar appears

continues

Type **ISLAND WATERSPORTS**	
Press Ctrl-T	The Artistic Text dialog box appears
At Si<u>z</u>e, *enter* **40**	
At Type, *choose* Zurich Blk BT	
Click on <u>S</u>pacing	
At <u>C</u>haracter, *enter* **-10**	
At <u>W</u>ord, *enter* **120**	
Click on OK	
Click on OK *again*	
You have the text and the path, so go for it!	
Click on the Pick tool	
Shift-click on ISLAND WATERSPORTS *and the inner text path*	
Click on Te<u>x</u>t	The Text menu appears
Click on Fit <u>T</u>ext To Path	The Fit Text To Path roll-up menu appears
At Fit Text To Path roll-up menu, click on Apply	ISLAND WATERSPORTS is set to the inner path

So how does the text look? It probably needs some tweaking and kerning. Take note of the places that need to be tightened or loosened and then click on Undo to break the text off the path. Now is the time to make those initial kerning adjustments. When you are done, refit the text to the path. Continue to use interactive kerning and the character attributes to rotate individual characters.

If you happen to do something to make Undo unavailable, you can use Straighten Text to do the job. Straighten Text is on the Arrange menu. Once again, the best strategy is to make a duplicate of any seriously tweaked chunk of text.

Now, set the text for the bottom of the logo.

Setting the Bottom Text

Click on the Text tool	The cursor becomes a +
Click on the page	The text I bar appears
Type **ESTABLISHED 1966**	
Press Ctrl-T	The Artistic Text dialog box appears
At <u>S</u>ize, *enter* **40**	
At Type, *choose* Zurich LT BT	
Click on <u>S</u>pacing	
At <u>C</u>haracter, *enter* **5**	
At <u>W</u>ord, *enter* **120**	
Click on OK	
Click on OK again	
Click on the Pick tool	
Shift-click on inner text path	
At Fit Text To Path roll-up menu, click on the Alignment down-arrow button	The alignment menu appears
Click on Top-Of Caps	
Click on Bottom button	
Click on Place on other side	
Click on Apply	ESTABLISHED 1966 is set to the inner path (see figs. 8.23 and 8.24)

This type might not need nearly as much refining as the type at the top of the logo. Feel free to do any kerning or rotating you think appropriate.

You are almost done, but you have a few things to tidy up. The two text paths should be nonprinting, and hence must be assigned an outline and fill of NONE. Alternatively, you can delete the text path outlines without disturbing the text. If you want to go back in and tweak some more, however, you have nothing to align to. The inner and outer outlines (which you do want to print) should be combined and given a fill of white and a two-point outline. The results should look like figure 8.25.

Figure 8.23:

Setting top-of-caps, on other side, and bottom alignments.

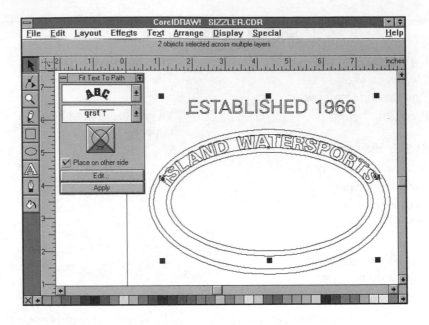

Figure 8.24:

The logo with type fit to path.

TIP

For best results when setting type to a tight curve, use a smaller point size.

Bring the Sizzler art into position, rotate and scale to fit, and save the file. The logo is done!

As you have seen, fitting text to path is a powerful feature that enables the user to make the final aesthetic adjustments. This exercise gives you just a taste of what the procedure is all about. Do not feel that you are done as soon as Draw has fit the text to your path. More often than not, you need to go in and adjust kern pairs, as well as character rotation. Avoid setting text to tight curves, if at all possible. If you must, try setting the type in a smaller point size.

Figure 8.25:
The finished logo.

Here is one general rule of advice with regard to character spacing. Text fit to the outside of a path should initially be set with a tight track. Text fit to the inside of a path should initially be set with a loose track, because outside text opens up and inside text closes up after they have been fit to their respective paths.

Now that you have the logo finished, move on to perspective, the final subject in this chapter.

Adding Perspective

The perspective effect was introduced in CorelDRAW! version 2.0, to great acclaim. This feature provides a means to apply one- and two-point perspective to any object (see figs. 8.26 and 8.27). If you are not familiar with perspective, briefly go over the theory basics presented here. If you are interested in learning more background information, consider taking a course in two-dimensional design.

There are many familiar examples to refer to when speaking about perspective. The most common might be the ubiquitous railroad tracks and telephone poles. Think how these objects fade off into the distance, shrinking to tiny spots on the horizon.

Figure 8.26:

One-point
perspective.

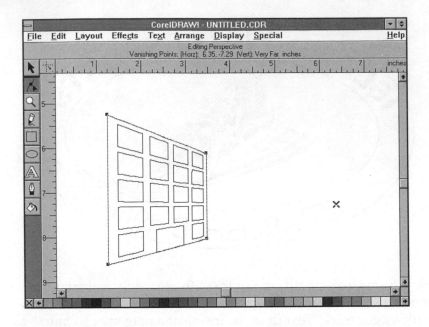

Figure 8.27:

Two-point
perspective.

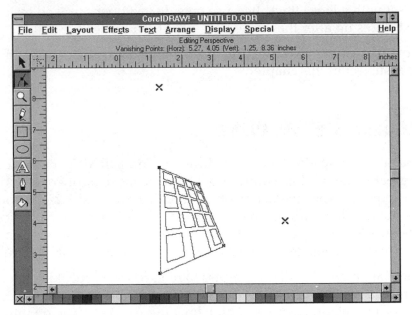

When working with perspective, two constants should always be
kept in mind. You must have a horizon line and at least one

vanishing point. The horizon line, as its name implies, is a horizontal "edge of the earth," whereas the vanishing point is the point of convergence on the horizon line. As objects get farther away, they grow vertically closer to the horizon line.

Remember that the horizon line is at eye level. If eye level is five feet and seven inches, so too is the horizon line. Consequently, any object that is at eye level—regardless of its location on the plane—hits the horizon line.

The best way to lay down a horizon line with CorelDRAW! is to drag in a horizontal guideline. Then, you can drag in a vertical guideline (or two) to set up your vanishing point(s). This method is especially handy when aligning the vanishing points of a number of objects.

Using the Perspective Effect

When you Add Perspective (on the Effects menu), CorelDRAW! applies a bounding box to the object, and the cursor turns into the Shape tool. To alter one-point perspective, drag a corner handle. If you want to constrain the movement horizontally or vertically, hold down Ctrl. To affect the perspective on two opposite handles simultaneously, hold down both Ctrl and Shift; the handles move in opposite directions.

To alter two-point perspective, drag a corner handle toward (or away from) the object's center. Watch for a pair of X markers on the screen; these markers are the object's vanishing points. After they are on-screen, you might find it easier to change an object's perspective by dragging the object's vanishing points rather than on the object's handles.

Not too surprisingly, one-point perspective enables for one (usually horizontal) vanishing point, whereas two-point perspective affords two (vertical and horizontal) vanishing points. You can use the click-and-drag positioning technique on either variety.

You can use the perspective effect on a single object, a group of objects, or a number of (ungrouped) objects. But if you want to apply perspective to an illustration of a building with doors and windows, for example, you should group the objects on each "face." Otherwise, the perspective is applied to each object rather than to the objects as a whole, and you would have to adjust the perspective for each object (see fig. 8.28).

Figure 8.28:

Remember to group before copying perspective!

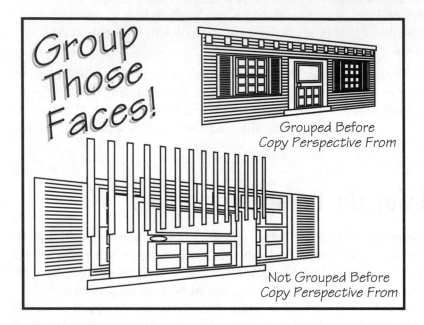

Group Those Faces!

Grouped Before
Copy Perspective From

Not Grouped Before
Copy Perspective From

Remember Copy Style From? You also can use Copy Perspective From! Select the object that you want to copy the Copy **P**erspective From (on the Effe**c**ts menu), and the From? arrow appears. Then click on the object you want to copy the perspective from. Instant perspective! Note that if you copy to a number of ungrouped objects, a separate perspective is applied to each object.

Right now, give the perspective effect a try. You take the finished Island Watersports logo and see how it looks on a shopping bag (see fig. 8.29). This exercise should ease you into perspective. You draw a couple of rectangles and a couple of handles, and set some type before you get around to applying perspective.

Figure 8.29:
The Island
Watersports
shopping bag.

Using Perspective To Put the Logo on a Shopping Bag

Set the grid to an easy 2 per inch, and turn it on. This exercise might remind you of the box kite you built way back in Chapter 2!

Click on the Rectangle tool	
Draw a rectangle 2 inches wide by 2 1/2 inches high	
Click on 20% tint	
Click on the Outline tool	The Outline fly-out menu appears
Click on the two-point rule	
Draw a second rectangle 1 inch wide by 2 1/2 inches high to the left and vertically aligned with the first rectangle	
Click on 30% tint	
Click on the Outline tool	The Outline fly-out menu appears
Click on the two-point rule	
Drag the horizontal guideline down 1.5 inches below the top of the rectangles	This is your horizon line
Drag the vertical guideline over 1.5 inches from the left of the rectangles	This is your left vanishing point

continues

Drag the vertical guideline over 2.5 inches from the right of the rectangles	This is your right vanishing point
Press Ctrl-Y	Turns off grid

Now, you set some text for the left side of the bag and draw a couple of handles:

Click on the Text tool	The cursor turns into a +
Click on the inside of the left rectangle	The Text I bar appears
Type **SURF** *and press Enter*	
Type **SKI &** *and press Enter*	
Type **MORE!**	
Press Ctrl-T	The Artistic Text dialog box appears
At Si<u>z</u>e, *enter* **24**	
Click on <u>C</u>enter	
Specify Swiss 921 BT	
Click on OK	
Click on the Pick tool	
Click on the skinny side of the bag	The text and the side of the bag are selected
Press Ctrl-A	The Align dialog box appears
Click on Horizontal Center	
Click on Vertical Center	
Click on OK	The type is centered on the side of the bag
Press Ctrl-G	The type is grouped with the side of the bag
Click on the Pencil tool	
Draw a pair of handles	Now it should look like figure 8.30

Okay, give this bag some perspective. You drag corner handles until the vanishing points appear, then drag the vanishing points onto the snap-to guideline intersections.

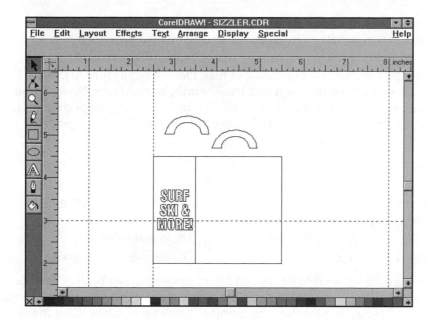

Figure 8.30:
Building the bag.

Finishing the Shopping Bag

Click on the Pick tool

Click on the skinny side of the bag   The text and the side of the bag
                                                     are selected

Click on Effects   The Effects menu appears

Click on Add Perspective   A bounding box appears around
                                                     the side of the bag

*Click and drag the top left handle
down until the vanishing point appears*

*Click and drag the vanishing point   The bag's left side
onto the left guideline intersection*   now has perspective!

Click on the bag's front side   Selects the bag's front

Click on Effects   The Effects menu appears

Click on Add Perspective   A bounding box appears around
                                                     the front of the bag

*Drag the top right handle down until
the vanishing point appears*

continues

Drag the vanishing point onto the right guideline intersection	The bag's right side has perspective, too! Figure 8.31 shows the results

Drag the handles into position and give them the appropriate tints of 40 and 50 percent for the front and back handle, respectively. Now all you have to do is add the logo to the front of the bag, copy perspective to it, and give it a tweak or two. Make sure that the logo has been grouped before you copy perspective!

Drag the logo onto the front of the bag	
Scale the logo to fit	
Click on Effe**c**ts	The Effects menu appears
Click on Copy Effect **F**rom	
Click on Copy **P**erspective From	The From? arrow appears
Click on the front of the bag	The perspective is copied

The logo might need to be resized after perspective has been added. Go ahead and resize as necessary. When you have it right, click on the Shape tool and reposition the vanishing point. Finish up by reshuffling the objects, and group when you are done.

Figure 8.31:

The bag gets some perspective.

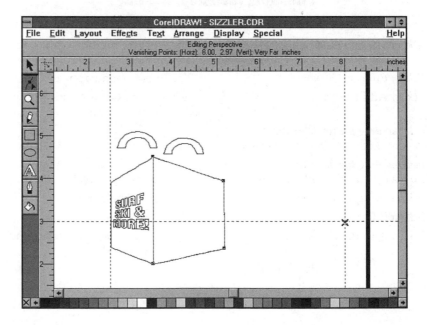

If an object's perspective gets out of hand, you easily can remove it with the Clear Perspective command. For objects with multiple perspectives, the command clears each perspective, one at a time. Clicking on <u>C</u>lear Transformations removes all perspectives (as well as envelopes) at once.

Like the Envelope effect, text that has been given a perspective remains in an editable state. You easily can change the wording on a packaging mock-up (like your shopping bag) or on a bill-board rendering.

Phew! That winds up this chapter. It covered a lot of ground, so take a break while Joe makes his big presentation to the marketing executives at Island Watersports (see fig. 8.32).

Figure 8.32:

Island Watersports marketing campaign.

Summary

CorelDRAW! is a relatively simple program that is capable of some very complex work. It takes a little talent and a general understanding of the concepts behind the program to be successful in its use.

In this chapter, you have focused on ways you can work more efficiently. Properly combining and grouping your work ensures that files redraw and print in a timely manner. Using the preview window to your advantage is another way to save valuable time. You also learned about Draw's Fit Text to Path command and how it can help you manipulate type in minutes instead of hours.

Even though artistic skill is one thing and electronic design know-how is another, the two are not mutually exclusive. Through a synthesis of both, Draw can help you achieve your goals in both art and business.

9

Special Type Effects

Remember Felix the Cat, the cartoon feline with his bag of tricks? This chapter is your equivalent to Felix's magic bag. When you run short of ideas, turn to this chapter for an instant concept, a creative jump-start, or a new way to solve a design dilemma.

The majority of this chapter is devoted to type effects. Some techniques might be familiar, but others might not be quite as obvious. Each effect is illustrated along with a quick how-to exercise, providing a fun and easy way to perfect your technique.

The chapter concludes by exploring backgrounds. Textures can come from a variety of sources. By using a scanner and a bit-map paint program, you can misappropriate any pattern from marble tile to spattered paint to achieve a unique look. And in the vector world, you learn to create a zooming grid by using the Perspective effect.

Using Typographical Pyrotechniques

As you have seen in previous chapters, CorelDRAW! enables users to produce a slew of impressive tricks with type. Serious design power comes into play when you use those effects to create multifaceted pieces of artwork. Images that are exhaustively time-consuming, incredibly expensive, or almost technically impossible to create conventionally can be produced on time and under budget. This fact does not mean, however, that projects require little time or effort!

This section investigates a number of effects that are not one-click endeavors, but require a bit of savvy and technical skill. As you work through the type effects, you soon realize that many of these tricks can apply to objects other than text. Most of the examples in this section strive to conjure up illusions of depth, texture, or motion.

With a depth effect, you can add a three-dimensional look to two-dimensional artwork. Draw enables you to quickly add pop to your work with effects like Extrude. To effectively add depth, you need to take the extrusion apart and apply different tints to each side of an object to add the illusion of lighting angles. The concept of lighting angles figures strongly in creating bevel type, embossed type, and tube type. The artist must fool the beholder's eye into accepting different tints as different faces of a multidimensional object.

This chapter uses a handful of the many fonts you can find on CorelDRAW! 4.0's CD-ROM disks. If you do not have a CD-ROM drive, you can substitute similar fonts, although Draw's huge font load might be all the justification you need to buy a CD-ROM drive!

Drop Shadows: Variations on a Theme

A *drop shadow* is a duplicate of an object filled with a different tint and placed behind the original object (see fig. 9.1). The fill can be lighter, darker, or a completely different color. The drop shadow is usually the first type embellishment discovered by neophyte desktop publishers, who sometimes overuse it brutally. In the right hands, however, a drop shadow is perfect for popping text off the page. When the drop shadow effect is correctly rendered, it makes type look as if it were magically suspended, floating above the page. Although drop shadows are commonly created with shades of gray, color adds far more subtleties than shades of gray alone can portray. In color advertising or packaging, the drop shadow is almost a necessity.

Plain Vanilla

Figure 9.1:

A standard drop shadow effect.

Even though a plain vanilla drop shadow is hardly worth writing (or reading) about, a few variations of the theme are definitely worth discussing. This section presents perspective shadows, knockout drops, and embossed type. A number of methods are available to create the drop shadow. CorelDRAW! enables you to use the Duplicate command (Ctrl-D), the Move command (with leave original), and Drag-duplicate. And don't forget that pressing the numeric + leaves a duplicate exactly on top of the original.

The Move and Duplicate commands offer the most accuracy. Move enables you to change the distance moved each time you use the command; you can change Duplicate's setting in the Preferences dialog box. When you work with a number of objects that all must have the same exact drop shadow, Duplicate is your most convenient choice.

If you are shadowing only one object, drag-duplicating (pressing the numeric + while dragging) is an excellent option. After the duplicate object is on the page, the Nudge function (when set at 0.01 inch) is the slickest way to reposition objects in fine increments.

Perspective Shadows

Figure 9.2 shows an example of a perspective shadow. The words are sitting on the horizon line, backlit by an offset radial fill. The foreground is a linear fountain fill with the fill angle set to flow from the focal point of the background. The perspective shadow completes the illusion by following the same imaginary light source.

Figure 9.2:

The perspective shadows effect.

The procedure to set a perspective shadow either behind or in front of a piece of type is simple. Contrary to popular opinion, you can create a perspective shadow without using the Perspective effect by using the Skew function.

You begin this exercise by drawing a pair of rectangles to form the background and foreground of your graphic. Draw the first rectangle using the Rectangle tool, and duplicate the second from it by using Ctrl-drag. Then add the type with its baseline resting on an imaginary horizon line. Pull a perspective shadow forward, and manipulate it using Skew. Finish up by setting the fill of each object.

Creating Long Shadows

Click on the Rectangle tool   The cursor changes into a +

Draw a rectangle 5 inches wide by 1 inch high

Click on the Pick tool

Drag the rectangle's top center handle down; hold down Ctrl and press +

Release the mouse button when the Y scale is (-100%)	A duplicate rectangle is created

The two rectangles should butt against each other. This line forms the horizon.

Click on the Text tool	The cursor becomes a +
Click on the center of the top rectangle	The Text I bar appears
Type **LONG SHADOWS**	
Press Ctrl-T	The Artistic Text dialog box appears
Change to 48-point Jupiter Normal	Changes the point size and face
Click on OK	A 48-point LONG SHADOWS appears
Click on the Pick tool	
Drag the text's top center handle down; hold down Ctrl, and press +	
Release the mouse button when the scale is (-100%)	A duplicate, mirrored LONG SHADOWS is created
Click on the mirrored LONG SHADOWS	The Rotate/Skew handles appear
Position the cursor on the center two-headed bottom arrow	The cursor becomes a +
Drag the cursor to the right	The cursor goes into Skewmode
Position the cursor for approximately 50 degrees of skew	
Release the mouse button	LONG SHADOWS has some pseudo-perspective
Click on LONG SHADOWS' base text	
Press Shift-PgUp	To bring the base type to the front
Click on **E***dit*	The Edit menu appears
Click on Select **A**ll	The status line reads `4 objects selected`
At the on-screen palette, right-click on No Outline	

continues

Drag the shadow into position, butting baseline to baseline, at the horizon line (see fig. 9.3). When everything is in place, assign object fills. Give the perspective shadow a 60% black fill, and the base type a black fill. Give the background (top rectangle) a radial fountain fill from 40% black to white. Use Center Offset to move the center, -50% in both x and y. The foreground (bottom rectangle) uses a linear fountain fill that runs from 60% black to 10% black at a 110-degree angle.

Figure 9.3:

The Long Shadows wireframe.

Shortcut

Click the right mouse button as you drag to leave an original.

Notice that the shadows fill is set to be as dark as the darkest point of the foreground, to ensure that it is, in fact, a shadow. Try setting the shadow to an intermediate tint (say, 40% black) for an interesting effect.

Knockout Drops

No, knockout drops are not leftover barbiturates from a 1940s spy movie. *Knockout* refers to the white outline of the text that knocks (or drops) out of the drop shadow (see fig. 9.4). You can use this effect when printing a multiple color job in which the drop shadow is a different color than the type itself and the printer's specifications call for loose register. This method is one way to avoid problems with trapping (see Chapter 12).

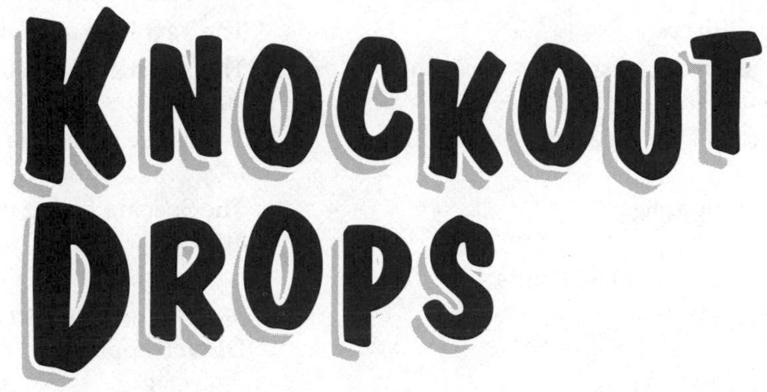

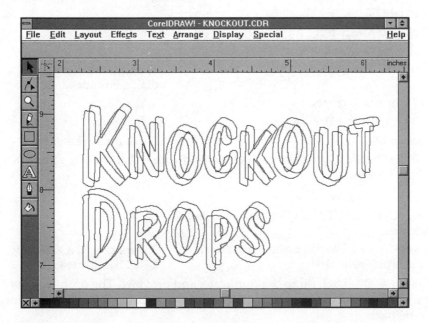

Figure 9.4:
The knockout drops effect.

This exercise is simple. Enlarge the size of the first letter in each word to give a small caps effect, and reposition a number of characters to make the type follow a jumpy baseline. Notice that when you create knockout drops, you select **B**ehind Fill in the Outline Pen dialog box. This extra step prevents the outline from choking the fill, avoiding an undesirable result. The results of this exercise are shown in figure 9.5.

Figure 9.5:
Knockout drops wireframe.

Creating Knockout Drops

Click on the Text tool	The cursor becomes a +
Click on the page	The Text I bar appears
Type **KNOCKOUT**, *press Enter, type* **DROPS**, *press Ctrl-T*	The Artistic Text dialog box appears
Change to 72-point Dom Casual BT	To change point size and face
Click on Spacing	The Spacing dialog box appears
Set Line Spacing to 80 Points	
Click on OK *twice*	A 72-point KNOCKOUT DROPS appears
Click on 100% Black	Fills text
Right-click on White	Outlines text
Click on the Outline tool	Outline Pen fly-out menu appears
Click on the Outline Pen Options tool	Outline Pen dialog box appears
Click on **B**ehind Fill *and* **S**cale With Image	
Click on Rounded Corners *and* Line Caps	
At **W**idth, *enter* **4 points**	
Click on OK	
Click on the Shape tool	
Drag a marquee around K and D	
Double-click on K's node	The Character Attributes dialog box appears
At Point Size, enter **100**	
At Vertical Shift, enter **-10**	
Click on OK	Initial caps are enlarged

Use the Shape tool to select and position individual characters to achieve a jumpy baseline:

Click on the Pick tool	
Drag KNOCKOUT DROPS down and to the left, then press +	
Release the mouse button when X and Y both are approximately -0.07	A duplicate KNOCKOUT DROPS is created

Assign a 20% black fill to the duplicate, and preview. The drop shadow is in front of the base text. Use Shift-Page Down to send the drop shadow to the back.

Embossed Text

Unlike standard drop shadows, which make type look as if it were floating above a page, embossed text makes type look as if it were pressed into the page (see fig. 9.6). This effect is useful when rendering type that should look as if it were set in stone. CorelPHOTO-PAINT! and other bit-map paint programs can apply an embossed look to text or artwork with a built-in command, but vector-based CorelDRAW! does not offer a one-click solution.

Figure 9.6:
The embossed text effect.

CorelDRAW! does, however, enable you to quickly emulate embossed text by setting two drop shadows—one above and one below the base text. This provides the illusion of highlight and shadow. Although this solution is not the most elegant, it is effective and easy to accomplish. You can create interesting effects by setting the base type with the same tint or color as the background, or by carefully highlighting sections of the embossed text with slivers of tint, color, or fountain fill. If you work from a textured background, you can achieve a granite look, especially if you bring in a granite scan!

Creating Embossed Text

Click on the Rectangle tool   The cursor changes to a +

Draw a rectangle 5 1/4 inches wide by 1 1/2 inches high

Click on 30% Black Fill

Click on the Text tool   The cursor becomes a +

Click on the center of the rectangle   The Text I bar appears

continues

Type **Emboss**	
Press Ctrl-T	The Artistic Text dialog box appears
Change to 96-point Arabia	Changes point size and face
Click on OK	A 96-point Emboss appears
Click on the Pick tool	
Click on 30% Black	Fills base Emboss with 30% black
Drag Emboss, press +	
Release the mouse button when X and Y are approximately 0.02	A duplicate Emboss is created
Press Ctrl-R	Creates a third Emboss
Press Ctrl-PgDn	Sends the third Emboss back one layer
Click on White	Fills highlight Emboss with white
Click on the leftmost Emboss	
Click on 50% Black	Fills the shadow emboss with 50% black
Drag a marquee around all three Embosses	
Press Ctrl-G	Groups Emboss
At on-screen palette, right-click on No Outline	The Embosses have no outline
Shift-click on the rectangle	The Emboss and the rectangle are selected
Click on **A**rrange	The Arrange menu appears
Click on **A**lign	The Align dialog box appears
Click on Horizontal **C**enter	
Click on Vertical C**e**nter	
Click on OK	The Emboss is centered in the rectangle (see fig. 9.7)

Figure 9.7:
Emboss wireframe.

In the previous example, the lighting angle is set to come from the upper right corner of the page. To change the way the embossing is lit (altering the angle by 180 degrees), give the leftmost Emboss a 10% black tint, and the rightmost Emboss a 40% black tint.

Neon Type

Neon signs are back in vogue. This part of American culture has made the jump from the real thing in Las Vegas and Times Square to hand-lettered signs, pickup trucks, and print advertising. CorelDRAW! makes it easy to create lettering with a neon look (see fig. 9.8). Such typography can work beautifully in black and white, spot, or process color. Certain typefaces work exceptionally well as neon type. One of the best faces to use is VAG Rounded; its rounded ends give the perfect tubular feel. For script faces, try Freestyle or Kaufmann. In general, use a face that is of equal weight throughout the letterform.

Figure 9.8:

Examples of neon
and tube type.

Building neon type with CorelDRAW! is not incredibly difficult, but it does take time, patience, and experimentation to get things perfect. The Outline Pen dialog box is essential when you create neon type. Be sure that you select <u>S</u>cale With Image, Rounded Corners, and Line Caps. This ensures that you can scale your neon type reliably and that it does not present any spiky outline surprises. Use the Blend effect, at its default setting of 20 steps, to create the illusion of neon.

Back in the summertime paradise of Seaside, your hero, Joe DeLook, has just landed a design contract with his favorite waterfront bistro, The Neon Newt. The first project they want Joe to create is a full-color menu cover (see fig. 9.9). The cover depicts who else but Ned, namesake of The Neon Newt, and is lettered in their corporate typeface, VAG Rounded.

Joe has decided upon a simple design for the menu cover, which is to measure 6 inches by 8 inches. To begin the exercise, create a custom page with Page Frame.

Figure 9.9:
The Neon Newt
menu cover.

Creating Neon Type

Click on **F**ile	The File menu appears
Click on **N**ew	A new page appears
Click on **L**ayout	The Layout menu appears
Click on Page **S**etup	The Page Setup dialog box appears

continues

Roll down, click on **C**ustom	
At **W**idth, *enter* **6.0 inches**	
At **H**eight, *enter* **8.0 inches**	
Click on **A**dd Page Frame	
Click on OK	A 6-by-8-inch page is created with a page frame
Click on the page frame	
Click on Fill	The Fill fly-out menu appears
Click on Uniform Fill	The Uniform Fill dialog box appears
Click on Custom Palette	The dialog box configures itself for Custom Palette Colors
Click on Show Color Names	The dialog box configures itself to show Color Names
Scroll down and select Deep Navy Blue	
Click on OK	Page Frame is filled with Deep Navy Blue
Drag vertical ruler to create a guideline 0.5 inches from the left margin.	
Drag vertical ruler to create a guideline 0.5 inches from the right margin.	
Click on the Text tool	The cursor becomes a +
Click on the page's top left corner	The Text I bar appears
Type **NEON**	
Press Ctrl-T	The Artistic Text dialog box appears
Change to 96-point VAG Rounded BT	To change point size and face
Click on **B**old	
Click on OK	A 96-point VAG Rounded NEON appears
Click on the Pick tool	
At the on-screen palette, click on No Fill	
Click on the Outline tool	The Outline Pen fly-out menu appears
Click on Outline Color	The Outline Color dialog box appears

Scroll down, select Deep Navy Blue	
Click on OK	NEON is outlined with Deep Navy Blue
Click on the Outline tool	The Outline Pen fly-out menu appears
Click on Outline Pen Options	The Outline Pen dialog box appears
Click on **S**cale With Image	
Click on Rounded Corners *and* Line Caps	
At Width, *enter* `0.222 inches`	
Click on OK	Base NEON has a fat outline, the same color as the background
Drag NEON *to butt against the left guideline*	
Click on the Shape tool	
Click on NEON	NEON is selected
Drag the letterspace arrow to the right guideline	NEON is letterspaced
Click on the Pick tool	
Drag NEON *to the bottom of the page*	
Hold down Ctrl and press + (on the numeric key pad)	
Release the mouse button	A duplicate NEON is created
Press Ctrl-T	The Artistic Text dialog box appears
Backspace over NEON *and type* **NEWT**	
Click on OK	NEWT is set in 96-point VAG Rounded

Now that you have set the type, get Ned the Newt! Use Draw's Symbol Library to summon the slimy creature:

Click on the Text tool, drag down and to the right	The Text fly-out menu appears
Select the Star (Symbol) and release	The Symbols roll-up menu appears
Click on Animals	
At Symbol #, *type* **77**	To select Ned the Newt

continues

At Size, *type* **8** *inches*	To change size of Ned the Newt
Drag and drop Ned the newt *onto the page*	A big newt appears
Click on the Pick tool	
At the on-screen palette, click on No Fill	
Click on the Outline tool	The Outline Pen fly-out menu appears
Click on Outline Color	The Outline Color dialog box appears
Scroll down, select Grass Green	
Click on OK	Ned is outlined with Grass Green
Click on outline	The Outline Pen fly-out menu appears
Click on Outline Pen Options	The Outline Pen dialog box appears
Click on <u>S</u>cale With Image	
Click on Rounded Corners *and* Line Caps	
At Width, *enter* **0.167** **inches**	
Click on OK	

At this point, all the base elements are on the page. You need to create the highlight elements into which you will blend the base elements. Corel-DRAW! has a handy one-button shortcut to place duplicates directly on top of their originals. You might remember pressing + while dragging an object to create a duplicate. You also can select any object and press + without moving the object to create a duplicate.

Click on NEON	
Press +	NEON is duplicated
Click on the Outline tool	The Outline Pen fly-out menu appears
Click on Hairline	
Click on the Outline tool	The Outline Pen fly-out menu appears
Click on Outline Color	The Outline Color dialog box appears
Scroll up, select Magenta	
Click on OK	Highlight NEON is outlined with Magenta
Drag a marquee around both NEONs	Both NEONs are selected
Click on Effe<u>c</u>ts	The Effects menu appears

Click on **B**lend   The Blend roll-up menu
                                                    appears

Use the default settings of 20 Blend Steps and 0 degrees Rotation.

Click on Apply   NEON is blended
                                                    (see fig. 9.10)

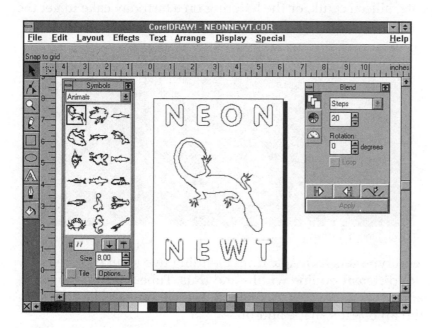

Figure 9.10:

Creating the Neon
Newt menu cover.

Now press F9 to look at what you have done so far. Notice that
the outline seems to fade into the background. If you recall, this
effect was created by using the same color for both the background and the type's base outline. Repeat the last steps (duplicate outline, change outline width and color, then blend) to
neonize the word NEWT. Then finish off Ned himself. Use a
Turquoise Hairline for Ned's highlight. Notice how different Ned
looks, as opposed to the type (refer to fig. 9.9). Ned appears to be
popping off instead of fading into the background because of his
base outline color.

Tube Type

Tube type is similar in concept, execution, and appearance to neon type. Once again, the Blend effect is used to create an illusion. But instead of a blend radiating outward, tube type grows inward to create a three-dimensional effect (see fig. 9.11). Think of gel toothpaste, silicon caulk, or the lettering on a birthday cake to get the gist of what tube type is all about.

Figure 9.11:

Tube type.

Neon type gets its magic from blending two similar pieces of type with different outline widths and tints. Tube type, on the other hand, does not necessarily use an outline. It works its wonders with an object's shape and fill.

To create tube type, start with a flowing script like Freestyle. Take care of any character pair kerning, duplicate the text string, and drag the duplicate off to the side (you use this for a drop shadow). Give the original text string a black fill/no outline, convert it to curves, and break it apart. Recombine any multiple path characters (such as A, B, D, and so on). Then, working letter by letter, create a duplicate of each letter. Make sure that the duplicate is on the top, and use the Shape tool to create a character just a little bit shorter and narrower, but, more importantly, thinner than the original.

Do not break the duplicate character apart to manipulate the individual paths! If you do, the blend does not work properly, and you go crazy trying to fix it. Fill the skinny character with a 10% gray highlight fill. Marquee-select the skinny character together with the original character, and use Blend to impart the illusion of depth.

Creating Tube Type

Instead of rendering an entire word of tube type, create only one letter: a 500-point Q. Working in large scale gives you greater precision in line placement, which is crucial in developing different lighting angles.

Click on the Text tool	The cursor becomes a +
Click on the center of the page	The Text I bar appears
Type Q	
Press Ctrl-T	The Artistic Text dialog box appears
Change to 500-point Freestyle Script	To change point size and face
Click on OK	A 500-point Freestyle Script Q appears
Click on the Pick tool	
At the on-screen palette, right-click on No Outline	
Click on 100% black	The Q is filled with 100% black, with no outline
Click on **A**rrange	The Arrange menu appears
Click on Con**v**ert To Curves	The Q is converted to curves
Press + on the numeric keypad	The Q is duplicated
Click on 10% black	The Q is filled with 10% black
Click on the Shape tool	

Move individual nodes inward and adjust control points to form a skinny Q inside the original. Take your time and adjust the control points as needed, pushing the highlight to the top right of the letter (see fig. 9.12). Remember, you can use the nudge feature to move selected nodes around or drag directly on a line. Do not break the duplicate character apart into its individual paths! Next, create the blend by using Draw's default (20 step) setting (see fig. 9.13).

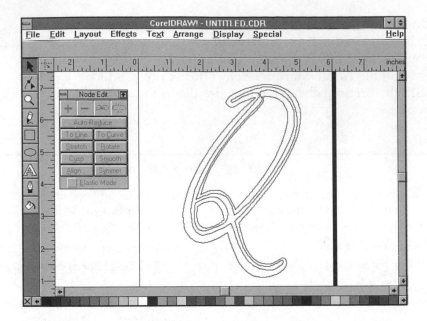

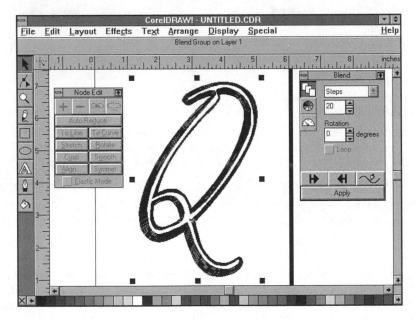

Creating the Blend

Click on the Pick tool	The skinny Q is selected
Shift-click on the original Q	Both Qs are selected
Click on Effe**c**ts	The Effects menu appears
Click on **B**lend	The Blend roll-up menu appears

Use the default settings of 20 Blend Steps and 0 degrees Rotation.

Click on Apply	A 20-step blend appears

Go ahead and preview the tube type Q. If you are not happy with the way the lighting angle looks, delete the blend, tweak the skinny Q, and blend again.

To finish off a piece of tube type, use the duplicate you made to set a drop shadow behind it; it will provide the extra oomph to pop the image off the printed page.

Tube type might seem like a long way to get the same effect as neon type, but it actually offers more. Although it takes more time and patience, tube type provides far more control over each individual character. It might take all afternoon to create a one-liner, but the results can be well worth the effort.

Shortcut

Click on the numeric keypad's plus symbol (+) to duplicate any selected object.

Punk Text

On occasion, you might need to use an informal typeface that looks as if it were hand-lettered. In these cases, you find that the standard-issue CorelDRAW! fonts do not fit the bill—until you pull a cheap trick out of the bag: punk text.

The name might conjure up visions of black leather and adolescent angst, but punk text is one of the best-kept secrets to create fast, easy, and distinctive display heads. Where would you use such unique typography? Just think rock and roll. T-shirts, concert flyers, compact-disc and cassette-tape packaging, and band logos all are fair game.

You can create punk text quickly. By using the Text tool, plug in the type in your choice of base typeface—sans-serif faces like Bauhaus Heavy are good choices. Next select the text and convert to curves. Switch to the Shape tool and drag a marquee around the entire text block. Double-click on any selected node to bring up the Node Edit roll-up menu, and change all the line segments to straight lines. There you go: punk text (see fig. 9.14).

Figure 9.14:

Punk type.

Tweaked Vogue Bold

Hand-Altered: R

Hand-Altered: B, C, E, G, O, R

You might need to tweak the type a bit—and this might take some time—but this is one of the slickest ways to create random lettering. Some characters fare better than others in the conversion process, as do certain typefaces. Angular characters, like A, E, and F, might not change at all, and require artistic persuasion. Use the Shape tool to finesse the letterforms. Certain effects require you to break apart and possibly recombine characters; for example, when using different colors/tints for each letter, or when rotating individual letters.

As a general rule, the more complex a face, the poorer a choice it is for creating punk text, because the results often are unreadable. On the other extreme, a face that already consists of purely straight lines—such as Machine—is not a candidate for conversion.

If you create a punk face you really like, you can always save it as a PostScript or TrueType typeface by using the Symbol/Typeface Export Filter. By doing this, you will save even more time when you set type for the same account. After you do this, you can export the font for use with applications that can't use PostScript or TrueType by converting the font with Ares FontMonger.

After you have created your punk text, you can apply any CorelDRAW! treatment. Just remember that when you convert text to curves, you will not be able to edit it, so be sure to check for typos before converting to curves. To finish things up, try using punk text with drop shadows or knockout drops.

Punk Text Revisited

Another quick way to create punk text is to duplicate a text string, drag the duplicate down the page, and change it to a completely different typeface. Then, use blend to mutate between the two different typefaces. Zingo...Instant punk text! The more blend steps, the more gradual the change. Separate the blend elements, ungroup the blend, and delete the iterations you don't need.

This technique surely leads you into uncharted typographical territory. Font creation has never been so immediate, not to mention random. Certainly, much of what you get with this technique is unreadable, but you are bound to create at least one usable style!

Figure 9.15:

More mutant punk type, courtesy of the blend effect.

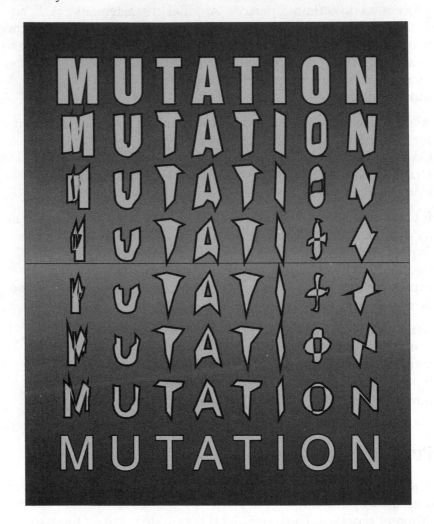

Bevel Text

Have you ever wanted your type to appear as if it had beveled edges? By following this straightforward but exacting process, you can create multidimensional type like a pro. To bevel a piece of type, you must add facets to each side (see fig. 9.16). You can accomplish this through diligent use of the Pencil tool, snap-to guidelines, and the Pick tool.

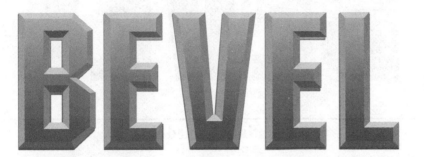

Figure 9.16:

The beveled text effect.

The trick to maintaining your sanity when creating beveled type is to start with a typeface that has a minimum of curves. Machine is a good choice, because it does not contain any curves at all. You also can try beveling punk text for an ultra-custom look. If the face contains curves, expect to spend extra time to get the curves to work out properly.

When you bevel text, the idea is to once again create the illusion of depth. To do this, use different tints of gray or base color on each side of a character. With process colors, you easily can add different percentages of black to the base CMYK mix. Spot colors (or good old black) can be altered with different screen densities. If you want to get real tricky (and spend an additional amount of time), you can use fountain fills on each facet, altering colors, angles, and edge padding appropriately.

In the following exercise, you bevel just one character, an E, set in 600-point Machine. Like the previous tube type exercise, this illustrates technique without becoming too cumbersome. Create the E with a full beveled surface, as opposed to a flat surface with beveled edges. You can try to create the latter on your own. Use the approach illustrated here, along with a variation of the tube type technique, to apply a flat surface bevel (see fig. 9.17).

Figure 9.17:
A slightly different bevel effect.

Creating Beveled Text

Click on the Text tool	The cursor becomes a +
Click on the center of the page	The Text I bar appears
Type E	
Press Ctrl-T	The Artistic Text dialog box appears
Change to 600-point Machine	To change point size and face
Click on OK	A 600-point Machine E appears
Click on Layout	The Layout menu appears

Make sure that Snap-to Grid is off and Snap-to Guidelines is on.

Click on the Zoom tool	The Zoom fly-out menu appears
Click on +	
Marquee-select E	To zoom up on E
Click on the Pick tool	
Position the cursor over the vertical ruler	
Drag the guideline to the left edge of the E, *and repeat for each vertical edge*	
Position the cursor over the horizontal ruler	
Drag the guideline to the top edge of the E, *and repeat for each horizontal edge*	

Now that the edge guidelines are in, draw the center guidelines by using a sneaky little trick. You might recall back in Chapter 5, you used nonprinting, guideline-layer ellipses to help balance your composition. This time, cut a few rectangles in half to determine the centerlines of the E. After the center guidelines are drawn, the rectangles are deleted (see fig. 9.18).

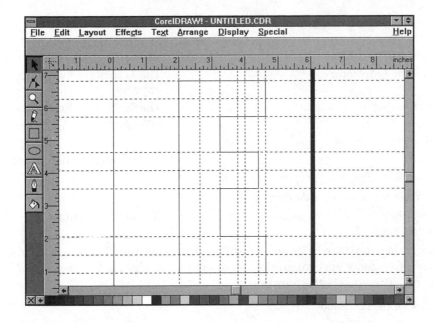

Figure 9.18:
Beveling the E on
the screen.

Drawing the Centerlines

Click on the Rectangle tool

Starting at the left side of the E, take the following steps:

*Click and drag a rectangle the width of the
E's downstroke*

Click on the Pick tool — The rectangle is selected

Click on Effects — The Effects menu appears

Click on **S**tretch & Mirror — The Stretch & Mirror dialog
box appears

At Horizontal, type **50**

Click on OK — The rectangle is half as wide

Snap the rectangle to the leftmost guideline

Position the cursor over the vertical ruler

*Drag the guideline to the rectangle's right
edge* — A centerline is drawn

Click on the Rectangle tool

Starting at the top of the E, take the
following steps:

continues

Drag a rectangle the depth of the E's top cross-stroke	
Click on the Pick tool	The rectangle is selected
Click on Transform	The Transform menu appears
Click on Stretch & Mirror	The Stretch & Mirror dialog box appears
At Vertical, type 50	
Click on OK	The rectangle is half as tall
Snap the rectangle to the uppermost guideline	
Position the cursor over the horizontal ruler	
Drag the guideline to the rectangle's bottom edge	A centerline is drawn

Use this procedure to draw centerlines throughout the E's cross-strokes. Drag two more vertical guidelines to denote the right side cross-stroke facets. Then delete the four boxes.

Click on the Pencil tool

Draw a series of three- and four-sided polygons to form the facets of the E (see fig. 9.19). Draw's Layer Control comes in handy on this project! This procedure is easiest if you create another layer for the facets and switch MultiLayer off.

Finish up by assigning a fill to each of the facets. Use an 80% black fill for all the southsides, a 20% fill for all the northsides, a 60% fill for all the eastsides, and a 40% fill for the westside (see fig. 9.20). Experiment with and without object outlines.

Chrome Type

The chrome look is almost as overdone as the common drop shadow, but many desktop designers are asked to set type in this style. Chrome type takes time and effort to render; it is not a point-and-click affair. Well-executed chrome type looks as shiny as the emblems on a custom show car, but poorly constructed chrome type can be complex and time-consuming to print. You must take two considerations into account: visual appeal and image engineering. If it looks great but does not print, you have not done your job. The same is true for the reverse scenario.

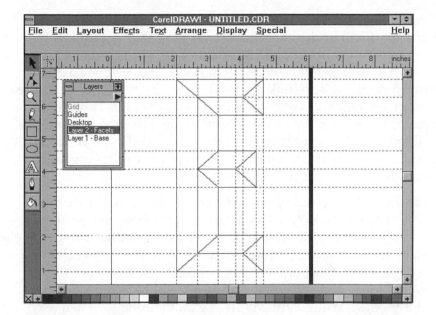

Figure 9.19:

Beveled E wireframe.

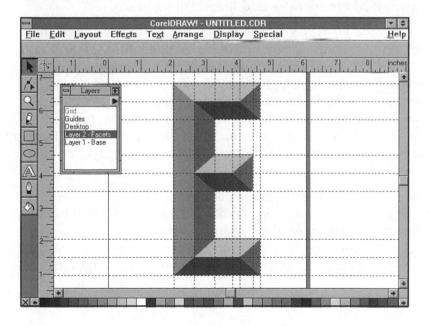

Figure 9.20.

Beveled E in full-
color mode.

Hopefully, after working (and reading) through the rest of this book, you will understand how to work with fountain fills to reap the rewards yet not choke your printer, or worse, your service bureau's imagesetter, which might result in overtime charges for intensive pages. The trick to creating chrome type that looks great and prints reliably is to construct the fountain fills as simple objects layered on top of the original type. Mindlessly fountain-filling large strings of type—as type—can needlessly tie up a printer's RIP. Your responsibility is to put your files together properly.

Traditionally, chrome type is rendered with an airbrush. But because CorelDRAW! does not have an airbrush tool, you must make do with a combination of methods. High-end chrome type is constructed by using both fountain fills and blends to achieve a metallic luster. Starbursts—glints of light—also can be built by using either a radial fountain fill or a blend between a fat and a skinny object, using a tube type-like methodology. When used sparingly, these sparkles add the finishing touch.

The method you are going to use makes heavy use of the Shape tool to break character outlines into smaller chunks. The chunks are then assigned different fountain fills, depending upon their geographical location upon the face of the character. At the very least, you might find that breaking a character into two chunks, upon a base character, provides a good foundation to build on. The bottom edge of the fountain fill of the top chunk can fade into the base character, while the top edge of the bottom chunk can contrast sharply with the base.

Once again, you create just one character—C—due to the complexity of the process. Good-looking chrome type takes a bit of effort and experimentation. To make your life easier, you can use Layer Control to orchestrate your drawing. When you are done with the letter C, try setting the rest of the word CHROME.

Creating Chrome Type

Click on the Text tool	The cursor becomes a +
Click on the center of the page	The Text I bar appears
Type **c**	
Press Ctrl-T	The Artistic Text dialog box appears
Change to 500-point Aachen BT	To change point size and face
Click on OK	A 500-point Aachen C appears
Click on **L**ayout	The Layout menu appears

Make sure that Snap-to Grid is off and that Snap-to Guidelines is on.

Click on the Zoom tool	The Zoom fly-out menu appears
Click on +	
Marquee-select the C	To zoom in on the C
Click on the Pick tool	
Position the cursor over the vertical ruler	
Drag the guideline to the left edge of the C's downstroke; repeat for the right edge of the C's downstroke	
Position the cursor over the horizontal ruler	
Drag the guideline to the bottom edge of the C's top serif; repeat for the top edge of the C's bottom serif	See figure 9.21
Press + on the numeric keypad	The C is duplicated
Press Ctrl-Q	The duplicate C is converted to curves

Click on the Shape tool

At each of the bottom two leftmost guideline intersection points, take the following steps:

Double-click	The Node Edit roll-up menu appears
Click on +	A node is added

After the two extra nodes have been added, take the following steps:

Marquee-select all four nodes that fall on the guideline intersection points

continues

At the Node Edit roll-up menu:

Click on **B**reak	The object is now four subpaths
Click on page	Deselects the nodes
Click on the top left node (of the four)	The node is selected
Click on **D**elete	The line segment is deleted
Click on the top right node (of the three)	The node is selected
Click on **D**elete	The line segment is deleted

You now have an object with just two subpaths.

Click on **A**rrange	The Arrange menu appears
Click on Brea**k** Apart	The duplicate C is now two separate (open path) objects
Click on page	Deselects the two objects
Click on the top half of the C	The top half of the C is selected
Click on the Pencil tool	The cursor becomes a +
Draw a line between the top half's two lower nodes	Closes the path
Click on the bottom half of the C	Selects the C's bottom half
Click on the Pencil tool	The cursor becomes a +
Draw a line between the bottom half's two upper nodes	Closes the path (see fig. 9.22)
Click on **E**dit	The Edit menu appears
Click on Select **A**ll	All the objects are selected
At the on-screen palette, right-click on No Outline	

You now have three separate objects: the original C, along with the top and bottom halves of the duplicate C. Give the original C a 10% black fill. Experiment with different linear fountain fills for the top and bottom halves of the duplicate C. Start with a 10% to 60% 90-degree fill for the top, and a 30% to 70% 90-degree fill for the bottom. Try adding a duplicate C, with an outline but no fill, and bring it to front. Then, add a neon effect for a glowing result, as shown in figure 9.23.

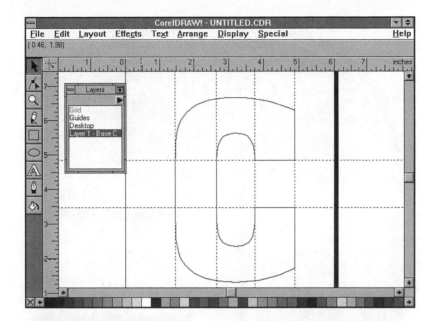

Figure 9.21:
The C with guide-lines drawn.

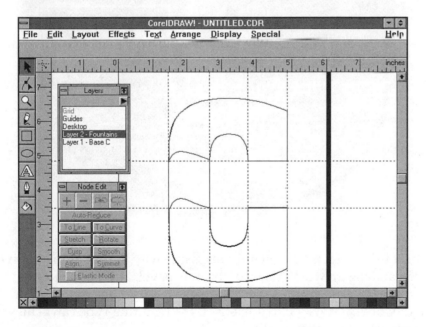

Figure 9.22:
The finished C wireframe.

Combining effects and techniques is one way to render distinctive,
eye-catching artwork. Use the chrome, bevel, and neon effects
together to yield impressive results. When used in combination
with CorelDRAW!'s Extrude effect, the resulting type can achieve
a near-photographic quality.

To achieve the ultimate in photo-realistic chrome type, you must use a three-dimensional modeling and rendering program. Unfortunately, Windows-based 3-D renderers are few and far between. On the forefront of 3-D rendering is Renderize from Visual Software, a 32-bit Windows program. You will find more information about Renderize in Chapter 10, "The Windows DTP Arsenal."

Spin Type

Spin type often is seen in program manuals and advertisements, but gets little work in the real world. This effect can be used to add the illusion of motion or depth to an object (see fig. 9.24). Spin type is fast and easy to do. You can use one of two techniques: the Multiple Repeat-Rotate-Leave Original technique or the Blend effect. Each technique has advantages. If you are not sure how much rotation you want, try the Multiple Repeat-Rotate-Leave Original technique. If you want to change tint as the type rotates, use the Blend effect.

Figure 9.24:

Spin type created using Multiple Repeat-Rotate-Leave Original.

Remember in Chapter 1 when you rotated the Corvette? Now you are going to move the object's rotation point and use Rotate to rotate the piece of type one degree while leaving an original. Then, repeatedly using the keyboard shortcut, Ctrl-R, repeat the step. You might be amazed at how fast you can grow a piece of spin type!

Using the Multiple Repeat-Rotate-Leave Original Technique

Click on the Text tool	The cursor becomes a +
Click on the center of the page	The Text I bar appears
Type SPIN TYPE	
Press Ctrl-T	The Artistic Text dialog box appears
Change to 48-point Century Oldstyle Italic	To change point size and face
Click on OK	A 48-point Century Oldstyle Italic SPIN TYPE appears
Click on the Pick tool	
At the on-screen palette, click on No Fill, right-click on 30% black	
Click on SPIN TYPE	The Rotate arrows appear
Position the cursor over the center of rotation	
Drag the center of rotation below and to the left of SPIN TYPE	
Position the cursor over the top right handle	The cursor's pointer becomes a +
Drag the top right handle up and left	A blue dashed box replaces the arrow handles. The status line shows amount of rotation in degrees
Press +	The status line reads Leave Original
When Angle is 1.0 degree, release the mouse button	A duplicate SPIN TEXT is created, rotated 1.0 degree from the original
Press Ctrl-R	Repeats the procedure

Use Ctrl-R another 28 times, and give the last object no outline and a 100% black fill.

The Multiple Repeat-Rotate-Leave Original technique used to create spin type also is valuable to create objects that radiate from a central point, such as petals on a flower or spokes on a wheel.

Next, try the same thing a little differently. This time, make use of the Blend effect to create your SPIN TYPE (see fig. 9.25). This next exercise uses the very first and last SPIN TYPEs you just created, so save the file if you want to hold onto it.

Figure 9.25:
Spin type created
using the Blend
effect.

To begin, select and delete all but the very first and last SPIN TYPEs. When you have done that, proceed with the following steps:

Using the Blend Effect

Click on the bottom SPIN TYPE

At the on-screen palette, click on
10% black, *right-click on* No Outline

Click on the top SPIN TYPE

At the on-screen palette, click on
50% black, *right-click on* No Outline

Shift-click on the bottom SPIN TYPE   Both SPIN TYPEs are selected

Click on Effects   The Effects menu appears

Click on **B**lend Roll-Up   The Blend Roll-Up menu appears

Click on Apply   A 20-step blend appears

Click on **A**rrange   The Arrange menu appears

Click on **S**eparate   The blend is separated

Click on page   To deselect the blend

Click on the top SPIN TYPE

Click on Fill   The Fill fly-out menu appears

Click on 100% black

Notice how the Blend effect SPIN TYPE differs from the first technique. Of course, the outline and fill characteristics were set up differently, but it is more than that. See how the Blend effect text moves in a straight line? Now take a look at the Multiple Repeat-Rotate-Leave Original type; it moves in a gentle arc. Try each technique with different fills, outlines, and rotation percentages. To have the spin layer in the opposite direction when using the Blend effect, select both originals and click on Reverse Order (on the <u>A</u>rrange menu, under <u>O</u>rder) before blending.

Two-Tone Type

Have you ever had the need for a piece of type that is half positive (black letters on a white background) and the other half reversed (white letters on a black background)? CorelDRAW! provides a straightforward way to accomplish this effect (see fig. 9.26). By combining the text with an object, you can create two-tone type in a matter of mouse clicks.

Figure 9.26:

Two-tone type.

This one is so easy that it might bring tears to the eyes of any graphics designer who ever had to do this using the old reversal stats and a technical pen.

Remember, after you combine text with any other object, it is not editable. Always make a duplicate of the type and objects you are about to combine for safekeeping. Drag duplicates off to the side, just in case you need to make an edit or adjust character kerning.

You also easily can add a spot color to the design by dragging a duplicate of the original shape behind the combined object. Change the tint/color of the duplicate object and send it behind the original.

Creating Two-Tone Type

Click on the Text tool	The cursor becomes a +
Click on the center of the page	The Text I bar appears
Type **TWO-TONE TYPE**	
Press Ctrl-T	The Artistic Text dialog box appears
Change to 72-point Exotc350 DmBd Bt, then click on **C**enter	To change the point size, face, and alignment
Click on OK	A 72-point TWO-TONE TYPE appears
Click on the Pencil tool	The cursor becomes a +
Draw a triangle taller than, but not as wide as, TWO-TONE TYPE	
Click on the Pick tool	
Shift-click on TWO-TONE TYPE	Both objects are selected
Press Ctrl-A	The Align dialog box appears
Click on Horizontal and Vertical **C**enter	
Click on OK	The objects are horizontally and vertically aligned
Press Ctrl-L	The Objects are combined
At the on-screen palette, right-click on No Outline, *click on* 100% black	

Preview your work. If it does not look quite the way you want it, immediately undo the combine. Then, adjust the elements and recombine.

Letterspaced Type

Letterspaced (or blown-out) type, also known as force-justified type, is a simple task with Draw's snap-to guidelines and interactive letterspacing. By dragging out a pair of vertical guidelines, you can adjust type to fit any width (see fig. 9.27). Set your type with the left side hitting the left guideline, and switch to the Shape tool. Draw displays the type's interactive spacing controls. Drag the horizontal (intercharacter) marker to pull the type out to the desired width. To set interword space, hold down Ctrl while you drag.

Figure 9.27:

Blown-out text.

DeLOOK DESIGN

S E A S I D E , U . S . A .   8 0 0 / 5 5 5 - 1 2 3 4

Creating Blown-Out Text

Position the cursor over the vertical ruler	
Drag the guideline to the left side of the page	
Position the cursor over the vertical ruler	
Drag the guideline four inches from the first guideline	
Click on the Text tool	The cursor becomes a +
Click on the left guideline	The Text I bar appears
Type **DeLOOK** (use 3 or 4 spaces) **DESIGN**	
Press Ctrl-T	The Artistic Text dialog box appears
Change to 24-point Eras Light	To change point size and face
Click on **N**one	To change justification
Click on OK	A 24-point, Eras Light DeLOOK DESIGN appears
Click on the Shape tool	
Drag DeLOOK DESIGN's *intercharacter marker to the right guideline and release the mouse button*	DeLOOK DESIGN is letterspaced
Click on the Text tool	The cursor becomes a +
Click on the left guideline	The Text I bar appears
Type **SEASIDE, U.S.A.** (use 3 spaces) **800/555-1234**	

Press Ctrl-T	The Artistic Text dialog box appears
Change to 12-point Eras Light	To change point size and face
Click on OK	A 12-point, Eras Light SEASIDE, U.S.A. 800/555-1234 appears
Click on the Shape tool	
Drag SEASIDE, U.S.A. 800/555-1234's *intercharacter marker to the right guideline and release the mouse button*	SEASIDE, U.S.A, 800/555-1234 is letterspaced (see fig. 9.28)

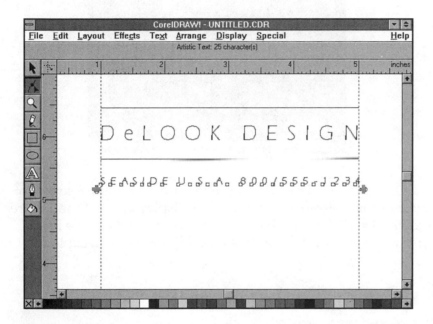

Figure 9.28:
Force-justified letterhead.

Texture Type

You fooled around with texture text in Chapter 7. Remember creating the Wave masked bit map? You can use the same technique along with a scanner to create some interesting texture type (see fig. 9.29). Of course, you can use bit maps with type, without masking. When combined with beveled, embossed, or a carefully extruded technique, texture type can be even more striking (see fig. 9.30).

Figure 9.29:

Texture type.

Figure 9.30:

Texture type
combined with other
techniques.

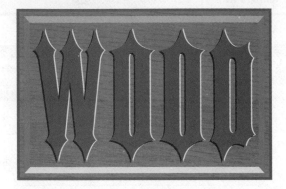

CorelDRAW! 4.0's Fractal Texture fills are a wonderful source of textures. The color plates in this book display all 44 of the textures in their default settings. Just try not to overdo it with the fractal fills, however, as your file sizes (and print times) can explode!

Exploring Backgrounds and Design Elements

As mentioned in the last section, bit-mapped textures add visual impact to the artwork you create with CorelDRAW! Many sources are available for bit-map images. You can use scanners to create images, or you can use paint programs like CorelPHOTO-PAINT! or Fractal Design Painter (and Sketcher) as well as high-end image retouching programs such as Adobe Photoshop, Aldus PhotoStyler, and Image-In-Color. You will find a number of Photo-Paint textures on the 3.0 CD-ROM disk. You also can find bit-map images in the public domain and from a variety of clip-art companies.

Using TIFF/PCX/BMP/GIF/TGA Textures

Some of the more popular textures are organics, such as marble, granite, and wood. A local tile or flooring store is an excellent source for marble patterns. Ask if you can borrow a few tiles to scan. When you return the tiles, bring your finished artwork with you. Although the store owners might be skeptical at first, you might end up with a new account after they see what you can do!

Non-organic textures, like drybrush (see fig. 9.31) or splattered paint (see fig. 9.32), also are quite popular. The drybrush and splattered paint techniques that have been all the rage in recent years have their popular base in custom car paint jobs and their inspiration in the work of Jackson Pollock. Although CorelDRAW! does not enable you to create drybrush or splattered effects from directly within the program, you easily can import TIFF or PCX scans of conventional artwork. After the TIFF or PCX image has been imported into Draw, you have the full range of color and tints. In the process of colorizing black-and-white (1 bit) line art, the fill color affects the (white) background, while the outline color affects the (black) foreground.

Crumpled paper is an interesting background that can be created quickly with a grayscale scanner. After being brought into CorelDRAW! as a TIFF, PCX, or BMP grayscale bit map, crumpled paper can be assigned a fill of any color or tint you want, becoming an intriguing design element (see fig. 9.33). An even slicker trick is to set a piece of type, print it on laser paper, crumple the print, and scan.

Figure 9.31:
A drybrush accent.

Figure 9.32:

A splattered
background with
punk type.

Figure 9.33:

The crumpled paper
effect.

The grid is one of the most overused graphics gimmicks in design. Nonetheless, you easily can create perspective grids with CorelDRAW!'s Perspective effect (see fig. 9.34). And when properly used with a tasteful fountain fill, the results can be so handsome as to make one forget that it has been done before (a zillion times).

True innovation is hard to come by. In many cases, tried and true not only gets the job done, but leaves the client feeling comfortable with what you have designed. Like all the other design effects reviewed in this chapter, the grid is an iteration of what other artists have repeatedly created.

Do not be afraid to innovate. But don't kill yourself for a client who does not appreciate, expect, or truly want innovative work; it can be too frustrating to attempt to convince someone who has no artistic appreciation. Do not waste their time or yours; if they expect formula, give it to them.

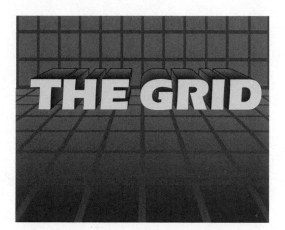

Figure 9.34:
The grid effect.

Summary

In this chapter, you have learned the basics behind a gamut of special effects, from the ubiquitous drop shadow through neon and punk type. Through it all you should come away with the realization that beauty takes time (and work).

CorelDRAW! has many built-in effects, such as Extrude and Blend. These magical implements can work wonders when used properly. But when an effect is used as an effect, without thought and overall design concept, you run the risk of losing focus. You easily can be caught up in the mechanics and technique (and fun) of creating a piece of electronic artwork and forget the real purpose of what you are doing.

Design should come first, not the computer. If you lose sight of your overall design concept, your finished product suffers. Use Draw's design power to your advantage. Do not let the constraints of the computer control your design.

You have a new set of brushes in your hands and a fresh canvas. Each time you approach a blank screen, you are faced with the same question that has faced artists since the beginning of time: how do I convey the message?

Part Three

Past Your Own PC

10

The Windows DTP Arsenal

he competition for graphics design work has never been tougher. More and more designers are going electronic—most of them arming themselves with the obligatory Macintosh. You have seen the TV commercials. You have read the magazine advertisements. You have heard the hype: you want to go DTP, you have to go Mac. Well, it just is not true. Not any more.

The information in the following pages should help to round out your perception of Draw's place in the DTP arsenal. This chapter touches on the subject of Windows (with more coverage in Appendix A). It also reviews the various export file formats, delves into fonts, and covers various programs and utilities. The chapter also includes a list of publications to help you obtain further information about the publishing field. Mosaic, Corel's visual file manager, is covered at the end of the chapter.

This chapter is dedicated to those professionals who have decided on the PC platform for their desktop publishing work. It presents resources that can be instrumental in helping you achieve success. Professionals must keep abreast of the ever-changing industry.

Graphic arts veterans can attest to the fact that systems go in and out with the seasons. The current crop of DTPers who feel a blind allegiance to any platform had better open their eyes.

When the next greatest system rolls along, well-heeled and far-sighted designers will jump from both ships. The rest will soon follow. While the Macintosh camp is presently entrenched and the PC troops are strengthening their position, you should watch for stray bullets.

Traditionally, the Macintosh has ruled the DTP market. In fact, it made the market. But it now runs the risk of losing the market. Prior versions of Windows have held back the PC, but with Windows 3.0, Microsoft had almost made amends. The latest incarnation of Windows, version 3.1, is faster and more stable and has incorporated TrueType. Although Macintosh still has the edge in many designers' eyes, the gap is narrower than it was. All the major graphics arts applications—XPress, Photoshop, Illustrator, and FreeHand—have finally been ported to Windows.

PC-based DTPers have a few distinct advantages over their Macintosh-based brethren. Their hardware choices are greater. They are not tied to the Apple mothership for systems. They can buy PCs at competitive prices from countless manufacturers, thus lowering overhead. Even the most staunch Mac user accepts the fact that a comparably equipped PC costs far less than a Macintosh.

PC-based DTPers are compatible with more computers. Far more PCs are installed than are Macs. This compatibility makes it easier to share files, not tears. Since the introduction of Apple's Super Drive, however, Macs have become far more compatible. They can easily read from and write to PC disks. Score one for Apple—it's not so easy to read a Mac disk on a PC.

Finally, do not forget: you have CorelDRAW!. And while there have been rumblings of a Mac version of Draw, as of this writing it has all been vaporware.

Taking Charge

As the year 2000 approaches, graphics communications are playing an increasingly important role in society. Once upon a time, people outside the publishing field knew little about type and design; the savvy businessperson of today, however, looks at the subject with a discerning eye.

Concurrently, society has begun to demand instant gratification. Witness the success of fax machines and overnight delivery services. These devices are not new developments, both having been used by the publishing industry for years. Today's business world, in fact, accepts these privileges as undeniable realities.

In addition to bringing design to the forefront and paving the field for faxes and overnight mail, newspapers and magazines were some of the first heavy-duty computer terminal users. For the industry, timeliness is everything. Business has borrowed heavily from the experiences of professional publishers.

In today's world, demanding businesspeople have begun to expect overnight design magic as well. You can probably blame this partially on those infamous computer commercials stating, "My department can do it." Although the computer has brought wonderful innovation to people's lives, it also has wrought havoc. People expect more from the designer, and they expect it faster. The aim of electronic artists is to stay competitive.

You are going into battle. Arm yourself. You need to become as cunning and shrewd as your competitors. You have to know what is out there and what works. You must form a strategy, yet be able to roll with the tide. Plenty of resources are available—it is up to you to use them.

Working with Windows

Because CorelDRAW! is a Windows-based program, it makes sense to outfit your software library with other Windows-based programs. In other words, to achieve the full potential of the environment, equip your computer with the proper software.

Just what docs that mean? Primarily, if you need a certain program to perform a particular function, you should choose a Windows-based program over a DOS- or other operating-system–based alternative.

Rebooting your computer to change from program to program is not fun and is an incredible strain on productivity. Although Windows 3.1 is far more forgiving and offers more alternatives than its earlier versions, it asks more from the machine it runs on. Previous generations of PC programs have been coded to run on the lowly 8088 processor. Windows programs are drawing the line between the power machine haves and have-nots.

Buying the Right Hardware

Windows eats up memory, both on the hard disk and in RAM. The first edition of this book (covering CorelDRAW! 1.2 and published in 1990) was written and illustrated on a 10MHz 80286 computer equipped with only a 20M hard disk and 2M of RAM. That machine wouldn't get you very far today. By comparison, Windows 3.1 must run on a more powerful computer equipped with a larger, faster hard disk and loads of RAM. Subsequent editions of this book were produced on a 33MHz 386 with 16M of RAM and a 124M IDE drive—barely a mid-level machine by today's standards. The current edition came to life on a number of machines, including a local bus 486/66 with 32M of RAM and a 245M hard disk (12 times the size of the disk in the original machine and still cramped!).

Historically, computers keep getting faster and cheaper. Prices drop as power rises—one of the lucky truths (at least for now) of the computer industry. Although prices for such commodities as memory chips tend to rise and fall due to market volatility, the general trend is toward more power for less money. The author's new machine costs no more (adjusting for inflation) than his old machine did just three years previously.

The best advice is to buy the fastest, most powerful computer you can afford. Do not take out a second mortgage to buy it, but do not scrimp on a few hundred bucks, either. The time you save is your own.

Buying the Right Software

Windows users naturally are prejudiced toward Windows software. Programs that share a common graphical user interface (GUI) (in this case, Windows) operate more intuitively and integrate with other programs that have been designed with the same interface. For example, why buy a word processing program that does not run in the Windows environment if you are already running Draw and, perhaps, PageMaker?

Although this is not the place to get into the Aldus PageMaker versus Quark Xpress versus Ventura Publisher argument, the marketplace tends to favor PageMaker. In this tumultuous industry, you constantly have to keep track of an ever-changing game. The ante is constantly being upped. More and more programs are being released in Windows-compatible format. As computers progress along the PC-GUI path, it is safe to say that Windows are becoming the norm.

Using Paint and Image Manipulation Programs

If you are reading this book, you probably already own one of the best object-oriented drawing packages available for the PC. You probably even use a page layout package or two. And even though Draw comes bundled with CorelPHOTO-PAINT!, you might want more firepower in the critical bit-mapped paint arena.

Adobe Photoshop

There can be no question that Adobe Photoshop is the de facto standard of professional-level image-manipulation programs. Adobe rolled out Photoshop for Windows in the spring of 1993 to great acclaim, assuring it of an increased foothold on the market. Photoshop features plug-in filters that enable users to employ third-party software that extends the program's capabilities.

Adobe also has allowed hardware developers to hook into the code, which has spawned a number of awesome video cards engineered to speed up specific Photoshop functions.

Adobe Systems, Inc.
1585 Charleston Road
P.O. Box 7900
Mountain View, CA 94039-7900
415/961-4400

Aldus PhotoStyler

If you have had the chance to use Adobe Photoshop on a Macintosh, you will find yourself right at home with Aldus PhotoStyler. Formerly marketed by U-Lead, PhotoStyler is one of the first high-end bit-map image-manipulation packages available for Windows. In the summer of 1991, Aldus acquired the rights to market PhotoStyler, and by fall had subsequently rebadged and repackaged the product.

PhotoStyler provides all the serious tools that you need to retouch, enhance, and compose full-color images on your PC. The program can read and write files in a number of formats, including BMP, GIF, PCX, TGA, and TIF. In addition, it can write files in EPS format. Scanners from Epson, Nikon, and Microtek are supported, along with most popular printers.

A number of built-in filters provide an array of smoothing, sharpening, and spatial effects. In addition, the program allows user-definable filters for ultra-custom work. The ubiquitous illustration tools—airbrush, paintbrush, pencil, and eraser—are included as well. This program, however, is designed for prepress work rather than image creation. PhotoStyler provides support for GCR (gray component replacement) and UCR (under color removal), essential tools for CMYK printing.

Aldus Corporation
411 First Avenue South
Seattle, WA 98104-2871
206/628-2320

Fractal Design Painter

Many PC-based artists have been frustrated by the lack of serious paint software for the Windows environment. This scarcity has been breached by an entry from a new software publishing firm formed by three veteran desktop software developers. Fractal Design Painter, from the Fractal Design Corporation, breaks new ground for Windows bit-map image creation. Its creators, Mark Zimmer, Tom Hedges, and Lee Lorenzen, are responsible for a few of the most powerful DTP programs available today. Zimmer and Hedges developed ImageStudio and ColorStudio; Lorenzen was a co-creator of Ventura Publisher.

Unlike Image-In-Color and Aldus PhotoStyler, Fractal Design Painter was developed as a tool for the fine artist rather than the prepress photo retoucher. Although the program can import images in a variety of file formats, you do not want to use it merely to remove dust and touch up scratches. Painter for Windows supports BMP, PCX, RIF, TGA, and TIF formats and is compatible with the Wacom tablets' pressure-sensitive pen.

When coupled with a Wacom tablet, Painter provides an environment so realistic that your nose might begin to twitch from the pastel dust, and your eyes might water from the turpentine. Painter's toolbox includes chalk, charcoal, crayons, felt-tip markers, and other amazingly true-to-life implements. The program even has settings that enable artists to paint in the brushstrokes of Van Gogh and Seurat! The canvas also is changeable, giving artists the freedom to alter the tooth of the work surface.

You would have difficulty finding a forgotten tool. Image cloning is supported with a twist; cloned images can be rendered in a variety of media, turning a photographic image into something far more organic. Painter includes electronic tracing paper and friskets to protect the original copy.

Painter, like other high-end programs, is demanding of the PC it runs on. It requires a 386 or 486 computer equipped with 6M of RAM, a suitably large hard disk, a high-resolution monitor, and a video card. Fractal calls for Super VGA/256 colors as a minimum. You will be happier with 32,768 colors or 24-bit color. This is one powerful program, and you need to load it on the most powerful machine you can muster. Fractal also offers a powerful black-and-white image editing program called Sketcher that does not require as much computer power.

Fractal Design Corporation
101 Madeline Drive, Suite 204
Aptos, CA 95003
408/688-8800

Image-In-Color Professional

Minnesota-based Image-In Incorporated has one of the hottest little programs on the PC publishing scene today. Positioned to go head-to-head with Adobe Photoshop and Aldus PhotoStyler, Image-In-Color Professional is fighting a David-against-Goliath battle for the PC-image retouching crown. Image-In-Color was the first Windows program to support the Wacom pressure-sensitive tablet.

With color separation controls developed in cooperation with AGFA Compugraphic, such as GCR, UCR, press gain compensation, and three color-absorption settings, Image-In is going after the serious prepress crowd. Color trade shops that have grudgingly accepted that the Mac is here to stay are in for a surprise. PC workstations are a whole lot more affordable!

Targeted at the high-end professional market, the program supports BMP, EPS, IMG, PICT, PCX, TGA, and TIF (including 6.0) formats, and can directly load Kodak Photo CD images. Color correction controls enable savvy users to create customized printer tone curves. A full range of more than 20 photographic filters is standard issue, as is the capability to create user-definable custom filters. The Wacom tablet's pressure-sensitive input is well-implemented in the program's painting tools, metering the flow of paint or density of a brushstroke.

Color scanners supported include Epson, Marstek, Microtek, Nikon, Nisca, Ricoh, Sharp, Howtek, and Umax. Options include an OCR package, Image-In Read, along with an autotracing package, Image-In Vect.

Image-In Incorporated
406 East 79th Street
Minneapolis, MN 55420
612/888-3633
800/345-3540

Using Other Drawing Programs

You might have asked yourself if there is any reason to use a
drawing program other than CorelDRAW!. There might be. For
the most part, Draw does a fine job, but it does fall short in a
number of places. The program's three chief competitors are
Adobe Illustrator 4.0, Aldus FreeHand 3.1, and Micrografx
Designer 3.1. Rather than a feature-by-feature comparison,
what follows are the strong points of those programs.

Adobe Illustrator 4.0

The latest incarnation of Illustrator more than makes up for the
dismal debut of the first version of the program. A number of
features are worth mentioning. The most convenient of these
features is that you can open multiple files (or versions of a file) at
one time. Just as important, masking is fully supported, and the
charting tool is built into the program—it is not called as a separate module.

As you might expect, Illustrator possesses the utmost level of
typographical refinement (to a thousandth of an em). The program allows an infinite number of characters in a text block. You
can automatically wrap text around objects and link text blocks.
Illustrator 4.0 lets you define leading in true points, and allows for
hanging punctuation. Text can be entered and edited directly on a
path.

Adobe Illustrator allows for more color selection choices. In addition to PANTONE spot, PANTONE process, and TRUMATCH,
you also can specify color with either the FOCALTONE or TOYO
color models. Adobe Separator offers a wealth of choices when

it comes time to actually generate color separations, and the program also supports monitor color calibration. The program is rock-solid, precise, and stable. Illustrator's Type 1 screen redraws are far faster than Draw's, and the output is reliable.

Adobe Systems Inc.
1585 Charleston Road
P.O. Box 7900
Mountain View, CA 94039-7900
415/961-4400

Aldus FreeHand 3.1

Developed by Altsys—the folks who brought you Fontographer—Aldus FreeHand 3.1 provides a number of amenities. As with WinIllustrator, FreeHand offers support for color calibration and enables you to paste objects inside other objects. Unlike Illustrator, however, FreeHand enables you to assign a default spread size. You can think of this feature as an autotrapping mechanism, although it is not the ultimate solution.

One of FreeHand's most notable features is the program's support for pressure-sensitive drawing tablets. FreeHand was the first vector-based Windows drawing program to use pressure-sensitivity, and the implementation is quite impressive. When you use the pressure tool, the harder you press, the fatter your drawn object becomes.

Aldus Corporation
411 First Avenue South
Seattle, WA 98104-2871
206/628-2320

Micrografx Designer 3.1

Prior to the arrival of CorelDRAW!, Micrografx Designer was the PC drawing program champ. Recent years have not been kind to the program's market share, but many of Designer's features still are enviable. Color is but one of them. Like Illustrator and FreeHand, Micrografx Designer supports color calibration. The program also has an autospread feature similar to FreeHand's; unfortunately, it does not support object-by-object overprinting.

Micrografx is legendary for its Windows printer drivers; the latest version of Designer continues that fine tradition. The program supports a huge 128×128-inch image area, and the company offers 24-hour support.

> Micrografx, Inc.
> 1303 Arapaho
> Richardson, TX
> 800/733-3729

Importing and Exporting Vector Files

As you have seen in past chapters, Draw imports and exports a wide variety of graphic file formats, be they vector or bit-map. Of the two, vector is usually preferable, if only for the fact that the subsequent images scale smoothly. Bit-map formats are covered in Chapter 7.

You have already learned how to import and export files in earlier chapters. Now turn your attention to some of the more interesting things that happen when you export vector files to other programs.

Draw is capable of exporting files in a plethora of file formats that meet almost every need. Regardless of the final destination for the graphic involved, you need not go without for want of the proper format.

AI/EPS

The most desirable export file formats are Adobe Illustrator (AI) and Encapsulated PostScript (EPS). These two provide the most information possible about an image.

Interestingly, Draw cannot reliably import (and subsequently edit) the files it exports as EPS files. This glitch makes it crucial to save all files in CDR format before exporting. By always saving your files as CDRs, you keep the door open for future revisions to your artwork.

CorelDRAW! 4.0 added an EPS Thumbnail import filter that allows it to place any EPS file into a CDR file. Placing is different from importing, however, in that the placed EPS thumbnails are not editable—they are only placeholders (represented by the EPS header). This works in a similar manner to the way Draw handles importing bit-map files such as TIFF, PCX, or BMP. Like imported bit maps, EPS files (imported as EPS thumbnails) are contained in the resulting CDR file. Furthermore, EPS Thumbnails are scalable and croppable, but are not editable.

Draw cannot import files that it has exported as EPS, because its EPS import filter only recognizes the Adobe Illustrator standard formats. Draw's EPS export filter includes more file information than the AI standards. Hence, the file contains too much information for the import filter to read. Part (or even all) of a file might appear, but the EPS import filter does not reliably import any but the Adobe Illustrator 1.1, 88, or 3.0 standards.

Of course, you always can export the file in AI format. CorelDRAW! enables you to export AI files in your choice of AI 1.1, 88, or version 3.0 file formats. A file exported from Draw in AI format can be reimported. In the next exercise, you can do just that.

Take the Monarch butterfly you created in Chapter 8 and export it as both an AI and an EPS file. Then, you try to import both (only the AI file imports), and save the imported version as a new CDR file.

What does all of this teach you? For starters, you see that the CDR format is far more compact than either the AI or EPS formats. You also learn that an imported AI file, originally created from a CDR file, yields a far larger file the second time it is saved.

Exporting and Importing AI/EPS Files

The last version you saved (without any scenery) was BUT9.CDR. If your most recent version is named differently, substitute your file name.

Click on **F**ile	The File menu appears
Click on **O**pen	The Open Drawing dialog box appears
Click on BUT9.CDR	
Click on **O**pen	BUT9 opens

Now you are going to export the file, first in EPS format and then in AI format. As you export, Draw assigns the appropriate file extension. It might look as if you are exporting to the same file, but you are not. The program takes care of that for you.

Exporting the File

First, export the file in EPS format:

Click on **F**ile	The File menu appears
Click on **E**xport	The Export dialog box appears
Click on Encapsulated PostScript, *.EPS	
Click on OK	The Export EPS dialog box appears
Click on OK	The file is exported as EPS
Now export the file in AI 3.0 format:	
Click on **F**ile	The File menu appears
Click on **E**xport	The Export Drawing dialog box appears
Click on Illustrator, *.AI, *.EPS	
Click on OK	The Export AI dialog box appears
Click on Adobe Illustrator V**3**.0	
Click on OK	The file is exported as AI

Image Headers

The Header Resolution option in the Export dialog box gives you a TIFF file embedded in the EPS file. The TIFF file provides a screen preview for the image when it is imported into a document prepared with another program, such as PageMaker, Ventura, or Xpress. The EPS Export filter allows you to choose between a Header Resolution of 0, 30, 75, and 300 dots per inch (DPI). In the exercise, you use the default resolution of 75 dpi, which provides an adequate screen representation. If you want the smallest EPS file possible, and don't need a screen preview, you can use the 0 DPI setting. On the other extreme, if you want the most precise screen preview possible, you can go with a 300-dpi header. The downside of a 300-dpi image header is a considerably larger EPS file size.

More importantly, high-resolution image headers can choke the program into which you are importing the EPS file. Your system might lock up, and you might need to reboot. For this reason, try to stick with lower-resolution headers. The EPS file is smaller, with the imported file displaying as a bounding box.

Fountain Steps

The Export EPS dialog box allows you to specify the number of Fountain Steps in your EPS files, from a minimum of 2 steps up to a maximum of 256 steps. The settings you use here depend on the screen frequencies and resolution of your output device. Chapter 11, "Printing Considerations," contains more information on setting fountain steps to avoid banding.

Text as Text or Text as Curves?

You might have noticed that the AI export filter asked the way you wanted to export text into the AI file. Although you did not have any text in the file, you still need to answer the question. Use Text as Text only if the fonts used in the file will be resident at the printer; otherwise, the printer substitutes the Courier font. The AI filter does something interesting to text with special character attributes—it breaks those characters into separate text objects.

The same is true for text on a path. Exporting text as curves can get around this by converting the text outlines to objects. However, the resulting object-text can be unacceptable; aberrations might crop up that, at best, affect the subtleties of type.

Now that you have exported to both EPS and AI formats, you see that it is currently impossible to import an EPS file that was exported from Draw. Clear up the screen by opening a new file.

Trying To Reimport a File

Click on **F**ile	The File menu appears
Click on **N**ew	A new file opens
Click on **F**ile	The File menu appears
Click on **I**mport	The Import Drawing dialog box appears

Click on Illustrator 1.1, 88, 3.0, *.AI, *.EPS

Click on BUT9.EPS

Click on OK

Draw attempts to open the file, but it might not be successful.

The file might not import successfully. In experiments with early beta versions of CorelDRAW! 4.0, the program imported the butterfly, but the illustration became slightly mangled in the process. You might meet with varying degrees of success.

Now that you have seen Draw's difficulty reimporting files that it has exported as EPS, try to bring in an AI file. You should meet with success this time.

Importing an AI File

Click on **F**ile	The File menu appears
Click on **N**ew	A new file opens
Click on **F**ile	The File menu appears
Click on **I**mport	The Import Drawing dialog box appears

continued

Click on Illustrator 88, 3.0, *.AI, *.EPS
Click on BUT9.AI
Click on OK

Notice how long it takes to import the file. Watch how the individual objects pop in one at a time, as opposed to the turbo-charged CDR file, which literally pours in. The AI format throws away all that valuable combining information. In addition, note that simple objects have been broken into smaller, segmented objects.

Now that the file has been reimported into Draw, resave it as a CDR file. Be careful not to overwrite the original file. You will name this file BUT9ASAI, to denote the Adobe Illustrator format.

Resaving the File as a CDR File

Click on <u>F</u>ile	The File menu appears
Click on Save <u>A</u>s	The Save Drawing dialog box appears
At File <u>N</u>ame, *type* **BUT9ASAI**	
At <u>I</u>mage Header, *click on* 1K (mono)	
Click on OK	The file is saved

Now, go out to the File Manager and take a look at the various sizes of the files you just created. You will be in for a surprise! As you can see, the original CDR file is quite compact at about 28K. The first EPS file jumped up to 80K. When exported through the CorelDRAW! 4.0 Adobe Illustrator export filter, the AI file grew to 102K, almost four times the size of the original.

The real revelation here is the size of the AI file that was imported and saved in CDR format. That file crept up to 114K. After this exercise, the advantages of storing files in the CDR format should be quite apparent. Unfortunately, none of the page layout programs support the CDR format.

AI/EPS Export Caveats

A few more things need to be mentioned (or reiterated) on the subject of AI/EPS file export before moving on to the other file formats. The first of these has to do with the computer bombing during file export. Over time, you might find that your computer will go out to lunch in the middle of file export. If so, the file you are exporting might be too complex. Always save the CDR file before you export it. You might need to go back into the CDR file to simplify things. If possible, pare down objects that contain a lot of nodes, and avoid combining large numbers of objects, especially if they are complex.

If you are having trouble accurately placing your EPS files into other programs (such as PageMaker), here's a little trick. Before you export your artwork, draw a rectangle (in the exact dimensions of the space you are importing the file into) around it, give the rectangle an outline and fill of none, and export the file. When you go to place the file, the bounding box should make placement an exact science. Just be sure to correctly position the artwork within the box *before* you export it. Doing so makes it easy to use the lowest resolution screen preview.

Export text as text when possible. This step ensures compact file sizes, and hopefully reduces the amount of time you spend waiting for (and possibly rebooting) your computer.

CorelDRAW! version 4.0 initially shipped with an EPS export filter that created files that could not be imported into Aldus PageMaker or Quark Xpress. This problem had to do with an oversight regarding the TIFF image header. A fix is available from Corel's CompuServe forum, however. The file name in the Corel Forum Library is EPSFIX.COM. This self-extracting file archive contains a new EXPEPS.DLL file.

Computer Graphics Metafile (CGM)

The CGM format has a compact, object-oriented structure. Unfortunately, the format uses no Bézier curves—only straight lines—to form images. This drawback can cause jaggies to occur when scaling up an image or when printing on a high-resolution output device. For some software packages, CGM might be the only choice. If so, you will have to use it.

One such example is earlier versions of Harvard Graphics. Although the program was extremely popular, it was notoriously hostile when it came to importing art. Harvard had the capability to convert only CGM files to its own format. To make matters worse, the conversion program does not like complex CGM files!

However, a shareware program written by Bob Cranford and known as LCD promises to simplify and fix CGM files so the Harvard conversion program can understand them. You can find it in CompuServe's IBMAPP forum, Library 10, under LCD.ZIP.

Newer versions of Harvard (3.0 and WinHarvard) have improved import filters, so you might want to use a more appropriate export filter. If you must use CGM, you should be aware that it does not support bit maps or PostScript texture fills. And if your file contains fountain fills, you can play with the banding by changing the Preview Fountain Stripes setting.

AutoCAD (DXF)

Engineers, draftsmen, and architects will be glad to know that Draw is capable of exporting to the DXF format. Although the export filter does pose severe limits, the results can be worth the effort.

The DXF export filter supports object outlines only. All fills, whether solid, texture, or fountain, are discarded, as are bit maps. In default mode, all Draw-exported text is converted to curves, which means it cannot be edited as text in the DXF file. You can export text as text by changing the ExportTextAsCurves setting to 0 (in the CORELDRW.INI file). Dashed lines and calligraphic pens are converted to 0.003" solid lines. Curves become polyline segments. Finally, you have your choice of converting your colors to either AutoCAD's standard 7 or full 255 color set.

Scan Conversion Object Description Language (SCODL)

SCODL is widely used in 35mm slide making. Chapter 11 touches on a bit of slide making. You might want to flip ahead a few pages for more information.

GEM

The compact, vector-based GEM format is an excellent choice for exporting to Ventura documents. You must take certain limitations into consideration, however. The first of these is a 128 nodes-per-object limit. Objects with more than 128 nodes are broken into strips and grouped, so remember to limit the number of nodes per object.

Another limitation of the GEM format has to do with color support. GEM is limited to only 16 colors; Draw has over 16 million. This presents more than a slight problem, especially with fountain fills. Draw attempts to get around this by dithering the color. If you are planning to export color files in GEM format, be prepared to go back to the original Draw file once or twice to get the colors in synch.

The GEM format does not support bit maps, whether they are scans or pattern fills. If your Draw file contains bit maps, you need to trace them or rethink the artwork. Dashed lines are nixed, as are PostScript texture fills (which become rather boring gray fills).

IBM PIF (GDF)

If you want to upload graphics into an IBM mainframe computer, you probably need the PIF/GDF export filter. This filter supports many of CorelDRAW!'s features, but, again, be aware of a few notable exceptions.

Because PIF is limited to a 16-color palette, stick to this restricted palette when designing your artwork. PostScript textures, pattern fills, and bit maps are not supported. Fountain fills now work, but results can be disappointing.

Windows Metafile (WMF)

Windows Metafile files can be thorny critters for page layout programs to import. These files impose a number of restrictions, such as no PostScript textures or halftones, no bit maps, and no patterns. Avoid these files if you can.

If Windows Metafiles still sound like a good idea, one more (big) caveat might change your mind. If you import WMF files into PageMaker and subsequently attempt to image those PM files on a Lino by using a Mac, you will be disappointed. The WMFs won't make the translation from the PC to the Mac. You'll be left with a bunch of bounding boxes and a bill from your service bureau. This problem has been somewhat resolved with PageMaker 5.0— the new version can convert WMF to PICT files on the Mac.

WordPerfect Graphic (WPG)

WordPerfect, one of the most popular word processing programs available today, boasts its own graphic format, WPG. You can use this format when exporting files to WordPerfect (5.0 and later) documents that will not be printed on a PostScript output device. Use the EPS export, however, if you plan to print the document on a PostScript printer.

The WPG format has its limitations. For starters, fountain fills are extremely crude, and PostScript textures and halftone screens are no go (for obvious reasons). In addition, bit maps are not supported, and Corel recommends that you convert all text to curves.

Draw's WPG export filter enables you to export either 16 or 256 colors. Although 256 colors might sound great, the results are subject to WordPerfect's screen and printer drivers. Stick to 16 colors for more reliable results.

Finally, image rotation should be done in Draw prior to exporting the file. Images rotated in WordPerfect might not print properly. Make sure the drawing looks right before you export it.

Searching for DTP Information

To get what you need to stay abreast of the DTP field, you must know where to look. The fact that you are reading this book shows that you have a thirst for knowledge and an appetite for information. The stronger that craving is, the more successful you will be.

The design revolution that has taken place since the advent of the Apple Macintosh, Adobe PostScript, and Aldus PageMaker is staggering. The immediacy of desktop publishing is now available to far more designers at increasingly affordable prices. Programs and computers have become more powerful than previously thought possible. And the trend shows no sign of subsiding.

The huge retail industry that has sprung up around the personal computer market is, to a large extent, mail order-based and service-oriented. You do not need to drive out to the store and lose a few hours of valuable time. Just pick up the phone, dial a toll-free number, place an order for whatever you could possibly need, and receive it the next day in the overnight mail.

Your job is to find resources and make contacts. Discover which programs and outlets are reliable, and support them. To that end, this section presents a selection of interesting products and firms that can make a difference in your day-to-day operations.

Clip-Art Connection: Clip Art by Modem

For those of you who do not have the resources—whether talent or time—to create art in a pinch, Clip-Art Connection from Connect Software (a division of Adonis Corporation) offers an exciting and innovative service: on-line clip art. Just boot up Clip-Art Connection and search for a graphic by category or by publisher.

After you find the correct image, use the built-in communications capabilities to access the on-line electronic clip-art database and download the art you need. The service runs 24 hours a day.

Clip-Art Connection enables users to preview the clip-art files by providing thumbnail images. The thumbnails are small, mono-chrome bit maps for preview purposes only. Adonis states that there are over 29,000 thumbnails in its library from 17 top ven-dors. By keeping thumbnails on the user's local PC, communica-tions charges are kept to a minimum. You do not need to buy complete clip-art collections just to get a single piece of art; per-piece rates can run on the high side, however. Adonis claims that the price usually ranges from about $1 to $25, although you can save money by not paying for any extra images that you will not use.

Although most subscribers to the service download and purchase individual files, you can also purchase complete collections. Although the complete collections are not downloadable—telephone costs and time factors make it prohibitive—Connect Software promises 48-hour shipping and competitive pricing.

Vendors include T/Maker, 3G Graphics, Studio Advertising Art, Metro Creative Graphics, ArtRight, Micrografx, ArtBeats, DreamMaker, MicroMaps, and others. Payment is billed through most popular credit cards.

Connect Software
A Division of Adonis Corporation
6742 185th Ave NE, Suite 150
Redmond, WA 98052
800/234-9497

Using Shareware

The personal computer shareware community is an oddity in today's society. Where else can you find people willing to give you their products without making you pay for them up-front?

Shareware is software that is distributed free of charge, with a proviso: you try it, you like it, you buy it. If you do not like (or use) the program, you need not pay for it.

The entire premise is based on trust. The shareware developers trust that if you like the program, you will buy it. They have no marketing, distribution, or production costs to speak of other than the cost of living. The registration fees they ask are paltry in comparison to the utility of their programs.

This type of personal computer program can be a boon to the electronic artist on a budget. There are literally thousands of programs out there for the asking. You can find them on computer bulletin boards around the world.

The disk supplied with this book contains a collection of some of the best shareware programs for the Windows DTP professional. Remember that shareware is try-before-you-buy. If you find that one or more of these programs fills your needs, make sure that you pay the registration fee(s).

PKZIP

One of the most wonderful shareware utilities available, PKZIP compresses files for cost-effective telecomputing, archiving, and storage. If you transmit files by modem, PKZIP can save you big bucks in telephone costs and on-line charges. PKZIP is available on many bulletin boards, including its own. It is commonly distributed in a compressed, self-extracting EXE format. The program contains utilities for compressing, decompressing, password encryption, and more.

Table 10.1 shows the results of running tests on some typical files. The files that were compressed included a database file, a word processing file, a file in native CorelDRAW! format, and various exported (EPS, SDL, CGM) versions of the Draw file.

Table 10.1
Compressed File Sizes

Type of File	Original Size	PKZIPPED Size
CDR	2584	1273
EPS	18606	6098
CGM	48088	23816
SCD	48916	24684
Database	85504	32918
Word Processing	54423	17759

Depending on your modem speed, you can save the cost of registration in no time at all. PKZIP is a utility that no telecomputing electronic artist should be without!

PKZIP
PKWARE, Inc.
7545 N. Port Washington Rd.
Glendale, WI 53217-3422
414/352-3670
BBS: 414/352-7176
Fax: 414/352-3815

Code To Code

Bruce Robey, a type shop owner, programming professional, and university instructor based in Washington D.C., offers two excellent shareware resources for typesetters and desktop publishers. The first of these two, Code To Code, is a typesetter/DTP utility collection.

Using Code To Code, you can update typesetter/DTP files without the hassle of reading through strings of obscure codes. A coded file, while fine for a typesetter experienced in editing around lengthy, intricate codes, can cause headaches for an editor who only wants to make text changes.

Although the program is not intended to be used with Draw, it certainly has a place in the DTP arsenal. Hard-core Ventura users, as well as high-end typographers, will find Code To Code to be of great use for removing delimited codes. You also have the option of storing removed codes that can be stored in a separate file.

Code To Code is shareware and is available for an economical $29.00 registration fee. The latest version and printed documentation are available through registration directly from the author. Code To Code also is available on a free trial basis by downloading it as CTOC21.EXE from the CompuServe IBMAPP forum LIB 12. The program also is available through BIX, GENIE, and MAGNALINE, and from disk distributors across the country.

AlphaQuote

Bruce Robey's other offering, AlphaQuote, is a DOS-based typesetting and DTP estimating and copyfitting program. The program was originally sold as commercial software and has been used by thousands of typesetters world-wide. AlphaQuote has been completely rewritten and re-released as shareware.

If you bill for your work, you will find AlphaQuote indispensable for estimating and copyfitting books, magazines, and newsletters. The menu-driven format is practical and easy to use. AlphaQuote Version 3.0 is available for $29.00. Interested parties might call for a registered version or download the shareware version from CompuServe, IBMAPP LIB 12 as AQ30.EXE.

> Code To Code 3.0
> AlphaQuote 3.0
> Bruce Robey
> AlphaBytes, Inc.
> 111 Eighth St. S.E.
> Washington, D.C. 20003
> 202/546-4119
> CompuServe ID: 71131,2734

Cubit Meister

After you start using Cubit Meister, you will never misplace your proportional sizing wheel again! Cubit Meister is an on-screen idiot wheel that painlessly computes reduction or enlargement percentages. In addition to providing you with fast, accurate sizing information, this handy program converts from one system of measurement to another.

Version 1.03 (included on the disk that accompanies this book) features a new three-dimensional look and can float on top of other active applications. Developed by graphic designer and *Inside CorelDRAW!* coauthor John Shanley, Cubit Meister provides essential functions for the Windows DTP professional.

> Cubit Meister
> Phoenix Creative Graphics
> 5 Clyde Road, Suite 101
> Somerset, NJ 08873
> Comp-Serve ID: 76535,3443

FontSpec

Have you ever wanted to create a catalog of type specimen pages for your personal type library? FontSpec makes it easy! The program enables you to display TrueType or PostScript typefaces on screen or on a printed page. You can create fully customized specimen pages, complete with header and footer information. FontSpec prints in your choice of single-column, two-column, or full-sheet samples. This neat little program is a great addition to your DTP arsenal whether you are a small, one person shop or a big design studio.

> Font Spec
> UniTech Corporation
> 2697 McKelvey Road
> Maryland Heights, MO 63043
> 314/770-2770

SetDRAW

The INI file situation in CorelDRAW! version 4.0 can be a tough nut to crack. David Brickley created SetDRAW in order to tweak Draw's INI files without using Notepad (or other text editors). The program allows you to check or alter Draw's most pertinent settings in its five INI files (CORELDRW.INI, CORELAPP.INI, CORELPRN.INI, CORELFLT.INI, and CORELFNT.INI). And it does so with point-and-shoot ease! Not only is the utility simple to use, it is also very safety conscious—you can restore your INI original settings at any time. The program features help at every step, so there's often no need to refer to Corel's documentation.

SetDRAW is a very cool thing—the utility that Corel Corporation forgot to provide. For more information, see Appendix A, which covers fine-tuning your system.

> SET DRAW
> Shooting Brick Productions
> P.O. Box 549
> Moss Beach, CA 94038
> 415/728-0244

WinPSX

Downloading PostScript fonts to your PostScript printer can save valuable minutes at print time (see Chapter 11). Unfortunately, while the CorelDRAW! 4.0 CD-ROMs contain somewhere in the neighborhood of 750 fonts, a font downloader is nowhere to be found. WinPSX to the rescue! Costas Kitsos' Windows utility is a no-nonsense PostScript font downloader that deserves a place on your hard drive.

Many features make dealing with the Windows font situation a much more pleasant experience. By clicking on Show Font Name, for example, you can select fonts by their real names (rather than by those cryptic eight-character alphanumeric hieroglyphics that Bitstream is so fond of). The program also enables you to create job lists for batch downloading. WinPSX is freeware, but Costas asks that, "If you find WinPSX useful and enjoyable, please plant a tree." This one's worth a forest.

WinPSX
Costas Kitsos
P.O. Box 64943
Los Angeles, CA 90064
Comp-Serve ID: 73667,1755.

WinZip

WinZip brings the convenience of Windows to the use of ZIP, LZH, and ARC files. It features an intuitive point-and-click interface for viewing, running, extracting, adding, deleting, and testing files in archives. Optional virus scanning support is included.

The Windows 3.1 Drag-and-Drop Interface is fully supported. You can drag-and-drop files from WinZip to other applications. WinZip extracts the files before it drops them on the target application. The target application treat the files as if they had been dropped by the File Manager. You also can drop archives on WinZip to open them, or drop files on WinZip to add them to the open archive.

WinZip includes built-in unzipping. It requires PKZIP to create ZIP files, and LHA, ARJ, and/or ARC to access files LZH, ARJ, and ARC files, respectively. WinZip is ASP Shareware.

WinZip
Nico Mak
P.O. Box 919
Bristol, CT 06011-0919
Comp-Serve ID: 70056,241

The Association of Shareware Professionals

Just because a program is shareware does not necessarily mean that it comes as is and without software support. The Association of Shareware Professionals (ASP) was formed in 1987 to bolster the image and ensure the future of shareware as an ongoing alternative to conventional/commercial software.

ASP software developers must subscribe to a code of ethics and commit themselves to the concept of shareware. The association publishes a regularly updated catalog of programs, which includes file descriptions, locations, and registration fees. The ASP catalog is available in Library 8 of the CIS IBMJR forum, and must be extracted from ARC format using the shareware program ARC-E.COM.

Although the ASP does not review members' software for functionality or usefulness—its philosophy is to let the users try before they buy—the association does provide an ombudsman to deal with any post-registration disputes. However, the ombudsman cannot provide technical support for members' products.

Organizations such as the ASP have all of your best interests in mind. The concept of shareware is simple, elegant, and fragile. Electronic artists must lend their support if it is to survive.

> The Association of Shareware Professionals
> P.O. Box 5786
> Bellevue, WA 98006

Publications for Publishers

Information-hungry electronic artists have many avenues to pursue in their quest for knowledge. To stay on top of developments, it is important to have a variety of information resources. Many publications are available on the subject of graphic design, typography, and DTP.

Aldus Magazine

Okay, okay, so this is a house organ. But it is still worth mentioning. This slick four-color publication—sent free-of-charge to registered Aldus users—is a testament to what can be done at the high-end of desktop design. Although the first issues were a bit unpolished, *Aldus Magazine* has evolved into a fine publication.

The original and ambitious premise behind the bimonthly *Aldus Magazine* was to use a completely new design with each issue. These redesigns were potential nightmares for its designers, but tasty pickings for those of you who might be short on ideas. The magazine has since settled down to a consistent layout, but is still full of great design! Subscriptions are available for those folks who are not registered Aldus users.

Aldus Magazine
Aldus Corporation
411 First Avenue South
Seattle, WA 98104-2871
206/628-2321

Corellation

Corellation, the official magazine of the Association of Corel Artists & Designers (ACAD), is an independent publication produced by Draw-loving publishing professionals. Each issue is full of information that suits Draw artists of all levels. The magazine includes articles and how-tos for everyone from beginners through advanced users. The monthly magazine includes listings for training centers and service bureaus, along with product reviews and interviews.

Randy Tobin, *Corellation*'s editor/designer, does a fine job. The magazine is light and airy, making good use of editorial white space. Both design and content are of high caliber. This magazine is exceedingly well-printed for one of its type, making good use of spot varnishes and soy inks. Yearly subscriptions are bundled with a yearly membership in ACAD (a non-profit group).

Association of Corel Artists & Designers
1309 Riverside Drive
Burbank, CA 91506

Electronic Publishing (formerly TypeWorld)

TypeWorld, founded in 1977 and edited by the venerable (and opinionated) Frank Romano, is now known as *Electronic Publish-*

ing, "the first and only newspaper for electronic publishing." Recently purchased by the PennWell Publishing Company, *Electronic Publishing* is published twice a month. Though not for the low-end DTPer, the newspaper provides pages upon pages of product information for service bureaus and electronic publishers. Chances are, a product hits the pages of *Electronic Publishing* before it hits the streets.

The newspaper also includes a good-sized classified section that lists equipment for sale, from low-end desktop stuff through six-figure high-dollar systems.

> *Electronic Publishing* Editorial Offices
> One Stiles Road
> P.O. Box 170
> Salem, NH 03079
> 603/898-2822

U&lc

A true treasure, *U&lc* (which is proofreader's code for upper- and lowercase) bills itself as the international journal of type and graphic design. *U&lc* is a quarterly celebration of the typographer's craft. Within its large format, you are treated to design at its best, whether black and white, spot color, or process color. Each issue brings incredible spreads that beg the mind for thorough consideration. Typographic history is taught here, and it is taught quite well.

Published by the International Typeface Corporation and available for a nominal fee, *U&lc* is a resource that you should not be without.

> *U&lc*
> International Typeface Corporation
> 2 Hammarskjold Plaza
> New York, NY 10017
> 212/371-0699

Using CompuServe Information Service (CIS)

Have a question that needs to be answered, and cannot afford to spend the time or money to call Ottawa? Try CompuServe.

CompuServe is one of the most amazing resources in the computer world. It is a support network, offering you thousands of people who are ready to offer advice on whatever your computer problems might be.

Type up a note that covers the problem in your favorite word processor. Then save it as an ASCII file and upload it to either the Corel or DTP Forums. Within a day, sometimes even hours, you will get the answer you need without waiting on hold or spending big bucks on telephone calls.

The Desktop Publishing Forum

The Desktop Publishing Forum (DTPFORUM) is the place where savvy desktoppers hang out to trade advice, talk shop, and shmooze. DTPFORUM includes the message board, with its winding threads of questions, answers, and conversations on topics ranging from DTP issues to what is the best Canadian beer. In the libraries, you can find demo programs, fonts, clip-art samples, and more. Every Tuesday night at 9 p.m. Eastern time, the DTPFORUM sponsors an on-line conference where DTPers can visit and trade information. To acess this forum, type **GO DTPFORUM** at the CompuServe menu.

The Zenith Forum

The Zenith Forum (ZENITH FORUM) originally was created to support owners of Zenith Data Systems computers, most notably the Zenith portables. It has since grown to support portables in general, as well as Windows products. ZENITH FORUM is an excellent place to scour for shareware programs from graphics converters to Windows utilities.

For the convenience of forum members, an up-to-date catalog of library files is posted on the first of every month. It is always LIBSUM.EXE in the New Files Library (Library 1). This forum is especially sensitive to the needs of new CompuServe users and holds a beginners conference every Sunday night to give them live help. To get to the ZENITH FORUM, just type **GO ZENITH**.

The Corel Forum

In late spring, 1992, Corel opened their own CompuServe forum. Just type **GO COREL**, and you'll be whisked to one of the most interesting forums on CIS! Here, you can ask specific Draw-related questions and expect a prompt response from a number of folks well-versed in the programs intricacies. You can even upload problem files, connect-time-free, for Corel's on-line sleuths. In addition to the message board, the Corel Forum includes libraries that contain bug-fixes, various CDR sample files, and a number of utilities.

> CompuServe Incorporated
> 5000 Arlington Centre Blvd.
> Columbus, OH 43220

Fooling with Fonts

In the not-too-distant past, the idea of purchasing a typeface from one manufacturer, loading that typeface onto a machine from another manufacturer, manipulating the typeface with a program from a third manufacturer, and printing it on a printer from yet a fourth was a wildly speculative concept. Today, it is a hard and fast reality. The key component in this tricky equation is what is known as the page description language (PDL). As you might have already deduced, the PDL that has made it all possible is Adobe Systems' PostScript language.

The arrival of the PostScript language has opened doors that were once locked with proprietary keys. In days gone by, if you wanted a new typeface for your particular printer, you had to go straight to the source: the printer's manufacturer. Typefaces from company A did not run on typesetters from company B, and vice versa.

Today, thanks to PostScript, you can buy fonts everywhere—even as shareware and, as you will see, from a mail-order firm dedicated to selling just fonts. In addition, you have the flexibility to create your own fonts on the PC platform using Altsys Fontographer or a combination of CorelDRAW! and Ares FontMonger.

Where Are CorelDRAW!'s Fonts?

CorelDRAW! version 3.0 changed the way that Draw accesses fonts. Previous versions of the program relied upon the proprietary WFN font format and included a utility program, WFNBOSS, to convert fonts between formats. Draw 4.0 uses either TrueType, PostScript, or WFN fonts.

Accessing Draw's fonts can be a problem if you do not have a CD-ROM drive on your computer. Approximately 50 fonts are supplied in TrueType format from the installation disks. In addition, there are 750 or so TrueType fonts on the CD-ROM disks distributed with every copy of Draw 4.0. And all 750 of the PostScript fonts are supplied on the CD-ROM. The symbol fonts are in WFN format.

Although Windows has a limit of 1000 TrueType fonts, Draw has an internal limit of 900 (which can be a combination of TrueType, PostScript, and WFN formats). If you have more than 900 fonts, you will want to use Ares FontMinder to manage your fonts.

Ares FontMinder

Need a way to control a burgeoning array of fonts? Ares FontMinder tames the font-beast by organizing your fonts into easily installable (and de-installable) font packs. These font packs can contain any array of Type 1 and/or TrueType fonts. You can arrange your fonts according to clients, recurring jobs, or opera-tors. With an easy way to swap between font loads, your system will operate faster and with less overhead. The idea is to load only the fonts you need, rather than the whole collection.

FontMinder evolved from the successful shareware program, FontManager. Developer Dennis Harrington's pet project became so popular that it attracted the attention of Ares, and has now grown into a full-fledged commercial application worthy of any serious DTPer.

Ares FontMonger

Ares FontMonger is one of the most useful pieces of software that a Draw power-user can own. The program is designed to convert, enhance, modify, and even create typefaces, and is a perfect complement to Draw's ability to export TrueType or PostScript Type 1 typefaces. However, FontMonger's font conversions are far more advanced and include *font hinting*, which improves the appearance of laser-printed text.

FontMonger can convert fonts from a slew of PC font formats: Win 3.1 TrueType, PostScript Type 1 and 3, Intellifonts, Nimbus Q, Corel WFN, LaserMaster LXO; not to mention NeXT PostScript Type 1, as well as Mac TrueType, PostScript Type 1 and 3. These typefaces can be converted into: Win 3.1 TrueType, PC PostScript Type 1 and 3, Nimbus Q, NeXT PostScript Type 1, along with Mac TrueType, PostScript Type 1 and 3. That covers just about all the bases!

Converting fonts between formats is a sticky legal issue. The Ares documentation states that the creation of beautiful and practical typefaces is an art rather than a science, sometimes requiring years of work for the creation of a single typeface. Ares Software sup-ports existing copyrights and the efforts of those who designed them and supports the work of the companies who publish fonts. You should check the license agreement for your fonts before using FontMonger to convert or alter them. For more information, please contact the supplier of your fonts directly.

As important as format conversions, the program enables you to do some serious modifications to existing fonts. You can build special fractions, symbols, or custom small caps. You also can import CorelDRAW! artwork into a font, so that you can create a logofont for distribution throughout your company. The power inherent in FontMonger is disproportionate to its price.

Ares Software Corporation
P.O. Box 4667
Foster City, CA 94404-4667
415/578-9090

FontHaus

FontHaus was born in Norwalk, Connecticut, in 1990 out of a desire to fill the growing needs of graphic designers. The firm is dedicated to providing timely, exceptional service and advice to the designer in need of a specific typeface. The only things they sell are fonts and font-related software. With over 6000 fonts in stock and ready to ship, FontHaus is a boon to the artist with heavy deadlines to meet.

In addition to being service-oriented from a delivery point of view, FontHaus offers unequalled depth and typographic expertise. While larger computer mail-order firms might offer just the Adobe library of fonts, FontHaus is a one-stop source for fonts from all the major foundries, as well as many small foundries. They offer typefaces from Adobe, Agfa, ATF, Autologic, Berthold, Bitstream, Elsner+Flake, The Font Bureau, ITC, Lanston, Letraset, Linotype-Hell, Monotype, Panache, and Treacyfaces (just to name a few). To complement the depth of their wares, the people answering the phones know type—they are not just order-takers.

Dedicated to pushing the design envelope, FontHaus also actively seeks new and leading-edge type designs from today's most prominent designers, which they issue under the FontHaus label. These fonts are not available anywhere else, and include exciting new designs as well as revivals of classic typefaces. Each and every font sold by FontHaus (regardless of foundry) is fully licensed, thus protecting the rights of the original designer and foundry. All told, FontHaus is a class act, and a resource that no typographer worth her pica gauge should be without.

FontHaus Inc.
15 Perry Avenue
Norwalk, CT 06850
800/942-9110
203/846-3087
Fax: 203/849-8527

Adobe Type Manager

One of the biggest things to hit the PC DTP market in 1990 (right after the arrival of Windows 3.0 and CorelDRAW! versions 1.2 and 2.0, that is) had to be the introduction of the Windows PC version of Adobe Type Manager (ATM).

The program uses vector printer fonts to produce screen fonts, eliminating the jagged or stick-like characters everyone had resigned themselves to for years. ATM makes on-screen type look the way it should. And, as a boon to folks who do not have access to PostScript printers, it enables you to print PostScript fonts, as well!

The publishing world speaks PostScript. CorelDRAW! version 4.0's CD-ROM provides an instant library of over 750 PostScript Type 1 format fonts that you can use with any other Windows programs, such as PageMaker or Word for Windows. If you use Windows and you do not have ATM, what are you waiting for?

Using Mosaic: Corel's Visual File Manager

CorelDRAW! enables the electronic artist to amass volumes of work in a short period of time. This productivity is a mixed blessing. Although it is easy to create stunning artwork, the sheer number of files can soon pile into an unmanageable tangle of obscure files. CorelMOSAIC! (first introduced in version 2.0) helps you to cut through the confusion in a number of ways, and adds even more versatility to CorelDRAW!.

The first means of file management is the Visual File Selector. This icon-based feature provides an instantly recognizable vignette (a compact bit-map screen representation) of the artwork contained in a file. Whether stored in a library or as a stand-alone file, each image can be summoned through strictly visual association. The need for the user to remember specific file names is greatly diminished. Scroll through a directory in Mosaic, find the image you want, double-click—and CorelDRAW! opens with that file.

Mosaic was greatly enhanced in CorelDRAW 3.0, and it has been beefed-up again in version 4.0. It can display images in a wide variety of formats. In addition to CDR, you can view thumbnails of AI, BMP, CCH, DIB, EPS, GIF, PCC, PCX, SHW, TIF, TGA, and even Kodak Photo CD format files. So you easily can sort through your files, regardless of the format, before you import them into Draw. Displaying all those files, however, can take some time. Thankfully, Mosaic allows you to turn off the bit-map preview in its Preferences dialog box by clicking on Text Mode Display.

Mosaic enables you to compress and organize your files. Compressing files and storing them in libraries saves on disk space. You can organize the libraries to suit your working style through the Get Info dialog box.

Using Mosaic Libraries

Mosaic libraries store CorelDRAW! artwork files in a compact, orderly manner. The Library function uses a compression routine when compressing files and when expanding them back to usable form.

Working with existing library files is a straightforward affair. To open a file contained in a library, double-click on the file name, select a directory to place the expanded file into, and click on OK. Alternatively, you can select the file and choose Expand File from the Edit menu. If you want to expand a number of files at once (to CDR format) without actually opening them in Draw, shift-click on the files and then select Expand File(s) from the Edit menu.

Creating Mosaic libraries and adding to existing libraries is simple. To create a Library, click on Edit, then click on New Catalog/Library. To add files to a library, select a number of CDR files, click on Edit, and click on Insert File(s). Unlike earlier versions, you must first create a library before you can add files to it.

Organizing and Annotating Your Files

In addition to compressed Libraries, Mosaic also allows you to create catalogs. Unlike libraries, however, catalogs are only fancy lists that enable you to visually group files together without compressing or moving them from directory to directory.

The Get Info (File Information) dialog box that you access through Mosaic's Edit menu enables you to add information to file listings in two powerful ways. The first involves *keywords*, which you can use to perform word or subject searches. By entering a number of descriptive words (separated by commas or plus signs) in the Keyword field of the Get Info dialog box, you can build a database of artwork that you can easily search by categories.

The second field in the Get Info dialog box is Notes. This field can include a variety of information relevant to a file, such as a color summary or other description, client information, and so on. Because Keywords and Notes are Windows text fields, you can cut and paste information into them from other Windows applications. The file information dialog box also lists a host of other important file information, such as date, time, and size. The most useful information, however, is a listing of font usage—checking this field before opening a file will save you plenty of time.

Gang Printing with Mosaic

Do you need laser copies of a number of Draw files? In Mosaic, Shift- or Ctrl-click on the required files, then click on Print Files. This step saves you the time and hassle of opening files one at a time and sending each to the printer. You set up the printer dialog box for the first image, and the rest of the pages print unattended.

Mosaic even enables you to extract and merge text from a number of selected files. For many people, this function can seem a bit obscure. But this can be a powerful tool for database-publishing everything from certificates to business forms.

Mosaic Thumbnails

One of the handiest things that you can do in CorelMOSAIC! is to print thumbnail representations of your files. This feature can be a great time saver and a boon to the production-minded. Mosaic's Page Setup dialog box enables you to title pages and images in your choice of typeface and justification. You can vary the size of your thumbnails—both on screen and on the printed page—by changing the thumbnail width using the Mosaic Preferences dialog box. These features came in really handy during the production of this book!

Printing thumbnails can be rather time- and memory-intensive. If practical, it is best to print large numbers of thumbnails at a time when your computer and printer are idle, such as during lunch or after working hours.

Summary

CorelDRAW! is but one of many weapons you can use in your electronic graphic arts arsenal. Thankfully, it does a tremendous job of integrating with many different packages. The trick is to know which packages to use and what to buy. The only way to do so is to stay current with the steady stream of information in this industry. You accomplish this feat not by keeping your ear to the ground, but by keeping your nose in the trades.

The resources presented in this chapter are a starting point. To be successful, you must be informed. The ultimate business weapon is knowledge. It is up to you to go out and get it.

Printing Considerations

aving a pretty picture on the screen is one thing, but getting it printed is quite another. This book has stressed the concept of working drawings. The ultimate goal is to assemble an image that can be reproduced in a timely fashion. To that end, this chapter covers the issues of working with Draw in a production environment. With all the power of Corel DRAW! 4.0 comes the dubious ability to easily create images too complex for just about any printer to output.

In the Monarch butterfly exercise in Chapter 8, you constructed a process color image that is a compact, streamlined file. Well-constructed images are the key to cost-effective printing. Not only do they image faster on the computer, they also should image faster on the output device, saving on "per-minute" charges.

Spot color images also should be carefully constructed. *Trapping*—the almost imperceptible overlap of different colors—is extremely important for many printing techniques, from screen printing T-shirts through fine art lithography. As you will see later in this chapter, you can set up traps with Draw, but only if the image has been put together with this in mind. While some artists may consider the extra work involved hardly worth the effort, others will welcome the ability to provide chokes and spreads.

This chapter focuses on getting your Draw files to the printer—not just the printer on the desk next to you, but also to the guy down the street who ultimately will print umpteen copies. Start out by taking a look at how Draw enables you to access its print options.

Using Draw's Print Options

CorelDRAW!'s print savvy is controlled by the Print dialog box. Please note that this means the print options as they relate to a PostScript output device. Although Windows can drive plenty of non-PostScript devices, it is hardly worth using CorelDRAW! with anything but a true Adobe PostScript-licensed printer.

The one exception is a relatively inexpensive color inkjet printer, which can be a real convenience when used as a design tool. However, do not use an inkjet printer as a prepress proofing device for images that ultimately will be output on a PostScript printer. The continuity just is not there.

Take a look at the various options that Draw gives you when printing files (see fig. 11.1). To access the Print dialog box, click on **F**ile and then select **P**rint, or press Ctrl-P.

Figure 11.1:

The Print dialog box.

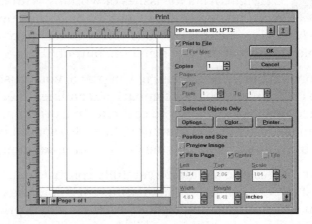

Print Dialog Box

- **Printer Selection edit box.** This box tells you for which printer Draw is composing its printer output. Next to this is a box with a **?** in it. When selected, this information-only box lists various properties about the currently selected printer. You do not have any control over the information in this list.

- **Print To File.** Selecting Print To File causes Draw to create a PostScript file that you can download to an imagesetter (commonly referred to as a "Lino," but other imagesetting equipment manufacturers exist) from any other computer. If the other computer is a Mac, you should select the For Mac check box. This option removes a pair of control characters that Draw normally includes in PostScript files. These characters are filtered out by the printing ports on a PC. If you are printing to a Mac and do not select this option, these characters are passed on to the printer and end up generating a PostScript error, keeping the pages from imaging.

- **Copies.** Simply lets you select to print more than one copy of your image. Note that this option doesn't work correctly on all printers. If printing multiple copies takes a long time, it probably means that CorelDRAW! is sending the complete print job to the printer multiple times instead of sending a command to just print multiple copies. In this situation, you should select the Printer button and set the number of copies in the printer's setup dialog box.

- **Selected Objects Only.** This time-saving option is valuable when working with images that consist of many objects. It works in a similar manner to Preview Only Selected. In this mode, the printer outputs only those objects you have selected when you open the dialog. If you want to print just one or a few objects without waiting for the printer to image all the objects, use Selected Objects Only.

- **Preview Image.** New in CorelDRAW! 4.0 is the capability to move the selected objects (as a group, not individually) around on the page using the image preview on the left side of the dialog box. You can move the image with the mouse or by typing new coordinates in the dialog box. You also can use this option just to get a peek at the image as it fits on the page.

- **Fit to Page.** This option is a subset of Scale. With one click, the oversized image is scaled up or down and centered to fit on the selected output page.

- **Tile.** The Tile option prints an image larger than the output device's largest paper size. For example, when proofing a tabloid-sized image on a printer whose paper size is limited to 8 1/2 inches by 11 inches, click on Tile. The printer breaks the image up into pieces (or tiles), which then can be taped together for proofing.

- **Scale.** Scale, like Tile, is a convenient way to print oversized images. Unlike Tile, however, Scale can fit the image on one piece of paper, although at a reduced size. The reduction percentages are variable.

In the middle of the dialog box, you find three buttons titled Options, Color and Printer. Take a look at the options available from each of these buttons.

Printing Options

When you click on the Options button, the Options dialog box opens (see fig. 11.2). This dialog box presents the following selections:

- **Set Flatness to.** *Flatness* governs the smoothness of curves in PostScript output files. The lower the setting, the smoother the curves (and the more difficult a file is to print). Complex objects sometimes can choke a printer. Raising the Flatness setting enables Draw to simplify the curves, making the file more palatable to PostScript printers. Printing to a high-resolution imagesetter can be more problematic than printing to a desktop laser printer because of printer memory constraints and the number of dots and points that the imagesetter has to manage. If you are finding that your files print OK on a 300 dpi PostScript printer, but fail on a 1200 dpi imagesetter you can *lower* the flatness setting to 0.25 here when printing to the laser printer (don't forget to set it back to 1 for final output for the imagesetter). This will simulate printing to the imagesetter, and may give you warnings about problem files before going out to your service bureau. If you find that raising the flatness helps many of your drawings to print, you may find that you have to break large curves into smaller segments.

Figure 11.2:
The Options dialog box.

- **Auto Increase Flatness.** This option was introduced in CorelDRAW! 3.0. As indicated before, Draw makes it too easy to create overly complex images that can be trouble at print time. When you choose this option, Corel takes control of printing by setting up the PostScript file to automatically increment the flatness setting by 2 (relative to the initial flatness setting) up to 5 times each time the printer returns a Limitcheck error when processing a clipping path in a print job. If the PostScript object is still too complex to print, the printer will skip the object and go on to process the next object in the page description. One of the downsides of this feature, though, is that it has the potential to increase printing time greatly.

- **Screen Frequency.** This option sets up the output device's halftone size for spot colors or composite color (screen frequency and angle for process color separations is controlled in the separations dialog box). Although the dropdown list has only a limited selection of screen frequencies, you can type in specific values. To ascertain the correct screen frequency to use, check with the printer (the person, not the machine) who ultimately will print the job. He should be able to give you complete specifications.

The Screen Frequency setting is overridden by any individual changes in the Outline or Fill PostScript screen options dialog boxes (for those objects only). Thus, you can use, for instance, a 110 screen for an entire image with the exception of the logo, which might require a special screen effect, such as a line pattern at 25 lpi. Please note that special screen effects do not rotate. If you rotate such a screened image, the lines do not rotate with the image. This can lead to some unexpected results if you print proofs on a PostScript laser printer in portrait mode, then print your final output on an imagetter that rotates the page to print across the paper in the printer.

- **Fountain Steps.** The Fountain Steps option governs the number of stripes in a printed fountain fill. Low values print faster (with visible banding), while high values look smoother (and take longer to print). For high-resolution imagesetters, Corel recommends 128 for 1270 dpi, and 200 for 2540 dpi. Set this option to a lower number to speed up proof printing (at the expense of exaggerated banding in fountain fills).

Below this section are the options you use to control the way images are printed. You should consult your print shop for directions on which selections to make. These options also are shown in figure 11.2.

- **Print Negative.** Print Negative sets the PostScript output device to invert the file image, turning black to white and white to black. You need this option when imaging negatives that will be directly burned to the printing plates. Film negatives give the highest possible quality, short of burning plates right on the Lino.

- **Emulsion Down.** When this option is selected, the image is printed upside-down and backwards. Your print shop might refer to this as "ReadRight" and "ReadWrong." The default output is "ReadRight" (emulsion up). Selecting Emulsion Down is the same as selecting "ReadWrong."

- **All Fonts Resident.** This option is another time-saving feature, and one that is important for the serious typographer who regularly uses a service bureau. This option sets up the output file so that it calls the fonts directly from the output device. If this option is not checked, the file contains all the font information as curves, not the actual font files.

Output files that contain several fonts can grow quite large. If you click All Fonts Resident, you (or your service bureau) must have the corresponding fonts already downloaded to the printer (either in RAM, ROM, or on a hard disk in the printer). Otherwise, two things can happen: the printer substitutes Courier for the missing fonts, or the file does not print correctly. Unlike other Windows programs, Draw never downloads fonts with its print jobs. The downside to this fact is that you have to go in and edit your CORELFNT.INI file if you are using fonts other than the ones that come with CorelDRAW!. (See Appendix A for more information on editing the Corel INI files.)

In addition to speeding up print time, selecting All Fonts Resident uses the actual PostScript font, rather than Draw's interpretation of it. This fact may not be important to many folks, but discerning typographers can tell the difference, subtle though it might seem.

The important thing to remember when using All Fonts Resident is that the required fonts must already be loaded on the printer. When you are using the standard 35 PostScript fonts, this is no problem for most printers. In fact, if your file contains only fonts from among the 35 standards, you do not need to select the option; Draw automatically uses the printer's resident fonts. But using, for instance, Ottawa without having Optima loaded on the printer results in font substitution. Make sure that your service bureau can provide a list of its available fonts. And don't forget to include a list of the fonts used with each file you submit to your service bureau.

- **Print As Separations.** This option is used for color imaging. Each color used is broken into its own plate. If you are using process color, you get separate plates for cyan, magenta, yellow, and black. With spot color, each spot color used has its own plate, too. This option also works with a combination of spot and process colors, just in case you want to pay for that seven-color press.

If you want, you also can ask CorelDRAW to convert your spot colors to CMYK process equivalents so that the job outputs as a four-color separation without additional spot color plates.

When Print As **S**eparations is selected, Draw automatically selects **C**rop Marks, **R**egistration Marks, Densito**m**eter Scale, and File **I**nformation. You can turn off these options (discussed next) as required.

Selecting Print As **S**eparations also enables the Se**p**arations button in the dialog box. When you click on Se**p**arations, another dialog box opens in which you can (but usually do not want to) change the halftone frequencies and angles. If you don't quite know to what these options refer, you definitely do not want to change them. Only do so under direct instruction from your printer (again, the person, not the machine).

- **Auto Trapping options.** Also included in the Separations dialog box are several Auto Trapping settings. When turned on, Draw automatically creates traps for objects that have no outline, have a uniform fill, and have not been set to over-print in the Object menu. You also can elect to Always **O**ver-print Black (even if the object does not meet the above three restrictions). While this option provides an "easy" solution to trapping, discuss trapping issues with your printer first for best results. She might want a set of negatives with no trap-ping (so her stripper can create the traps manually) or might ask for an Encapsulated PostScript (EPS) file that can be processed through a stand-alone trapping solution (such as Aldus TrapWise). Please refer to the section later in this chapter on manual trapping for more information on the trapping process.

Back at the Options dialog box, take a look at the References section.

- **C**rop Marks. This option adds marks to the output image that tell the pressperson where the actual edges of the page should be if the page has to be trimmed from a larger sheet of paper.

- **Registration Marks.** These "bull's-eye" marks are imperative for aligning the printed image on the press and are absolutely necessary for color printing. You can select <u>R</u>egistration Marks only when you have selected to print separations.

- **Calibration <u>B</u>ar.** The calibration bar is a series of color swatches that print in the margin of the drawing. These swatches help you calibrate your monitor to the actual output colors.

- **Densito<u>m</u>eter Scale.** This selection prints a grid that shows the range of color from 1 to 100 for the current color separation plate. The Densito<u>m</u>eter Scale option is available only when printing separations.

- **File <u>I</u>nformation.** This option prints all pertinent file information on the page with the image, including the name of the file, the plate color, the screen frequency and angle, and the time and date the file was printed. This data is printed outside the image area unless you select <u>W</u>ithin Page. If <u>W</u>ithin Page is selected, this information might print over parts of your illustration, so be careful.

NOTE

To use any of these reference marks, you must be printing to a paper size that is larger than the page size of your drawing.

Color Options

The second button in the Print dialog box cluster is C<u>o</u>lor. This button opens what is probably the scariest looking dialog box in CorelDRAW!. The Color dialog box and its associated buttons include helpful color separation and prepress tools like Gray Component Replacement (GCR), Undercolor Removal (UCR), and Dot Gain.

In the Color dialog box, you are presented with two images of your document. The original document is on the left, and a color-corrected image appears on the right (see fig. 11.3). Below these images is a list of all the colors used in the document. You can choose which specific color or colors you want to view in the right side window from this list. You also can view each color as a 256-level grayscale image by selecting the Show as <u>G</u>rayscale box (which is only available when individual colors are selected in the color list).

Figure 11.3:

The Color dialog box.

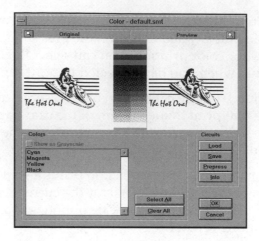

This dialog box is your doorway to CorelDRAW's prepress tools. Most of the tools here are beyond the scope of this book. Instead, you should discuss these elements in detail with your commercial printshop. The following discussion provides some basic information on Draw's prepress tools, which you can access by clicking on the **P**repress button. Also note that as this book was going to press, Corel was preparing an update to CorelDRAW! 4.0 that mihgt include changes to the prepress capabilities of the program. The following represents the shipping product as of this writing:

- **Gray Component Replacement (GCR).** This color separation technique reduces the three process colors (yellow, magenta, and cyan) in an entire document by replacing them with more black ink. The three process colors combine to form black, so by replacing a percentage of their coverage with black, you end up with less ink coverage. This lessening leads to improved sharpness and increased contrast along with an easier press setup, lower ink costs, and better consistency.

  In the Prepress Tools dialog box, you can set the GCR value along the tonal range of the document. Setting GCR to a higher value in the shadow areas generally improves the separations, but too much GCR in the shadows can decrease the apparent depth of the shadows and dark colors.

- **Undercolor Removal (UCR).** This option employs a technique that reduces cyan, magenta, and yellow in dark and neutral shadow areas, replacing them with increased black coverage. This technique alleviates problems of too much total ink coverage (which causes ink drying and other problems). The UCR is entered as a total percentage of ink coverage. 400% allows all inks to print over each other; this maximum, however, works only in a theoretical environment. In real-world applications, the total area coverage (TAC) should be limited to a maximum of 300%.

  GCR and UCR sound very similar, but their effects do differ. GCR substitutes the graying component in a three-color separation with black ink, while UCR reduces the amount of process colors in neutral gray areas by adding black. GCR takes place throughout the image, while UCR is applied only in shadow areas. GCR makes the pressperson's job a little easier when trying to maintain a neutral gray area, because she only needs to monitor the blank ink coverage instead of watching the CMY balance.

- **Black Point.** This option specifies the blackness level in the image. Although Cyan, Magenta, and Yellow combine to form a three-color black, it is not as dark as a four-color black (adding black ink). By selecting a black point between 0.0 (same as a three-color black) and 1.0 (four-color black) you can specify the apparent darkness of black. The actual percentages of color are determined by the CGR and UCR settings.

- **Dot Gain.** By the time an image goes from film to plate to paper, the halftone dots tend to spread slightly in size. This spreading leads to more intense or darker colors than what was intended. Dot gain is most apparent in the shadows and midtone areas, but also can occur in the highlights. Different types of presses and different quality papers all affect the amount of dot gain. The dot gain control allows for a general (Master) reduction in dot size, or specific (CMY or K) control. Enter a positive number in the dot gain box to indicate the percentage of decrease in pixel sizes.

NOTE

To load the printer circuit COREL3 (included on Disk 1 and at the root of the CD-ROM Disc 1), copy COREL3.SMT, COREL3.RGB, and COREL3.CMY into the COREL40\CUSTOM directory, then load the circuit by clicking on the **L**oad button in the Color dialog box.

Any changes that you make to the prepress settings can be saved in a circuit (SMT) file so that you can call them up again as needed. CorelDRAW! 4.0 handles color printing much differently than earlier versions did. Version 4.0 includes a set of files to simulate the color circuits of version 3, but they are not exact. You might notice that colors print quite differently in version 4. One of the things promised in the next revision of Draw is an option to turn off the prepress controls so that you can handle colors as you did in earlier versions.

Remember, discuss each of the prepress tools with your commercial printer. The particulars of printing presses, imagesetters, paper types, and so on. all have an impact on the settings to be made in this section.

Setting Up the Printer

The last button in the Print dialog box is the **P**rinter button. This button simply opens the Windows Printer Setup dialog box, in which you can change paper sizes and orientation (portrait or landscape). Note that Draw normally alerts you if the page and printer orientation are not set the same. It also automatically changes the orientation of the printer for you. You can click on the **A**bout button here to find out which version of the printer driver you are using.

Windows 3.1 Print Driver Woes

Early versions of Microsoft's Windows 3.1 PostScript printer drivers have been problem-ridden. The 3.5 version that originally shipped with Windows 3.1 was revised a few times during the last year or so, and the latest version is 3.56. You should be running with the latest release of the driver. You can download the latest PostScript drivers from Microsoft's BBS at 206/936-6735 or from the MSL section of CompuServe. The drivers are found in LINO.EXE, a self-extracting archive file that includes the latest PostScript driver along with various Windows PostScript Description (WPD) files for Linotronic support and/or PSCRIPT.EXE (just the PS driver and license agreement). Note that if you are going to be using Aldus PageMaker 5.0, the 3.56 (or newer) PostScript driver is required.

Printing in Color

Unless you are lucky enough to have a color printer, the only way to check your images is to send out for a color proof. You have three options. The first is to send out for a color print from a service bureau that offers color PostScript output from a color PostScript printer such as the QMS ColorScript. These devices offer 300-dpi proof, which is suitable for comp work (but not prepress proofing) and can emulate either process or PANTONE colors. But rather than use these devices for *final* proofing, consider them marvelous, though costly, design tools.

The second, and preferred, color proofing option is to have your service bureau burn negatives on its Lino. Then, if you are using process colors, have the negatives made into a DuPont Chromalin color proof (commonly referred to as a "chrome"). For PANTONE colors, there are similar proofing systems.

The final option for color proofing is to have your printer show the color breaks with transparencies—such as 3M Color Keys— prior to running the job. Regardless of method, you always should have proofs made before going to press.

Negatives are a necessary step for high-quality printing. If your printer does not work with negatives, he is probably using direct-to-plate technology. He might think that this is high-tech, but it is not usually suitable for high-quality color printing. Look for another printer.

Process color is an intricate, expensive affair. If you intend to use CorelDRAW! to produce process color separations, make sure that you have plenty of time and money before proceeding. Each set of separations and chrome can easily cost more than $100. Do not expect to save by scrimping on the proof print. The dollars you save might cost you fifty times that if a press job must be rerun.

Manual Trapping

Trapping, or *spreads and chokes*, as the procedure is commonly called, is the way printers compensate for variations in press registration when running multiple color jobs. Quite simply, one color is spread out, or the other color is choked in. This creates a slight overprint and counteracts any fluctuations in registration while a print job is running.

Figure 11.4 shows a simple trap. The darker outline color overprints the lighter fill color, resulting in a trap.

Figure 11.4:

An example of a trap.

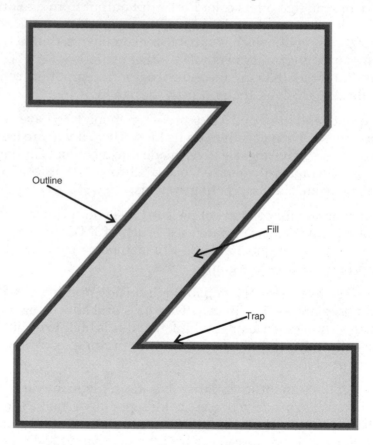

There is good news when it comes to traps. In version 2.0, CorelDRAW! introduced a semi-automated capability for trapping artwork. However, it is a tricky business—a manual, trap-by-trap procedure—that should be approached with caution. The secret is in the way you construct your images.

Each press and pressman has different trapping requirements. Some need no traps at all and are perfectly content with butt registration. Others require varying spreads and chokes. Ink and paper types also have a lot to do with the trap amplitude.

If a color image can be separated into layers by colors, it might be possible to set traps. In a multiple color image, each color becomes a layer. By using outlines of the same color as the object's fill, a trap can be drawn. The secret here is to use the Overprint option in the Options dialog box (accessed through the Outline Color dialog box).

As with anything of this nature, have multiple copies of your file, just in case. Leave the original file untouched and play around with a duplicate.

You are going to see how to build traps with Draw—not necessarily easy, but possible. Remember the Thurston's Bait & Tackle T-shirt design you built in Chapter 5? Trot that file out now and complete it.

Screen printing in general, and T-shirts (or other textiles) in particular, tend to require more trapping than precise offset presses. To this end, you begin with the Thurston's design as a way to explain the simplest of traps. Because all you are dealing with is outlined type, the principles should be rather obvious. The more intricate an image becomes, the more difficult it is to trap.

The object here is to make the lighter color overprint the darker color just slightly. This trick is not done with mirrors, just different outlines! In this first example, the trap happens in a flash. All you need to do is click on overprint and select an appropriate line width.

Trapping the Thurston's Design

After you have gone through the following exercise, you get the idea behind the trap solution. You use a pair of suitable aquatic colors to bring the design to life.

As you can see, trapping with Draw can be a tricky maneuver. Sometimes it is simple and obvious; other times complex, puzzling, and ultimately impossible.

Setting a Simple Trap

You start out by opening up the last version of the Thurston's file. This one happens to be TBT8. Substitute the name of your completed file if it is different.

Click on **F**ile	The File menu appears
Click on **O**pen	
Double-click on the file name	The file assembles itself on-screen

You need to group the words "Thurston's Bait & Tackle" so that they can be modified easily.

Shift-click on all elements in Thurston's Bait & Tackle	
Press Ctrl-G	The words are grouped

Next, you need to give the type a spot color fill and an overprinting outline.

Click on the Fill tool	The Fill fly-out menu appears
Click on Uniform Fill	The Uniform Fill dialog box appears
Click on PANTONE Spot Colors	
At Model, click on Names	Dialog box configures for names
Click on PANTONE Process Blue CV	To fill with PANTONE Process Blue CV
At Tint, *enter* **100**	
Click on OK	
Click on the Outline tool	The Outline fly-out menu appears.

Click on the Outline Pen *icon*	The Outline Pen dialog box appears
Click on the round corner	
Click on the round line cap	
At Width, *enter* **0.04** inches	
Click on OK	
At Color, *click on* **M**ore	The Outline Color dialog box appears
Click on **S**pot	
Roll down and click on PANTONE 316	
At Tint, *enter* **100**	
Click on PostScript **O**ptions	The Options dialog box appears
Click on **O**verprint	
Click on OK	
Click on OK again	
Click on OK one last time	

You have created an outline that overprints the fill by .02 inch. Now, you are going to print that outline to a file. You test this setup on your desktop laser printer.

Click on **F**ile	The File menu appears
Click on **P**rint	The Print dialog box appears
Click on Print As S**e**parations	
Deselect Film **N**egative	You are printing positives
Click on Print To **F**ile	
Click on For **M**ac	
Click on OK	

The Color dialog box appears. The only colors that should be present are PANTONE Process Blue CV and PANTONE 316 CV.

Click on **A**ll Colors	
Click on OK	The Print to File dialog box appears (see fig. 11.5)
Click on OK	The Printer on FILE-NAME dialog box appears

continues

The print file automatically is assigned the same prefix as your current file, but with a PRN file extension.

Click on OK   The Thurston's sign is
                                                 printed to a file

The PostScript Printer on FILENAME dialog box enables you to set up your file for a specific media size. To choose an imagesetter such as the Linotronic 300, you must load the imagesetter's drivers on your system through the Windows Control Panel.

Figure 11.5:

The Print to File dialog box.

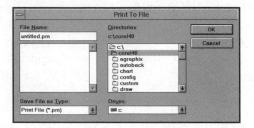

Congratulations, you just created a simple trap using CorelDRAW! In this exercise, you printed your image to a file rather than to a laser printer. These files would be taken to a service bureau for film positive output. The film positives would then be used to produce the photo stencils required for screen printing. By contrast, lithographic printing usually requires film negatives.

Because you were preparing the file for screen printing, the trap you set was very large and very obvious. If you have a laser printer, send the separations to it, so you can see the trap. Remember to reset your printer options!

NOTE

Do not click on Behind Fill in the Outline Pen dialog box, or you will be left with no trap at all.

Although the preceding example is admittedly the most rudimentary of chokes and spreads, it illustrates the concept. Every day, artists all over the world are creating traps using Draw. Here is a salute to all those groundbreakers willing to take the arrows in the forehead!

More complicated traps require that you duplicate objects, giving the duplicate (trap) no fill and an overprinting outline in either the fill or background color. Things can get quite complicated. One of the best ways to keep your head is to set up your images in overlays.

Avoiding Traps

No one is twisting your arm into trapping. In fact, many printers would rather handle the traps themselves rather than try to correct what you have attempted. There are far more sophisticated trapping solutions than what is included with CorelDRAW! 4.0. If you are not comfortable with trapping your work, don't. Talk with your printer, color trade shop, or service bureau; they might be able to offer a solution that can save everyone time, headaches, and cash.

Designers and artists should not have to worry about the way the ink hits the paper, just the end result. Unfortunately, the current situation requires that you *must* worry about it, although you don't have to worry about it alone. If you do not possess print production expertise, find people who do. If your printer does not have the electronic smarts to help you, check around. If you have a good relationship with your printer, let him know what you need. He can be an excellent resource, even if he can't handle everything in-house.

High-end systems, such as Scitex, set up traps after the image has already been ripped into a huge bit map. This procedure can be the most expeditious method for trapping an intricate multicolor design. You need serious computer power and prepress expertise to do it right! The high end might not be for you, however. If you use a lot of hairlines in your work, you might not be pleased with the results. Once again, the best plan is to consult with folks who know the game. Let them guide you through the process, but expect to pay for their expertise. The costs are trivial when compared to what it costs you for a print job gone bad.

Playing with the Bands

If you have been working with CorelDRAW! for any significant amount of time, you are bound to have been disappointed at times by fountain fill *banding*. This unwanted phenomenon creates visible stripes in what should be smooth transitions of gray (or color) in images printed on a PostScript printer. Banding is due to the restrictions of the PostScript language and the resolution of your output device.

Avoiding Banding in PostScript Fountain Fills

In many cases, banding can be eliminated by following a few basic rules. These caveats have to do with the imaging capabilities of your (or your service bureau's) printer, along with the optical capabilities of the human eye.

Unfortunately, the secret to avoiding banding requires that you perform a mathematical equation or two. You can use the Windows Calculator to handle all the hard work. All you have to do is apply the rules.

The fundamental rule regulates the number of fountain fill stripes available to the printer. This figure depends upon the printer's resolution (dpi), the screen line frequency (lpi), and the percent of gray change. The *gray change* is the difference between the starting and ending percentages:

$$\text{Number of stripes} = (\text{dpi}/\text{lpi})^2 \times (\% \text{ gray change})$$

For example, typical desktop laser printers image at 300 dpi/60 lpi. A fountain fill that went from black to white—100-percent black to 0-percent black—would be a 100-percent gray change.

$$25 \text{ stripes} = (300/60)^2 \times (100-0)/100$$

If you were to print the same image on a Lino at 1270 dpi/110 lpi, you would have a greater number of stripes, due to the increase in resolution.

$$133 \text{ stripes} = (1270/110)^2 \times (100-0)/100$$

As shown in table 11.1, the number of stripes goes down as line frequency (lpi) at any given resolution goes up. Although it might be advantageous to avoid banding by lowering the screen frequency, remember that the screen dots are larger and more noticeable. Instead, it might be worth your while to run the file at high resolution. For example, if you are having trouble with banding in a fountain fill at 1270 dpi/120 lpi, running the same file at 2540 dpi/120 lpi might alleviate the problem by providing a significantly larger number of stripes. The file takes longer to print, however; consequently, your service bureau will probably charge a higher rate for high resolution.

Table 11.1
Number of Stripes at Various Resolutions

% Gray Change	dpi: 300 lpi: 60	1270 90	2540 120	133	120	133	150
10	2	19	11	9	44	36	28
20	5	39	22	18	89	72	57
30	7	59	33	27	134	109	86
40	10	79	44	36	179	145	114
50	12	99	56	45	224	182	143
60	15	119	67	54	256	218	172
70	17	139	78	63	256	255	200
80	20	159	89	72	256	256	229
90	22	179	100	82	256	256	256
100	25	199	112	91	256	256	256

A boundary does exist, however. Notice that at higher resolutions, the PostScript interpreter sets a maximum limit of 256 stripes. This limit is apparent in longer fountain fills and those with smaller amounts of gray change—which leads to the next important item.

The human eye disregards bands that are 1/32 inch (0.03") or less. So what does that mean in the real world? Simple. You get visible banding when individual bands are wider than 0.03 inch. Hence, banding is usually noticeable in longer fountain fills. Why? Multiply 0.03 inch by the maximum allowable number of bands (0.03" × 256 = 7.68"). That result is why you always get a degree of visible banding in a large fill—even at high resolution (2540 dpi). Because lower-resolution printers have far fewer stripes, banding is far more prevalent.

Before you print a fountain-filled object on a Lino, try running the numbers through the "Number of Stripes" equation. Then, multiply the number of stripes by 0.03. If the resulting number is larger than the length of the fountain-filled object, it is a good candidate for banding. You might want to rethink the fill and use a lower screen frequency, larger gray change, or run the file at a higher resolution.

Because the maximum number of stripes is limited by resolution, laser printers are far more prone to banding than are high-resolution imagesetters. Even so, a quick check with the calculator can save you money at Lino time. Now that you have the basics of black-and-white fountain fill banding characteristics, take a look at the way it works with color fountain fills.

What about Color Fills?

In the last section, you learned the basics of avoiding banding in black-and-white fountain fills. With color fountain fills, you follow the basics and add one last equation. Before you can determine the gray change percentage for a color fountain fill, you need to come up with gray values for the starting and ending colors. The good news here is that CorelDRAW!'s color palette makes it easy to perform the equation.

Although you might be working with CMYK or PANTONE colors, the PostScript language deals with your colors in their Red/Green/Blue (RGB) equivalents. Draw's color palette enables you to instantly change a color from its CMYK or Pantone values into RGB values. With your starting fill color selected in the dialog box, change the fill type from its original setting to RGB. Presto! The color's RGB values appear. Write the values down, cancel out of the dialog box, and repeat the procedure for the ending fill color. Then, plug the numbers into the following equation for each of the colors. (This equation is reprinted from the *PostScript Language Reference Manual*, Second Edition. Published by Addison-Wesley Publishing Company, Inc. Copyright © 1985-1988, 1990 Adobe Systems Incorporated. All rights reserved.)

%Gray = 30%(Red Value) + 59%(Green Value) + 11%(Blue Value)

With the gray value of the starting and ending fill colors calculated, proceed with the first equation you learned: The number of stripes = $(dpi/lpi)^2 \times$ (% Gray Change). Then, multiply the number of stripes by 0.03 inches to determine whether or not you are going to get any banding.

In Short...

Your budget and time frame dictate the way you handle fountain fills. Laser printers produce bands on everything but the shortest fills. Printing files on a higher resolution output device results in an increase in quality—up to a point. By following the rules set forth in this section, you can alleviate many unhappy surprises when you get your printed output back from the service bureau.

Printing Other Items with CorelDRAW!

One of the beauties of CorelDRAW! is that the images you create can be taken to many platforms and output on many devices. But the attraction is not solely in the range of printers that Draw can drive. The depth lies in the imaging possibilities, or more appropriately, the potential of what can be done with the output images.

By now, you probably have used Draw to prepare a variety of printed material, and you might even have a few different digitized logos on hand. You probably have a knowledge of laser printers and high-resolution imagesetters like the Linotype L-300 as well.

As you have seen in the last exercise, images can easily be made into Lino film positives and screen printed.

Print Merge

At some time, you may be asked to produce boilerplate prints merged with variable data, such as diplomas or awards (see fig. 11.6). You are in luck. CorelDRAW! version 2.0 introduced Print Merge, a marvelous feature that enables you to combine a data file that contains a number of records with a static layout (including art and typographic effects) on the fly.

Figure 11.6:

The BITE diploma.

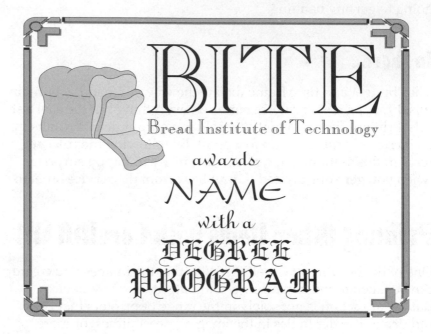

Print Merge applies most, but not all, of Draw's effects to variable data. Specifically, merged text cannot be fitted to a path, blended, or extruded. Most other attributes apply. This feature is incredibly powerful, although it might yield questionable results when used with some of the more intricate effects, such as envelope.

The merge file must be saved in plain-vanilla ASCII format with a TXT file extension. You can use Notepad, Write, or any other word processor capable of producing a clean ASCII file.

All merge files must follow the same general format. The first line lets Draw know how many data fields are to be replaced. The lines that follow are the fields (separated by beginning and ending backslashes) with the exact words to be replaced in the boilerplate file. After a blank line, the variable records start. Each individual field is separated by backslashes. A blank line separates each record.

The following example is a file prepared for the Bread Institute of Technology:

```
3
\NAME\
\DEGREE\
\PROGRAM\

\Harry Pumpernickel\
\Doctor of\
\Yeastology\

\Rhonda Rye\
\Master of\
\Grainology\

\Sonny Sourdough\
\Bachelor of\
\Crustectomy\
```

35mm Slides

Back in Chapter 6, you put an image together for a 35mm slide presentation. You learned the basics of slide setup; you might remember that Joe DeLook sent the files off to a slide service bureau.

A staple of the typical board meeting, 35mm slides are a costly proposition for most businesses. Many companies send their sketches out to slide houses and pay hefty bills for the service they receive. Some large companies have expensive, dedicated, in-house departments and systems to churn out the celluloid.

Many firms are finding that they can control their own destinies by producing quality slide images with a desktop system and a qualified operator. Images built in CorelDRAW! can be sent to a 35mm slide service bureau in much the same way you would send files to a Lino service bureau. You do not need to switch to another software package. You can continue to use Draw to integrate and enhance elements originally generated in other programs.

If your company produces slides in volume, you might consider purchasing your own desktop slidemaker. These handy devices enable you to output directly to 35mm film, which you then take to a local photo lab for processing. If you are interested, a wide range of cameras are available. Prices start in the low four-figure range, while a high-end camera can easily cost more than $20,000.

If you intend to produce slides, as in Chapter 6, you should be aware of a few things. For starters, it is a wise idea to use a slide service bureau that is familiar with CorelDRAW!. Second, allow plenty of time; you do not want to be experimenting at deadline time. Finally, it helps to know the lingo, so here is a bit of the buzz.

Imaging Formats

When your slide service bureau images your files, they probably will ask for the file in one of three formats. These formats are (beginning with the least desirable) CGM, SCODL, and EPS. Some caveats go with all three of the popular slide formats.

The CGM (Computer Graphics Metafile) format does not support bit maps, nor does it support PostScript textures. In addition, fountain fills are not fully implemented. Linear fountain fills are no problem as long as they are applied to nonrotated rectangular objects. But if you have to export CGM, and your files contain other types of fountain fills, you will get your best results by using a masked fill rather than a filled object. Use the CGM format only if you absolutely must.

For slide work, the SCODL (Scan Conversion Object Description Language) is far preferable to the CGM format. If Include All Artistic Attributes is selected, SCODL supports any type of object corners, pen shapes, calligraphic pen effects, and fountain fills with the same limitations as CGM. Bit maps are not supported, nor are PostScript Fills. Only rounded or butted line caps are supported. SCODL does not recognize dotted or dashed lines.

SCODL supports certain fountain fills, but only linear fills on rectangles and radial on circles. The best way to use a fountain fill with SCODL files is to build a clipping mask. Be wary of radial fills, because they overprint the circle by approximately ten percent—which leads to the next SCODL caveat.

When exporting SCODL files, do not leave any objects outside the page. If you do, your slides do not image properly. If you have objects lying outside the page area when you try to export in SCODL, CorelDRAW! issues an error message. Take heed and correct the problem.

The best way to image slides is in PostScript EPS format. Post-Script slides support all of CorelDRAW!'s features. Check with your slide service bureau to see if it can work with EPS before sending your files in one of the lesser formats. EPS slides are more expensive than SCODL or CGM slides, but the results are well worth the extra expense.

CorelDRAW!'s *Technical Reference Manual* covers each of the export file formats in depth. You can find the information you need in the "Exporting Graphics Files to Other Software Packages" section of the manual.

The Image Center

One of a rare breed, the Roanoke, Virginia-based Image Center is an authorized CorelDRAW! imaging center. This status is not bestowed on just any slide bureau.

While most slide bureaus accept Draw-generated SCODL files, few can offer Image Center's flexibility and amenities. Unlike most bureaus, Image Center can work with native Draw files. Just send them a CDR file, and they will image it at 8,000 lines resolution. Eight thousand lines is twice the resolution of most bureaus, at a very competitive price.

Image Center also can provide PostScript slides in addition to the more pedestrian formats. This fact ensures that your slides are imaged with all the good stuff intact. Anything that can be output as EPS will image: fountain fills, dashed lines, and so on. Image Center does not ask for the EPS file, only the CDR, saving on communication time and, ultimately, cost.

In addition to the convenience of transmitting either SCODL or CDR files, Image Center accepts other formats like CGM, PCX, PIC, GIF, and the ever-popular TGA (Targa) files.

Image Center uses Matrix MVP raster image processors and MGI Solitaire digital film recorders to image your CorelDRAW! slides, assuring you of the highest possible quality. If you require Ektachrome color overheads, they can be shot at 4,000 lines resolution on Kodak Ektachrome 8-inch × 10-inch film.

By using Image Center, you have the accessibility of on-line file transfer. You can transmit your files one day and have slides the next. They promise delivery within 24 to 48 hours. You do not even need to buy any communications software—Image Center provides a copy of its own communications program free of charge! The program is called IC-COM, and it accompanies your free user kit. Along with the program, you will find easy-to-follow instructions that will have you uploading your Draw files in minutes. Simply dial and telecommunicate your images. Very few slide bureaus offer this much utility and value.

> Image Center, Inc.
> P.O. Box 2570
> Roanoke, VA 24010
> 1011 Second Street, S.W.
> Roanoke, VA 24016
> 800/433-8829
> 703/343-8243
> 703/343-0691 (FAX)
> 703/344-3549 (MODEM)

Vinyl Lettering

One of the lesser known uses for CorelDRAW! is that of producing vinyl lettering for signmaking. A software program known as CADlinkPlus from ThermaZone Engineering, Inc., makes vinyl cutting from Draw files a reality.

CADlinkPlus can import files and enable the user to scale drawings by percentages or by forcing the size to a specific dimension. This scaling alleviates Draw's page size limitation. The drawings can then be sent to plotters from over ten different manufacturers. But CADlinkPlus (and vinyl cutters in general) supports object outlines only; none of Draw's fills are usable.

ThermaZone also offers an Outline/Inline/Distortion module program, which can apply some pretty tricky effects to the imported images. The text/graphics distortion software is capable of impressive three-dimensional perspective distortions, convex or concave arch distortions, fit to globe, and many other valuable effects. The software module enables the user to combine up to ten different distortions. And, as an added bonus, CADlinkPlus images can be converted into DXF or EPS files and reimported into Draw.

Vinyl cutting from Draw images is expensive; you obviously need a vinyl cutting plotter as well as CADlinkPlus to do the task. Unfortunately for most users, the cost of vinyl cutting plotters can be prohibitive. You easily can spend more than $5,000 on the additional hardware and software required to cut vinyl.

> ThermaZone Engineering, Inc.
> 2285 St. Laurent Blvd. Unit D-8
> Ottawa, Ontario, Canada K1G 4Z7
> 613/523-2715
> 613/523-0932 (FAX)

Colossal Graphics: Large-Format Output

Have you ever needed a huge print of a CorelDRAW! or other PostScript/EPS file? If so, you probably had a hard time finding a way to image those big files, especially when considering Draw's maximum image area. Luckily, a company has broken the barrier to large-format output. Colossal Graphics, Incorporated of Palo Alto, California, has pioneered the service by selling the PowerScript workstation, which enables printing Colossal Color Prints—full-color images up to 40 inches × 12 feet in one piece! Even larger images (billboards, anyone?) can be created by tiling a single EPS page into multiple panels with precision accuracy using PosterWorks, a program from S. H. Pierce & Co.

Although a color PowerScript system can be quite expensive (in the same ballpark as an imagesetter), you do not have to own one to take advantage of its virtues. A local PowerScript bureau can output your file on premium bond paper or 4 mil clear film at a maximum resolution of 400 dpi. The prints then can be dry mounted or laminated for durability.

PowerScript output should not be thought of as prepress proofing. Instead, it is a way to economically print a short run of posters, meeting/trade show signage, flip charts, in-store displays, architectural renderings, or site plans. The possibilities are inexhaustible. Output costs start at roughly $7 per square foot for black-and-white output, and around $10 per square foot for color. Considering the cost of conventional alternatives, imaging files at a PowerScript bureau can save thousands of dollars and plenty of time.

Colossal provides a thorough step-by-step CorelDRAW! user's guide for creating large-format artwork. Basically, you need to provide a scaling percentage to "blow up" your images, along with font usage information. Although Colossal provides a scaling formula, a graphic arts proportional scaling wheel—or the Cubit Meister Shareware Program (on the *Inside CorelDRAW!* floppy disk)—makes it even easier to calculate percentages.

The following list of PowerScript Imaging Centers can help you locate a bureau in your area. If none are close by, do not fret; they all are linked together with high-speed modems, so you never have to leave your studio! Colossal will gladly ship your Colossal color prints by overnight mail.

POWERSCRIPT Imaging Centers

Corporate headquarters:
Colossal Graphics, Inc.
437 Emerson Street
Palo Alto, CA 94301
415/328-2264
415/328-0699 (24-hour BBS)

A&E Products
4235 Richmond Avenue
Houston, TX 77027
713/621-0022

Atlanta Blue Print
1025 W. Peachtree Street, NW
Atlanta, GA 30309
404/873-5911

Blair Graphics, Inc.
1740 Stanford Street
Santa Monica, CA 90404
213/829-4621

Blue Print Service Company
149 Second Street
San Francisco, CA 94105
415/495-8700

Carich Reprographics, Inc.
412 S. Harwood Street
Dallas, TX 75201
214/939-0009

National Reprographics, Inc.
44 West 18th Street, 3rd Floor
New York, NY 10011
212/366-7075

Reprographic Plus
176 Main Street
Norwalk, CT 06852
203/847-3839

Reprographic Technologies, Inc.
2865 South Moorland Road
New Berlin, WI 53151
414/796-8162

Riteway Reproductions, Inc.
22 W. Monroe Street
Chicago, IL 60603
312/726-0346

San Jose Blue Print
835 West Julian Street
San Jose, CA 95126
408/295-5770

Triangle Company
314 S. Cincinnati Street
Tulsa, OK 74103
918/628-0400

Triangle Reproductions
2203 Cee Gee
San Antonio, TX 78217

Veenstra Reproductions
850 Grandville Avenue SW
Grand Rapids, MI 49503
616/452-1495

Waterfront Reprographics Ltd.
903 Western Avenue
Seattle, WA 98104
206/467-9889

European Imaging Centers

Colossal, LTD
Bournend Business Center
Coref End Road
Bournend, Buckingham, UK
SL8 5AS
628 8509 01

Colossal Trading Company
Cardiff, Wales

No Limits
London, England

The Crawfords Group
London, England

Pronto Prints
London, England

Printronix
London, England

Using Service Bureaus

When picking a service bureau, remember that when you buy cheap, you get cheap. In other words, if you are shopping for Lino output strictly on per-page charges, you are doing yourself (and your clients) a great disservice.

At the risk of infuriating those folks who have plunked down big bucks on a "Mr. Printo" franchise, avoid them—unless they can prove that they are knowledgeable about high-end DTP. The person running the Lino might not know the first thing about PostScript, film densities, or typography. Do not choose bureaus by price alone. Service is what is important.

Be careful of Macintosh-only bureaus. While these folks might know their stuff, they might not be able to help with any Draw-related problems. Familiarity with CorelDRAW! and PCs is more than helpful. When sending files to a Macintosh-only bureau, be sure to click on For **M**ac; otherwise, you must remove the very first and last character in the PRN file by editing the file as an ASCII text file (these characters look like a skinny rectangle). If you do not, the file will not print. This step can be done easily using Windows Write—just remember to save as text only!

Another convenient way to send files to a Macintosh-only bureau is to export the Draw images in EPS format and import them into a PageMaker document. Because PageMaker converts smoothly from the PC to Mac platforms (and the reverse), this method can be a convenient way to include multiple graphics in one file. However, this method should be used only for black-and-white (or monochrome) images; for color separations, print to a file.

Always include a list of the fonts used in each file if you want to use the service bureau's printer-resident fonts. And one more word of caution: Macs do not like PCX bit maps—use a TIFF file instead.

So What Makes a Good Service Bureau?

This question is a tricky one. Due to the nature of the business, service bureaus tend to be hectic places. Time *is* money to these folks. If your bureau spends time with you making sure that the files you send them print properly, they are saving everyone a lot of grief (and shekels). It is most important for you to have a good line of communication. Don't expect to sit and have tea, but if you can't *talk* to your bureau, you should consider a change.

A good service bureau should provide a number of things in addition to support. They should have at least the full Adobe font library so that you do not always have to send your fonts along with your files. Additional font libraries are a bonus, and can be indicative of the shop's commitment to their clients. The bureau should be responsive to your suggestions and offer answers to your questions.

Once again, it's a good idea to deal with a bureau that is more than just PC-literate. A Mac-only house can be trouble, and in reality, is a dying breed. Savvy bureaus have a PC or two hanging around (along with the latest versions of the most popular programs). In fact, the smart bureaus are running print servers like COPS' PServe.

You should take a number of heavy-metal hardware issues into consideration. Ask what kind of imagesetter they are using. If you are doing process color separations, look for a Linotype-Hell 330 (or better), Agfa SelectSet, or Scitex Dolev. These babies deliver the goods—tight register and optimized screens (which lessen the chance of any undesirable moire effects). Lesser machines cannot deliver the quality needed for process work. Be sure to find out what type of color proofing methods they offer; it makes the most sense to get your separations and proofs under one roof.

How serious are they? Even if you are just doing spot color work, you want to know that they are competent. Is their imagesetter calibrated? Do they use a replenishing film processor? Can they guarantee film density (dmax) and halftone dot accuracy? Ask what brand of film and paper they use; if they use Dupont, there's a reason why their per page prices may be a bit more expensive. Quality materials cost more, and value is not determined by price alone.

Solving Printing Problems

You already might have run into the horrible reality of a file that will not print. To be honest, this problem does happen, but it usually is not fatal. Although it can be frustrating, especially at deadline, you simply (more or less) tweak the file or the printer setup to work things out. By using the methods covered in this book, you should reduce the likelihood of nonprinting files.

Are You Hooked Up Correctly?

If you are having trouble printing *any* Draw files, check out your printer setup. To begin, make sure that your selected printer matches the default printer. Set the Transmission Retry Time to 600, and set Device Not Selected to 0. You also can try turning Windows Print Manager off. While you might lose the convenience of this feature, it might be necessary if you are short on disk space. (The Print Manager spools printer jobs to the hard disk before sending them to the printer.)

Windows provides a means to monitor what is happening with your PostScript Printer. This mechanism is known as the

PostScript Error Handler. You can access this feature by going to Draw's Print Setup dialog box and clicking on **O**ptions, and then **A**dvanced. When the Advanced Options dialog box appears, make sure that Print PostScript Error Information is selected. The error handler report can be used to diagnose a problem file (if you know PostScript programming). Corel's technical support team can interpret the results and suggest solutions to problem files.

Draw also includes its own PostScript Error Handler routine in the form of a printer TSR file that you can download to the printer before printing. This error handler remains in the printer's memory until it is reset or turned off. The file and directions for its use are found in the \COREL4\DRAW\EHANDLER directory. Corel's technical support team can interpret the results and suggest solutions to problem files.

Typical PostScript errors are LIMITCHECK, RANGECHECK, and TIMEOUT. About 30 possible error messages exist, but these are the most common. If you get LIMITCHECK errors, check the complexity of your curves, use AutoReduce to eliminate unneccesary nodes, and do not fountain fill complex shapes. If you continue to get TIMEOUT errors, you might need to adjust the printer timeout by adding timeout=999 to the [named printer,port] section of the WIN.INI file.

Note that PostScript clone printers have been known to be rather cranky. True Adobe-licensed PostScript is now cost-competitive with the clones, but so far, most of the 600 dpi PostScript printers are *not* Adobe PostScript. Know what you are getting into when you shop for PostScript printers.

Making Sure Your Files Run

As mentioned throughout the book, try to build streamlined files. Avoid using too many fountain fills or fountain-filling complex objects. Use Combine, but do not overuse it; try to limit the number of objects combined to twenty in each clump.

Exploit the power of Bèzier curves. Reduce the number of nodes in your objects; you get smoother curves, smaller file sizes, faster printing, and better performance. If you still have problems printing, try using a higher Flatness setting (or try using Auto Increase) in the Print Dialog box.

When you build your collage, try to keep things clean so that you easily can go back in and adjust things if need be. Remember, you actually are writing computer programs that run on your printer's internal processor. If you write a bad program, it will not run. You must be able to go in and make sense of what you have created.

Summary

The reason most people purchased Draw was to produce slick-looking print graphics. In this chapter, you have seen ways to control Draw's print functions to give the best possible images. In addition, you have learned that the program can be used for far more than just conventional printed imagery. It can be used just as effectively for 35mm slidemaking, serigraphy, and signmaking.

Draw opens doors. Because it works with so many programs and can interface so easily with so many other programs, its possibilities are endless. This chapter has tried to illuminate some of the program's less obvious imaging capabilities and show you how to get those files printed.

Part Four

OLE... Fighting the Bull

CorelPHOTO-PAINT!

n the current release of CorelPHOTO-PAINT!, the capabilities of this application have been greatly enhanced. No longer just a simple paint program, Photo-Paint now is a much more powerful photo-retouching program than it was in the past. In fact, this new and improved Corel module gives its competitors, such as Aldus Photoshop, a run for their money in many aspects. Major enhancements to the program include the filtering and image manipulation capabilities. By employing the new and generous supply of filters, you can use the program to create a wide range of special effects. In earlier versions of Photo-Paint, these effects were very, very difficult—if not impossible—to create.

If you have used Photo-Paint in the past, this chapter shows you the many ways in which the program's capabilities have been improved. Along with the new creativity tools, Photo-Paint now enables you to create four-color process images that you can output directly from Photo-Paint or export to other programs. You also can preseparate Photo-Paint images and use them in programs that support OPI (Open Prepress Interface) format. This format rapidly is becoming the standard for image sharing in the entire publishing industry. Thanks to these expanded tools, filters, and features, Photo-Paint now provides you with greater latitude to create artistic effects.

Understanding System Requirements

Along with all these great new features, however, comes a downside to the program. Although you can run the program on a 386 computer with 4M of RAM, a VGA monitor, and an 80M hard drive, a more powerful system is highly recommended. If you really want to get into the full extent of Photo-Paint's retouching capabilities, you should run this module on a power user's workstation.

The following system setup is recommended:

- 486DX33
- 256M cache
- 21-inch color monitor driven by a 24-bit True Color Graphics Card with at least 1M of Video RAM
- 510M hard drive
- At least 8M of RAM—preferably more
- Syquest 44 or 88 removable drive

Why use such a killer workstation? Color production is not a lightweight process. It requires serious number crunching and is very processor-intensive. The nature of the image files migrating to the Windows desktop is changing. These files are beginning to resemble the files used in the high-end environments such as Scitex in their size and complexity. Just how intensive might these files become? Consider the following scenario.

You are working on a 10-image montage image for a presentation cover. The final printed piece will be an 11-by-17-inch spread for the front and back covers of a book. The job will be printed at a 150 lpi line screen, so your images need to be scanned according to the "dpi × 2" rule of thumb (thus, at 300 dpi).

Because you did not know the final sizes in advance, you had all the images scanned at approximately 150%, or 7 inches by 10 inches. At 300 dpi, these factors calculate to some huge files—probably in the 20–30M range each.

While you work on the collage, you might need to open as many as five images at once, which requires an extra 300M of disk space. Also, don't forget that you have the whole Corel drive package loaded on this workstation. This package eats up another 20M or so for all the modules. Windows 3.1 takes up a good 6M. Add to that all the other programs that you might have on the same machine—word processor, spreadsheet, database, PIM, and fax/modem software. (Don't forget Tetris!) When all the applications are accounted for, you maybe need about 400M of ROM to make this baby hum.

After you copy all the scans onto your hard drive and launch CorelPHOTO-PAINT!, you open the first image—a picture of the front of the corporate headquarters building. The day the photographer took the picture, the sky was overcast. He didn't really filter his shot as he should have, so that gray sky looks really foreboding. Also, no one told physical plant about the shoot. The day before, they had a landscaping crew in to prepare part of the lawn for resodding. All the bad sod was removed before the end of the day. In addition to these other problems, the position of the company's new sign looks odd in relation to the building itself.

Because this image is the centerpiece for the front cover, it really needs some work. Add a little more blue to the sky. Recombine the corrected plates. Clone the patches of dirt with grass from elsewhere. Increase the saturation and hue. Move the sign closer to the sidewalk. Blend it into its new home. Now clone in grass and sky where the sign used to be. Crop out the parking lot. (It doesn't look that great with the high cyclone fence and the razor wire.) Now save the new image.

Whew! Did you really think that you were going to do all that on the relative beast of a 386? Leave that dinosaur for the page layout crew from now on.

Configuring Your Hardware and Software

Before you can use Photo-Paint, you need to set up your equipment and software needs for optimum running condition. Make sure that Windows is running in the ideal configuration for the work that you are doing. If you haven't upgraded to Windows 3.1, you should seriously consider doing so. Windows 3.1 provides a much more stable working environment. Your applications are less prone to experience unrecoverable application error messages, and Windows 3.1 has a good memory management scheme.

Setting Up Your Hardware

Because of the way Photo-Paint allocates memory resources, you should enable the virtual memory module in Window 3.1. If you used the default setup for Windows, your swap file most likely is not set up as a permanent file. Unless you have a space availability issue on your hard drive, you should set up at least a 10M permanent swap file.

Enabling Virtual Memory

Click on the Control Panel *icon*	The Control Panel dialog box appears
Click on the 386 Enhanced *icon*	The 386 Enhanced dialog box appears
Click on Virtual Memory	
Click on Change	The dialog box expands to show the recommended swap file size and the maximum value

It can't hurt to use more than the recommended size, but go with at least the minimum recommended memory.

In the lower left corner might be the Use 32-Bit Access check box. If this option is not present, your disk controller does not support a 32-bit disk access. If it does appear, click on it to further improve the access speed (see fig 12.1).

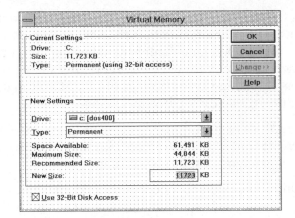

Figure 12.1:
Virtual Memory
dialog box.

Setting Photo-Paint Preferences

After you have optimized Windows, you can set up the preferences for Photo-Paint. Preference settings enable you to tell Photo-Paint the way you want to open the application and what kind of measurement system you want to use.

If you have used previous versions of Photo-Paint, you will notice several changes to the Preferences dialog box. Many of the functions have been changed, combined, or moved elsewhere (you learn more about these changes later).

From the **S**pecial menu, select **P**references. In the Preferences dialog box, you see two edit boxes: **A**t Startup and **U**nits (see fig. 12.2).

Figure 12.2:
The Preferences
dialog box.

At Startup enables you to choose what you want Photo-Paint to do after it launches. The default choice, About, is a waste of mouse strokes. If you select this option, the program opens with the Corel splash screen, and you have to click the mouse button to begin using the actual application. The Nothing option launches the program and waits for direction from you. New assumes that you never want to open an existing file when starting up. More often than not, you do want to open an existing image file, so choose Open. By using this option, Photo-Paint automatically presents the Open File dialog box at startup.

Like most graphics applications, Photo-Paint also enables you to choose a default unit of measurement. Click on the drop-down list button and choose your preferred setting.

The next option you need to adjust is the *gamma* (screen brightness) setting. From the Display menu, select Calibrate. GAMMA.PCX, which is included in the file samples that loaded when you installed the software, is the screen image you use to make this judgment. To load this image from the File menu, select Open, scroll down to GAMMA.PCX, and click on OK. The range threshold for setting Gamma is 1.0 to 2.0 with a .01 increment. (Apparently, Corel expects you to use an arbitrary value in that range until you find a brightness that you like.)

Note that there is no Apply button in the dialog box. Each time you adjust the gamma, you must save the curve and switch to the GAMMA.PCX to evaluate the change—a process that can be tiresome and time-consuming. After the gamma is set the way that you like it, adjust the Red/Green/Blue (RGB) values to level off the grayness of the window's vertical strip. Adjustments of two or three units either way should provide acceptable results. This process translates to a smoother transition between the monitor's colors.

Remember, the goal here is long-range consistency. This methodology does not give a color-accurate screen model. By saving the setting to a file, however, you at least have a consistent value to use as a benchmark each time you load it. Next week and next month, the image colors will look the same as when the job was started. By setting these default standards, you consistently can manipulate image colors even if you have to wait days or weeks between sessions.

Exploring the CorelPHOTO-PAINT! Filters

Filters are predefined effects you can use to alter the appearance of an image. The newest version of Photo-Paint offers you an extensive variety of filters. These filters serve two distinctly different purposes.

The first set of filters is for *special effects* editing. You can make alterations as simple as adding a tonal cast to the overall image or a more substantial change, such as masking and embossing a particular element of the image. You can, in fact, take an image from the real world and modify it so completely that it no longer resembles those real-world criteria. The special effects filters are described in table 12.1.

NOTE

For a thorough discussion of these filters and their associated options, consult the CorelPHOTO-PAINT! user manual.

Table 12.1
Special Effects Filters

Filter Name	Description
Artistic/**P**ointillism	Gives the image a "dotty" appearance
Artistic/**I**mpressionism	Applies impressionistic brush strokes to the image
Edge/**E**dge Emphasis	Highlights the edges between the various colors in the image
Edge/Edge **D**etect	Creates an outline effect
Edge/**C**ontour	Outlines the edges of a picture with lines
Edge/**O**utline	Outlines the selected area or the entire image
Emboss	Creates a 3D relief effect
Invert	Like photo negatives, inverts the image colors

continued

Table 12.1
continued

Filter Name	Description
Jaggie Despecle	Scatters the image colors
Motion **B**lur	Creates the appearance of movement
Noise/**A**dd Noise	Creates a granular texture effect
Noise/Add **M**ore Noise	More of the same, with specific options
Noise/**R**emove Noise	Softens edges and reduces speckles and splotches
Noise/Ma**x**imum	Lightens the image by reducing the number of colors
Noise/Me**d**ian	Removes noise from grainy images
Noise/Mi**n**imum	Darkens the image by increasing the number of colors
Pixelate	"Enlarges" the pixels, creating a block-like effect
P**o**sterize	Lowers the resolution to give the image a rough, "fuzzy" look.
P**s**ychedelic	Randomly changes image colors for a 1960s look
So**l**arize	Reverses the color of any selected pixels below the set threshold

These filters are considered the "fun" filters. Although no set standards exist for acceptable results, you can find several suggestions in the Photo-Paint user manual. These special effects filters are highly interpretive in nature and provide very artistic results. You might, for example, use a filter to blur the area behind a runner to promote the feeling of motion.

The other class of filters are the *retouching* filters. You use these filters to make an image look better than it appeared originally. These filters are based on traditional retouching skills and require a greater understanding of the characteristics of an image to be used effectively. The program can't just do it for you. The retouching filters are described in table 12.2.

Table 12.2
Retouching Filters

Filter Name	Description
Color/**B**rightness And Contrast	Lightens or darkens a picture and/or changes the distinction between dark and light areas in the image
Color/**T**hreshold	Changes image to solid colors
Color/**G**amma	Adjusts middle grayscale values to enhance detail
Color/**H**ue and Saturation	Self-explanatory
Sharpen/**S**harpen	Enhances edges and brings out detail
Sharpen/**E**nhance Detail	Analyzes pixel values and applies greatest amount of sharpening
Sharpen/**U**nsharp Mask	Accentuates edge detail and sharpens smooth areas
Sharpen/**A**daptive Unsharp Mask	Accentuates edge detail without changing or affecting other parts of the area
Smooth/**S**mooth	Tones down differences in adjacent pixels
Smooth/**So**ften	Tones down harshness but does not lose detail
Smooth/**D**iffuse	Scatters image colors

continued

Table 12.2
continued

Filter Name	Description
S̲m̲ooth/B̲lend	Smoothes and softens colors and transitions
T̲one/C̲olor/Gray Map	Adjusts for lighting inaccuracies
T̲one/E̲qualize	Redistributes color shades

Above all, the name of the game for these filters is "Practice!" If you don't understand the fundamentals, you can waste a lot of time and effort and still end up with mediocre images. The only way to acquire a skill base is by using the tools.

Understanding Fills and Canvases

Fill and canvases are just what their names imply. You use *fills* to fill areas; you use *canvases* as backgrounds over which you place other images. Both objects ultimately become part of the final image. The way in which you create them is where they differ.

Fill

A fill can be manufactured from bit-mapped patterns or bit-mapped textures. *Bit-mapped patterns* are used with tile fills and can be any bit-map image that you can think of. If you have a photo of a car, for example, you can scan it into Photo-Paint and save it as a bit map. You then can use this image as a tile fill (much like the Wallpaper feature of Windows). A *bit-mapped texture*, on the other hand, is a repetitive effect, like the color weave in a piece of cloth.

Bit-mapped textures are used to create texture fills. An extensive set of base textures is provided with the application. You can edit these existing textures to create the texture value that you want to use as a fill. Although the range is not limitless, you can create an almost limitless list of effects. You can, for example, add or subtract colors, increase softness, or change the transparency of existing textures for a whole new look.

Canvas

Canvas patterns are tile patterns that are applied to the entire image. After you apply a canvas, its pattern shows through any additional painting that is done to the image. The degree to which it shows through depends on the percent of transparency and embossing. Remember that the canvas is not saved with the image until it has been merged. This feature is especially useful if you want to use your favorite car (the one that you were using as a tile fill) as a single background to the whole image.

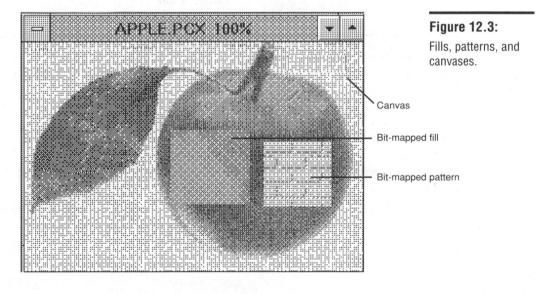

TIP

Remember that the image you want to use as a tile fill must be no larger than 128 pixels square. Other information is truncated and lost as a tile. To effectively use an entire image as a tile, you must select the image area that you want and resize it so that the final fill area is no larger than 128×128 pixels.

Figure 12.3:

Fills, patterns, and canvases.

Introducing the Photo-Paint Toolbox

Corel provides you with over 40 tools in this version of Photo-Paint. Although some tools are more useful in their application than others, Corel obviously has put a great deal of time and effort into enhancing the Photo-Paint toolbox. The following sections describe some of the more helpful tools included in the toolbox. For more information on tools, refer to your Photo-Paint user manual.

Masking, Selection, and Effects Tools

You use these tools to select areas for masks and retouching. By using them in combination, the tool set enables you to manipulate the image in almost limitless combinations. These tools are shown in table 12.3.

Table 12.3
Masking, Selection, and Effects Tools

Tool Name	Description
Rectangle Selection	Selects an area to mask by selecting opposing corners
Magic Wand Selection	Selects mask area according to tonal value; range sensitivity is defined using Tolerance
Lasso	Cuts a mask by drawing around an object
Polygon Selection	Cuts a mask according to irregular geometric shapes (similar to Lasso, but no curves)
Hand	Moves an imported or masked element
Zoom	Magnifies the image

Tool Name	Description
Locator	Opens a small duplicate of the zoomed-in image
Eraser	Removes all tone from selected image area
Eyedropper	Selects a color from an image area to use with other tools
Local Undo	Cancels the most recent effect on a masked area
Color Replacer	Erases selected area with a color value
Freehand Contrast	Increases contrast in a local area without masking
Freehand Brighten	Brightens a local area without masking
Tint	Tints an area locally using the currently selected outline color
Smear Paintbrush	Locally blends hard edges together
Frechand Smudge	Locally distorts image data and breaks up regularity
Sharpen	Sharpens a local fuzzy or soft image area

The following exercise demonstrates one way you can combine the use of these tools. Suppose, for example, that you want to replace a splotchy area with a flat tone or a color selected from elsewhere on the image.

TIP

Many tools have menu alternatives. Sometimes using these tools as menu selections is easier than selecting them from the toolbox.

Using Tools in Conjunction

Click on the Rectangle Selection tool

Click the left mouse button to anchor the selector and drag pointer to include desired color area

continued

Release mouse to select area	A dotted line (marquee) appears that defines the color area
Click on Display, then select Zoom	The Zoom fly-out menu appears
Click on 200%	The selected area is enlarged by 200%
Click on the Eyedropper tool	
Right-click on desired color	This color becomes the selected color fill
Select Normal (100%) zoom	Screen redraws to normal view
Click on the Lasso tool	
Click the left mouse button and drag the cursor around the area to be masked	A marquee outlines the selected area
Select 1600% zoom	Selected area is magnified 1600 times and a pixel grid appears (see fig. 12.4)
Click on the Color Replace tool	
Move cursor to the area you want to color	
Click in each pixel box to be colored	The color changes in the selected area
Zoom out to normal	
From the File menu, click on Save As	The Save As dialog box appears
Give the file a new name and click on OK	

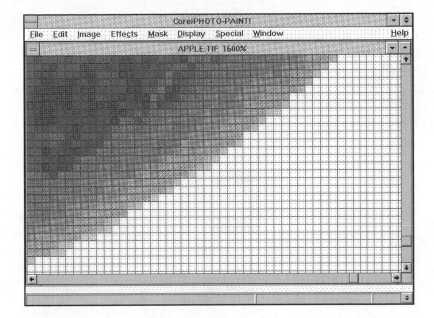

Figure 12.4:
The image zoomed in 1600%.

Painting Tools

Included in the painting tools are four very useful paint brushes. These creative tools enable you to add the appearance of brush strokes to an image:

- Freehand brush
- Impressionist brush
- Pointillist brush
- Air brush
- Spray can
- Artistic brush

Although most of these tools' effects are self-explanatory, two of the brushes are very specific in their effect and are defined by their traditional art theory names: Pointillist and Impressionist. The *Pointillist* brush gives the effect of dipping only the brush tip in paint and dabbing on circular areas of paint to make up the image. The other brush is the *Impressionist* brush, which places broad strokes of multicolors to the canvas.

TIP

Press L when you use the Lasso tool to change to Magic mode. This mode enables you to tightly mask oddly shaped items. You must have a tight color tolerance to do it.

Because each of these brush strokes is made up of a different set of components, the settings for each brush are very different. The Artistic brush, for instance, has only two setup options (see fig. 12.5). You can select an oil pattern (with a choice of 13 patterns) and use **W**idth to determine the size of the brush. The Impressionistic brush, on the other hand, has several options available to create different types of brush strokes (see fig. 12.6).

Figure 12.5:

The Tool Settings dialog box for the Artist brush option.

Figure 12.6:

The Tool Settings dialog box for the Impressionist brush.

The brush tools are very creative in nature. Unless you have a specific use in mind, however, they are merely extra appendages. As you learn to use Photo-Paint, leave these four techniques for last. The time required to learn them usually outweighs the gain in versatility for most of your needs. On the other hand, if you want to use the program to creatively develop new images on screen that replicate the traditional painting process, this is the place to start.

Cloning Tools

Of all the tools available, the cloning tools probably are second only to the masking tools in their importance in the retouching arsenal. *Cloning* is the process of copying the color and texture of one area of an image directly to another, along with the pattern of variability. You can choose from the following tools:

- Clone

- Impressionism Clone

- Pointillism Clone

The impact of the tools' uses is immense in scope. Consider their application. Suppose that you want to use a scan of a man's face. The face is a very rugged, cowboy-type face—highly chiseled features, aquiline nose, five-o'clock shadow. Unfortunately, the face has a blemish on the side of the nose, and a slight scar runs parallel to the nose line.

If you use a color copy to get rid of these problems, the patch would not keep the shape or variations of the skin. By using the Clone tool on the area a few pixels to one side of the trouble spot, you can eradicate the problem but still maintain the color, texture, and variation of the skin. This procedure makes the chore of fixing the face a very easy and uncomplicated process. Again, the key is to intelligently define the size and shape of the cloning tool. Use a zoomed ratio of 200–300% to work in close up.

The difference with Pointillist or Impressionist cloning is in the nature of those effects. The cloning process is the same, like the brushes of the same name; however, the clone has the added aspect of the respective style. The result is a creatively distorted clone.

Text Tool

Another useful tool in Photo-Paint is the Text tool. If you are using text heavy with images, you might be better off adding text in a program designed for page layout. On the other hand, if you are adding the text for its artistic value, then Photo-Paint presents the best way to place the text. The reasoning is not immediately obvious, but is worth considering.

In page layout, the assumption is that the text will be moved, edited, changed, rearranged, and generally altered. Photo-Paint, however, assumes that after you place the text and save, you want the text to become part of the final integrated image. When the file is saved, text becomes just that—an element of the artwork. You no longer can adjust the text outside the framework of Photo-Paint.

When you select the Text tool, a fly-out menu appears. This menu enables you to choose a font, the point size, and font attributes (bold, italic, and so on). On the surface, this menu appears to offer a very limited selection of options. Remember, however, that Photo-Paint uses integrated scroll bars. By using the Color tool, for example, you can select a color based on various color models. By selecting different colors for background, fill, and outline, you can vary the typestyle further. The combination of tool usage enables you to create a range of different type formatting.

Understanding Calibration

Several calibration procedures are built into Photo-Paint to ensure that the output is as accurate as possible. Monitor or gamma calibration was discussed earlier in this chapter. Another calibration option is tone map. The *tone map* is a definition of the visual correction of the images as a balance between what you are seeing on the monitor and what is seen in the printed product. When editing a tone map, the goal is to create a set of predefined corrections that you can use for images with similar characteristics.

Suppose that you have a number of scans that are images of a forest at dusk. Although the images are obviously different, they have similar characteristics: low contrast, lots of shadows, and so on. After you view the printed piece, it appears that the shadows are still plugged up and the midtones appear too weak. One approach to solving this problem is to load each scan individually and make a series of baseline corrections. Of course, to be consistent, you need to write down the changes (or have the memory of an elephant) so that you can apply the same changes to the remaining images. Because all the images have consistent tonal values, you can use a very handy shortcut—edit a tone map. After you make the necessary changes to one image, you can use the tone map to apply the same set of general corrections to all the images.

Editing a Tone Map

Load the corrected image to use as a guideline.

From the **F**ile *menu, select* Edit **T**one Map	The Tone Map dialog box opens (see fig 12.7)
Click on **E**dit *and open the scale bar*	The default values appear in 10% increments
Edit the value numerically at each percentage break point. Type a new numerical value for the different tonal levels in each text box	

The changes that you make are seen on the tone map as you make them. To attain special effects, however, the resulting visual map generally should retain regularity, not bounce up and down as you move across the map.

Click on **A**pply	Image shows adjustment
Repeat the two preceding steps	Image changes to reflect edits
When finished, save the file	Map is saved as a distinct tone map file

Figure 12.7:

The Tone Map dialog box and Options submenu.

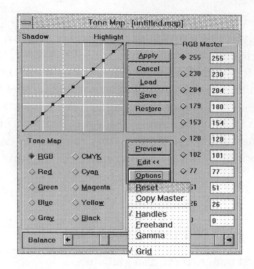

You can use three other methods to edit the value. After you click on **O**ptions, a submenu gives you three choices: **H**andles, **F**reehand, and **G**amma. Although these alternatives are available, the numerical method described earlier is the most accurate way to go. The other options are easy to use, but they do not give true results.

Among the other tone map editing choices is the color model. This selection is done according to the scan (if it is black-and-white, gray is your only option) and the final output (separation into CMYK, used as a slide, or composite print).

Generally speaking, if the file is to be printed CMYK, then work in CMY**K** mode. For all other uses, select **R**GB. Also, consider whether the inaccuracy effects only a single color or is global in nature. If the problem is a single color (the shadows are predominately black in CMYK mode, for example), then edit the tone map for just the single color first.

Remember also that this is a cumulative process. If you edit one color and the problem still exists, make similar adjustments to other colors or to the master curve. Almost all adjustments should be subtle in nature, as a gross shift only results in highlighting a color inaccuracy at one end of the curve. Remember, too, that you can apply the correction in preview mode as you work. Use it often. This procedure is a subjective process done with objective tools. The numbers don't tell the whole story. In the end, it comes down to your interpretive skills and experience.

After you are satisfied that the curve you have edited will do the job, give it a unique name and save it. Do not save it as the default. You want the baseline default as a starting point in the future to generate other curves and to build your library of corrections. If you save the correction curve with the name default, all future tone maps need to overcome this curve beyond the errors inherent in the subject curves.

The following exercise outlines the simple process of applying your newly created tone map to images.

Applying the Curve

Open the image to which you wish to apply the curve.

Select Edit **T**one Map *from the* **F**ile *menu*

Click on **L**oad

Select the appropriate map

Click on **A**pply   The image is adjusted according to the map you loaded

If the image appears correctly, save it (as always with a new name) and go on to the next.

If the image does not look right, you always have the option of tweaking the image. Keep in mind that Photo-Paint does not have in-line densitometer. "Rightness" is a visual process. So, if the image looks okay, it probably is best at this point to leave it alone.

Preparing for Prepress

If the image is for CMYK output, the next step is the prepress setup. Photo-Paint's P**r**epress option is found on the **F**ile menu. As you learned in Chapter 11, the prepress controls enable you to define some characteristics that will be part of the final separation films produced from a PostScript imagesetter. To use these controls properly, you must understand the press environment you are using and have at least a rudimentary knowledge of the techniques of UCR and GCR.

The first thing to determine is whether to use an imagesetter or a printer. If you are going to the trouble of outputting separations, you really should output film from an imagesetter. If you output to a printer with the intent of having film shot, you add an additional generation to the process. After the images move from digital (your computer) to analog (the media), each *generation* (subsequent reproduction) experiences a loss of image quality. Remember that cartoon your friend in the accounting department sent you? It looked like a copy of a copy of a copy of a copy. Same idea here.

Briefly, the prepress controls include the following. For more information on using the <u>P</u>repress options, refer to Chapter 11, "Printing Considerations," or your software documentation.

- **Gray Component Replacement.** An important consideration if the overall image is very saturated. A portion of the cyan, magenta, and yellow that make up the gray components of the image can be removed without affecting the appearance of the image.

- **<u>U</u>ndercolor Removal.** Assumes that some portion of cyan, magenta, and yellow are being mixed to create the black. A good portion of this undercolor can be replaced to reduce the CMY ink percentages.

   In both GCR and UCR, the same principle applies: the less ink used, the better the quality of the colors that are printed.

- **<u>D</u>ot Gain.** This option enables you to control halftone dot spread based on type of press.

- **Quality.** Choose <u>B</u>etter or B<u>e</u>st. Better than what? Because this option is a highly subjective differentiation, the <u>B</u>etter button makes no sense. Go for B<u>e</u>st.

- **Calibrate.** This option is supposed to aid you in matching printer swatches to the screen. The methodology appears arcane and confusing, however, and the results are questionable. For best results, skip this step.

When you save the setup, the process invoked converts RGB values to CMYK. This task is very, very processor-intensive. Even with a 486/66, it takes some time. A 486/66DX2 with 16M of RAM took 20 minutes; a 386/33 with 5M took almost 100 minutes. Thus, do not create a new prepress setup on a short deadline. Consider making this task one that is started at the end of the day. Before you walk out the door, you can turn off the monitor, leave your computer on, and let it merrily churn away to its heart's content.

Calibrating Your Printer

Another type of calibration process involves the output device itself. In addition to preparing for output using the prepress controls, you (or your service bureau) should perform the calibration procedures outlined in this section.

A vital printer calibration sets the device's linearity (also known as "d-max"). *Linearity* is the ideal "straight" line value of image density and is measured in equal increments from 0–100% ink coverage. Although no image device ever attains precise linearity, this control attempts to adjust for perfection.

Calibrate is an option of the File menu's Print command. When you open this dialog box, you see yet another visual curve map. On the left side is an 11-step gray strip with a text box next to each step. If you do your own output, you need a densitometer to read the test strip. A *densitometer* is a special device used to measure the actual density of output film or paper. It reads the opacity of the ink coverage as a percentage of a base line of 100% light transparency. This reading reports on the variance of the imaging device from that 10% linear increment. Each step represents an equal 10% value starting with 0% and continuing on to 100% (thus, 11 steps). You need to output a density strip that gives you at least that many steps. You need a set of density readings for each type of output that you do—RC paper, negative film, positive film, emulsion up, emulsion down, and any other combination.

After you check the density and adjust the variations, save the new settings. This step enables you to always use the appropriate settings for the output method, ensuring the best possible linearity. Although you should check this information regularly, a well-maintained device in a stable environment should not drift excessively.

Printing the Image

After your device is calculated and your image is properly set up for prepress, you are ready to actually print the image. From the File menu, select Print, then Print. When the dialog box opens, you see several controls. If you are going to create separated films, you need to know how to use these controls. To begin, click on Options. The Options dialog box appears as shown in figure 12.8.

First, take a look at what you can and cannot do. You can make grayscale or color separations; you can print directly to an imagesetter or create a print file to download later.

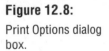

Figure 12.8:

Print Options dialog box.

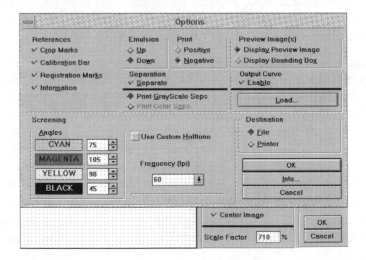

Buried within the Print menus is the option to create a SEP file. Although it is not clear in the Corel documentation, this option apparently means a Tiff 6.0 file format. You cannot create a preseparated file format such as DCS to use in a page layout program, however. If the page layout environment that you use does support Tiff 6.0, you might want to try it. Although it is not a page layout program by definition, CorelDRAW! does support the SEP format. Among the Windows-based page layout programs, the only one that does support Tiff 6.0 is Aldus PageMaker 5.0. But no guarantees. Corel uses a different nomenclature for its Tiff 6.0. It remains to be seen whether this means that the file format is fully compliant, or if it has been altered drastically enough to make it a non-compatible format.

Now move on to the other options in the dialog box. If your output is a composite, do not check Separate. If the final is separated, then obviously, check this box. In the upper left corner are check boxes for Crop Marks, Calibration Bar, Registration Marks, and Information. You always should select all four of these options to simplify the stripping and proofing.

The lower left corner of the dialog box contains the screen angle information edit boxes. In these boxes, you can set specific angles for each of the four plates that you are printing. With this release, Photo-Paint does not allow for the separation of additional plates. Thus, you cannot create matte plates, varnishes, or any other type of touch plate.

In the center is the Frequency (lpi) setting. This value is decided by several issues such as paper type and press type. Along with the emulsion direction and the print type options at the top center, you should discuss these settings with your printer early in the process.

After you make the appropriate selections, click on the OK button (the long one above Info) to return to the Print dialog box. In the upper right is the Printer list box. If you do not select the correct printer or output device, your printed file will not be accurate. If you are printing a file to a PostScript device for which you do not have a specific driver, you must install the PostScript Printer driver in Windows. You usually can use this generic PostScript driver with no problems.

After all is said and done, the last thing to do is select Print. If you are outputting to a printer, the dialog box shows you the status on the print job for each plate. On the other hand, if you selected File as the destination, another dialog box appears. Nothing out of the ordinary here; make the appropriate entries and click on OK.

Putting It All Together: A User Model

Jason Jacks is the director of creative services at the AppleWorks Goodfood Restaurant Corporation. Last week, AppleWorks's CEO announced the acquisition of a new operation division. This division runs restaurants throughout the Pacific Rim. As a result of this merger, AppleWorks now is a multinational operating company with a least one operating unit in every time zone throughout the world. The VP of Shareholder Relations has come to Jason with a rush project. The stockholders meeting is next week. Clearly, this change in the company structure is going to quickly become a major issue of discussion at the meeting. As such, the entire presentation must be redone to reflect the agenda change. Further, the marketing department wants to immediately launch into a new PR campaign announcing this change to the business community. This will be done both in the trades and in the financial newspapers such as the *Wall Street Journal*.

The VP is not asking very much. Just develop a single image idea that is usable throughout the transition for all operating units and the marketing group. Oh, and by the way, have it in finished form in about five calendar days. Jason is told about this at noon on Wednesday. He immediately calls on his good friend, Joe DeLook.

After some very quick discussions with the group doing the shareholder presentation and the marketing people, Jason and Joe prepare their plan of attack. In the thumbnails Jason has drawn, the ad shows a picture of the Earth with an apple as its moon, and some text appears across the face of the planet. Not an extremely complex idea, but a slick image if done correctly. Three different versions of the announcement are needed. One must be full-color RGB for the shareholder presentation. Next will be a four-color version for the trade magazines (this one will be TIFF CMYK format so their ad agency can incorporate it into a larger page layout). Next is a grayscale TIFF, also going to the agency. This format is needed for the cover of the Annual Report insert that is being added as a last-minute handout.

Where To Start

The first place to go is to an electronic image house. Why an electronic image house rather than a traditional operation that delivers images as 4×5 transparencies? Joe's view is very pragmatic. He does not have a high-resolution scanner, but he does have CorelDRAW! 4.0. Thus, he can use Photo-Paint to convert almost any image format that he might receive into a format that will work for him. Also, he has a modem.

Only two images are needed for this project: an apple and a picture of the planet Earth taken from high altitude (fortunately, NASA had several of these photos that have been made available to the public). After several calls, Joe finds the two images that he wants at image banks at opposite ends of the country. The two that he settles on are from two different image companies. The Earth image is from a company that delivers files in GIF format. The apple is available as a PCX. Downloading the two images, Joe is now ready to begin.

Step one is to standardize the images. Joe opens each image in Photo-Paint and saves it as a TIFF 5.0 file. This selection was made purely by personal preference, because Joe is most comfortable working in the TIFF format.

Joe looks at his two images. The image of the planet Earth looks fine just as it is. Before he can use the apple (see fig. 12.9), however, Joe needs to get rid of the stem and the leaf.

Figure 12.9:
The apple image.

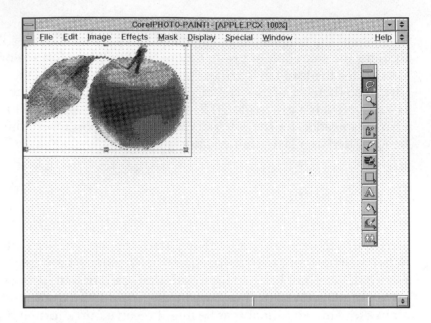

Figure 12.9:

The apple image.

Paring Down the Apple

Load the image you want to edit.

Select Zoom from the Display menu	The Zoom fly-out menu appears
Click on 400%	The image is magnified 400%
Click on the Lasso tool, then press L	The cursor changes to a +; you now are in Magic mode
Click on Special, then select Color Tolerance	The Color Tolerance fly-out menu appears
Set the color tolerance to +5/_% in all colors using the Identical Values box checked	Sets a tight color tolerance when you select an object to mask
Draw a line around the apple, "slicing off" the stem and leaf as close as possible	Draws a mask line around the apple
Double-click when finished	
Click on Mask, then select Crop to Mask	Truncates all data outside the mask and creates a new image file (see fig. 12.10)

Figure 12.10:
The cropped apple.

Each time you make a major change to an image (not just a color or effect shift), Photo-Paint automatically generates a new image. If you don't like the way it looks, simply close it without saving. The original image returns to the screen, ready for another try.

Remember, however, to save work in progress by using the Save **A**s command and assigning a different name to the file. If you do not change the file name, you write over the original image.

Polishing the Apple

After cropping the apple, Joe needs to get rid of any leftover stem material. For this operation, he selects the cloning tool. This is probably the most effective and highly efficient tool for cleaning up the interior of an area that includes a texture.

Cleaning Up the Image

Click on the Clone tool	The cursor changes to a +
Click and hold down the left button in the area you want to clone	The + and brush move synchronously, copying values from relative areas to relative areas
*From the **F**ile menu, select* Save **A**s	
Enter new file name and click on OK	Photo-Paint redraws the image in a new window

So far, everything is going smoothly, and Joe's stress level is not too high. The next step is to combine the two images into one file.

Combining the Images

Click on <u>E</u>dit, *then* <u>C</u>opy From	A dialog box similar to the File Open dialog box appears
Select the apple file	The apple image is imported into the destination file (EARTH.GIF)
Click on <u>F</u>ile, *then select* Save <u>A</u>s	
Enter a new name	The images now are saved as a new file (see fig. 12.11)

Figure 12.11:

The combined images before cleanup.

Joe sees two problems with the new image. First, the apple is too large to make the intended image dimensions work. It is about 25% the size of the Earth orb. The second problem is that the image imported with its bounding box intact. This means that while Joe cut a mask to crop to and create a new apple without the leaf and extended stem, that mask did not stay with the image. After the image was cropped, it was redefined with a new bounding box, always a rectangle. If no color has been defined to fill that space, the image color will be white by default. Photo-Paint does not enable you to save a path with the file format and use it as a silhouette.

Solving the two-part problem will involve several steps. First, he needs to scale the apple in relation to the planet by using the Rectangle Selection tool. By positioning the pointer at one of the image's corners, the size of the overall image can be enlarged or reduced on screen. This command does not have any constrain key, however, so be careful not to distort the image horizontally or vertically.

After Joe settles on the relative size of the Apple, he saves the new image. Now he can work with the clone to get rid of the white areas. The best approach is to work in two steps. First, do the rough work—clone in large areas that don't really approach the edges of the apple (see fig. 12.12). For this part, use a relatively large brush size—maybe an 8 or 9. The shape of the brush would vary according to the context of the area in question. In the case of Joe's apple, a square brush proved to be the most expedient.

After the rough clone work is completed, the time comes to do the detail cloning. The detail work is just that—very detailed. This step requires a very fine tool size, probably a 2 or a 3. Again, the type of work suggests staying with a square shape. Now, however, the display magnification needs to be increased greatly. The most efficient size to use in this instance is 600% zoom.

Figure 12.12:

Magnified view of the cleanup area.

Although 1600% provides a pixel-level grid, for this project that magnification makes no sense. Cloning the edges all around the apple at that magnification would be tedious. Further, the shape of the apple is far from perfect in any sense. If the apple deviates slightly from its natural contours, the impact on the final image is negligible at best. The 600% magnification enables you to work at a near-pixel level but to actually clone several pixels at a time.

You want to use a hard tool edge for tasks of this sort. If the tool is soft, there might be too many pixels right near the edge of the apple that are far too light, adding to the potential of creating halo.

The operative word is save, and save, and save. Even though the progress is not as tedious as 1600% magnification, it still takes some time. At this point, recloning a third or more of the edge of the image because something went wrong at the end could throw your schedule way off. Better to spend a few seconds repeatedly saving the file than to spend an hour or more redoing work that was done right the first time.

After Joe finishes working on the apple (see fig. 12.13), he decides to do some more general cleanup. He feels the images need more separation between the blackness of space and the Earth and apple. By adding some contrast and brightness, he easily adds the needed delineation.

Next, Joe applies an adaptive unsharp mask to soften the harshness of the edges—particularly around the apple—and make the "suspension of disbelief" more likely.

Although he feels that adding text should be next, instinct tells Joe to do otherwise. The grayscale versions would be printed at 300 dpi on a laser printer and 85 line screen on newsprint; the four-color was being imaged at 175 lpi in the ad and at 300 lpi for RGB slide output. Separating the text from the background in grayscale probably would not hold up very well if the text were placed as color type before the image was converted. As such, Joe decides to convert to grayscale first and to add the text for both versions independently.

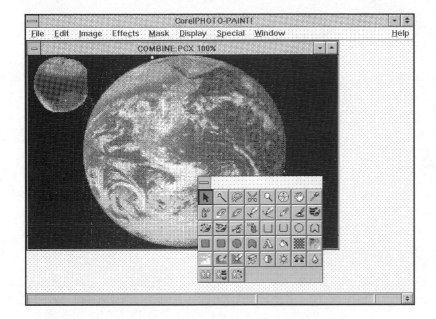

Figure 12.13:
The combined images after initial cleanup.

Going to the menu bar, Joe pulls down the Image menu and clicks on the Convert To command, then selects Grayscale (8-bit). After this selection is made, the image is converted. Of course, the next step is to save the conversion. Joe now has two images to work with for text: a black-and-white image and a color one. Applying the text copy to both is an identical process except for the selection of color. For the 24-bit version, Joe selects red type; for the grayscale version, black.

Inserting Text

At the **D***isplay menu, select* Colo**r** Selection Roll-Up	The Color roll-up menu appears
Click on the roll-down arrow	The Color roll-down menu opens
Click on the right arrow, select CMYK	Text boxes along top change from RGB To CMYK (the K is grayed)

continued

In the CMY boxes, enter the following values:
140 C
230 M
30 Y

Repeat for Background and Fill Outline by clicking on the bar on the lower right	The display adjusts to show the changes
Click on the Text tool	A window opens with a text dialog box on the top
Enter the text	
In lower portion, select the desired type face, style, and size of font desired	A sample of the selected font format appears in the display
Click on OK	The formatted text is applied to image
Move the cursor to the text position and resize it using the text's handles	
When finished, double-click	The handles and perimeter lines disappear, leaving the text in place
Click on File, then select Save **A**s; *type the new file name*	The image is saved with a new file name (see fig 12.14)

Figure 12.14:
The finished
product.

Preparing the Final File Formats

Joe breathes a sigh of relief. The hard part is over! (And it really wasn't that hard, was it?) All that remains is to convert the image to the various formats.

He decides to start with the presentation slide. Because this file will be sent to a high-end slide recorder, maximum color depth should be used. In this case, True Color.

The next file, the four-color, takes a little more forethought. The trade magazine needs 175 lpi. He also learns that separations will be made as part of the final page output. He'll leave the screen angles alone. The agency has already advised Joe that the service bureau uses a Linotype-Hell L630 with a RIP 60. Additionally, the ad agency plans to work with the file in PageMaker 5.0 for final layout. With this information in hand, Joe can set up the print options:

- He selects Crop Marks, Calibration Bar, Registration Marks, and Information.

- He sets Frequency (lpi) to 175.

- He selects Emulsion Up and Print Negative.

- For the color separations, he clicks on Separate and Print Color Seps.

- Because the image will be output elsewhere, he selects Destination File.

- At the Print Menu, Joe select L630 as the printer type.

- Finally, he selects Scale 100% and Center Image.

- When the Print window appears, Joe enters a file name and then selects the format as four-color sep (*.SEP) to generate TIFF CMYK images.

- For the grayscale version, he saves the file only as a TIFF.

Joe gives the completed work to Jason. After he checks it over, Jason delivers the TIFF files to the ad agency and sends the RGB and grayscale composite to the presentation group.

The project is completed ahead of schedule, the VP is happy, and Joe and Jason celebrate over frosty mugs.

Summary

Although it sounds easy, you must remember that color production is not a natural process. To consistently achieve natural-looking results, you must gain experience with Photo-Paint. In order to gain experience, you must practice (and study the theory of color production).

Most of all, communicate with your output service, whether in-house or an outside vendor. If you are not sure how to do something, ask them. If you are attempting something that you have never tried before, discuss it with them first. No one likes having to run the job a second time under the gun, even if they are billing you for it.

As you use Photo-Paint effects, look at the results of the application of the various effects. If they don't look appealing to you, or they don't attain the result you wanted, don't do it. Aesthetics are just as important as the content. Ugly graphics are just that ... ugly graphics.

CorelMOVE!

orel Corporation's quest is to provide a package that produces every kind of graphic image you might need. CorelMOVE!, the newest module to be integrated into CorelDRAW!, fills the need for a multimedia authoring tool. CorelMOVE! enables you to create full-fledged multimedia animation sequences.

Like the screen shows produced by CorelSHOW!, the animations you create with CorelMOVE! are transportable to other computers running Windows. With the proper MCI drivers installed, you can play back your animations by using the Microsoft Media Player. The Media Player was automatically installed in the Program Manager's Accessories Group.

Now that CorelSHOW! can import CorelMOVE! files in addition to sequences created in Autodesk's Animator program, you can add animation sequences to all your screen shows.

CorelMOVE! animations are developed by rendering graphical elements—*actors* and *props*—as separate components. These components are assembled and edited into finished sequences. Sound effects and cues are then added to complete a multimedia production. This modular concept offers you the flexibility to

TIP

CorelMOVE! files have a CMV extension. Autodesk Animator files have FLI or FLC extensions.

"mix and match" the elements you create. These elements can be organized into libraries for easy retrieval and use in other animated productions.

Thanks to CorelMOVE!, the exciting world of sound and motion is within the grasp of anyone with the desire to learn and experiment.

This chapter teaches you the basics of CorelMOVE!. It also introduces you to the fundamentals of animation and explains how these relate to CorelMOVE!. You see how simple animation can be and get an idea of the powerful features CorelMOVE! has to offer to the budding animator.

Exploring Animation

Animation is the process of bringing to life that which is inanimate. Animation is based on the way live-action motion is photographed for movies. In a movie, scores of photos are snapped every second to capture motion in progress. Each separate picture is called a *frame*. When played back, the projected image appears to be moving.

In animation, artists create the individual frames. The artist must study and draw, in sequence, every progressive part of a movement (see fig. 13.1). Sound like a lot of work? It is! Computers and programs like CorelMOVE!, however, make it much less difficult.

Figure 13.1:

Renderings needed to animate walking motion.

Walt Disney, perhaps the most famous animator of all time, elevated the process of animation to an art form. He perfected techniques used to make animated characters seem more lifelike. He combined his characters with perfectly coordinated sound tracks, placed them on stunning background paintings, and painstakingly recorded his masterpieces on film.

For many of us, the most familiar form of animation is the common cartoon. You can while away many hours of a Saturday morning digesting the surreal antics of talking dogs, muscle-bound super heroes, and zany aliens. The techniques used to produce these "not-quite-Disneylike" features are closely related to CorelMOVE!'s special style of animation.

With CorelMOVE!, you create and coordinate the same three basic animation elements Disney worked with: actors, props, and sounds. Sound is not really a necessity. In fact, only those who have sound boards installed in their computers can use sound in CorelMOVE!. Now you have a great excuse to buy that sound board you have been drooling over.

Actors

Actors are the most important elements in your animated creations. They are also the most complex items to develop. Actors are made up of several cels depicting each phase of a movement. *Cel* is short for cellulose acetate—the clear material on which traditional animators paint their characters. The material must be transparent so that the background painting shows through as each frame of the progressive motion is photographed in sequence.

You must know what your actors do so that you can map out and dissect their movements. Then you are ready to render your individual cels. This important planning stage, called *storyboarding*, is discussed later in the chapter.

Props

Props are rendered just like actors. They do not, however, need to show different stages of motion, so they are rendered on a single cel only. A prop is still very versatile. It can be completely stationary or manipulated with Move's built-in transitions during the course of your movie. *Transitions* are special effects that enhance the way props enter and exit your animation. Good use of props adds depth to your animations.

Backgrounds

Backgrounds are the scenery against which the actors and props move. Background paintings often are major productions in big-budget animations. You also need backgrounds in CorelMOVE! animations because you don't want your actors and props cavorting around a stark white screen. As far as CorelMOVE! is concerned, backgrounds are considered props. Usually, you render them at a size that covers your animation window and place them on the bottom layer.

Layers

TIP

An actor can never be placed behind a prop. Props always appear on a layer behind actors.

CorelMOVE! uses the same concept as CorelDRAW! when it comes to layering items. You can move an element to the front of everything else, to the back of everything, or anywhere in between. CorelMOVE! makes it exceedingly easy to rearrange the layering of animation elements.

Sound

If you have a sound board installed in your system, background sounds can be incorporated into the show to make it much more exciting and professional. As you become a more experienced animator, you can even synchronize recorded voices with a character's movements to make it appear that the character is talking.

Storyboarding

The first step in producing your animation is planning. Answer the questions who, what, when, and where before you start the actual animation process; this saves a tremendous amount of time redoing work later. The traditional term for this step is *storyboarding*. You plan your animation by drawing single frames and placing them in the order they appear in the animation. Only key frames need to be rendered: those that show a different view of an actor, a new prop entering or exiting the scene, or the beginning of a new scene.

How much work should you put into storyboarding? If your animation is simple and you are working alone, your storyboard can be simple and sketchy. If you are working with many others on an elaborate project, the storyboard must be detailed enough to give everybody involved enough information to "see" the movie and be able to complete their specific tasks.

So then, talking dogs, muscle-bound super heroes, and zany aliens parading around your computer screen are only a few steps away, right? Yes and no. Some factors that affect the overall quality of your productions must be considered.

For the best possible animations, you need better-than-average computer power. CorelMOVE! is carrying out many instructions and is pushing tons of pixels around on your screen. The number of cels in your actor, the speed you want your animations to move (frames per second), the number of actors and props used in your show, and the incorporation of sound are factors that have a dramatic effect on your computer's performance. Even a simple animation sequence can bring a weak CPU with a small, slow hard disk and minimal RAM to a crawl. Do not neglect the importance of a fast video system. Accelerator cards and systems that incorporate Local Bus architecture keep your animations zipping along.

If you are serious about animation, buy the biggest and fastest hardware you can afford. You won't regret it. If you are simply getting your feet wet, experiment with CorelMOVE!. See what you can do with the resources you have. You will undoubtedly be surprised by what you can accomplish.

Another factor is experience. Animation is an art. Walt Disney honed his skills over time; it paid off. Your practice will too. Reading imparts to you the experience of others. Go to the library and find some books on animation. Subscribe to magazines that specialize in multimedia.

Study the work of other animators. To this end, the samples supplied with CorelMOVE! are an invaluable source of information. Open them up. Examine them closely. Look at all the actors and the cels that make them move.

Finally, have patience. Consider that one minute's worth of animation in a typical high-quality animated film is composed of 1,440 cels. In CorelMOVE!, you don't make anywhere near that amount of cels, but the basics still apply. The work can be tedious. Take your time, and you can produce professional-looking animations.

Joe DeLook Goes Multimedia

Joe's old pal, Rip Raster, has another project for DeLook Design. Rip wants something really eye-catching to draw people's attention to the new swimwear boutique he has opened at the rear of his surf shop.

Joe recently has been experimenting with CorelMOVE!, so he suggests that a multimedia show running on the computer at the front of the store should do the trick. Rip, with visions of MTV videos in his head, is sold.

Joe sits down to plan out his visuals. All he knows for sure is that he needs a beach scene, a surfboard, and Rippin' Surfboards' logo. Now what?

Joe's project in CorelMOVE! is the basis for the exercises you follow here. After you finish this chapter, take a look at what Joe created for Rippin' Surfboards. If you are interested in receiving a disk file of the completed CorelMOVE! exercise, consult the mail-in disk offer at the back of the book.

If you are ready, pull up your director's chair, put on your favorite beret, and grab your megaphone. Next stop—Movieland!

Starting CorelMOVE!: Lights, Camera, Action!

First you must start up CorelMOVE! and become familiar with its tools. Then you can work through a simple example to see the way an animation, with actors and props, is created.

Upon installation, CorelDRAW! 4.0 creates a Program Group in Program Manager called Corel 4. In it, you find the CorelMOVE! icon. Double-click on the icon to start the program. After a few seconds CorelMOVE! stares you in the face.

Understanding the CorelMOVE! Workspace

CorelMOVE! has two work areas: the Animation Window and the Editor. Unfortunately, when you start CorelMOVE! you are in neither. You see only a bleak-looking, marble-textured backdrop and an anemic menu bar. All the menu titles except File are inaccessible. You do not have much choice here. You need to start a new file (see fig. 13.2).

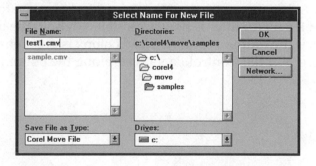

Figure 13.2:
Starting a new file.

Starting a New Move File

Click on <u>F</u>ile

Click on <u>N</u>ew   The Select Name for New File
                                                             dialog box appears

In the File Name textbox, type **Test1**   The CMV extension is automati-
                                                             cally added to the end of the file
                                                             name

Use Dri<u>v</u>es and <u>D</u>irectories to store the file where you will remember it.
Do yourself a favor and don't choose a floppy disk.

Click on OK   You now are in the Animation
                                                             Window, and the name of your
                                                             file is displayed in CorelMOVE!'s
                                                             title bar

Touring the Animation Window

The global parameters of your animation are set in the Animation
Window. These parameters include how big (in pixels) your
animation is; how many frames long it runs; and how fast it plays
back. This workspace is where you assemble and arrange the
elements of your animation. You assign actors movements (paths)
across the frame and specify the entering and exiting transitions
for your props. This is not where you create the actors and props;
that is done in the Editor.

Now is the best time to become familiar with the Animation
Window. At the top, notice that the menu bar has come to life. All
but one of the menu titles is now accessible. Right in the middle of
the screen is the Frame Window. The Toolbox is positioned along
the left side, and the Control Panel rests along the bottom (see
fig. 13.3).

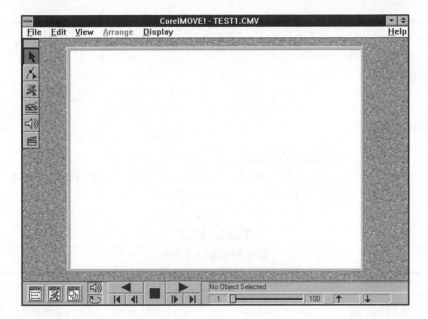

Figure 13.3:
CorelMOVE!'s
Animation Window.

Menus

Now you can drop down each menu and get a look at the available options. This is your chance to play Sherlock Holmes and investigate. You can't do any harm if you click on Cancel to get out of any dialog boxes. Take note of Import in the File menu and Insert New Object under the Edit menu. Although they look the same, they have slightly different purposes. If you select the Timelines, Cel Sequencer, or Library roll-up menus under Display, more toys appear. You get to use these options later.

Frame Window

All the elements of your movie are assembled and played back inside the frame window area. You can change the height and width of the frame from the Animation Information dialog box under the Display menu. Keep in mind that your animations are played on other computers that might not run the same video resolution as yours. If yours produces an animation with a frame size of 800x600, and play it back on a system with 640x480 (VGA), 120 pixels on the right side and 140 pixels on the bottom of your creation are lopped off. Remember what was said earlier about planning?

Toolbox

Six tools are available in CorelMOVE!: the Pick tool, Path tool, Actor tool, Prop tool, Sound tool, and Cue tool. Table 13.1 shows each tool and its purpose.

Table 13.1
The Toolbox Tools

Icon	Tool Name	Use
	Pick tool	For selecting or moving actors and props; works just like the Pick tool in CorelDRAW!.
	Path tool	For selecting actors and applying paths to them; also for selecting and editing existing paths. Similar to the Node Edit tool in CorelDRAW!.
	Actor tool	For creating new actors. It opens a dialog box that enables you to choose the editor of your choice: Move's paint editor, PhotoPAINT!, or CorelDRAW! 4.0.
	Prop tool	For creating new props. It opens a dialog box that enables you to choose the editor of your choice: Move's paint editor, PhotoPAINT!, or CorelDRAW! 4.0.

Icon	Tool Name	Use
	Sound tool	For importing sounds. It opens a dialog box that allows you to use CorelMOVE!'s Wave Editor to record and modify WAV files.
	Cue tool	For creating cues. The Cue Information dialog box appears. Cues enable you to automatically start, stop, or pause your animations. Cues enable you to "chain" different animation files together and add that "interactive" touch.

Control Panel

Starting on the far left of the Control Panel are icons that display the Timelines, Library, and Cel Sequencer roll-up menus. These are tools you use to fine-tune your animations; they are the same roll-ups you saw under the Display menu.

In the middle is a cluster of seven VCR-style push-button controls. These are used to play your animation in a variety of ways. To the left of these playback controls are two more controls. The top sports a speaker, and the bottom has a circular-shaped arrow. Table 13.2 shows these controls and their functions.

Table 13.2
Control Panel Controls

Icon	Control Name	Function
	Stop	Stops playback of your animation
	Forward	Plays back your animation (with sound, if enabled)
	Forward One Frame	Plays back one frame each time you click on it
	Reverse	Reverses playback of your animation (without sound, even if enabled)
	Reverse One Frame	Reverses playback, one frame each time you click on it
	First Frame	Moves to frame one
	Last Frame	Moves to last frame of animation
	Loop	Provides continuous playback of your animation until the Stop button is clicked
	Enable Sound	Enables sound during normal forward playback (has no effect if you do not have a sound board installed)

Rounding out the Control Panel is a slider control that enables you to move through the frames comprising your animated production. The numbers on either side of the slider inform you of the frame you are viewing and the total number of frames in your animation. Other status fields on the Control Panel display important information about the currently selected actor or prop. You are kept aware of the selection's type, name, amount of cels, and which frame it enters and exits the animation.

Creating and Modifying Actors and Props

The other workspace you use to create animations is the Editor. CorelMOVE! is unique among animation packages because it offers a choice of three different editors for creating or modifying actors and props: the built-in Move bit-map editor, the PhotoPAINT! module, and CorelDRAW! 4.0. Which one should you use? It depends.

The Move editor and PhotoPAINT! are bit-map–based paint programs. If you are comfortable with these types of programs and their tools suit your needs, by all means, use them.

When you use CorelDRAW! as your editor, you get the power of a vector-based drawing package. All the tools available in Draw are at your disposal. This pushes CorelMOVE! ahead of the pack.

As you examine each editor's tools and functions, you realize that each has strengths and weaknesses. The beauty of CorelMOVE! is that you are not locked into using just one editor. Use them all; what works for you is the right tool for the job!

To examine the editors, you need to have something to edit. Tell CorelMOVE! that you want to create or modify an actor or prop.

Creating a New Actor

Click on the Actor tool	The New Actor dialog box appears

In the Object **N**ame *text box, type* **Ball1**

All elements in your animations should have unique names to make them easy to identify. These are not file names, only labels.

Click on the **C**reate New *option*
Click on CorelDRAW! 4.0 Graphic *in the* Object **T**ype *list*

Click on OK	CorelDRAW! starts

Through the magic of OLE, CorelDRAW! starts and a link is established between it and CorelMOVE!. *OLE* stands for object linking and embedding. This Windows feature enables you to create files that share and transfer information between OLE-capable applications, such as Move, Draw, and Paint. OLE makes it possible to dynamically edit animation elements created in Draw or Paint directly from Move. If you look closely, you see that this is not an ordinary instance of CorelDRAW! (see fig. 13.4).

Figure 13.4:

Using CorelDRAW! as the editor.

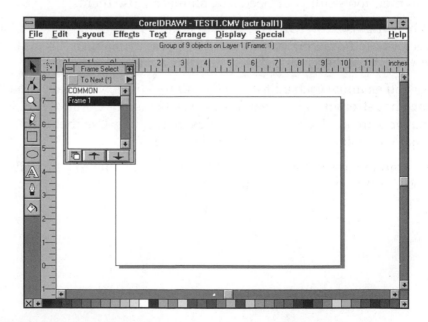

The text in the title bar at the top indicates that the file it is linked to is Test1.CMV. It also reveals the actor and its name.

A new roll-up menu—Frame Select—also is conspicuous. Think of it as a modified version of the normal Layers roll-up menu. This roll-up provides everything you need to use CorelDRAW! as your animation editor.

Some more changes are under the File menu. Update initiates the "rendering" function and uses OLE to transfer all your work from Draw to Move. Exit & Return does the same thing; however, it closes this instance of Draw. If you are sure that you will not do any more editing to this actor, or you are running low on Windows resources, use Exit & Return. Save Copy As enables you to save the drawing as a native CDR file.

Take some more time to look around, then choose Exit & Return. When you are presented with the Update the embedded object? message, just say NO!.

Now create a new actor using PhotoPAINT!. The same types of changes have been made to Paint's File menu and title bar. The biggest difference between this editor and Draw or the Move editor is the lack of support for making the individual frames that comprise an actor. What PhotoPAINT excels at is making elaborate scenery that moves because it is really an actor moving along a path.

Creating Your First Actor

You are ready to create your first actor and breathe life into its nostrils. Cancel everything else you have done to get back to the Animation Window. Take a deep breath and push the Actor tool on the Toolbar one more time.

Name your actor Ball1. Choose CorelDRAW! 4.0 Graphic as your Object Type. Make sure that Create New is still selected and click on OK.

When CorelDRAW! is up and ready, follow the directions in the next exercise to render your actor—a simple beach ball.

Remember, to make a perfect circle using the Ellipse tool you must hold down the Ctrl key.

Creating a Beach Ball

Click on the Ellipse tool	The cursor becomes a +
Place the cursor anywhere on the page and drag out a circle approximately 2 inches in diameter	A circle is drawn
Click on the Outline tool	The Outline tool fly-out menu appears
Click on the Pen Nib *icon*	The Outline Pen dialog box appears
Select Points *from the drop-down list of measurements*	
In the **W**idth *text box, type* **3** *points*	
Click on OK	Your circle has a 3-point black outline

If your outline color is not black, change it in the Pen Color dialog box. Also, make sure that **E**dit Wireframe under the **D**isplay menu is not checked, and that you select the circle before the next steps.

Click on the Fill tool	The Fill fly-out menu appears
Click on the Color Wheel *icon*	The Uniform Fill dialog box appears
Click on the drop-down list next to Show *and select* Pantone Spot Colors Model	The visual color palette changes
Click on the Show Color Names *option*	A check mark appears
Select Pantone Red 032 *from the color list*	
Click on OK	The circle has turned red

Next, you make the different colored sections of the beach ball. The ball has four series of red, blue, and white sections for a total of 12 sections. Each segment needs to have an arc of 30 degrees.

The basic steps to accomplish this are: **C**opy the red circle and use **P**aste to bring another one in directly on top. Change the color of the top circle. Next, make a 30-degree pie slice out of it. Then use Rotate on the pie slice, and be sure to use "keep the original."

Finally, make the segments the correct colors and get rid of any unnecessary pie slices. The following exercises take each procedure step-by-step.

Making the Segments

Select the red circle and click on **E**dit	The Edit menu appears
Click on **C**opy	A Copying box flashes on and off; the circle is now on the Windows Clipboard
Click on **E**dit	The Edit menu appears
Click on **P**aste	The screen flickers as it draws another red circle directly on top of the first
Click on the Fill tool	The Fill fly-out menu appears
Click on Uniform Fill	The Uniform Fill dialog box appears
Select Pantone Blue 072 *from the color list*	The New color display turns blue
Click on OK	The top circle turns blue

You are going to make the first pie segment now. Use the Zoom tool to get in fairly close. Remember to keep the Shape tool inside the circle's outline.

Click on the Shape tool	
Click and hold down the mouse button on the circle's node	The node is highlighted
Move the node in a clockwise direction until you make a 30-degree wedge	The status bar reads `Total angle = 30.0 degrees` (see fig. 13.5)

Now duplicate and rotate the pie slice. Make sure that the blue slice is selected.

Click on Effe**c**ts	The Effects menu appears
Click on **R**otate & Skew	The Rotate & Skew dialog box appears
In the **R**otation Angle *text box, type* **30**	
Click on **L**eave Original	
Click on OK	Another blue pie slice is drawn

continues

Press Ctrl-R nine times

Eleven blue slices are on top of
the red circle (see fig. 13.6)

Figure 13.5:
Thirty-degree blue
segment.

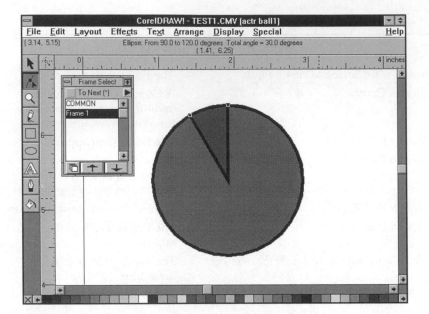

Figure 13.6:
Ball1 with 11 blue
segments.

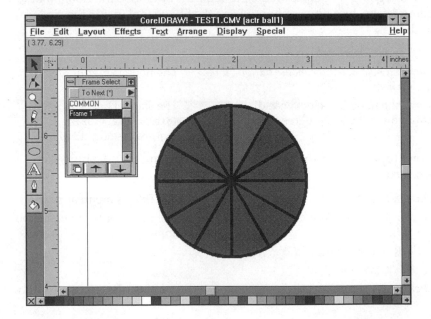

To make the final changes, you assign every third segment a light gray color. This is necessary because Move translates pure white into transparent. A 5% black appears to be opaque white when translated by Move. Working clockwise, select the segment next to the red one.

Making the Finishing Touches

Click on the Fill tool

The Fill fly-out menu appears

Select the Uniform Fill *icon*

The Uniform Fill dialog box appears

Select black from the list

In the percentage text box, type **5**

Continue filling every third segment with 5% black. Complete the red, white, and blue sequence by deleting any blue segments covering segments which need to be red. After you finish, group all your elements. Figure 13.7 shows your ball.

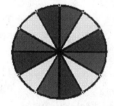

Figure 13.7:

The completed beach ball.

There you have it, your basic beach ball! Now you have to animate the ball's rolling motion, which is fairly simple: just show the ball in different degrees of rotation on each cel.

Using the Frame Select Roll-Up Menu

Whether you realize it, you have been working on the first frame of your animation sequence. Notice that Frame 1 is highlighted in the Frame Select roll-up menu. A frame is also labeled COMMON. Any element you want repeated on every frame of your animation should be drawn here.

The motion of any round object is highly repetitive. This means you only need to make key frames and copy them to other frames to complete the sequence. Irregularly shaped objects are not as simple to animate.

To start the beach ball rolling, you need to insert more cels into your actor's sequence. You only need enough cels to show one complete rotation of the ball—three frames. Two more renderings of your ball, besides the original, is sufficient. You use the Frame Select roll-up menu.

The Frame Select roll-up menu (shown in fig. 13.8) has a small black triangle indicating that another fly-out menu is accessed by clicking on it. From this menu you can easily insert cels, delete cels, and copy items from one cel to another.

Animating the Beach Ball

On the Frame Select roll-up menu, click on the fly-out meno button (a triangle)	The fly-out menu appears
Click on Insert after	The Insert new frames dialog box appears
Type **2**	
Click on OK	The Frame Select roll-up shows a frame count of 3
Select Frame 1 *from the Frame Select roll-up*	The beach ball reappears
Select the ball and click on the Frame Select fly-out menu	
Click on Copy To	The TO? arrow appears
Click on Frame 2	You are now on Frame 2, and the ball has been copied
Click on Effe**c**ts	
Click on **R**otate & Skew	
In the Rotation **A**ngle *text box, type* **30**	
Click on OK	The ball rotates 30 degrees
Click on the Frame Select fly-out menu	
Click on Copy to	The TO? arrow appears (see fig. 13.9)

Click on Frame 3	The ball is copied to Frame 3
Click on Effects	
Click on **R**otate & Skew	

In the Rotation **A**ngle *text box, type* **30**

You have made three cels that illustrate one complete rotation of the beach ball.

Figure 13.8:

The Frame Select fly-out menu.

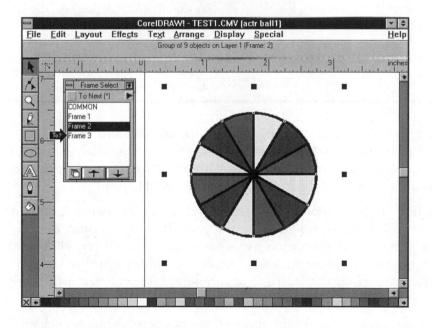

Figure 13.9:

Copying rotated Ball1 from Frame 2 to Frame 3.

You now can use the up- and down-arrow buttons on the bottom of the Frame Select roll-up menu to cycle through your cels, or use the Preview button (the button to the left of the up arrow) to see a preview of the cels in motion.

If you have copied the wrong rotation rendering to a cel, it appears to have a jerky motion. Find the rendering that is out of sequence and delete the existing ball first. Then copy the right rendering to the cel.

Getting Back to Move

Using CorelDRAW!'s great drawing tools to create the ball animation was much easier than using any of the paint-type editors. Now you must get the ball back to Move. This is a snap.

Returning to MOVE

Click on File	The File menu appears
Click on Exit & Return	A CorelDRAW! dialog box appears, prompting you to update the embedded object
Click on Yes	The Rendering status indicator appears and shows the progress of its exporting functions

OLE takes care of shutting down CorelDRAW! and placing the actor in the Animation Window. You see another dialog box that shows Move's progress in importing the actor's color information. If all goes well, Ball1 is ready to show you its stuff.

Click on the forward VCR button on the Control Panel and watch the ball spin. Round and round it goes. If the Loop push-button is depressed, the animation plays continuously until you click on the Stop button. Let it run, and observe the slider control move and the Frame Counter status fields change. After you are sufficiently dizzy, click on the Stop button.

When you need to make changes to your actor, double-click on it. This brings up the Actor Information dialog box. You can modify almost every aspect of the actor by changing the values in the text boxes. This dialog box also is the gateway back to CorelDRAW!. Click on the Edit Actor button at the lower left, to launch back to

Draw. The actor is loaded and ready to edit. The same procedure is used for props.

Now give the ball a little push in the right direction. First, move the ball to a good starting point. You can do this by selecting and moving it with the mouse or by changing the Start Position coordinates in the Actor Information dialog box; the latter method makes it easier to work through the example.

Moving the Starting Position

Double-click on Ball1   The Actor Information dialog box
                                           appears

In the **H**orizontal *text box, type* **339**

In the **V**ertical *text box, type* **7**

Click on OK

Ball1 is now positioned in the upper right corner of the Animation Window. To get it to move across the screen, it needs a path to follow.

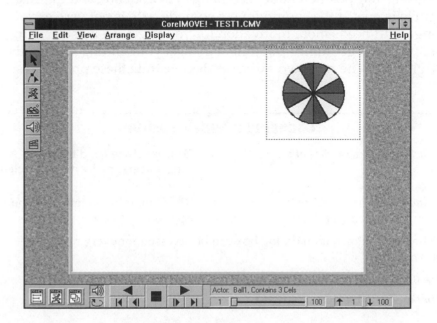

Figure 13.10:

Ball1 after moving the start position.

A simple path needs only two points: a beginning and an end. The coordinate your actor starts from is the *beginning node*; the coordinate your actor finishes at is the *end node*. A very active actor has a complicated path with many intermediate nodes.

To assign a path to an actor, select the actor with the Path tool. Path nodes can be set anywhere in Move's Animation Window or gray marble backdrop.

Using the Path Edit Roll-Up Menu

Select the Path tool from the Toolbox and click on Ball1. The Path Edit roll-up menu appears, and the ball is surrounded by a bounding box with a black circle at the upper left corner. This black circle indicates the corner of the actor that moves along the assigned path. Move your mouse to the left edge of the Animation Window and click once about halfway down the side. If a new node is not made, make sure that the Allow Adding Points option at the bottom of the Edit Path roll-up menu is checked. Then try it again.

The starting position node has changed to a square, and the black circle is now at the end node. A two-node path is not very exciting. Ball1 needs more motivation for you to get the most from it; more nodes get things popping. First, get your ending node in the right spot. The next two exercises demonstrate these procedures.

Changing a Node's Position

Click on Ball1 *with the Path tool*	Ball1 is selected and the beginning and end nodes are connected by a line
Double-click on the end node	The Point Information dialog box appears

The Point Information dialog box can be accessed for every node on a path.

In the <u>H</u>orizontal *text box, type* **5**

In the <u>V</u>ertical *text box, type* **202**

If not already checked, select the Loop To Here
option

Click on OK   Ball1 repositions

Adding More Nodes to a Path

Click on the +/- button on the Path Edit   The Scale Path dialog
roll-up menu   box appears

In the **D**esired *text box, type* **12**

Click on OK

Now you have placed 12 nodes on the path, and the ball has
moved to the second one (see fig. 13.11). Push the Forward button
on the Control Panel and watch the fun. The Scale Path dialog box
is used to delete, as well as add, nodes to a path.

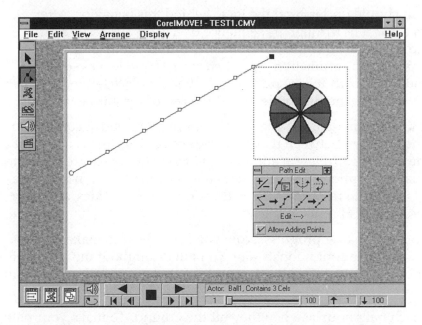

Figure 13.11:
Path with 12 nodes.

Why is the ball running downhill and spinning away at the
bottom? Because you set the last node to be the Loop To Here
node. The Loop To Here node performs a special function. See

what happens when you change its location to another node on the path. For the sake of brevity, Loop To Here is abbreviated as LTH.

Changing the Loop To Here Node

Click on Ball1 *with the Path tool*

Double-click on the first node on the path   The Point Information dialog
                                                     box appears

Click on the Loop To Here *option*

Click on OK

Now play back your animation. As you see, changing the LTH node makes a big difference in the way your animation works. Experiment by changing the LTH node setting to different nodes on the path.

You should understand the logic behind this behavior. After an actor runs through its sequence of cels (in this case 12), it moves to the LTH node and finishes out its allotted amount of frames in the animation. So, when the LTH node was set at the end of the path it just spun away; it had no place left to go. When it was set to the first node, it had the rest of the path left.

If the LTH node is set to a node other than the end, a connection line is drawn between it and the end node. This line is now part of the actor's path. If you add nodes to the path, nodes are added to this line segment. This may not be what you want. If not, set the LTH node to the end of the path, add your new nodes, and then reset the LTH node.

You are making progress. Now you know how to make your actors move continuously along a path throughout the length of your animation. This continuous loop, however, will get on your nerves in short order.

Beach balls bounce when they hit the ground. To make your path reflect an arcing motion, reposition the nodes. This makes your ball act more realistically, and is the next step to realism for your animation.

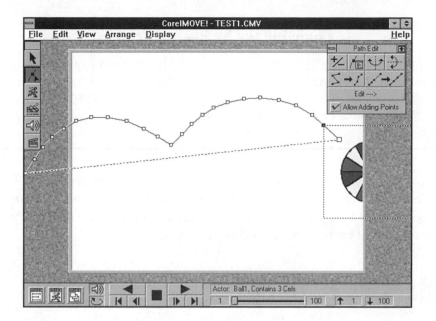

Use the Path tool to position your actor's nodes like those shown
in figure 13.12. Note how the end of the path extends out of the
Animation Window. Before you start, increase the amount of
nodes to 24, giving a smoother appearance to your ball's motion.

Run your animation and keep tweaking the nodes until you are
satisfied. A proper understanding of how paths and nodes affect
your animation is important. Take your time and experiment.

Of course, other factors affect the quality of your animation. One
factor is the amount of frames that your show displays.

If you look closely at your animation as it is playing, you notice
the ball's motion is pretty smooth until you get to frame 100; then
it jumps. To understand why, think about the arithmetic involved.
You created Ball1 with three cels and put it on a path with 12
nodes. Then you increased the node count to 24. These numbers
are all multiples of the amount of cels in your actor. Therefore,
changing the total frames in your animation to any multiple of
three makes it look smoother.

TIP

You can move a
series of consecutive
nodes by selecting
them using the Shift-
Click technique.

Changing the Number of Frames

Click on **D**isplay	The Display menu appears
Click on **A**nimation Info	The Animation Information dialog box appears

In the **N**umber of Frames *text box, type* **96**
Click on OK

Push the forward playback button and enjoy the fruits of your labor. The ball no longer jumps at the end of your show. As you see, lengthening or shortening your animation may be necessary to achieve a certain effect and is very simple to do.

Backing It All Up

Ball1 looks rather lonely on a blank screen. A background does wonders at this point. What is a beach scene without sand and sky? Because neither element needs to move, they will be props. Creating both of these props is a snap with CorelDRAW!.

Making the Beach

Go to Frame 1

Click on the Prop tool in the Toolbox	The New Prop dialog box appears

In the Object **N**ame *text box, type* **Beach**
In the Object **T**ype *list, click on* CorelDRAW! 4.0 Graphic
Select the **C**reate New *option*

Click on OK	CorelDRAW! starts

Select the Rectangle tool

Drag out a rectangle approximately 9.80" x 2.5" and position it at the bottom of your page.

Click on the Fill tool	The Fill fly-out menu appears
Click on the Texture Fill tool (top row, sixth from the left)	The Texture Fill dialog box appears

Select Styles in the Texture **L**ibrary
drop-down list

Select Mineral.Speckled 2 Colors from the
Texture List

In the Texture # *edit box, type* **5469**

Use the 1st Mineral and 2nd Mineral color selectors to create a combination of colors that reminds you of a sandy beach. When you change a value, click on the Preview button to see what your combination looks like. When you are satisfied with the look, click on OK.

Click on the Outline tool	The Outline fly-out menu appears
Click on the Pen Nib *icon*	The Outline Pen dialog box appears

In the **W**idth *text box, type* **6**

Select **B**ehind Fill

Click on OK

A beach is seldom perfectly flat. Convert the rectangle to curves, and add a few nodes and curves to make it look similar to figure 13.13.

Click on **F**ile

Click on E**x**it and Return

Click on Yes *in the Embed Object dialog box*

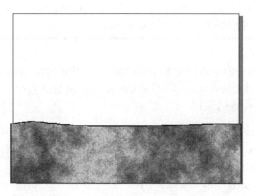

Figure 13.13:
Creating the beach.

Back in Move, position your beach at the bottom of the Animation Window. View your animation and see how it looks.

Creating the sky is even easier than creating the sand. For the sky, a fountain-filled rectangle does nicely. Select the Prop tool, name your prop "Sky," and click on OK to start CorelDRAW!.

Creating the Sky

Click on the Rectangle tool

Drag out a rectangle approximately 9.8" x 5" and position it at the top of the page.

Click on the Fill tool

Click on the Fountain Fill tool	The Fountain Fill dialog box appears
*Click on **O**ptions*	The Fountain Fill Color Options dialog box appears
*Click on **C**ustom*	
Choose a sky blue color from the Palette	
Click on OK	The Fountain Fill dialog box reappears
*In the **A**ngle text box, type* **-90**	The color display shows dark blue at the top and white at the bottom

Click on OK

Use the Outline tool to remove any outline that can be assigned to the rectangle before selecting E**x**it and Return.

The Sky prop should be positioned at the top of the Animation Window and then sent to the back using the **A**rrange menu, as shown in figure 13.14.

You now have your own little piece of the seashore. Add whatever else you like; some clouds moving through the blue sky or a bright sun up in the corner would be appropriate. Small details, like shadows under the ball when it hits the sand, are finishing touches that make your animation come alive. Now use the **T**imelines roll-up menu to fit your elements together.

Using the Timelines Roll-Up Menu

The Timelines roll-up menu is crucial to get that "top-down" view of your animation. It lists all the elements of your animation by category: first come actors, next props, third sounds, and finally, cues. Each section is separated by a line. As you can see, Ball1 is on top with Sky and Beach underneath. If you do not see them in the listing, check to see if the Actor and Prop buttons at the top of the Timelines roll-up menu are depressed.

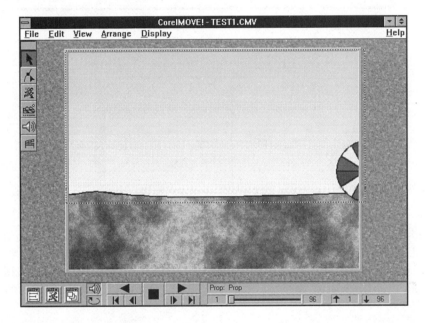

Figure 13.14:
Positioning the sky.

Click on the arrow button at the top, to the right of the icons. The roll-up expands and displays multicolored timelines. Each time-line indicates the frame at which an element enters the animation, in how many frames the element displays, and at what frame it exits.

The Timelines roll-up menu is very intuitive. You can modify the timing aspects of all components from this roll-up. This is more efficient than jumping to many different dialog boxes to accom-plish the same results. Your cursor shape changes as it passes over a timeline. Your cursor can take three different shapes, indicating what part of the timeline you are changing. Use the following exercise to arrange Ball1, Sky, and Beach.

Moving Timelines

Click and hold on the left end of the Beach timeline	The cursor turns to an arrow pointing left
Drag the end of the timeline to Frame 1	The status bar at the bottom reads 1

If you have problems grabbing the end of a timeline, use the slider at the top of the Timelines roll-up menu to zoom in on the line you need to modify (see fig. 13.15).

Figure 13.15:

Using the slider control to zoom in on timelines.

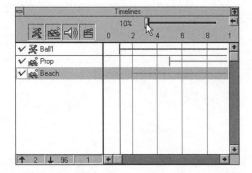

Use the same technique to change the starting position of Sky and Ball1. Play with each element's timelines, then play back your animation to see the results. In this way, you become familiar with the versatility and control built into this very useful roll-up menu.

The Cel Sequencer Roll-Up Menu

TIP

The Cel Sequencer effects can be applied only to actors. If a special effect is needed for a prop, use a transition.

CorelMOVE! provides special functions that enable you to make your actors more dramatic without redrawing them. Learning to use the options found on the Cel **S**equencer roll-up menu saves time and helps you to produce more advanced animations. You can apply these built-in special effects to your actors with a few mouse clicks. Use one of these effects now to see how it automatically makes your ball appear to bounce into the distance.

Making the Cels Smaller

Click on the Path tool

Click on Ball1

Click on the Cel Sequencer *Icon in the*
Control Panel or click on Cel **S**equencer
Rollup *under* **D**isplay

The Cel Sequencer roll-up
menu appears (see fig. 13.16)

The first drop-down list controls which frames in your animation are
affected when you click on Apply. You can choose to affect all the
frames, one frame, or a range of frames. The Effect Type list box changes
depending on the frame selection method you choose. The type of
options available for each effect also changes accordingly.

Select All Frames *from the Apply To drop-down list*

In the Effects Type list box, select Scale Sequence

In the Effects Option list, select Large To Medium

Click on Apply

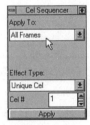

Figure 13.16:

The Cel Sequencer
roll-up menu.

Play back your animation and watch the beach ball bounce away
toward the horizon. Play with the various effects the Cel Sequencer has to offer.

One very powerful effect is Unique Cel. This effect enables you to
display the actor's cels out of sequence. A practical application for
this feature is to make an actor appear to pause and then continue.
To accomplish this, select your actor and set a certain number of
consecutive frames to the same cel number. The more consecutive
frames you assign to the same cel number, the longer the actor
remains motionless.

The Library Roll-Up Menu

The key to CorelMOVE!'s flexible nature is its capability to save and organize animation elements. You collect your actors, props, and sounds and save them in libraries. When you need an element you have created previously, you simply load the library that contains it and then place it into your new production.

The **L**ibrary roll-up menu provides the functions needed to manage your libraries and their members (see fig. 13.17).

Figure 13.17:

The Library roll-up menu.

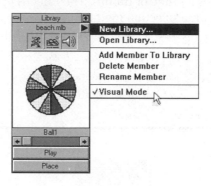

Making Use of a Library

Click on the Library *icon in the Control Panel or click on* **L**ibrary Rollup *under* **D**isplay	The Library roll-up menu appears
Click on the black arrow at the top of the roll-up menu	The pop-up menu appears
Click on New Library	The New Library dialog box appears
In the File **N**ame *text box, type* **beach**	
Use the Directories and Drives areas to choose where you want to store your library	
Click on OK	
With the Pick tool, click on Ball1	A bounding box appears around Ball1
Click on the black arrow on the **L**ibrary *roll-up menu*	The pop-up menu appears

Click on Add Member To Library	Ball1 is placed in the Beach library; Ball1 is displayed in the status line under its picture

If a picture of Ball1 is not displayed, choose Visual Mode from the pop-up menu. Click on the Play button to watch Ball1 run through its cels, and click on Stop when you are finished. Repeat the preceding steps for each member you want to add to the library. Use the scroll bars under the status line to view each member in the library.

To place Library members in other animations, open the library, scroll through the members to find the one you need, and select Place.

Adding Sound

With a sound board installed in your computer, you can elevate your animations to multimedia extravaganzas. Well, almost.

By using the Sound icon in the Toolbox, you can use Move's internal Wave Editor to record, manipulate, and place files into your animation. If you have access to other sources for WAV files, you can use the Import command on the File menu.

NOTE

WAV files come in several different "flavors." If your WAV file does not play, it may not be 100% compatible with Microsoft's specification for WAV files.

Use the Timelines roll-up menu to start and end the sound at the appropriate frames. Make sure that you allow enough frames in between the start and stop positions to accommodate the length of your file. Placing simple sounds in your animation is not very complicated; however, it takes a good deal of experimentation to synchronize your sounds with the visual elements of your animation.

Summary

Congratulations! You have learned the basics of CorelMOVE!'s magic. CorelMOVE! has many more features to exploit. Soon you use prop transitions for special effects and merge your animations into CorelSHOW! screen shows. With a little more experience, you add cues to interactively start one animation from within another. These advanced techniques set your Corel-MOVE! animations apart from the pack.

You gain experience by experimenting. Have fun. The next time you sit down to watch some of those Saturday morning cartoons, you probably will appreciate them in a totally new way.

CorelSHOW!

orelSHOW! stands out as unique among the modules that comprise the CorelDRAW! family of applications. You use CorelSHOW! to assemble pieces of information (objects) that you created in other applications. You might think of Show like a factory assembly-line area; it provides a simple workspace in which separately made parts are bolted on or welded together to make something bigger than the sum of its parts. Where were these parts created? You can create the elements with programs such as CorelDRAW!, CorelCHART!, CorelPHOTOPAINT!, and CorelMOVE!, to name just a few.

CorelSHOW! ideally is suited for creating and managing on-screen presentations. This module provides an application area that benefits greatly from Show's capability to incorporate graphics, sound, and animation files.

Additionally, you can use Show to automate printing jobs, such as overhead and 35mm slide presentations. Rather than using CorelDRAW to open and print myriad overheads, you can make a presentation out of them in Show. You can rearrange the order of the overheads and need to issue only one print command.

Now you can walk away and make yourself a peanut butter-and-jelly sandwich while Show and the printer do the rest.

Getting To Know OLE

Show's capability to work its wonders is based on something that is built into Microsoft Windows. This underlying functionality is called OLE. If you worked through Chapter 13 on CorelMOVE!, you already are familiar with OLE. Because OLE is such an integral part of Show, however, this discussion provides a good opportunity to get some rudimentary information on its operations.

OLE stands for *Object Linking and Embedding*. Its purpose in the Windows world is to keep track of mundane information such as which files or programs you used to create objects in a document. Microsoft thinks this is intuitive computing. It is, but you must play by the rules and not move applications and files around on your computer. Also, applications must be designed to utilize the capabilities of OLE. Thankfully, Corel has endowed its suite of program modules to be OLE-capable.

To successfully transfer information using OLE, the two programs must cooperate closely. In this process, one program is called the client and the other is termed the server. The *server* is the program that originates the information and "serves it up" to the *client*. The client then uses the transferred information as it needs to. Microsoft does not force any program to adopt all the functionality of OLE; therefore, an application can be OLE-capable and be only a server, only a client, or both.

You are probably thinking, "What's the big deal? I've been using the Windows Clipboard to transfer information to and from applications for years." True, but transferring items by using the Clipboard often changes their construction—sometimes a lot. The item also becomes disconnected from the application that created it. If you need to revise something that went over the Clipboard, you might experience some problems.

First, Embedding

The power of OLE lies in its capability to create and maintain a connection between programs that share objects. If you need to make a change to your object, select O**b**ject from the client applications **E**dit menu. This process launches the server and loads your original file. Make your revisions, save the file, issue an Update command from the server and presto! Your changes appear in the client application. No fussing with exporting, importing, and intermediate files strewed all over the hard drive. This part is the *embedding* half of OLE. What could be quicker and easier?

Second, Linking

Suppose that you want to change every place you used your company logo on 150 35mm slides. No problem. The *linking* capability in OLE comes into play in this situation. If you used a link function when you added the company logo in the slide assembly process, the client application automatically looks to see whether the master logo file has changed and then updates each slide. Now that is slick!

Third, the Uh-Oh in OLE

As mentioned earlier, you must play by the rules in the OLE world. If you move the master file, the link is broken. Keep that master logo file in the same spot. You also must plan which type of transfer to use for a new document: a static embedded transfer (that you maintain) or a dynamically linked transfer (that is automatically updated). Another point to remember: don't move those OLE server applications. Generally, their location is added to the registration database at the time each program is installed so that Windows can keep track of where servers and clients can be found when their services are needed. (You didn't really think it was magic, did you?)

Finally, the last sticky wicket in the OLE scheme: OLE 2.0. Yes, Microsoft upgraded OLE and, as of this writing, it was not bug-free. So, CorelDRAW! modules that utilize OLE 2.0 functions might be less than reliable. The following is an excerpt from the README.WRI file in the COREL4 directory:

> *"The Microsoft OLE 2.0 redistributable files supplied with this package can produce certain operational problems. These problems should be cleared up when Microsoft ships a maintenance release of OLE 2.0, currently planned for the summer of 1993."*

Hopefully, by the time you read this, the fix will be out. If you are experiencing OLE2-related problems, you should contact Corel Corporation and request the fix. How do you know if you are having OLE2 problems? Just use Show for a while—it is an OLE client application that will reveal any problems in short order.

Starting CorelSHOW!

Enough talk of embedding, linking and what-not. The time has come to mouse your way over to Program Manager and double-click on the CorelSHOW! icon in the Corel Graphics program group. After the colorful title screen disappears, Show displays the Welcome To CorelSHOW! dialog box. This dialog box enables you to choose Open an Existing Presentation or Start a New presentation. Because Corel did not supply any sample Show presentations with this release, you must start a new presentation.

Starting a New SHOW Presentation

Click on Start a New Presentation *option button*	The Start with Slides option becomes visible
In the Start with Slides *textbox, type* **3**	

If Page Settings are not 11 by 8 1/2 inches and Landscape, use the Page Setup button to change them:

Click on Page Setup	The Page Setup dialog box appears

At Orientation, *select* <u>L</u>andscape
At Page Size, *select* Scree<u>n</u>

Click on OK   The Welcome to
CorelSHOW! dialog
appears

Click on OK   A new presentation
window appears

You now are ready to create a three-page screenshow. The next section helps you become familiar with the tools that Show offers.

Touring the Presentation Window

The CorelSHOW! Presentation window supplies the blank pages and basic tools needed to assemble and view your presentation elements. The following sections describe the various components of the Presentation window (see fig. 14.1)

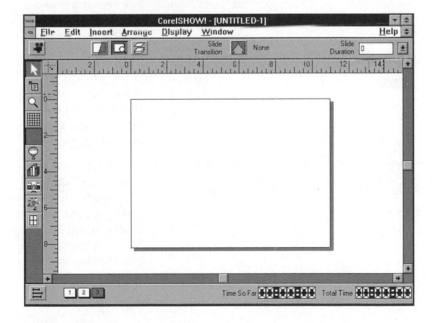

Figure 14.1:
The CorelSHOW! screen.

The menu bar provides selections for most of the functions used in Show. Select each menu and examine the choices offered. The File menu contains the commands to save your presentation files and open existing ones. Pay particular attention to the Insert, Arrange, and Display menus. You use the functions available under these menus to complete your Show projects.

Below the menu bar is a gray ribbon bar on which you find five buttons and a textbox with a drop-down list. Table 14.1 shows each item and its purpose.

Table 14.1
The Ribbon Bar Elements

Element	Name	Use
	Screenshow button	For viewing your presentation on-screen.
	Background View button	For viewing and editing background objects.
	Slide Viewer button	For viewing and editing foreground objects on individual slides in the presentation (Show's default view).
	Slide Sorter button	For viewing and arranging thumbnail versions of all the slides in your presentation. When this button is pressed, the Number button appears on the ribbon bar, which you can use to rearrange the pages in a presentation.

Element	Name	Use
	Transition button	For adding built-in effects that make the transition between pages more interesting.
	Slide Duration Setting	For setting the amount of time an object or page displays on-screen.

Continuing down the left side of the CorelSHOW! screen, you see the Toolbar. Click on these icons to access the tools you need to create or modify the elements in your presentations. Table 14.2 lists these buttons and their uses.

Table 14.2
The Toolbar

Icon	Tool Name	Use
	Pick tool	For selecting, moving, and resizing objects.
	Pop-up menu	For accessing a pop-up menu of options. The choices available on the pop-up menu change depending on the type of object selected.
	Zoom tool	For changing the viewing magnification of the page.

continues

Table 14.2
continued

Icon	Tool Name	Use
	Background Library tool	For accessing libraries of backgrounds.
	CorelDRAW! tool	For accessing CorelDRAW! to create objects.
	CorelCHART! tool	For launching Chart to create objects.
	Corel PHOTO-PAINT! tool	For using Photo-Paint to create objects.
	Insert Animation tool	For inserting an animation file (the same function as selecting **A**nimation from the **I**nsert menu).
	OLE tool	For launching other OLE-capable applications on your system that can create valid objects.

Along the bottom of the Show window is another gray area that offers more tools to control your presentation.

The first control on the far left is the Timelines button. This button is very similar to the Timelines roll-up in CorelMOVE!. Selecting this icon brings up a window that graphically displays the slides in your presentation (see fig.14.2). From this window, you quickly can see if a slide has a cue assigned to it and for how long the slide is set to display. Any sound objects you insert in the presentation also are shown here. You can limit the types of objects displayed in the window by selecting or deselecting the icons at the top-left. The button on the far right enables you to magnify the scale of the timelines portion of the window. This tool is handy for grabbing the lines to manually adjust the time duration of each slide or sound.

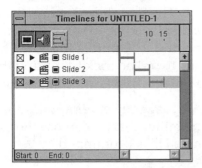

Figure 14.2:
The Timeline window.

To the right of the Timeline button are icons that represent the pages in your presentation. Clicking on these icons moves you from page to page. Note that the page icons disappear and are replaced by the word Background when you select the Background button on the top ribbon bar. Because backgrounds apply to all the pages in your presentation, you do not need to switch from page to page. If you want to use a different background on a slide, select the slide, then select the **O**mit Background command from the **E**dit menu. Choosing this option disables the master background on that slide. You then can create another background and place it on the foreground layer of the slide.

The last two controls in the lower portion of the screen are time displays. The first control shows how much time the presentation takes up to the page you are currently viewing. The second display keeps track of how much time your total presentation takes. Don't set your watch by these counters, they are not very accurate. They do, however, provide a close estimate of your presentation length.

Now that you have experienced the who, what, and where of CorelSHOW!'s interface, it is time to move along and create a simple screenshow.

Developing a Buildup Screenshow

A *buildup* is a series of slides displayed in succession. Each new slide adds more information to the previous slide. Bullet charts are ideal candidates for use of the buildup technique.

The following exercises work through making a three-bullet buildup screenshow. The first slide displays the first bullet point. As the next slide is displayed, it appears as if the second point is simply added to the first. The third slide adds the final bullet point to the previous two. The trick to making this technique work is to create the slide that displays the complete bullet list first.

You use CorelDRAW! as your server application to create a background and the bullet charts. You use the CorelDRAW! tool and the Insert menu's Object command.

Creating the Background

Screenshows need colorful backgrounds to make the displayed information more interesting. The following exercises are designed to produce dark blue bullet points on a yellow background. Feel free to substitute a color scheme that suits your taste.

Creating a Background

Click on the Background tool on the ribbon bar	The word Background replaces the page icons
Click on the CorelDRAW! tool	The cursor becomes a +
Click on the cursor anywhere on the blank page	CorelDRAW! launches and comes to the front of CorelSHOW!
Click on Layout	The Layout menu appears
Click on Page Setup	The Page Setup dialog box appears

If your page size is not Letter or the orientation is not Landscape, select these options now.

Click on **A**dd Page Frame	
Click on OK	You are back in the Draw page window and the page border is high-lighted
With the page border highlighted, click on the Outline tool	The Outline tool fly-out menu appears
Click on the Outline Color *icon*	The Outline Color dialog box appears
In the Show drop-down list, select PANTONE Spot Colors	The color pallet changes
Click on Show Color Names	Color pallet is changed to display color swatches and PANTONE names
Select PANTONE Yellow CV	The New color display is changed to yellow
Click on OK	The page border is now yellow
Click on the Fill tool	The Fill fly-out menu appears
Click on the Color Wheel *icon*	The Uniform Fill dialog box appears
Click on Show Color Names	Color pallet is changed to display color swatches and PANTONE names
Select PANTONE Yellow CV	The New color display is changed to yellow
Click on OK	The page is now filled with yellow
Click on **F**ile	The File menu appears
Click on E**x**it & Return to CorelSHOW!	A dialog box asks if you want to update the embedded object
Click on **Y**es	CorelDRAW! disappears and you are back in CorelSHOW!

Through OLE, the CorelDRAW! background object has been transferred and embedded into your presentation. If you need to change the background for any reason, simply double-click on it. CorelSHOW! launches CorelDRAW! and automatically loads the background object for you.

continues

Notice that the size of the yellow background is very small. The next step is to make the background fit perfectly.

Click on **A**rrange	The Arrange menu appears
Click on Fit Object to **P**age	The background is sized to fill the entire page
Click on the Slide View tool in the ribbon bar	The page icons at the bottom reappear

Now that you have created a background, navigate through the page icons to confirm that each page displays the yellow background.

Using Background Libraries

If you create a background that you would like to use again, use the Save **B**ackground command under the **F**ile menu to store your background in a Background Library file (SHB). You can create new libraries or select the Insert in Library option to add a background to an existing SHB file. When you want to use a saved background again, click on the Background tool, and the Background Library window appears. You can use the Change button and browse the hard drive to locate the SHB file that contains the background you want. After you locate the file, you can access all the backgrounds stored in that library. Simply click on the background of your choice and it is placed into your presentation. You need to click on the Done button to close the library window.

Creating a Bullet Chart

As mentioned earlier, the bullet chart you create has three bullet points. You use CoreDRAW!'s text roll-up, automatic bullet-making, and paragraph functions to make the slide.

Some items to remember about the interaction between Show and Draw: the size of objects transferred are not to scale (you saw how the background came in very small) and interaction through OLE might be slower than expected. As far as the first point goes, the workaround is to place a page frame border around all your objects. Remember the way we put the page frame around the background page? This technique, used in conjunction with the Fit Object to Page command, assures that all objects reposition properly when you resize them. Regarding the slowness of OLE operations: we can only hope the improvements Microsoft comes up with in the future will improve the situation.

Making Your Bullet Points

Click on the page 1 *icon*	The page 1 icon turns gray
Click on the CorelDRAW! *icon in the toolbar*	The cursor becomes a +
Click on the cursor anywhere on the blank page	CorelDRAW! is launched and comes to the front of CorelSHOW!
Click on **L**ayout	The Layout menu appears
Click on **P**age Setup	The Page Setup dialog box appears

If your page size is not Letter or the orientation is not Landscape, select these options now.

Click on **A**dd Page Frame	
Click on OK	You are back in the Draw page window, and the page border is highlighted
With the page border highlighted, click on the Outline tool	The Outline tool fly-out menu appears
Click on the Outline Color *icon*	The Outline Color dialog box appears
In the Show *drop-down list, select* PANTONE Spot Colors	The color pallet changes
Click on Show Color Names	Color pallet is changed to display color swatches and PANTONE names
Select PANTONE Yellow CV	The New color display changes to yellow

continues

Click on OK	The page border now is yellow
Click on and hold the Text tool	The Text tool fly-out appears
Select the Paragraph Text *icon*	The cursor becomes a +
Starting at the top left corner, drag out a rectangle approximately 9 3/4 inches wide and 7 1/2 inches high	The paragraph text frame appears and the text cursor is placed in the frame

You are ready to type the three sentences that make up the bullets. Remember to start each sentence with a Tab and press Enter only at the end of the sentence

In the text frame, type `<tab>This is bullet number one.<enter><tab>This is bullet number two.<enter><tab>This is the final bullet, making a total of three.`

Click on and drag the cursor to highlight all the text in the frame

Click on **T**ext	The Text menu appears
Click on Text **R**oll-Up	The Text roll-up menu appears

In the Font Name and style drop-down lists, make sure that AvanteGarde BK BT and Normal are selected. These fonts normally are the defaults, but you might have changed them.

In the Measurement Type *drop-down list, select* points

In the Size *textbox, type* **66**

On the Text roll-up, click on Paragraph	The Paragraph dialog box appears

Make sure that Spacing is selected under the Cate**g**ory section on the left of the dialog box. Select any of the three measurement system drop-downs and change it from % of Char. Height to Points.

In the L**i**ne *textbox, type* **68**

In the **B**efore Paragraph *textbox, type* **66**

In the **A**fter Paragraph *textbox, type* **25**

At Cate**g**ory, *select* Tabs	The Paragraph dialog box changes to display a tab ruler and settings options

Click on the Clear **A**ll *button*	All the tab markers disappear from the ruler display
In the textbox next to the **S**et *button, type* **0.88**	
Click on **S**et	A tab marker appears in the ruler display
At Cate**g**ory, *select* Indents	The Paragraph dialog box changes to display indent settings options
In the **R**est of Lines *textbox, type* **0.88**	
At Cate**g**ory, *select* Bullet	The Paragraph dialog box changes to display bullet option settings
Select B**u**llet On	The list of bullet types becomes active
From the list of bullet types, select CommonBullets	The display of bullets changes to reflect those available in the CommmonBullets font
At Symbol #, *type* **93**	A checkmark-in-a-box is highlighted
At Size, *type* **82**	
Click on OK	The Paragraph dialog box disappears
On the Text roll-up, click on Apply	The settings are applied to the text
Click on the Fill tool	The Fill fly-out menu appears
Click on the Color Wheel *icon*	The Uniform Fill dialog box appears
Click on Show Color Names *option button*	Color pallet is changed to display color swatches and PANTONE names
Select PANTONE Reflex Blue CV	The New color display is changed to blue
Click on OK	The text now is filled with blue

You now should have a screen that looks very similar to figure 14.3. This slide is the final one in the three-part series. You save it as a CDR file and use it as the template for the first two slides that make up the series.

continues

Figure 14.3:
The Bullet Chart.

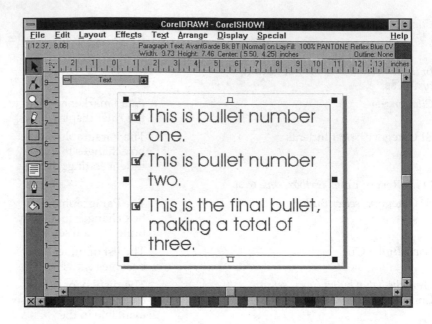

Click on **F**ile	The File menu appears
Click on Save Copy **A**s	The Save Drawing dialog box appears

Use the **D**irectories area to navigate to a directory you will remember.

At File **N**ame, *type* **BULLET3**

Click on OK	The Save Drawing dialog box disappears
Click on the Text tool	The cursor turns to an I-bar
In the paragraph text frame, click on the cursor after the period in the last bullet point. Hold down the mouse button and select the entire third bullet point, including the check mark	The text is highlighted
Press Del	The highlighted text disappears

If the checkbox for the last bullet point does not disappear, move the text cursor to the end of the second bullet point and press Del again.

Click on **F**ile	The File menu appears
Click on Save Copy **A**s	The Save Drawing dialog box appears

If not already there, use <u>D</u>irectories to navigate to the directory in which you saved BULLET3.CDR.

In the File <u>N</u>ame *textbox, type* **BULLET2**

Click on OK	The Save Drawing dialog box disappears

Finally, use the preceding steps to delete the second bullet point and save the file as BULLET1. This CorelDRAW! object, consisting of a border and the first bullet point, now is transferred to CorelSHOW!.

Click on <u>F</u>ile	The File menu appears
Click on E<u>x</u>it & Return to CorelSHOW!	A CorelDRAW! dialog box asks if you want to update the embedded object
Click on <u>Y</u>es	CorelDRAW! disappears and you are back in CorelSHOW!

Notice that the size of the object is very small.

Click on <u>A</u>rrange	The Arrange menu appears
Click on Fit Object to <u>P</u>age	The object is sized to fill the entire page

Now that you have the first slide in Show and the files needed to create the next two slides saved on your hard drive, you are ready to finish off the presentation. The following steps use a new means of placing the objects into the next two slides in the series: the <u>I</u>nsert menu's <u>O</u>bject command. Using this command, you can link and embed files that already exist, or you can start OLE-capable programs to create objects for your use.

Inserting an Object From a File

Click on page 2 *icon*	Page 2 icon turns gray and page 2 in the presentation appears
Click on <u>I</u>nsert	The Insert menu appears

continues

Click on **O**bject	The Insert Object dialog box appears
Select Create from **F**ile	The dialog box changes and displays a **F**ile textbox, a **B**rowse button, and a **L**ink option box
Click on **B**rowse	The Browse dialog box appears

Use the **D**irectories areas to move to the directory in which you saved BULLET2.CDR. Use the File **N**ame list to select the file.

Click on OK	The Browse dialog box disappears and the path for BULLET2.CDR has been inserted in the File textbox
Click on OK	The Insert Object dialog box disappears; you are back in Show and the cursor has changed to a +
Click anywhere on the page	The CorelDRAW! object appears, very small on the page
Click on **A**rrange	The Arrange menu appears
Click on Fit Object to **P**age	The object is sized to fill the entire page

Use the same process to insert BULLET3.CDR onto page three of the presentation.

If for any reason, the BULLET2.CDR and BULLET3.CDR files do not import properly, try this workaround. Insert them into the presentation using the CorelDRAW! tool as you did when you created and inserted the first slide. You do not need to create the slides from scratch; just use the CorelDRAW! **I**mport command under the **F**ile menu to load the existing CDR files. Finally, choose E**x**it & Return from the **F**ile menu, answer **Y**es to the embed object question to return to CorelSHOW! and continue with the exercise from there.

Saving Your Presentation

You have done quite a bit of work so far; you need to save your presentation.

Saving the Bullet Presentation

Click on File	The File menu appears
Click on Save	The Save Presentation dialog box appears

Use **D**irectories to move to the directory in which you want to save your file.

In the File **N**ame textbox, type **BULLET**

Click on OK	The Save Presentation dialog box disappears and your file is saved to disk

---

Displaying Your Screenshow

Now that you have three slides in your show, take a look at what you have created. Several options under the **D**isplay menu affect the way your presentation displays on the screen.

Under the **D**isplay menu, choose the **P**resentation Options command and the Presentation Options dialog box appears (see fig. 14.4). From here, you can select one of two options that control the timing of your screenshow: **A**utomatic Advance to next slide or **M**anual Advance to next slide.

Figure 14.4:

The Presentations
Options dialog box.

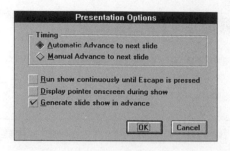

Automatic Advance uses the time shown in the Slide Duration textbox to display the current slide for the set time period. It then automatically displays the next slide for its set duration. This procedure continues until the end of your show. If you want to lengthen or shorten the duration of a slide's screen time, simply click in the textbox and type the value you want. Alternatively, you can choose from one of the preset values in the drop-down list next to the textbox. The default setting for slide duration is 5.

TIP

If you set a slide and all objects on it to a duration setting of 0, the display of that slide is suppressed during the screenshow.

The Slide Duration textbox has two functions. If you select the slide border or workspace background (not an object on the slide), it controls the time of display for that slide. If you have selected an object on the slide, the caption of the textbox changes to read `Frame Duration`. Now you are controlling how long the high-lighted element displays. Using this feature, you can have two elements on a slide and set the total length of the slide display to 10, with the first element set to display for 5 and the second element for a duration of 8. This staggering of display times is a way to add more interest to your screen presentations.

Choose the **M**anual Advance option button for hands-on control of how long each page in your show displays. To move to the next page, simply double-click on the left mouse button or press any of the following keys: PgDown, down or right arrow, F6, Enter, or the Spacebar. To move backwards in a presentation, double-click on the right mouse button, or use any of the following keys: PgUp, up or left arrow, or F6. Move to the first slide in the presentation using the Home or F9 keys. Jump to the last slide using the End or F10 keys. Press Esc in Automatic or Manual mode to end the screenshow.

The next three option settings in the Presentation Options dialog box control other aspects of the show.

Run show continuously until ESC is pressed is pretty self-explanatory. **D**isplay pointer on-screen during show enables you to use the arrow cursor to point to objects during the screen display. If this option is not selected, the cursor does not appear at all during the screenshow. Finally, a very important option: **G**enerate slide show in advance. This setting allows Show to compose the screenshow before you run it. This option eliminates any gaps in moving from one slide to the next. Sometimes you might need to deselect this option; for most shows, however, it should be used.

The time has arrived to start your screenshow. Make sure **A**utomatic Advance and **G**enerate screenshow in advance are selected before proceeding.

Running the Screenshow

Click on the Screenshow icon on the ribbon bar at the top of the screen	The Generating Slides dialog box appears. After the status bar shows that the slide show has been generated, another dialog box asks if you want to start the screenshow
Click on OK	The CorelSHOW! window disappears and the screenshow starts

Your presentation takes up the full screen of the monitor and should advance from the first bullet-point slide to the last. If your show starts over because you have selected the continue option, press Esc to stop it. After the screenshow ends, you are returned to CorelSHOW!

If you noticed that any of the bullet points seemed to move or jump when the next point was displayed, the text object probably was moved slightly. This problem is easy to fix: move to the slide that doesn't appear right, select the text object, and use the Fit Object To Page command. This step repositions the slide properly.

Adding Transitions

Now that you have the basic show together, you need to add a little pizzazz. A transition will do nicely. A transition is a special effect that controls the way a slide or the objects on it enter or exit the screen display. Finish off the three-bullet-point slide show by adding a transition to the last slide.

Adding a Transition To End With a Bang

Click on page 3 *icon*	The page view changes and the page 3 icon is grayed
Click on the text object	The transition button caption changes to Frame Transitions, None, None
Click on the Frame Transitions *button*	The Transition Effects dialog box appears
In the Closing *list, select* WipeUp	
Click on Preview	The Preview display shows a small preview of the effect
Click on OK	The Frame Transition caption now reads None, WipeUp

---

You cannot see the effects of your transition until you run the screenshow. Go ahead and run it and watch as the last slide "rolls up and away" at the end.

Transitions can be applied to the slide or to the separate elements on the slide. This concept is the same as the time duration feature. When a transition is set for a slide, the background displays the effect. The effect is not noticeable if a common background is applied to all the slides. You need to use the Omit Background command and substitute another object as a background to see the background special effects.

Transitions are much more noticeable on objects like graphics and text. Objects can have opening and closing transitions, but slides have only closing transitions. If you are trying for a specific look using several transitions on several objects contained on the same page, it is important to know how Show paints the objects on your screen. It does this by painting the back layers first and the top layer last. If you want an object to appear last when the page is displayed, select the object and use the commands under the **A**rrange menu to bring it to the front. This idea of layers is not hard to grasp, because other Corel modules use it as well.

Modifying Your Presentations

You have gotten to see most of the creation features of Corel-SHOW!. Now you need to learn to do some fine-tuning and modify your shows. What if you need to add or delete slides or pages from your presentation?

The following exercises demonstrate how easy these task are to perform.

Adding Pages

Click on page 3 *icon*	The page 3 icon turns gray
Click on **I**nsert	The Insert menu appears
Click on New **P**age	The Insert New Page dialog box appears
In the Insert pages *textbox, type* **2**	
Select After current	
Click on OK	The page icons on the bottom bar have increased to five

That is all there is to adding pages in a presentation. How about deleting, you say? All right, let's do it.

No menu command exists for deleting pages. This task must be taken care of from the Slide Sorter mode. The next exercise shows the way it is done.

Deleting Pages

Click on the Slide Sorter button on the ribbon bar	The view window changes to show thumbnail versions of the presentation (see fig. 14.5)
Click on the page 5 *icon*	The page is highlighted
Press Del	The page disappears

Figure 14.5:

The Slide Sorter view.

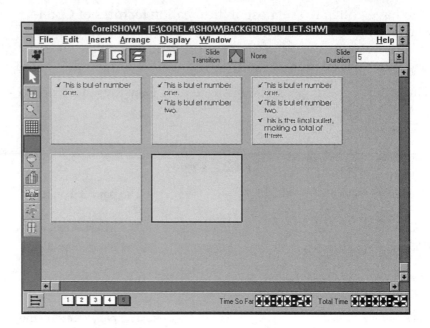

This presentation business is getting simpler all the time, isn't it? How about a hard one, like rearranging the order of your presentation? Surely that is a tough one. Not with CorelSHOW!. Take a look at the next exercise, but first make sure you are still in Slide Sorter view.

Moving Pages Around

Click on and hold on the page 1 *icon*	The page is highlighted
Drag it past the last slide	A gray bar appears after slide 4
Release the mouse button	Slide 1 is placed at the end and all previous slides move up one position

An alternative way to rearrange slides is to use the Numbering tool.

Click on the Numbering tool in the upper ribbon bar	The tool icon depresses
Click on the slides in the order that you want them	The slides are high-lighted
Click on the Numbering tool again	The slides are rearranged

As you have seen, modifying and fine-tuning your presentations are extremely easy tasks utilizing the built-in tools that CorelSHOW! supplies.

Adding Other Objects

The principles and techniques shown earlier to embed graphics objects apply to all the different objects with which Show can work—whether it is a background created in Photo-Paint or an animation created in Move. Some points to keep in mind regarding sound and animation are outlined in the next sections.

Sounds

You can use the Sound or Object commands under the Insert menu to embed sound files in your Show presentations. You can only incorporate Microsoft-compatible WAV files. If you have WAV files that do not play in Show, it is because they do not meet Microsoft's specifications completely. Bear in mind that you won't be able to hear sounds unless you have a sound board installed in your system or have installed Microsoft's poor man's solution: the PC speaker driver.

The *PC speaker driver* is a software solution that enables you to play WAV files through the small speaker in your computer. You can find this driver on many bulletin boards or get it directly from Microsoft. It is by no means a quality sound solution, but it does work. You might be surprised at how many persons are impressed by even the simplest bells and whistles.

Animations

If you read the previous chapter on CorelMOVE!, you should be familiar enough with the things that animation can do to liven up a presentation. Mixing the movements of animation with charts, graphs and word slides makes for a very memorable and impressive presentation.

Show can accept files saved in the following formats: CorelMOVE! (CMV), Autodesk Animator (FLI, FLC) and Quicktime (MOV). You can use the Animation Tool in the toolbar or the **A**nimation command under the **I**nsert menu to call up the Insert Animation dialog box. This dialog box gives you access to any animation file on your system. Click on the **O**ptions button to reveal settings that you can use to get the most out of your animation files. Some types of files cannot make use of all the options shown. Such is the case with CorelMOVE! files, which cannot be set to display F**u**ll Screen—they simply do not resize. Some Autodesk Animator files can take advantage of this option, but the result might not look very good on your monitor. You have to experiment to find optimal settings for your presentations.

TIP

You cannot make changes to a presentation after it is saved as a screenshow file. Save a new presentation as an editable file first, then as a screenshow file. For existing presentations, save the screenshow file under a different name or in another directory.

Taking Your Shows on the Road

CorelSHOW! enables you to save a presentation so that it can only be run as a screenshow and cannot be edited or changed by the viewer. This is the best way to distribute your presentations to others. In addition to running on your computer, the screenshow also can be shown on another computer.

To save a file as a screenshow, choose Save **A**s from the **F**ile menu, select the Screenshow Only option box, and give it a unique file name. If you are going to distribute your presentation on a floppy disk, click on the **S**egment File for Portable Media button, then choose the appropriate disk size option. Click on OK. If your screenshow is too large to fit on one floppy disk, CorelSHOW! asks you to insert additional ones. Should your presentation contain links to other files on your system, CorelSHOW! asks you if it should copy or ignore those linked files.

If you are going to display your presentations on computers that do not have CorelSHOW! installed, you need to distribute the portable screenshow player program, SHOWRUN.EXE and several other files. The following procedure is recommended by Corel:

NOTE

In order for SHOWRUN to operate, the system must have Microsoft Windows version 3.0 or higher installed.

1. Copy the SHOWRUN.EXE file from the CD-ROM to a \TEST\ directory on the target system. Copy the COMPOBJ.DLL and OLE2*.* files from your \WINDOWS\SYSTEM\ directory to the \WINDOWS\SYSTEM\ directory on the target system.

2. Copy the following files from your COREL40\PROGRAMS\ directory to the \TEST\directory of the target system:

AAVGA.DLL	CMVENS40.DLL	CDRSHW40.DLL
CDRSMC40.DLL	CDRUTL40.DLL	CDRFLT40.DLL
CAAPLAY.DLL	CDRCMF40.DLL	CDRCPT40.DLL
CDROLE40.DLL	CDRFNT40.DLL	CDRGFX40.DLL
CDRMEM40.DLL		

3. Next, register OLE2 by double-clicking on OLE2.REG.

4. Finally, copy your screenshow file to the target system. Start SHOWRUN.EXE by double-clicking on it in File Manager or by choosing **R**un from the Program Manager **F**ile menu. After SHOWRUN starts, select **O**pen from the **F**ile menu and select the screenshow file you want to run.

Summary

CorelSHOW! offers you the tools to create presentations and screenshows that use state-of-the-art features. Using OLE-capable server applications opens up great possibilities. As the number of programs being upgraded to take advantage of OLE's functionality grows, the ability to combine objects that previously were incompatible becomes a major attraction.

Part Five

Appendixes

Working with Windows

ecause CorelDRAW! runs under the Windows environment, it is essential to become comfortable with the Microsoft interface. If you think, "Well, all I use is Draw; I don't need to know Windows," you are selling yourself short. A thorough knowledge of Windows will make you a better Draw user. Although this appendix does not pretend to be the ultimate Windows reference, it can help make your work with Draw—and Windows—more pleasant and productive.

At its simplest, using Windows to your advantage means taking advantage of the mini-programs (like Windows Write and Paintbrush) that come with the package. In addition, you should learn how to navigate the tricky waters of Windows' lesser-known features like Recorder, Character Map, and its built-in screen-capture utility.

Fine-Tuning Corel's INI Files

Draw uses INI files (short for initialization files) to store configuration settings that Draw and the other modules need to start up and perform many of their functions. These files control details like which fonts need to be downloaded to your printer, export/import filter options, which roll-ups are present on starting a module, and where vital Draw files are stored on your system.

A word of caution: editing these INI files is not a step to be taken lightly. You should not be afraid to touch them, but do so only after you learn about them. The best approach to making any manual changes to an INI file is to shut down the CorelDRAW! module whose INI file you want to modify, make a copy of the INI file, then make your changes to the original file. When you start up your module again, the changes take effect. If something goes wrong and your module does not start properly, simply rename your backup copy to get back in business.

These INI files are plain-vanilla ASCII text files that you can edit using Windows Notepad, Write, or SysEdit. If you use Write, however, do not convert any files to Write format. The simplest way to edit an INI file is to double-click on its icon in the File Manager so that the file opens in Notepad. Some files, such as CORELFNT.INI, are too big for Notepad, however. Write's capability for handling larger files comes in handy in these cases.

Previous versions of CorelDRAW! stored most configuration settings in the CORELDRW.INI. This file was found in the subdirectory in which CorelDRAW! was installed. No longer. Due to the expansion of the program and its modules, a new management system for initialization information has been implemented.

As you inspect the CorelDRAW! directory structure, you will see the CONFIG subdirectory. In this directory, you find CORELDRW.INI, CORELAPP.INI, CORELFNT.INI, CORELFLT.INI, CORELPRN.INI, and an INI file for each of Corel's modules. Several of these files include settings that you can modify to suit your needs. Some settings can be changed while you are inside the applications. These settings are saved automatically when you shut down the module. Some options, however, simply are not available through the module's dialog boxes and must be changed manually in the INI file. Table A.1 lists each INI file and which areas of CorelDRAW! 4.0 its settings effect.

Table A.1
CorelDRAW! 4.0 INI Files

File Name	Description
CORELAPP.INI	Information needed by all modules, such as directories for program files and spelling and hyphenation dictionaries
CORELDRW.INI	Settings specific to Draw module functions
CORELFLT.INI	Import and export information used by Corel modules
CORELFNT.INI	Information for fonts and symbols supplied by Corel; font downloading information for PostScript printers and font mapping assignments for converting pre-version 4.0 files
CORELPRN.INI	Printing information shared by all Corel modules
CORELCHT.INI	Startup preferences and template information for Chart
CORELMOS.INI	Mosaic's preference settings
CORELMOV.INI	Move's configuration information
CORELPNT.INI	Photo-Paint's preference settings and filter configurations
CORELSHW.INI	Startup settings needed by Show

Much of the information and settings in these INI files are not of much interest unless you have nothing else to do with your life. Thus, the following sections discuss only the notable portions of the CORELAPP.INI, CORELDRW.INI, CORELFNT.INI, and CORELPRN.INI files.

The structure of an INI file is very predictable. The format was determined by Microsoft when it developed Windows. Each INI file has sections, enclosed by square brackets, with option keywords and their values listed below the section title. Tables A.2 and A.3 list sections of note from the four main INI files. Each keyword is given along with its available options. The last column lists the keyword's default setting after normal installation.

Table A.2
CORELAPP.INI: [Config] Section

Setting	Options	Default
ProgramsDir=x	Directory for program files	C:\COREL40\PROGRAMS
DataDir=x	Directory for data files	C:\COREL40\PROGRAMS\DATA
CustomDir=x	Directory for custom files	C:\COREL40\CUSTOM
DrawDir=x	Directory for CorelDRAW! files	C:\COREL40\DRAW
ChartDir=x	Directory for CorelCHART! files	C:\COREL40\CHART
ShowDir=x	Directory for CorelSHOW! files	C:\COREL40\SHOW
PhotoPaintDir=x	Directory for CorelPHOTO-PAINT! files	C:\COREL40\PHOTOPNT
MoveDir=x	Directory for CorelMOVE! files	C:\COREL40\MOVE
TraceDir=x	Directory for CorelTRACE! files	C:\COREL40\TRACE
MosaicDir=x	Directory for CorelMOSAIC! files	C:\COREL40\PROGRAMS
FontsDir=x	Directory for WFN fonts	C:\COREL40\SYMBOLS
FiltersDir=x	Directory for filters	C:\COREL40\PROGRAMS
FountainPresets=x	Fountain fill information file	CORELDRW.FFP
SpellLanguage=x	English, French, German, Swedish, Spanish, Italian, Danish, Dutch, Finnish	English
SpellDict=x	Spelling dictionary file	IENM9150.DAT
HyphenateDict=x	Hyphenation dictionary file	HECRP301.DAT
ThesaurusDict=x	Thesaurus dictionary file	COM_THES.DIS
BigPalette=x	0 (no) or 1 (yes)	0
BigToolbox=x	0 (no) or 1 (yes)	0
FontRasterizer=x	0 (no) or 1 (yes)	1
3DLook=x	0 (no) or 1 (yes)	1
TTFOptimization=x	0 (no) or 1 (yes)	1
TextureMaxSize=x	0 (no) or 1 (yes)	257

The following sections explain in more detail the listings in table A.2.

Setting Up Directories

The first 12 entries under the [Config] heading dictate where the various CorelDRAW! program files were stored on your system at the time of installation. If you move any CorelDRAW! 4.0 files, you might have to modify these path statements.

Fountain Presets

This file was created by CorelDRAW! and contains the fountain fill information file used to create linear, radial, and conical fills. If you save any custom fountain fills, the new information is added to this file.

Leaving Dictionary Settings Alone

Do not change the default settings for *SpellDict*, *HyphenateDict*, and *ThesaurusDict* entries. These lines assign the proper spelling, hyphenation, and thesaurus dictionaries, for the language in which your computer was set up at installation.

Backing Yourself Up

Everyone knows the value of backing up files. CORELDRW.INI offers several choices for configuring the way Draw automatically backs up your files. The *AutoBackupMins* entry can be set for anywhere from 1 to 99 minutes. The number represents the number of minutes that pass before Draw automatically makes a backup of the file you are currently working on. The file is saved with an ABK extension in the directory pointed to by the AutoBackDir entry. You can disable the AutoBackup feature by setting this entry to 0. The frequency you decide on depends on your working style and personal preferences. The default setting is 10 minutes. If you experience a crash while working in Draw, simply rename the ABK version of the file with a CDR extension, and you will only be a few minutes behind schedule.

The *MakeBackupWhenSave* entry has a default setting of 1. By default, Draw creates a backup (BAK) file each time you save a previously saved CDR file. This feature can be a lifesaver if you errantly save a job you really wanted to rename. To open up disk space, however, you should check your Corel subdirectories periodically and remove any unnecessary BAK files. If you like to work without a safety net, you can turn off this feature with a setting of 0.

Sizing the BigToolbox and BigPalette

The *BigPalette* and *BigToolbox* entries control the size of their respective screen representations. You might want to set these options to 1 if you are using a high-resolution video display card with a 14- or 15-inch monitor. This setting provides a larger, more useable toolbox and palette. With a larger monitor (16-inch or more), both entries should be set at the default of 0.

Font Rasterizer

This setting enables or disables the internal font rasterizer. The rasterizer improves the appearance of CorelDRAW! fonts printed at small sizes. You might need to disable the font rasterizer for some printers that do not print properly with it enabled. The rasterizer also slows screen redraws and printing times dramatically.

The 3D Look

If you don't like the 3D interface look of Corel applications, you can set this option to 0. The Color options in the Windows Control Panel now take effect for the screen elements that formerly were 3D.

TrueType Font Optimization

This feature speeds up access to the Windows TrueType font engine. Some printer and screen drivers might not work well when this feature is enabled. If you encounter screen or printer problems only when you use Corel modules, try changing this setting to 0.

Maxing Out Your Textures

The TextureMaxSize setting determines the maximum width (in device pixels) of an object that can be filled with a fractal texture. Because a fractal of fill actually is a bit-mapped image, it can take up large amounts of memory and can lead to bloated printer file sizes. These files can take literally hours to print. The TextureMax Size defaults to a value of 257. Set this value higher to allow for longer filled areas. The texture generator works faster if this number is equal to a power of 2 plus 1 (257, 513, 1025, and so on). If you use a number below 129, however, you slow down the screen preview.

Table A.3
CORELDRW.INI: [Config] Section

Setting	Option	Default
AutoBackupDir=x	Directory for ABK files	
AutoBackupMins=x	0 = Disabled, 1 or more = number of minutes	10
CalligraphicClipboard=x	0 (no) or 1 (yes)	1
CMYKPalette=x	CMYK Palette Filename	CORELDRW.PAL
DelayToDrawWhileMoving=x	Delay in milliseconds	500
INKPalette=x	Ink Filename	CORELDRW.IPL
MakeBackupWhenSave=x	0 (no) or 1 (yes)	1
MaxCharsToDrawDuringKern=x	Number of characters	25
MaximizeCDraw=x	0 (no) or 1 (yes)	0
ShowObjectsWhenMoving=x	0 (no) or 1 (yes)	0

continues

Table A.3
Continued

Setting	Option	Default
TextOnClpMetafile=x	0 (no) or 1 (yes)	0
TemplateDir=x	Directory for templates	C:\COREL40\ DRAW\TEMPLATE
AutoReduceOnImport=x	0 (no) or 1 (yes)	0
MinCharsToBreak=x	Number of characters	3
EditTextOnScreen=x	0 (no) or 1 (yes)	1
FullScreenBmpThumbnail=x	0 (no) or 1 (yes)	0

Greater details of the settings in table A.3 are contained in the following sections.

Controlling the Clipboard

CorelDRAW! provides superior Clipboard support with two entries in CORELDRW.INI. The *TextOnClpMetafile* entry controls whether or not text cut or copied to the Clipboard is output as text or as "converted-to-curve" objects. Use the default setting of 0 for text as text; use a setting of 1 for text as objects. The *CalligraphicClipboard* default setting of 1 maintains any calligraphic outline effects; a setting of 0 ignores the effects.

Locating Palettes

The settings for both the *CMYKPalette* and *InkPalette* entries are reset each time you exit CorelDRAW!. Consequently, any changes you make to either of these settings are overwritten the next time you close Draw with a different color palette active.

Seeing What You Are Doing

Seeing what you are clicking on and dragging can be an advantage, but it can be a drag as well. Sometimes just a bounding-box display is sufficient to tell you that an object is moving. With the ShowObjectsWhenMoving entry set to its default of 0, the object is not redrawn as it is dragged—an advantage when you are manipulating complex objects or large bitmaps. If you want to see the objects as you move them, set this entry to 1.

The MaxCharsToDrawDuringKern entry governs whether or not characters are displayed when kerning with the Shape tool. To display interactive kerning, the number of characters being kerned must be equal to or less than the specified number for this entry. The default setting is 25, and MaxCharsToDrawDuringKern must be set to at least 10.

With these two entries controlling what is redrawn, you also can control how responsive the redraw is. The DelayToDraw WhileMoving entry controls how long you must stop your movements before the object redraws. This setting is extremely fine— you can set it from 1 to 32,000 milliseconds. The default is 500.

How much you see of Draw when it starts up also can be determined by the MaximizeCDraw setting. If you want Draw always to fill the screen when it opens, set MaximizeCDraw to 1. The default setting of 0 starts Draw at its default window size. This setting allows some room at the bottom of the screen to access the Windows desktop when necessary

Support for New Features

CorelDRAW! 4.0 introduces several new features that need configuration information. The TemplateDir, for example, is a pointer to the directory location for those timesaving Templates that you can create.

AutoReduceOnImport is useful when importing vector graphics. It automatically reduces the number of nodes on curves without significantly altering the shape. If you need to keep all the nodes when importing vector files, disable this feature by setting it to 0.

MinCharsToBreak tells Draw how many characters to maintain at the end of a line of paragraph text when it is flowed into an envelope. Using the default value of 3 means that Draw does not start a new line without at least three characters on that line.

The EditTextOnScreen option is meant to make things speedier on computers that have slower redraw times. Changing the setting from the default of 1 to 0 disables your ability to edit text in the main window. In lieu of the main window, you are presented with the Edit Text dialog box for all your text tool functions.

Finally comes the FullScreenBmpThumbnail setting, which effects display of rotated bit maps in Full-Screen Preview. Changing the default setting to 1 causes Draw to display a smaller bit map. This variable can speed up screen redraws dramatically. If screen image quality is important, however, stick with the default of 0.

Table A.4
CORELPRN.INI: [Config] section

Setting	Option	Default
PSBitmapFontLimit=x	0 to 250	8
PSBitmapFontSizeThreshold=x	Height of character in pixels	75
PSComplexityThreshold=x	# of nodes (20 to 20000)	1500
PSOverprintBlackLimit=x	0 to 100	95
WarnBadOrientation=x	0 (no) or 1 (yes)	1
DumpEntireBitmap	0 (no) or 1 (yes)	0

Corel has moved all printer information to an INI file dedicated strictly for printing functions. Details regarding the options listed in table A.4 are discussed in the next sections.

Allowing for Complex Paths

You might need the PSComplexityThreshold entry if you have ignored some of the basics of CorelDRAW! repeated many times in this book: **Keep your paths simple! Delete unnecessary nodes! Easy on the fountain (and other complex) fills!** (You can think of this book as a really fat Strunk and White's *Elements of Grammar*, if you want.)

If a filled path has a *value* (number of nodes) of more than the number specified in the PSComplexityThreshold entry, Draw breaks up the path into simpler paths, without modifying the path's appearance. If you are getting PostScript LimitCheck errors with the default setting of 1,500, set the PSComplexityThreshold to 200 or so. This entry can be set from 20 to 30,000.

Specifying PostScript Printer Settings

A few printer options are available to fine-tune PostScript printer specifications. CorelDRAW! can send your fonts to the printer as mathematical curves or as bit maps. For small type on lower resolution devices, sending as bit maps might produce better-looking type. Bit-mapped fonts, however, steal printer memory that otherwise could be used to image a page. So, the PSBitmapFontLimit entry comes in handy. It has a default setting of 8, but can be set from 0 to 250. This value specifies the number of bit-map fonts Draw can create for printer versions of the fonts you are using in your file.

The PSBitmapFontSizeThreshold controls another aspect of text sent to the printer as a bit map. This value determines the number of printer pixels (dots per inch, or dpi) a character can be before it is no longer able to be sent as a bit map. Other criteria also make text ineligible to be bit-mapped: the text in question must be untransformed, nonoutlined, and uniformly filled. Also, it cannot be a printer–resident font. You might find bit-mapped fonts worthwhile on low-resolution laser printers, but on high-resolution imagesetters they are pointless. Low-resolution printers have far fewer pixels per equivalent type sizes.

For users preparing color separations, the PSOverprintBlackLimit will be of interest. This setting has a range of 0 to 100. It represents a percentage of trap or overlap added to items on the black layer of a color separation. If you set this value to a number lower than the default of 95, you might get white areas in your finished printed materials because Draw did not automatically add enough trap.

LaserJet 4 Support

The LaserJet 4 PCL driver allocates a fixed amount of memory for every raster image processed. When sending a bit map one line at a time, the driver keeps allocating memory (far too much memory) for every line. Enable this switch if you are receiving memory overflow errors. This setting changes the way Draw sends the raster data to eliminate the problem. Note that other printer drivers use the same memory-handling techniques; if memory overflow errors are occurring at the printer, these drivers also benefit if you enable this switch.

If Only You Had Been Warned

The WarnBadOrientation entry is a convenience feature. When set to its default of 1, Draw warns you when your printer is set for landscape and you are printing a portrait page (or vice versa). When set to 0, Draw does not give you any fair warning.

Using WFN Fonts

Versions 1 and 2 of CorelDRAW! used the proprietary WFN font format. By contrast, versions 3 and 4 provide access to TrueType, PostScript Type 1, and Corel WFN fonts. You might have created custom WFN fonts in an older version of Draw. If so, you can use these fonts as they are or convert them to TrueType or PostScript format by using the Ares FontMonger.

In loading order, Draw's internal Font Manager first accesses TrueType, then PostScript (assuming that Adobe Type Manager—ATM—is enabled), and finally, WFN fonts. If you have fonts with the same name in more than one format, the Font Manager uses the first one it finds and disregards the rest.

The method you use to add fonts depends on the font type you are using. TrueType fonts are added through the Fonts section of the Windows Control Panel. PostScript fonts should be added through the ATM Control Panel.

Adding WFN fonts is not quite as straightforward. If you are adding a standard previous-version font, however, the process is still relatively simple. Just roll down to the [Fonts] section of CORELFNT.INI, and delete the semicolon in front of the font you want to access. Not many of the previous versions' WFN fonts are listed, so you might have to open the CORELDRW.INI file from version 2 or 3 and copy the font entry in [CorelDrwFonts] section. Next, make sure that that font has been copied into the directory you have specified in the FontsDir entry of CORELAPP.INI. The next time you launch Draw, your WFN fonts are available.

Typefaces created in earlier CorelDRAW! versions and exported as WFN fonts can be used in version 4.0. As stated in the previous paragraph, you need to add a line for each of the WFN fonts you want to use in version 4.0 in the [Fonts] section. Enter each line exactly as it appears in the [CorelDrwFonts] section of your version 2.*x* or 3.0 CORELDRW.INI file. The next step is to add a line in the [FontMapV20] section for each font family you created in versions 2.*x* or 3.0. The line you add will look something like this:

```
Filename.WFN=FONTname www,bbb,iii,ooo
```

Filename.WFN is the custom font file. *FONTname* is the version 2.*x* or 3.0 font's name as found in the previous version's CORELDRW.INI (not the font's file name). A font's name usually is not the same as the font's file name; it is not case-sensitive and must be the same as the name you entered in the [Fonts] section.

The *www,bbb,iii,ooo* part of this line refers to the space-character width for the normal, bold, italic, and bold-italic version 2.*x* fonts. You can determine the space-character width by using the DOS-based WFNSPACE.EXE utility supplied with Draw 3.0. The utility is found in the DRAW directory; copy it into the directory in which your version 2.*x* WFN fonts are located. At the DOS prompt, type **WFNSPACE** *fontname*.**WFN**. The program responds with the space-character widths for the font specified by *fontname*.**WFN**. Use this information to complete the font family line you want to insert into the [CORELDRW20FontMap] section.

Not too hard, but the best solution still might be to convert the WFN font to TrueType or PostScript format using FontMonger.

Font Mapping from Previous Versions

Two sections in CORELFNT.INI deal with determining the ways in which older files are remapped when opened in CorelDRAW! 4. The first is [FontMapV20]. This section determines the way in which version 4.0 interprets and assigns font settings from version 2.*x* files. If you are upgrading from version 3.0 and have made any changes to the CorelDRAW! version 3.0 CORELDRW.INI [CORELDRW20FontMap] section, you should copy them over to the [FontMapV20] section of the CORELFNT.INI. This step ensures that custom WFN fonts, whether self-created or converted from other formats, are assigned properly. If you are upgrading from version 2.*x*, you have to follow the instructions for adding WFN fonts outlined in the previous "Using WFN Fonts" section. In either case, if you do not follow the instructions properly, Draw cannot recognize which typeface to use when opening your file, and will respond with a `Bad or Missing Font File` message. In that case, you get AvantGarde BT as a replacement font. The process of assigning 2.*x* WFN fonts to font names that are recognized by CorelDRAW! 4.0 really isn't impossible, just tedious— especially when you have a large number of custom fonts.

After the [FontMapV20] portion follows the [FontMapV30] section. This section is the largest part of CORELFNT.INI, because it attempts to reassign all the previous version fonts to one of the 750 included in the new release.

The strategy behind CORELFNT.INI is that if the CDR file opened is a version 2.*x* file, it picks up its new font assignment from the [FontMapV20] section. The next step is to proceed through [FontMapV30] and get reassigned to one of the BitStream faces provided with version 4.0. You might not have installed all the BitStream fonts that [FontMapV30] references, however (the default installation certainly doesn't install them for you). Again, Draw substitutes AvantGarde BT for each font it cannot recognize.

The next thought you might have is that it should be easy to edit the [FontMapV30] section of CORELFNT.INI to point to another font that is already installed on your system. This procedure would eliminate the necessity to install those BitStream faces. An example would be changing Toronto-Normal=Dutch801 Rm BT-Normal to Toronto-Normal=Toronto-Normal. The concept sounds reasonable in theory, but the initial 4.0 release does not handle it this way—at least with version 2.*x* files. Corel has stated that this inconvenience will be rectified in a newer revision. The work-around, for the time being, is to open any version 2.*x* files in version 3.0, save them as version 3.0 files, then bring them in to version 4.0.

Specifying Printer-Resident Fonts

If you are lucky enough to have a font-loaded hard disk attached to your printer, you might want to make changes to the [PSResidentFonts] section of CORELFNT.INI. This change has to do with whether Draw uses the printer's fonts or its own. Each font description line ends with a 0, 1, or 3. These numbers refer to the font's printer-residency status. If the line ends in 0, it means that the font is not a printer resident and, consequently, Draw downloads this font to the printer. A line ending in 1 denotes that the font is one of the "original" LaserWriter fonts (for example, Times Roman or Helvetica). A 3 denotes that the font is one of the standard 35 fonts found in most Adobe PostScript-licensed laser printers.

If you have a printer-resident font not among the standard 35 (many models available from QMS, for example, have more than the base 35 installed as resident), you can replace the 0 at the end of its font description line with a 3. This setting tells Draw to use the printer-resident font rather than the Draw font. Using printer-resident fonts results in faster print times and better type quality because of PostScript Type 1 font hinting. *Font hinting* helps make small type look smoother when printed on a low-resolution laser printer.

In addition to ITC Zapf Dingbats and Symbols fonts, the standard 35 LaserWriter fonts include the following:

ITC Avant Garde Gothic Book

ITC Avant Garde Gothic Book Oblique

ITC Avant Garde Gothic Demi

ITC Avant Garde Gothic Demi Oblique

ITC Bookman Light

ITC Bookman Light Italic

ITC Bookman Demi

ITC Bookman Demi Italic

Courier

Courier Oblique

Courier Bold

Courier Bold Oblique

Helvetica

Helvetica Oblique

Helvetica Bold

Helvetica Bold Oblique

Helvetica Condensed

Helvetica Condensed Oblique

Helvetica Condensed Bold

Helvetica Condensed Bold Oblique

New Century Schoolbook Roman

New Century Schoolbook Italic

New Century Schoolbook Bold

New Century Schoolbook Bold Italic

Palatino Roman

Palatino Italic

Palatino Bold

Palatino Bold Italic

Times Roman

Times Italic

Times Bold

Times Bold Italic

ITC Zapf Chancery

Another scenario that would require you to edit the [PSResident] section of CORELFNT.INI is that you regularly download a particular Type 1 font to your printer and therefore it is considered printer-resident. You can add a new entry for this font to your CORELFNT.INI with a 3 appended to the entry. This tells Windows to use the downloaded, printer-resident font instead of having Draw rasterize the font or convert it to curves at print time.

The needed entry for a downloaded font is somewhat tricky. You need three parts to put together. Parts one and three are easy to get from other sources; part two you need to figure out on your own. The three parts are defined as follows:

```
<FamilyName><-Weight>=<PSFontname>
```

The *<FamilyName>* portion can be gleaned from the ATM.INI file (if you have properly installed the font using ATM first). Just open it up in Notepad and browse until you find the font you need, then copy everything on the left side of the equal sign. Take Eras Light as an example. In ATM.INI the entry might look like:

```
ErasLight=c:\psfonts\pfm\erl____.pfm,c:\psfonts\erl____.pfb
```

You would copy `Eras Light` and add it as a new entry to the [PSResident] section of CORELFNT.INI. Add an equal sign to the end of the entry, and part one is over with.

Now you get part three: *<PSFontname>*, from the PFM file referenced in the Eras Light entry in ATM.INI. Use Write to open up (with no conversion) the ERL_____.PFM file. The file displays with lots of garbage characters. Don't worry; the only information you need is intact and found five lines down. Move along until you find the word `PostScript` and a square box; after that you should recognize the name of the font (the same as you copied from the ATM.INI file) and a square box character. Next you see the PostScript font name for the font. You need to highlight and copy this font name from just after the square box to just before the next square box (see fig. A.1). In our example using Eras Light, we need to copy `ItcEras-Light`. Now insert it after the `Eras Light=` entry in CORELFNT.INI. Part three is over with!

Figure A.1:

The selected PSFontname in Eras Light PFM file.

Part two, *<-Weight>*, comes from your head. If the font you have installed and downloaded is regular, then the weight would be `-Normal`. If it is an italic font then it would be `-Italic`. `-Bold` and `-BoldItalic` are the other weight entries you can specify. Now, your completed Eras Light entry would look like the following:

```
Eras Light-Normal=ItcEras-Light 3
```

This entry causes CorelDRAW! to use the Eras Light font outline resident in the printer to print your job. If Draw cannot place Eras Light in residence on your printer for any reason, Courier is substituted. This error is a sure clue that the font is not available on your printer's hard drive, the font was not downloaded to the printer, or the CORELFNT.INI entries are wrong.

Using What You Paid For

Throughout this book, you used many of the different programs that came bundled in the Windows 3.1 package. In the chapters on setting type, you saw how easy it was to copy text from Windows Write into the Draw text entry box. In the section on bit maps, you used Windows Paintbrush to create some snazzy bit-mapped images.

The following sections touch on some of Windows' less obvious features. Microsoft's programmers have come up with a couple of great new ideas. By the time you are finished with these sections, you are likely to have some ideas of your own.

Using the Recorder for Ultra-Macros

Windows 3.1 includes a supercharged replacement for Draw's dearly departed (but basically useless) macro function (which disappeared in version 2.0). Get ready for fun, because Microsoft has built a new rollercoaster on the Windows boardwalk, and its name is Recorder.

Recorder is a utility that enables users to register all movements within a screen or window. Try a simple exercise to illustrate the versatility Recorder adds to Draw. This exercise sets up a continuous loop that takes an ellipse, duplicates it, moves it, rotates it, and changes its color. Before you start this exercise, make sure that the Uniform Fill dialog box is in Process Color/CMYK mode.

A Ghost in the Machine

Click on Draw's Minimize button	CorelDRAW! is minimized to an icon

In the Windows Program Manager, take the following steps:

Double-click on the Accessories *icon or window*	
Double-click on the Recorder *icon*	
Click on Recorder's Minimize *button*	Recorder is minimized to an icon
Drag the Recorder icon to the bottom of the screen	Icon must be at least partially visible while Draw is running to perform this exercise
Double-click on the Draw icon	Draw returns to a full screen
Click on **S**pecial	The Special menu appears
Click on Pr**e**ferences	The Preferences dialog box appears
At Place Duplicate, *enter* **0,6 horz.** *and* **1,0 vert.** *picas, points*	
Click on OK	
Click on the Ellipse tool	
Draw an ellipse at the bottom of the page	Make it about 1 inch high by 0.5 inch wide
Click on the Fill tool	The Fill fly-out menu appears
Click on Uniform Fill	The Uniform Fill dialog box appears
Click on **P**rocess	
At Cyan, enter **100**	
At Magenta, enter **100**	
At Yellow, enter **20**	
At Black, enter **0**	
Click on OK	
Click on the Outline tool	The Outline fly-out menu appears
Click on the two-point rule	

Now that you have your first ellipse on the page, you use the Record Macro dialog box (see fig. A.2) to build a continuous loop to duplicate the ellipse and place each duplicate one pica above and six points to the right of the last. Then scale the duplicate horizontally 110 percent, and fade the color in 2 percent increments for cyan and 4 percent increments for magenta. Because the loop is continuous, you can start the macro and come back later to see what the program has done. During this exercise, be careful not to take the pointer outside the Active Border Tool Box. If you do, Recorder stops the program each time at the point at which you went out.

A Ghost in the Machine, Part 2

Click on the ellipse	The ellipse is selected
Double-click on the Recorder icon	
Click on **M**acro	The Macro menu appears
Click on **R**ecord	The Record Macro dialog box appears (see fig. A.2)
At Record Macro Name *enter* **Twister**	
At Shortcut Key, *enter* **z**	
At Playback To, *click on* Same Application	
At Playback Speed, *click on* Fast	
Click on Continuous Loop	
Click on Enable Shortcut Keys	
At Record **M**ouse, *click on* Everything	
At **R**elative to, *click on* Window	
Click on **S**tart	The macro begins recording
In the Draw Window:	
Click on **E**dit	The Edit menu appears
Click on **D**uplicate	The ellipse is duplicated
Click on Effe**c**ts	The Effects menu appears
Click on **S**tretch & Mirror	The Stretch & Mirror dialog box appears

continues

Click on the up horizontal arrow twice	Registers 110 percent
Click on OK	The ellipse is stretched horizontally 110 percent
Click on the Fill tool	The Fill fly-out menu appears
Click on Uniform Fill	The Uniform Fill dialog box appears
Click on the Cyan down arrow twice	
Click on the Magenta down arrow four times	
Click on OK	
Click on the Recorder icon	The Macro Recording Suspended dialog box appears; the Save Macro option is already selected
Click on OK	The macro is saved

Congratulations! You have created your first Recorder macro. Now play it back. Just start it up and watch it do its trick.

Press Ctrl-Z	The macro begins
To stop the macro, press Ctrl-Break	
To save the macro, go to the Recorder's F*ile menu and select* Save **A**s	

If everything went as planned, you have created a little twister that looks like figure A.3. You hope that it is not headed toward the town of Seaside and your old friend Joe DeLook.

Now you have seen that Recorder works in a most intriguing manner that deserves some experimentation on your part. The preceding exercise should whet your appetite and start you off in a new direction.

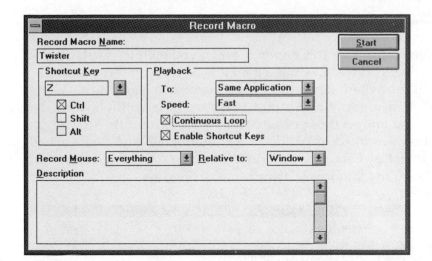

Figure A.2:
The Record Macro dialog box.

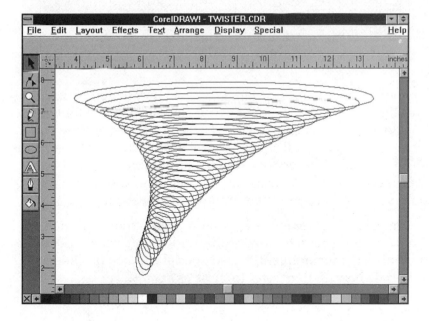

Figure A.3:
Twister.

Finding Those Dingbats with Character Map

Remember back in Chapter 3, when you built those playing cards? Perhaps you recall what a pain it was to key in those arcane, unintuitive Alt keystrokes to gain access to high-bit characters. Well, fear not... the Windows Character Map utility makes it easy to find and set those peculiar characters. This nifty little device was introduced in Windows 3.1, although it pays homage to the Mac's Key Caps, and to Norton Desktop's Key Finder. Figure A.4 shows the Windows Character Map window.

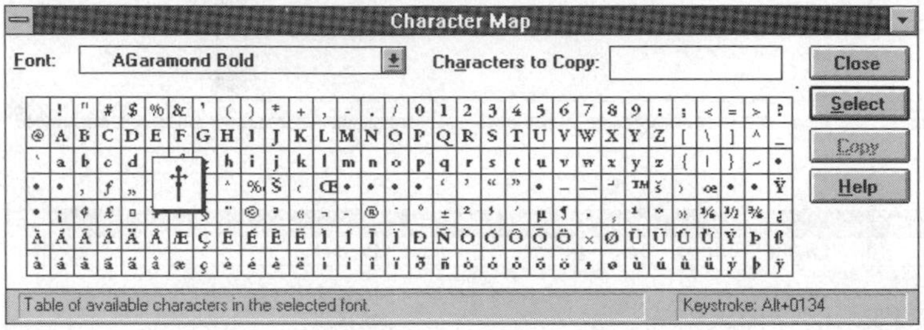

Figure A.4:

Finding a dagger with the Character Map utility.

When you run Character Map, you quickly can identify and select any character in any (TrueType or PostScript Type 1) font you have loaded. You then copy the character to the Clipboard and paste it into your application. After the character has been pasted, you then change the character to the applicable font, and *voilà!* You have your special character without having to resort to looking at hard copy or memorizing Alt-key sequences.

If you want to get really slick, you can use a combination of Recorder and Character Map utilities to build a number of mnemonic macros for frequently used special characters. Old-time, code-based typesetters refer to these as *pi calls*.

Capturing Screens with Windows

The folks at Microsoft were very generous when they endowed Windows with a built-in screen capture (or screen grab) utility. This utility is extremely useful in situations where you need to use a screen shot for advertising or documentation.

Capturing screens with Windows is fairly simple, although it lacks the ease and automation found in a dedicated screen capture utility program such as Hotshot. To capture a screen, just press Print Screen or Alt-Print Screen, and presto-chango, the screen is copied to the Clipboard. Once the image is in the Clipboard, it can be saved in Clipboard format or pasted into an appropriate Windows program such as Paintbrush. Be sure to configure Paintbrush's image attributes for your computer's video card resolution (VGA, 640×480; Super VGA, 800×600).

Some Windows programs can accept these Clipboard files while others cannot. The author has successfully pasted screen captures into PageMaker using this method.

Take a look at figure A.5, which shows a computer within a computer within a computer. This graphic was produced using Draw and the Windows screen capture utility. The Clipboard picture of the computer was imported into Draw, then the Print Screen button was pressed to capture the screen to the Clipboard. This image was pasted back into Draw and resized to fit inside the first computer's monitor. The paste procedure was applied again to place the smallest computer. If you want to save screen captures to use in Draw later, paste them into a program that can save them as BMP, TIF, or PCX files. Do not save them as Windows Clipboard files (CLP), because Draw does not have a CLP import filter.

If you are having trouble capturing screens, you might want to check a few things. The application from which you are copying screens might have its Program Information File (PIF) set for No Screen Exchange. If this is true, turn off the option, restart the application, and try again. The Print Screen or Alt-Print Screen keys might be reserved combinations for the application from which you are trying to capture screens. If so, go back to the program's PIF and turn off the Reserve Shortcut Key options. Another item to consider is the program's video mode. Take one more trip back to the PIF and try a higher setting.

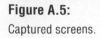

Figure A.5:
Captured screens.

Capturing Screens with CCapture

CorelDRAW! 4.0 includes a crude little screen capture utility of its own. Corel Screen Capture (or CCapture) is an improvement over the built-in Windows screen capture utility, but falls far short of the better screen capture utilities on the market. CCapture offers three screen grab choices. The first choice, PrtScrn, captures the entire Desktop, and does pretty much what the built-in Windows screen capture feature does. The other two choices, Alt+PrtScrn and Alt+Pause, capture just the currently selected window, or the client area of the currently selected window, respectively.

If you need a large number of screen grabs, get serious and ditch CCapture. To crank out large numbers of screen shots, you need automation, control over image quality, and a choice of file formats. You would do best to look at a commercial package such as Collage.

As with any type of publishing, you must determine whether the manufacturer of the program whose screens you are capturing requires permission for publication of their screen images. At the very least, you would be wise to include a disclaimer in the advertisement or in the front pages of any other published work.

Running Windows 3.1 on a Tight Ship

Is your computer underpowered and saddled with a wimpy little hard disk? You are not alone. The first edition of this book was written and illustrated on a lowly 10MHz 286 PC equipped with a meager 20M hard disk. Although this did create some problems, they were more aggravating than insurmountable. In contrast, the next three editions of this book were blasted out of a 386/33 machine, and the edition you are reading now was created on a number of machines, including a 486/50 and a 486/66. Speed does make a difference! Quite frankly, it would be a mean feat (if not an exercise in futility) to attempt to run Windows 3.1 and CorelDRAW! 4.0 on the earlier machines.

Make the most of your system, especially when system resources are limited. People with yesterday's technology must be prudent with their disk space. A couple of megabytes of extra junk on a 330M hard disk is nothing to worry about, but on an 80M hard disk, it might be the factor that causes you to miss your deadline.

Deleting Unnecessary Windows Files

Windows can gobble up lots of valuable disk space if all its options are installed. If storage space is a problem, go back in and delete the files and applications you do not absolutely need.

The best strategy to follow here is to cover yourself. Instead of merely deleting unnecessary files, copy them to floppy disks, then remove them from the hard disk. This way, you easily can restore a file if you need it at a later date—if you finally get that big hard disk. Until then, floppy disks are easy on the wallet. At less than a dollar per megabyte of storage (for high-density 5 1/4-inch disks), they cost far less than hard disk storage.

For safety's sake, do not remove any Windows files not specifically mentioned in the following sections.

Deleting Leftover TMP Files

If (or when) your system locks up while running Windows, the currently open programs leave behind temporary (TMP) files. These files can accumulate to the point where they take many megabytes of storage. Periodically, delete all TMP files from the TEMP directory where they are stored. Do not do this while Windows is running, however, or you might delete files currently in use. Exit Windows before deleting the TMP files. If you do not have a separate directory for TMP files, set one up; if you do, your housekeeping chores are less of a hassle.

Deleting Wallpaper Files

You might want to remove the bit-mapped files that Windows users refer to as *wallpaper* for your desktop. These files are identified by the file extension BMP. Although these files can lend a jazzy look to your Windows desktop, they eat up plenty of space—over 420K (if you have installed over a previous version of Windows). The following wallpaper files are located in your WINDOWS directory:

256COLOR.BMP	PARTY.BMP
ARCHES.BMP	PYRAMID.BMP
BOXES.BMP	RIBBONS.BMP
CHESS.BMP	TARTAN.BMP
CHITZ.BMP	WEAVE.BMP
MARBLE.BMP	WINLOGO.BMP
PAPER.BMP	

NOTE

Be sure to use the Windows Control Panel to set desktop wallpaper to None before removing any BMP files.

Be careful not to delete any BMPs you have created... you might need them! The best strategy is to store your own BMPs (other than those you want to use as wallpaper) in their own directory.

Deleting Game Files

The next group of files that you might want to eliminate are the two Windows game files, Minesweeper and Solitaire, along with their associated help files. Removing these files nets more than

235K. You might even find yourself becoming more productive by taking these files off your system. Solitaire is known to have addictive qualities. If you have not played it yet, deal yourself a hand before you remove it! These files are fun to have on your system, but feel free to remove them if you need the space. The game files and their help files are titled:

SOL.EXE	WINMINE.EXE
SOL.HLP	WINMINE.HLP

If you are using Windows for Workgroups, you have another game that is dispensable. Unless it is close to your heart or to another user on the network, you can remove the following files for the Hearts card game and reap another 121K of disk space:

MSHEARTS.EXE
MSHEARTS.HLP

Deleting Unnecessary Help Files

Although Help (HLP) files can be beneficial, they also take up a lot of space. It is perfectly acceptable to run an application file without having its associated HLP file. And because Windows comes with comprehensive documentation, the HLP files are expendable. To this end, you can remove many of the help files from your WINDOWS directory and save almost 1M of space! For example, you can run quite well without the following HLP files:

CALC.HLP	PBRUSH.HLP
CALENDAR.HLP	RECORDER.HLP
CARDFILE.HLP	WRITE.HLP

Deleting Other Applications

The last group of possible files you can delete includes any of a number of Windows application files, along with their help files. It is not recommended that you remove any of these files, but if you need the space, do what you have to do. If you are happy with your communications program, you probably are safe in deleting TERMINAL.EXE. Do you already have a Windows-based word processor like Word for Windows or Ami Professional? Then you can delete WRITE.EXE. Remember that the Windows application files listed here are among the last you should delete to free up additional disk space:

CALC.EXE	TERMINAL.EXE
CALENDAR.EXE	PBRUSH.EXE
CARDFILE.EXE	WRITE.EXE
CLOCK.EXE	

Optimizing Your System for CorelDRAW!

You can set up the Microsoft Windows operating environment in a multitude of ways. Different computer configurations require different arrangements. To get the best performance out of Draw, you should be using a 486 or Pentium computer with plenty of RAM (8M minimum), a serious video card (preferably a Windows accelerator), and a large, fast hard disk. If you have a multiple-computer environment, put the fastest machines on the desks of the people doing design and DTP work. Move the slower machines to the desks of those who are doing less processor-intensive tasks such as word processing. This setup maximizes all your resources.

Getting Serious about Video Display Cards

On the subject of video display cards and high-resolution monitors, take heed. Generally, the higher resolution your card and monitor, the longer it takes for the screen to rewrite. You could grow old waiting for that beautiful image. Faster cards now are on the market, however. In addition to on-board memory, some of these cards feature graphics processors or coprocessors that can speed things up greatly.

There are scads of display cards on the market, from $50 no-name VGA cards, to high-end 24-bit cards that sell for thousands of dollars. Do yourself a favor: stick to the brand names. You will save yourself plenty of trouble down the road (like when Windows NT increases in the software market). You want to be very sure that you can get updated video drivers when you need them.

As of this writing, decent VGA cards can be had for $75, while respectable SuperVGA cards are in the $125 to $200 range. Accelerated cards configured with graphics coprocessors (for Windows) start at around $275. When buying video cards, remember this generalization: the more memory, the more colors, the more cash. You must ask yourself: "What kind of work do I do?" and budget accordingly. If you are creating mostly black-and-white work, a SuperVGA 1024×768 card fits the bill. If you can, spring for an accelerated card—you will appreciate the performance improvement over a vanilla card. For basic layout and design work, you easily can get away with 256 colors... just be sure to always specify colors with a swatch book. If you are doing high-end work such as photo retouching, go for a 24-bit card.

Diamond SpeedStar24X

Through the production of the latest edition of this book, a number of video cards were used. The bare minimum configuration for CorelDRAW! 3.0 is a VGA monitor and display card. Most folks are far happier with a display card that supports multiple resolutions, however. The Diamond SpeedStar24X display card covers that ground quite nicely. This Windows accelerator can switch among VGA, SuperVGA, and 1024×768 resolutions. In addition, the SpeedStar24X offers 24-bit color in the 640×480 resolution. At the high-resolution settings, however, only 256 colors are available, because the board is configured with only 1M of video RAM. The SpeedStar24X performs reliably in all modes when configured with the supplied WinSpeed Win3.1 drivers.

Orchid Fahrenheit VA

Another fine graphics accelerator card that also was used during the production of this edition of *Inside CorelDRAW!* was the Fahrenheit VA from Orchid. This card has very similar specifications to the Diamond SpeedStar24X, with one notable addition. The VA in the name stands for voice annotation. The Fahrenheit VA comes with a small microphone that plugs into the back of the card. Using this mike and the supplied software, you can add your own voice to any application utilizing OLE very easily. The card comes configured with 1M of video RAM. VGA, SuperVGA, and 1024×768 resolutions are supported, with up to 16.8 million colors available in VGA mode.

Radius MultiView 24

At the high end, a Radius MultiView 24 demonstrates what serious 24-bit color is all about. Radius built their reputation in the Macintosh market, and has brought all its smarts to the PC side with aplomb. The MultiView 24 is an expensive card, but it is a professional tool, not a toy, providing 16.8 million colors at 1024×768. It comes configured with 3M of VRAM and 3 graphic coprocessors for the utmost in 24-bit performance. Because the MultiView 24 is a pass-through card, a Diamond SpeedStar (not the 24X) card was used to provide VGA capabilities—cabling was a straightforward affair. The pass-through arrangement allows for a dual-monitor configuration. The Radius card was extremely stable, a joy to behold, and a pleasure to use.

Understanding a Bit More about Monitors

If you decide that you want to run at high-resolution, consider a monitor larger than 14 inches. Using an 800×600 or 1024×768 driver with a smaller monitor can give you a case of severe eyestrain. To be fair, most video card manufacturers (Diamond, Orchid, and Radius) supply two sets of drivers for high-resolution: one with small fonts and one with large fonts. With a small screen and low-resolution driver, use the small font driver.

On large monitors at high resolutions, the large fonts should be easier to read.

Buying More RAM

How much RAM should your system have? As much as you can afford. Although Corel recommends a minimum of 4M, you really should have at least 8M. In general, Windows applications are far happier with gobs of memory, and image editors like Corel PHOTO-PAINT! use all the memory you can throw at them. With enough RAM, you can turn virtual memory off and reap a speed reward: RAM is far faster than virtual memory. Consequently, if you have plenty of RAM available, you have no need for a swap file.

To turn off Swapfile, open the Windows Control Panel. Click on the 386 Enhanced icon, and then click on the Virtual Memory button. The dialog box that appears shows your system's current settings. To alter the settings, click on the Change button, and then enter your new settings. To turn off virtual memory, go to the Type option and click on None, and then click on OK. Click on Yes at the warning box, and you're on your way.

Most PC clones come equipped to use SIMM RAM chips. You usually find two banks of four SIMM slots each. You must fill complete banks with like chips. Both 1M and 4M SIMM chips are readily available, and 16M SIMM chips are just entering the market. Check your system documentation for the speed and size SIMM chips your machine requires. With two full banks of 4M SIMM chips, for example, you can cook with 32M of fast silicon for about $1,200.

Using SmartDrive

The newest version of Windows SmartDrive—the Windows Disk Cache—runs rings around its predecessor. The previous version was so notoriously slow that it spawned a slew of third-party disk-caching software, such as Hyperdisk and Super PC-Kwik. The third-party houses now are scrambling to hot-rod their products to a higher level of performance. SmartDrive is now a full-blown, well-mannered read/write cache. If you are not using SmartDrive, you are sacrificing performance.

Taking Care of Your Hard Disk

Personal computer hard disk drives are ticking time bombs. Users develop a sense of security at the ease with which files can be stored "in the computer." Many folks simply ignore the care and well-being of their hard disks until trouble hits. The following sections describe a couple of practices that can make your hard disk hold more information and run smoother and faster.

Using PKZIP

To fit more files on a hard disk, you can compress files using a utility like PKZIP, discussed in Chapter 11. PKZIP can dramatically reduce the amount of space required to store a file. Remember one important caveat, however: compressed files are not immediately accessible, because they first must be uncompressed. Compression is not practical for files needed with any frequency, so use PKZIP with discretion.

Of course, you can use CorelMOSAIC! to compress CDR files (into library files), but you still need a general compression utility. PKZIP (or WinZip, the Windows version) fits that bill very nicely.

Running CHKDSK

CHKDSK is a DOS utility used to analyze a disk's storage capacity and status. It also can fix lost file clusters that might be wasting space on your computer's hard disk. Every time your system bombs, temporary files are left that, over time, can squander valuable room on your hard disk. Do not confuse these temporary files with the Windows TMP files described earlier. These temporary files are of a different sort.

Always run CHKDSK after you remove large numbers of files. CHKDSK is another utility that should be run from DOS rather than Windows. By typing **CHKDSK /F** at the DOS command line, you tell DOS to correct any errors CHKDSK discovers. This procedure stores bad files and gives them the CHK extension. After CHKDSK is done, look at and remove any unneeded CHK files. For more information on CHKDSK, refer to a DOS manual.

Running a Disk Optimizer

Running a disk optimizer is especially important on a small hard disk. Disk optimization can encompass a couple of different procedures and requires you to purchase a utility package such as the Norton Utilities Advanced Edition or PCTools (for Windows or DOS).

In general, disk optimization consists of *defragmenting* or repacking your hard disk, along with possibly changing your hard disk's interleave.

Files are stored in sectors. When a disk (be it hard or floppy) is new and files are stored for the very first time, they are saved in sequential sectors. As the disk fills up and the files are updated and appended, the files are no longer stored sequentially, and they become fragmented. The File Allocation Table enables DOS to monitor the status of all the sectors on a disk. The more times a disk is used, the more fragmented and less efficient it becomes.

Disk fragmentation is easy to correct by running a disk "defragger," such as Norton's Speed Disk or PCTools Compress. These utilities reorganize the placement of files and directories on a disk, thereby reducing the amount of read-write head movement and increasing the speed with which data can be read off the disk.

Disk interleave can compensate for a computer that does not match the performance of its hard disk. Changing disk interleave can improve disk performance, but it is a tricky procedure best left to hard-core techies.

Summary

Windows is it—at least as far as getting graphics done on the PC platform, that is. Microsoft has provided a rich and diverse repertoire of utility programs with the Windows package, and an ever-growing number of Windows applications are available. But Windows has upped the ante, and it is very demanding of the computers that run it.

As you have seen, you can optimize Windows performance on any platform with a minimum configuration of an 80286 computer with 2M of RAM and a 40M hard disk. To get even better performance in the Windows environment, you need to beef up your platform. For many, a powerful 80386 (or 486 or Pentium) computer, lots of RAM, and a large, speedy hard disk have become a necessity. The old computer axiom goes something like, "software sells hardware." In the case of Windows 3.1, this statement has never been more true.

Beyond the Mouse

ach day brings yet another innovative tool with the promise of mastering the graphical user interface (GUI). Gadgets such as trackballs, touchpads, touchscreens, and other pointing devices seek to win our favor. Many do a fine job for most GUI tasks, but the graphic artist's needs are far more demanding. Zipping from window to window is small potatoes compared to creating complex artwork.

Electronic artists need precision and flexibility. Design concessions based on the limitations of hardware are a sad truth for many artists. Because mice, trackballs, and the like are not conducive to drawing in an intuitive manner, many a work has been compromised. It need not be that way.

An artist should be liberated, not imprisoned, by his tools. Imagine a paintbrush chained to a canvas, or a stick of charcoal wired to a sketch pad—not exactly an artistically stimulating thought. The computer and its peripherals should stimulate artistic creativity.

Throughout the creation of this book, the author experimented with a variety of input devices. Different stages of the production process brought out the good and bad points of each device. This appendix discusses the pros and cons of several input devices with which the author is particularly familiar. Use this information to help you determine the best input device for your needs.

The Microsoft Mouse

Without question, and for good reason, the Microsoft Mouse is one of the most popular input devices available today. In the past, Microsoft bundled the mouse with software, such as Windows/286 or Paintbrush. This bundle made the purchase an attractive package, so truckloads of mice were sold. More than good marketing is involved, however.

The venerable Microsoft Mouse offers a streamlined, ergonomic design. Many people consider it the most natural-feeling mouse available today. Microsoft's designers have done a fine job of perfecting the mouse's mechanism and feel. The mouse fits comfortably into the palm of your hand, as if (amazing as it may seem) it was designed specifically for the task (and it was).

With a real Microsoft Mouse, you never need to worry about software compatibility, especially when you are running under Windows. In short, if a program uses a graphical interface, it is compatible with the Microsoft Mouse.

No mouse, however, can be considered a tool for serious electronic illustration. Drawing with a mouse is unnatural and cumbersome for most artists. To truly realize your own artistic potential, consider some of the other input devices on the market and save your mouse for backup duty or for non-artistic computing tasks like spreadsheet work.

The IMCS PenMouse

The most unique input device tested was the IMCS PenMouse. This strange-looking creature is best explained as a miniature mouse grafted to a pen-like appendage. Although the IMCS

PenMouse is definitely not for everyone, it does hold promise for use in specialized circumstances.

The PenMouse is very conservative in its appetite for workspace, making it worthy of consideration for users with laptops or limited desktop real estate. With a long 9 1/2-foot cord, the PenMouse has a conveniently long reach. In fact, one of the most pleasant things to do with the device is to mimic a conventional pen. With a pad of paper in your lap, you can use the PenMouse like a normal drawing tool and draw in a relaxed, seminatural position.

Although the PenMouse is intended to be held between the middle finger, forefinger, and thumb like a pen, the large angular case is too bulky for some people's liking. Tracing is inconvenient, because the PenMouse's base obscures the drawing you are tracing.

The PenMouse runs flawlessly with Windows 3.1. Because the device uses the standard Microsoft Mouse driver, you do not even need to use Windows Setup to install the PenMouse. Hookup is simple using IMCS's distinctive cable adapter, which couples a mouse bus connection to DB-9 and DB-25 serial ports. The author routed the PenMouse through both a mouse port and the more pedestrian DB-25 connection with equally favorable results.

The PenMouse is finicky about the surfaces it is used on, however. The hard plastic roller does not like the smooth veneer tops of typical office furniture. Taping a piece of paper to the top of the desk or using a mouse pad alleviates the lack of traction. The roller ball is easily removed for cleaning through a hinged plastic door.

In everyday use, the PenMouse is not quite adequate for object-oriented illustration work. It is vague and imprecise when working with tight tolerances. For general Windows work, however, the device operates soundly. Although it is not recommended as your sole input device for artwork, the PenMouse deserves a look if your needs include laptop computing.

The Trackball

The device that first rode to fame in the video game arcade has become commonplace on personal computers all over the world. What is a trackball, you ask? For the uninitiated, think of a trackball as an upside-down mouse. To move the cursor, you roll the orb around. Not quite as much fun as the orb in Woody Allen's *Sleeper*, but quite effective for desktop computing.

In general, trackballs can be an excellent alternative to the mouse. They take up little desk space and, when used for general-purpose click-and-drag computing, trackballs perform well. However, when put to the task of freehand drawing, the trackball falls far short. As a drawing tool, it is even less intuitive than the mouse. Although the trackball does not hold up to the task of freehand drawing, it is fairly proficient for node-tweaking chores.

Graphics Tablets

To extol the virtues of one brand of mouse over the other, or to investigate everything from trackballs to touchpads, is a waste of time. For serious design work, put the mouse, its siblings, and its cousins on the shelf.

Only one serious mouse alternative for electronic design exists: the digitizing (or graphics) tablet. Although a mouse might be inexpensive compared to a tablet, the mouse can never hope to offer the tablet's drawing precision. With a graphics tablet, freehand drawing becomes a genuine reality rather than a bad joke. Try a good tablet. The cost difference soon becomes meaningless. The proper tablet enables you to draw in a natural manner rather than in a clumsy tangle of mouse and cord.

These statements might invoke the ire of mouse loyalists. Spend some time working with a quality graphics tablet like the ones described in the next section, however, and you will come to the same conclusion: drawing with a mouse is like painting with a brick.

The Wacom Family of Cordless Digitizers

On the forefront of digitizing tablet manufacturers, Wacom, Inc. offers high-quality products at reasonable prices. Although less-expensive graphics tablets are available, they offer far fewer amenities. All of Wacom's tablets are cordless, for example. No cords connect the *stylus* (pen) or *cursor* (puck) with the tablet itself, so the user can hold the pen or puck in the most natural manner possible. Cordlessness alone makes Wacom tablets specialized devices. Few cordless tablets are on the market, and certainly none with the same feel or features.

You can economize by purchasing a smaller (and less expensive) tablet. Wacom offers a full line of digitizing tablets, running from the compact 6-by-9-inch SD-510 to the monster 35-by-47-inch SD-013. For DTP work, a 12-by-12-inch tablet is the largest tablet you will need.

Throughout the production of this book, the author had the good fortune to work with a Wacom SD-420 12-by-12-inch digitizing tablet equipped with a cordless pen.

Right out of the box, the tablet was a joy to work with. Everything functioned properly, and installation was a simple, three-step process. Initially, the author ran the tablet with Windows/286 and was favorably impressed with the digitizer's performance. Windows 3.0 was released the week after the SD-420 arrived. Two days after the release of Windows 3.0, the updated Windows 3.0 mouse driver arrived. The tablet continues to operate flawlessly with Windows 3.1. CorelDRAW! 4.0 requires the new Pen Windows drivers.

Throughout testing, the author ran into only one drawback to the cordless design—it was easy to pick up the pen and forget where he left it. To minimize this problem, Wacom provides a handsome storage case and also offers an attractive desktop pen holder.

In addition to the standard model SD-420, Wacom offers two variations on the same platform, the SD-421L and SD-422L. The SD-421L adds an electrostatic surface, which enables you to hold papers to the tablet surface through electrostatic adhesion, avoiding the need for tape. This feature can be a boon for artists who trace artwork regularly. The SD-422L features a transparent menu that protects heavily used menu sheets from abuse. Although there are no Wacom menus for CorelDRAW! as of this writing, it would not be an insurmountable task to build your own.

The quality-conscious yet budget-minded artist would be wise to look at Wacom's 6-by-9-inch SD-510 as a viable alternative to either a mouse or a full-sized tablet. The SD-510 provides many of the same features as its larger siblings at an affordable price.

The SD-510 is available in two configurations. The SD-510B features a PC bus card controller and is invaluable for situations in which an extra serial port is not available. This model draws power from the PC's bus, alleviating the need for an external power cord. For computers with an extra serial port but no extra expansion slots, consider the SD-510C, which operates off an RS-232C serial port. Unlike the SD-510B, the SD-510C requires an external power source.

CorelDRAW! 4.0 now supports pressure-sensitivity through the PowerLine tool. Corel also boasts pressure support in PHOTO-PAINT!. The number of PC-based programs that support pressure-sensitivity is on the rise. On the bit-map side, Adobe Photoshop, Image-In-Color, Fractal Design Painter, and Sketcher do a fabulous job. In the vector world, Aldus FreeHand's pressure tool is wonderful, as is the implementation in Altsys Fontographer. The PC community has finally embraced pressure-sensitivity!

> Wacom Technology Corp.
> 501 S.E. Columbia Shores Blvd.
> Vancouver, WA 98661
> 1-800-922-6613

Glossary

A

Anamorphic scaling. Reducing or increasing one dimension (height or width) of an object without changing the other dimension.

Ascender. The part of a lowercase letter that extends above the x-height. See also *Descender, x-height.*

B

Baseline. The implied boundary on which a line of type sits.

Bézier curve. A mathematical formula for the description of a curve drawn between two anchor points (or nodes, in Corel terms). Each curve has a set of tangent (control) points to delineate the curve's path. The curves were developed in the early 1970s by French mathematician Pierre Bézier.

Bit map. A dot-by-dot method of rendering images. Common file formats include BMP, GIF, PCX, TGA, and TIFF.

Bleed. The illusion of printing to the edge of the paper. Accomplished by printing on an oversized piece of paper and then trimming to size.

C

Caps. Uppercase or capital letters.

Color separation. Separating a color original (photograph or illustration) into the four process colors—cyan, magenta, yellow, and black. See also *Process color.*

Color trade shop. A firm that specializes in printing prepress, specifically process color work. Usually employs a combination of traditional stripping techniques along with high-end graphics systems, such as Scitex, DS, Linotype-Hell, or Crosfield. See also *Stripping.*

Comp. Abbreviation for *comprehensive*. The designer's term for a mock-up of a finished job. Used for presentation rather than production purposes.

Condensed. A narrow version of a font, with a high character-per-line-count. CorelDRAW! can produce a pseudo-condensed version of any font through the use of anamorphic scaling. Use with caution, however—readability can be affected. See also *Anamorphic scaling, Extended.*

Continuous tone. Refers to an image with a smooth transition in tone, as in original photographs, charcoal drawings, or watercolor paintings. Cannot be rendered through any printing process. See also *Halftone.*

D

Decorative. An overdone typeface with a distinctive look. Used mainly for headlines; not normally used for text.

Descender. The part of a lowercase letter that extends below the baseline. See also *Ascender, x-height.*

Desktop publishing (DTP). The use of a personal computer as a system for producing typeset-quality text and graphics. The term reportedly was coined by Aldus chief Paul Brainerd.

Dot-matrix. An inexpensive printer that uses a print head commonly consisting of from 9 to 24 pins. Typically an office printer, a dot-matrix printer does not have high enough resolution to be used for computer graphics work.

DPI. Stands for *dots per inch*. Used in reference to the resolution of an output device or scanner. The higher the device's dpi, the higher the quality of the image.

Dropout (or Knockout) type. White type that "drops out" of a black or darkly colored background. Often referred to as *reverse type*.

E

Em dash. A dash approximately as wide as the letter M (most often used in text).

En dash. A dash as wide as the letter N (most often used with dates or numbers).

Extended. A wide version of a font. CorelDRAW! can produce a pseudo-extended version of any font through the use of anamorphic scaling. See also *Condensed*.

F

Family. All the fonts of the same typeface in various sizes and weights. Typically includes Roman, italic, bold, and bold-italic.

Flush. A term (as in *flush-right* and *flush-left*) referring to type set with an even margin on the right or left side. Also commonly referred to as *quad left* or *quad right*, alluding to the metal-type days when such lines were filled out with blanks known as quads.

Font. A set of characters of one typeface, weight, and size. In the hot-metal days, the term referred to a particular font of a particular size and style, such as 10-point Times-Roman. With the advent of digital composition, a font is thought of as the style throughout its complete range of sizes.

H

Hairline. A fine rule or line of one-half point or less.

Halftone. A method of visual trickery used when printing photographs. A halftone image fools the eye into thinking that black and white can produce gray by breaking down the tones into a series of noncontiguous dots. Dark shades are produced by dense patterns of thick dots. Lighter shades are produced by less-dense patterns of smaller dots. Can be produced photographically or electronically. See also *Continuous tone*.

High-res. Slang for *high-resolution*. Refers to an output device's capability of rendering images at 1270 dpi or higher.

I

Inferior figures. Small numbers, letters, or special characters set below the baseline.

J

Justified type. Type set with even left and right margins. High-end composition programs hyphenate and justify (H&J) copy by using both dictionary and algorithm methods.

K

Kerning. Reducing or increasing space between character pairs to compensate for character shape. Some examples of character pairs commonly kerned are *AW*, *LY*, *Te*, and *Ve*.

L

Leading. The amount of space between lines of type. Pronounced "ledding," the term comes from the actual strips of lead placed between lines in the hot-metal era.

Letterspacing. Increasing or decreasing the space between all characters. Current use of the term commonly refers to the act of opening up space, as opposed to *tracking*, which refers to the tightening up of space.

Ligatures. Character pairs, such as *ae, fi, fl, ff, ffi*, and *ffl*, combined to form one character for aesthetic reasons.

Line length. The column width of a block of type, normally measured in picas.

Low-res. Slang for *low resolution*. Refers to an output device's limitation of rendering at 400 dpi or less.

O

Oblique. A variation of italic.

Overprint type. Black or dark-colored type printed over a lighter underlying color, halftone, or light-gray tint.

Overprinting. Printing over an area that has been printed with a previous color. (The only way to trap with CorelDRAW!.) See also *Trapping*.

P

PANTONE Matching System (PMS). The printing industry's standard method of mixing inks and describing spot colors.

Pica. The printer's basic unit of measurement. An inch contains approximately six picas.

Point. There are 12 points to one pica; approximately 72 points to one inch.

Point size. The measurement used to describe type height. Refers to the approximate distance between the top of the ascenders and the bottom of the descenders.

PostScript. The de facto standard page-description language used in laser printers and other output devices. This Adobe Systems product revolutionized the typesetting and graphic art worlds.

Process color. The process used to produce the illusion of "full-color" printed pages. The image is produced using four printing plates, with one color (cyan, magenta, yellow, or black) on each plate. See also *Spot color*.

R

Ragged. A term (as in *ragged-left* or *ragged-right*) that refers to type set with an uneven margin on one side. Depending on client preference, ragged type can be set with or without hyphenation.

Registration Marks. The bull's-eyes (or cross-hairs) used by printers to align multicolor jobs when stripping negatives.

S

Sans serif. A typeface without serifs, such as Helvetica. See also *Serif*.

Script. A typeface rendered with a calligraphic style, such as Zapf Chancery. Commonly used for wedding invitations.

Serif. A typeface with end strokes, such as Times Roman. See also *Sans serif.*

Service bureau. A firm that specializes in high-resolution output of PostScript files. Commonly equipped with a combination of imagesetters, color printers, and other proofing equipment.

Set solid. Type set with a leading equal to the point size. Best used in larger display sizes with all caps.

Small caps. Type set in all caps smaller than the standard upper-case capital letters of the font. Small caps are drawn to sync with the normal x-height.

Spot color. Printing with more than one color, but not process. Ink is mixed to attain the precise color. See also *Process color.*

Spreads and chokes. Swelling and shrinking negatives to compensate for press variations. Commonly referred to as *trapping.*

Standing head. A "department head" that identifies a standard feature column in a periodical.

Stripping. The craft of assembling film negatives prior to printing. This art is best left to the professional.

Subscript. Small numbers, letters, or special characters set below the baseline.

Superior figures. Small numbers, letters, or special characters, such as the dollar sign, aligned with (or higher than) the top of the caps. See also *Superscript.*

Superscript. Small numbers, letters, or special characters, such as the dollar sign, aligned with (or higher than) the top of the caps. See also *Superior figures.*

T

Thumbnail sketches. The first stages of a project. Simple scribbles, often done on whatever paper might be available at the time—including coffee-stained restaurant napkins.

Tracking. Tightening the space between all characters, as opposed to *kerning*, which affects only the space between two characters.

Trapping. Slightly overlapping adjoining colors to prevent gaps when printing.

TrueType. An attempt by Apple and Microsoft to quash the Adobe Type 1 font-format standard. Dead for all intents and purposes on the Mac, its implications on the PC market remain to be seen.

TruMatch. A system for defining process color.

Typography. The craft of designing with type.

U

U&lc. Type set in uppercase and lowercase. Also, an excellent magazine published by the International Typeface Corporation.

V

Vector-based art. Drawings based on mathematical equations rather than bit-by-bit representations. This genre of electronic art can be scaled at will without loss of resolution.

X

x-height. The height of a lowercase letter *x*. Two typefaces can be the same point size, but have different x-heights.

CorelDRAW! Keyboard Shortcuts

+ (on the numeric keypad). Leaves the original object in place when moving, stretching, mirroring, rotating, or scaling. Also places a duplicate object behind the selected object, without any other actions

Alt-F4. Quits CorelDRAW!

Alt-F7. Accesses the Move dialog box

Alt-F8. Accesses the Rotate & Skew dialog box

Alt-F9. Accesses the Stretch & Mirror dialog box

Alt-A. Drops down the Arrange menu

Alt-F10. Aligns to baseline

Alt-Backspace (also Ctrl-Z). Accesses the Undo command

Alt-C. Drops down the Effects menu

Alt-D. Drops down the Display menu

Alt-E. Drops down the Edit menu

Alt-Enter. Accesses the Redo command

Alt-F. Drops down the File menu

Alt-L. Drops down the Layout menu

Alt-S. Drops down the Special menu

Alt-Tab. Switches between active programs

Alt-X. Drops down the Text menu

Click the right mouse button as you drag an object. Leaves the original object

Ctrl-F1. Accesses Help on the current command

Ctrl-F2. Accesses the Text roll-up menu

Ctrl-F3. Accesses the Layers roll-up menu

Ctrl-F5. Accesses the Style roll-up menu

Ctrl-F7. Accesses the Envelope roll-up menu

Ctrl-F8. Accesses the PowerLine roll-up menu

Ctrl-F9. Accesses the Contour roll-up menu

Ctrl-F10. Accesses the Node Edit roll-up menu

Ctrl-F11. Accesses the Symbol roll-up menu

Ctrl-A. Accesses the Align dialog box

Ctrl-B. Accesses the Blend roll-up menu

Ctrl-C (also Ctrl-Ins). Copies to the clipboard

Ctrl-D. Duplicates an object

Ctrl-E. Accesses the Extrude roll-up menu

Ctrl-Esc. Accesses the Windows Task Manager

Ctrl-F. Accesses the Fit Text To Path roll-up menu

Ctrl-G. Groups objects

Ctrl-Ins (also Ctrl-C). Copies to the clipboard

Ctrl-J. Accesses the Preferences dialog box

Ctrl-K. Breaks apart combined objects

Ctrl-L. Combines objects

Ctrl-N. Opens a new CorelDRAW! file

Ctrl-O. Opens an existing CorelDRAW! file

Ctrl-P. Accesses the Print dialog box

Ctrl-PgUp. Moves selected object forward one

Ctrl-PgDn. Moves selected object backward one

Ctrl-Q. Converts an object into curves

Ctrl-R. Repeats the last command or function

Ctrl-S. Saves the current drawing to disk

Ctrl-Spacebar. Enables the Pick tool

Ctrl-T. Accesses the Edit Text dialog box

Ctrl-U. Ungroups objects

Ctrl-V (also Shift-Ins). Pastes from the clipboard

Ctrl-W. Refreshes the screen

Ctrl-X (also Shift-Del). Cuts to the clipboard

Ctrl-Y. Turns Snap to Grid on and off

Ctrl-Z (also Alt-Backspace). Access the Undo command

Ctrl while drawing an ellipse or rectangle. Constructs a perfect circle or square

Ctrl while moving. Constrains movement to horizontal or vertical

Ctrl while rotating or skewing. Constrains movement to 15-percent (default) increments

Ctrl while stretching, scaling, or mirroring. Constrains movement to 100-percent increments

Del. Deletes a selected object or node

Double-clicking a character node. Accesses the Character Attributes dialog box

Double-clicking the page border. Accesses the Page Setup dialog box

Double-clicking the ruler. Accesses the Grid Setup dialog box

F1. Accesses Help

F2. Zooms in

F3. Zooms out

F4. Zooms to fit all objects in window

F5. Enables the Pencil tool

F6. Enables the Rectangle tool

F7. Enables the Ellipse tool

F8. Enables the Text tool

F9. Switches between full-screen preview and edit mode

F10. Enables the Shape tool

F11. Accesses the Fountain Fill dialog box

F12. Accesses the Outline Pen dialog box

PgDn. Moves object backward one

PgUp. Moves object forward one

Shift-F1. Accesses Help (on current screen or menu)

Shift-F4. Zooms to fit page in window

Shift-F8. Enables the Paragraph text tool

Shift-F9. Switches between Full-Color and Wireframe mode

Shift-F11. Accesses the Uniform Fill dialog box

Shift-F12. Accesses the Outline Color dialog box

Shift-Del (also Ctrl-X). Cuts the selected object to the clipboard

Shift-Ins (also Ctrl-V). Pastes the selected object from the clipboard

Shift-PgDn. Moves object to back

Shift-PgUp. Moves object to front

Shift-Tab. Selects the previous object

Shift while drawing. Erases when the mouse moves backward along a curve

Shift while drawing an ellipse or rectangle. Stretches or scales from the middle of the object

Spacebar. Toggles between the currently selected tool and the Pick tool

Tab. Selects the next object

Clip-Art Compendium

his appendix presents a brief list of electronic clip-art vendors. You might recognize some of the names from the collection that accompanies CorelDRAW!. Before you buy any clip art, make sure that you know what you are getting. Feel free to request brochures and samples from the manufacturers.

To get the most value for your clip-art dollar, install a CD-ROM drive. Every copy of CorelDRAW! 4.0 includes two CD-ROM discs. These discs contain thousands of clip-art images, from such vendors as ArtRight, Image Club, MicroMaps, One Mile Up, Tech Pool, and Totem. The money you spend to install the drive is far overshadowed by the wealth of high-quality artwork—not to mention the abundance of additional fonts!

21st Century Media PhotoDisk

Volume 1: Business & Industry
Volume 2: People and Lifestyles
Volume 3: Backgrounds and Textures
Volume 4: Science, Technology, and Medicine

Volume 5: World Commerce and Travel
Volume 6: Nature, Wildlife, and Environment
Volume 7: Business and Occupations

Now you can afford to design in full color by using professional digital stock photos. 21st Century Media's PhotoDisk™ collections consist of high-quality images on CD-ROM. Every photo is model-released and ready to use for advertising, promotions, newsletters, presentations, and multimedia. These images are award-winning stock photographs that have been scanned from transparencies and are provided in high-resolution TIFF format for desktop applications. Each volume includes the Lightbox browsing utility, which manipulates on-screen images to search, retrieve, store, view, copy, and paste.

> PhotoDisk, Inc.
> 2013 4th Ave., Suite 200
> Seattle, WA 98033
> 800/528-3472

Arroglyphs

Arroglyphs Environment Collection 1

Based on original hand-drawn images, the "Environment Collection" consists of 200 black-and-white EPS (AI 1.1 format) images covering environmental issues such as pollution, recycling, and life on Earth. Subject matter includes acid rain, global warming, ozone depletion, and so on. Beautifully rendered in a number of diverse styles, the package consists of six floppy disks and a comprehensive *User's Guide* that includes technical tips, page layout suggestions, and a detailed image catalog.

> ARRO International
> P.O. Box 167
> Montclair, NJ 07042
> 201/746-9620
> Fax: 201/509-0728

Artbeats

Backgrounds for Multimedia, Volumes 1 and 2
Marble and Granite Collection
Full-Page Images

Artbeats offers beautiful vector-based and bit-mapped background art for multimedia and desktop-publishing applications. "Backgrounds for Multimedia" are 8-bit and 24-bit images specifically designed for video, slide, animation, and texture mapping. The "Marble and Granite Collection" is an awesome, two-disc CD-ROM set of bit-mapped images in TIFF, TGA, PCX, and BMP formats. It includes 40 high-resolution images for prepress work; 120 multimedia backgrounds that you can use in slides and presentations; and 160 seamless tiles and floor tiles, which are ideal for three-dimensional renderings. The high-resolution TIFFs are highly recommended for four-color process printing.

The "Full-Page Images" collection (available on disk or CD-ROM) consists of a six-volume set (including Dimensions, Potpourri, and Natural Images) of EPS files, available as individual volumes or as a complete set. Each set consists of 10 images. The majority of these images are provided in black-and-white format, with high- and low-contrast (or light and dark) versions of each design.

> Artbeats
> 2611 S. Myrtle Road
> Myrtle Creek, OR 97457
> 503/863-4429
> Fax: 503/863-4547

ArtMaker

ArtMaker has a four-volume disk art library that has, all told, over 250 illustrations to round out your collection of 300 dpi PCX files. You get an antistatic disk storage sleeve, a pictorial index guidebook, and a free disk of your choice with your purchase.

> The ArtMaker Company
> 500 N. Claremont Blvd.

Claremont, CA 91711
714/626-8065
Fax: 714/621-1323

BBL Typographic

Volume 1: Westminster Abbey
Volume 2: Pontificale of John I
Volume 3: The Golden Bible
Volume 4: St. Mary of Soest
Volume 5: Paris Book of Hours
Volume 6: Musica Antiqua

From "The Land Down Under" comes a series of well-rendered medieval and renaissance letter forms and ornaments. Each volume contains a full alphabet of initial caps, in addition to decoratives, borders, and other period artworks. More than 70 images per volume, these volumes are available in CorelDRAW! version 2 format.

BBL Typographic
137 Narrow Neck Road
Katoomba, NSW 2780
Australia
011-61-47-826111
Fax: 011-61-47-826144

Casady & Greene

One of the more popular small electronic type foundries, Casady & Greene specializes in calligraphic, classic, and continental-flair typefaces. Their latest type collection, "Fluent Laser Font Library 2," contains 120 fonts in your choice of PostScript or TrueType formats. The company also produces a limited amount of clip art. "Special Events" is a charming little collection containing Dorothea Casady's Meow Cat Alphabet along with a variety of electronic art files suitable for holiday use. Perfect for calendars, lighter newsletters, and so on.

Casady & Greene
22734 Portola Drive
Salinas, CA 93908
408/484-9228
Fax: 408/484-9218

Church Mouse Electronic Illustration

ArtSource: The Ultimate Youth Ministry Clip Art Series
Volume 1: Fantastic Activities
Volume 2: Borders, Symbols, Holidays, and Attention Getters
Volume 3: Sports
Volume 4: Phrases and Verses
Volume 5: Amazing Oddities and Appalling Images
Volume 6: Spiritual Topics

As you might guess, these collections are ideal for churches or
organizations. "Fantastic Activities," for example, is more than
just clip art... it's an inspiration for fun events, such as pizza
parties, food drives, summer safaris, and more! Capture kids'
attention with the whimsical and cartoony renderings in the
"Sports" and "Amazing Oddities" collections. "Spiritual Topics"
is filled with topical and thematic clip art. All images are digitized
300 dpi TIFF files.

The Church Art Works
875 High Street NE
Salem, OR 97301
503/370-9377
Fax: 503/362-5231

Clipables

Clipables
Statements
Travel and Vacation

"Clipables" contains more than 1,300 professionally drawn black-and-white EPS files. This particularly versatile collection spans some of the following topics: animals, borders and ornaments, computers and business machines, children, construction, dingbats and symbols, display banners, drop cap toolbox, expressions, famous people, holidays, humor, maps and flags, medical, music, portfolio, sports, and transportation. Fortunately, this extensive library comes with a user's manual featuring a pictorial index that includes every image in the library. Available on disk and CD-ROM, this product is a good value when you consider the excellent cost-per-image ratio.

"Statements," along with the "Travel and Vacation" collection, are the two latest releases from C.A.R. The "Statements" collection consists of 150 skillfully rendered and emotional illustrations, ranging in content from humorous to serious. The "Travel and Vacation" collection contains 80 travel- and leisure-oriented illustrations.

C.A.R., Inc.
7009 Kingsbury
St. Louis, MO 63130
800/288-7585
314/721-6305

Clip-Art Connection (Subscription)

Clip-Art Connection is an electronic catalog, ordering, and fulfillment software package that runs under Windows. This subscription service provides modem access to over 29,000 clip-art images from 17 top vendors. Users can quickly locate and preview images using the keyword search feature. Individual images can be purchased by means of credit card and downloaded within minutes for instant use.

Connect Software
A Division of Adonis Corporation
6742 185th Ave. NE, Ste. 150
Redmond, WA 98052
800/234-9497

Clipatures

Clipatures Volume 1: Business Images
Clipatures Volume 2: Business Images 2
Clipatures Volume 3: Sports
Clipatures Volume 4: World Flags
Clipatures Volume 5: Borders

Clipatures offers five collections of EPS artwork targeted specifically for the business user and desktop publisher. The business collections are populated with lots of people in office settings. "Volume 1" includes credit cards, icons, and a good number of business-specific cartoons. "Volume 2" includes silhouettes, computers, and airplanes. "Volume 3" contains many male and female athletes, as well as sports icons, graphics, and symbols. "Volume 4" features over 300 flags (national, territorial, organizational, and code flags). "Volume 5" contains a wide variety of border styles, from Art Deco to Contemporary.

Dream Maker Software
925 West Kenyon Avenue, Suite 16
Englewood, CO 80110
303/762-1001
Fax: 303/762-0762

DataTech

Federal Logos, Symbols & Seals

Doing work with the Fed? "Federal Logos, Symbols & Seals" contains almost 700 logos and other images that pertain to the United States government. You will find logos for all your favorite government agencies, such as the Internal Revenue Service, the Veterans Administration, and the United States Postal Service. These images are 300 dpi PCX files.

DataTech Distributors
55 South Progress Avenue
Harrisburg, PA 17109
800/788-2068 or 717/652-4344
Fax: 717/652-3222

DesignClips: Natural Environment Series

DesignClips is a thorough, well-planned library of black-and-white graphic symbols perfect for use as design elements. The "Fish" collection, for example, includes (from A to D): Albacore, Anchovy, Angelfish, Bandtail Puffer, Barracuda, Bluefin Tuna, Blue Marlin, Bonito, Butterflyfish, Cod, and Dolphin. Each collection consists of 50 files, along with a comprehensive pictorial index. These images were originally designed as object-oriented art; therefore, the collection is available as EPS files. TIFF and PCX files are also available. LetterSpace is a subsidiary of David Curry Design, a New York-based graphic design firm.

> LetterSpace
> 338 East 53rd Street #2C
> New York, NY 10022-5254
> 800/933-9095 or 212/935-8130

Dynamic Graphics

Subscription:
Electronic Clipper
Electronic Print Media Service
Designer's Club

Electronic Clipper is Dynamic Graphics' premier all-purpose electronic art and idea service. Each month, subscribers receive over 70 TIFF and EPS files through floppy and CD-ROM. This service also includes *Options*, a monthly magazine filled with electronic design tips and layout ideas. Electronic Print Media Service is a monthly CD-ROM targeted for retail advertising and promotion; each disc includes over 100 TIFF and EPS files per month in seasonal and topical themes. Designer's Club provides over 55 general-purpose EPS images per month.

Non-subscription:
ArtAbout
Designer's Club Annual CD-ROM
Electronic Clipper Annual CD-ROM

"ArtAbout" is a series of themed clip-art collections made available on a single purchase, non-subscription basis. Each collection includes over 100 TIFF and EPS images. Subjects include sports, healthcare, food, seasons, business, education, graphics and symbols, and dining. The Designer's Club and Electronic Clipper Annual CD-ROMs offer previously released Dynamic Graphics artwork in convenient CD-ROM format. Each Designer's Club CD-ROM contains over 500 EPS images covering assorted subjects and in a variety of styles. The Electronic Clipper Annual CD-ROM contains over 800 images (60 percent TIFF and 40 percent EPS) in a wide variety of contemporary styles and themes.

Dynamic Graphics, Inc.
6000 N. Forest Park Drive
Peoria, IL 61614-3592
800/255-8800
Fax: 309/688-5873

Federal Clip Art

Federal Clip Art I: A Congress of Artwork
Federal Clip Art II: Air Combat
Federal Clip Art III: Naval Combat
Federal Clip Art IV: Ground Combat
Federal Clip Art V: Army Insignia
Federal Clip Art VI: Diplomatic Art
Federal Clip Art VII: State Art
Federal Clip Art VIII: European Art
Federal Clip Art IX: NASA Art
Federal Clip Art X: Book of Seals
Federal Clip Art XI: Naval Insignia
Federal Clip Art XII: Air Force Insignia
National Archives CD-ROM

Serious newspaper publishers, along with government and defense contractor DTPers, will be very pleased with these 12 packages. Each collection contains over 300 meticulous illustrations of various military hardware, insignias, and other U.S. government-specific items, including aircraft, missiles, and naval vessels. You will find lots of great One Mile Up clip art on the CorelDRAW! 4.0 CD-ROM disks. This art is black-and-white EPS, but packages also include Pantone and CMYK settings for exact government colors. The packages demonstrate an impressive attention to detail. The international and state flags found in the "Diplomatic Art" and "State Art" collections, for example, are trapped for accurate color printing.

> One Mile Up, Inc.
> 7011 Evergreen Court
> Annandale, VA 22003
> 703/642-1177
> Fax: 703/642-9088

Fine Art Impressions

Fine Art Impressions Art Library

A highly stylized package of hand-created illustrations. These 177 black-and-white detailed illustrations are available in CDR, EPS, CGM (for PC PageMaker users), and GEM (for Ventura Publisher users) formats. The package includes "Image Extras" (hardcopy illustrations not found on the disks), The "Designer's Desktop" (a step-by-step layout and design guide), The "Illustrator's Portfolio" (large printed samples of each image), a *Troubleshooting Guide*, and even a full-color three-ring binder to store it all in! Titles in the library include "Money & More Money," "Making Headlines," "Professional Workforce," "Borders & Boxes," and "Occupational Themes."

> Best Impressions
> 3844 W. Channel Islands Blvd. #234
> Oxnard, CA 93035

FM Waves

Marketed as "Clip Art with an Attitude," FM Waves offerings come in all flavors: PC or Mac, and EPS or 400-dpi TIFF. "DTPro" provides a wealth of images on a CD-ROM disc. "Graphic Originals" contains everything from icons, design elements, and arrows through beautiful fashion pen-and-ink renderings—all done with style. The "Graphic News Network" is intended for desktop publishers who need timely political cartoons, editorial graphics, and other hard-to-find artwork. Overall, FM Waves provides a formidable wealth of quality images.

> FM Waves
> 70 Derby Alley
> San Francisco, CA 94102

FontHaus Picture Fonts

Set No. 1: Transportation & Travel
Set No. 2: Commerce & Communication
Set No. 3: Holidays & Celebrations
Set No. 4: Food & Drink
Set No. 5: Household Items
Set No. 6: Animals

FontHaus calls their Picture Fonts "pictures you wouldn't expect from your keyboard," and that's quite an accurate description. Scalable, PostScript fonts, the first two sets in the series offer nice collections of symbols and borders. You can build your own train set (each car is a character), and create wonderful coupons and advertisements. Borders are created directly from the keyboard, using an old typesetter's trick. FontHaus Picture Fonts are thoughtfully designed, whimsical, and of high quality.

> FontHaus, Inc.
> 1375 Kings Highway East, Suite 240
> Fairfield, CT 06850
> 800/942-9110

Image Club

DigitArt Volumes 1-3, 8: Miscellaneous
DigitArt Volumes 4-5: Cartoon People
DigitArt Volume 6: Business & Industry
DigitArt Volume 7: World Maps
DigitArt Volume 9: Design Elements
DigitArt Volume 10-11: Design Letters
DigitArt Volume 12: Symbols & Headings
DigitArt Volume 13: Food & Entertainment
DigitArt Volume 14: Occasions
DigitArt Volume 15: Lifestyles
DigitArt Volume 16: Office & Education
DigitArt Volume 17: Universal Symbols
DigitArt Volume 18: Celebrity Caricatures
DigitArt Volume 19: Silhouettes
DigitArt Volume 20: Design Backgrounds
DigitArt Volume 21: Fabulous Fifties
DigitArt Volume 22: Business Cartoons
DigitArt Volume 23: Borders & Ornaments
DigitArt Volume 24: Science & Medicine
DigitArt Volume 25: Wood Cuts
DarkRoom Clip Photography
PhotoGear, Volume 1
Art & Type Vendor 2.0

DigitArt is a collection of 25 volumes of EPS art, available by volume or in combination. The volumes are also available as a complete collection, the ArtRoom CD-ROM, which contains over 9,000 images. The work ranges from slick and stylized to fanciful cartoons; for example, the "Wood Cuts" collection is designer-chic while the "Fabulous Fifties" collection is sheer camp.

"DarkRoom Clip Photography" is a stock photo library for CD-ROM. This collection consists of over 500 ready-to-use grayscale TIFFs. Subjects include business, lifestyle, sports, and travel. You can use the photos in black and white without paying additional royalties—provided the photographer is credited. Color photos can be requested for a royalty fee.

"PhotoGear" is a CD-ROM disc filled with 30 RGB TIFF files for high-quality, full-page offset printing. Image Club is also known for its massive collection of over 600 PostScript fonts, with an unabashed focus on display faces. The "Art & Type Vendor" is the original unlocking font and clip art CD-ROM, and is a great choice for DTPers on a budget.

> Image Club Graphics, Inc.
> #5, 190211th Street S.E.
> Calgary, Alberta, Canada T2G 3G2
> 800/661-9410 or 403/262-8008
> Fax: 403/261-7013

Images With Impact!

Accents & Borders 1 & 2
Business 1
Graphics & Symbols 1
People 1
Places & Faces 1
Images With Impact! CD-ROM v2.0

The award-winning "Accents & Borders 1" contains 270 design elements, including seasonal, geometric, historical, and contemporary designs; "Accents & Borders 2" contains 300 decorative and representational images. "Graphics & Symbols 1" covers a broad range of subjects. Ditto for "Business 1," which includes people, computers, financial success, and hands at work. "Places & Faces 1" includes illustrations of people of many ages and cultures, along with the world's top travel destinations and high-contrast recreational graphics. The CD-ROM contains all six Images With Impact! titles on one disk. Available in EPS, WMF, and 75-dpi BMP file formats.

> 3G Graphics
> 114 Second Avenue South, #104
> Edmonds, WA 98020
> 206/774-3518 or 800/456-0234

Innovation Advertising & Design

AdArt:
Logos & Trademarks, Volumes 1-11
Logos & Trademarks, Automotive Edition
Logos & Trademarks, Real Estate Edition
Logos & Trademarks, 500—Vinyl Edition
Cars & Light Trucks
Real Estate Art
International Symbols & Icons, Volumes 1 and 2
Flags of the World
Medical Symbols
Transportation
Credit Card Art
Business Symbols Collection
Vinyl Cutters Collection
Safety & Packaging Collection
Recycled Art—Environmentally Safe Clip Art
Accents & Attention Getters
AdArt: Clip Art for Advertising CD-ROM 2.0
AdArt: Logos & Trademarks, Volume 1-11 CD-ROM 2.0

This clip art should be standard issue for those who build advertisements or signage. AdArt is a superb idea: EPS logos for every company that you can think of! If you have ever spent hours searching out a logo for use in a newspaper ad, you will find this series indispensable. It includes graphics appropriate for businesses that sell or use autos, credit cards, insurance, real estate, and so on. "International Symbols & Icons" includes over 300 EPS files perfect for business charts, maps, and packaging. This collection is bread-and-butter electronic clip art. The CD-ROM package offers exceptional value—everything on one disk!

Innovation Advertising & Design
41 Mansfield Avenue
Essex Junction, VT 05452
800/255-0562 or 802/879-1164
Fax: 802/878-1768

Logo SuperPower

This collection is not clip art, but a set of over 2,000 electronic EPS design elements developed with logo and publication creation in mind. You can combine and tweak design elements for an infinite number of combinations. What formerly took days for an artist to render with pen and ink can be executed in a fraction of the time. An excellent choice for electronic designers who need to crank out logos at a moment's notice.

> Decathlon Corporation
> 4100 Executive Park Drive #16
> Cincinnati, OH 45241
> 800/648-5646
> Order Fax: 606/324-6038

MapArt

MapArt Volume 1: International & USA
MapArt Volume 2: US States by County
MapArt Volume 3: Global Perspectives
MapArt Volume 4: Metro Area Maps - USA
MapArt: World Data Bank (12 regions)

These versatile, comprehensive map collections are essential for many business situations. In fact, you might find that these packages pay for themselves the first time you use them. They might not quicken your pulse, but they will pay the rent. Excellent for creating everything from simple line art to complex information graphics. You can find a nice selection of Cartesia's maps on the CorelDRAW! 4.0 CD-ROM disk.

> Cartesia Software, Inc.
> P.O. Box 757
> Lambertville, NJ 08530
> 609/397-1611

[metal]

General Collection
General Collection II
Animal Collection
Pattern Collection

Designed by designers for designers. [metal] Studio offers four intriguing visual element collections. The "General Collection" contains 167 unique EPS images, covering subjects such as food, travel, animals, architecture, the oil industry, tools, and special events. The "General Collection II" contains 92 EPS files including cubist elements and line drawings with an emphasis on fun, travel, entertainment, and holidays. The "Animal Collection" consists of 72 EPS images rendered with a distinctive line and curve style. The "Pattern Collection" is made up of 15 TIFF images in a variety of stylistic and abstract patterns.

> [metal] Studio, Inc.
> 131 Memorial Drive #222
> Houston, TX 77079
> Info: 713/932-6088
> Order: 800/858-5254
> Fax: 713/932-6087

Metro ImageBase

Metro, one of the leaders in printed clip art, has published a large body of quality bit-mapped images. Over 31 collections are available, most consisting of 100 files. Collections include "Art Deco," "Borders & Boxes," "Food," "Team Sports," "The Four Seasons," and many others. Each collection comes with a printed ImageIndex for selecting files. These files are in 300-dpi PCX or TIFF format. A new CD-ROM also is available.

> Metro ImageBase
> 18623 Ventura Boulevard
> Suite 210
> Tarzana, CA 91356
> 800/525-1552 or 818/881-1997
> Fax: 818/881-4557

Moonlight Artworks

A cost-effective choice for those who work with display retail advertising (for example, newspaper ad designers). These sets use EPS files. Additional Moonlight Artworks, Logomaster, and Retail Ad sets are soon to be released.

> Hired Hand Design
> 3608 Faust Ave.
> Long Beach, CA 90808
> 213/429-2936

NOVA Cube

Pix
Military Art

"*Pix!*" includes stylized design elements (line art) over a wide range: anatomy, appliances, buildings, flowers, food, medicine, people, and more. "*Military Art*" is designed to meet the needs of professional military and defense industry users. This collection includes aircraft, equipment, symbols, and weapons. Both "*Pix!*" and "*Military Art*" arc available in EPS format.

> NOVA Cube
> 5600 El Campo
> Ft. Worth, TX 76107

PolyType

Volume 1: Ornaments
Volume 2: Corners
Volume 3: ArtDeco
Volume 4: Images

PolyType images are in font format, so that you access ornaments or objects from your keyboard instead of by importing a file. Each volume contains 130 images (in five fonts). All fonts are supplied in Adobe Type 1 format, along with character outlines in EPS format.

PolyType
P.O. Box 25976
Los Angeles, CA 90025
310/444-9934
800/998-9934

Presentation Task Force

A collection of over 3,500 files in object-oriented CGM format
from one of the ground-breakers in electronic imagery. As the
name implies, these images are perfect for presentation work,
including 35mm slides. Almost half the images are color. Subject
matter centers on business. The latest version (4.0) comes with a
conversion utility that converts color artwork into black and
white.

New Vision Technologies, Inc.
Box 5468, Station F
Ottawa, Ontario, Canada K2C 3M1
613/727-8184

ProArt

Multi-Ad Services, Inc., is a 46-year veteran in the clip-art industry. The electronic ProArt collections contain over 100 images. The
13 collections available are "Holiday," "Business," "Sports,"
"Food," "People," "Borders & Headings," "Health & Medical,"
"Educational," "Religious Images," "Christmas," "Animals,"
"Generic Products," and "Business 2." These EPS files are available on floppy disk or CD-ROM.

Multi-Ad Services, Inc.
1720 W. Detweiller Drive
Peoria, IL 61615-1695
800/447-1950 or 309/692-1530
Fax: 309/692-5444

Quick Art

Quick Art Deluxe: Volume 1 CD-ROM
Quick Art Lite: Volume 1 CD-ROM

"Quick Art Lite" consists of over 1,700 black-and-white images, in a wide variety of subjects including animals, borders, flowers, food, holidays, mail, maps, money, numbers, office/media, people, science/energy, sports/exercise, and travel. "Quick Art Deluxe" contains over 3,300 images (including all the images in the "Lite" collection) with buildings/landscapes, celebrations, clothing/sewing, education, entertainment, farm, gardening, health/medicine, insects, mail, maps, music, mystery, plants, religion, tools, toys/games, transportation, and weather. Both collections come with an illustrated user's manual. Individual subjects are available on floppy disk. The majority of images are in 300 dpi TIFF, IMG, and PCX formats.

> Wheeler Arts
> 66 Lake Park
> Champaign, IL 61821-7101
> 217/359-6816
> Fax: 217/359-8716

Santa Fe Collection

Designers and desktop publishers in search of Native American and Southwestern art will be pleased by the quality and value of the Santa Fe Collection. Originally developed on the Macintosh and now available in PC EPS format, this collection is one of the most complete and affordable genre libraries around. The many designs—including birds, bugs, fish, lizards, and motifs (over 100!)—show care, research, and sensitivity to Native American culture. An excellent value (almost 35M of art!), especially considering the low cost. The Santa Fe Collection Professional Version in EPS includes over 500 images and 125 preconstructed borders. As a bonus, the collection ships with RT's Santa Fe Font (a display typeface in both TrueType and Type 1 formats) as well as LOOKaRT, RT Graphics' EPS file viewer.

RT Computer Graphics
602 San Juan de Rio
Rio Rancho, NM 87124
800/245-7824 or 505/891-1600
Fax: 505/891-1350

Steven & Associates

One thousand images are found in this volume. Topics include architecture, birds, holidays, insects, mythology and fantasy, religion, semiconductors, symbols and signs and obviously, many more. All images are 300 dpi PCX files.

Steven & Associates
5205 Kearny Villa Way, #104
San Diego, CA 92123

The SunShine Graphics Library

Visual Delights

SunShine's Visual Delights is a large collection of over 60 affordable sets of black-and-white 300-dpi TIFF images. Each set covers one topic and contains approximately 68 pictures. Topics include men, women, children, designs, humor, borders, music, dance, mythology, Native Americans, Africa, the Middle East, American West, China, Japan, knighthood, royalty, angels, landscapes, fantasy, decorative letters, silhouettes, flowers, trees, plants, and other hard-to-find subjects. Animal sets include realistic and stylized mammals, birds, reptiles, insects, and sea life. Besides separate Jewish, Catholic, and Christian sets, plus Valentine's Day, Christmas, and Easter, many elaborate borders, cartouches, friezes, and other decorative elements are included.

Most images are line art, although some are delicate halftone images. Rights to use the images are granted for almost all purposes. Each set comes with a printed catalog that shows all the images along with a listing of their physical dimensions and file size.

SunShine
Box 4351
Austin, TX 78765

Taco Clipart Company

Animals Collection
Aquaculture and Fish Collection
Background Collection
Business Collection
Cellular Industry Collection
CompuServe "You asked for it, you got it" Collection
Court Related Collection
Ethnic Collection
Ethnic Business Collection 1-3
European Landmark Collection
Factory Collection
Food Collection
Hands Doing Things Collection
Holiday Collection
Icon Collection
International Finance Collection
Misc Collection
Money Collection
Pizza Collection
Relaxation Collection

Need a specific custom image, but can't afford to spend thousands of dollars? Or perhaps you are designing a program and need special buttons? Your prayers have been answered. Taco Clipart Company is a professional art-generating and -archiving company that specializes in custom artwork, delivered in your choice of formats. Taco's clipart is available in standard PC formats such as AI, EPS, GIF, TIF, DRW, CDR, TGA, WPG, GRF, and PIC (among others), as well as programming bit-map formats, like BMP, ICO, and DIB.

Most of the images offered by Taco have been paid for by commissioning companies, but each company paid a lesser price than standard by allowing Taco to retain the rights to the images. In return, Taco promises each company exclusive use of the image (usually six months) and then offers the images to their subscribers for use in their publications. Some of the original images were billed at $4,000. Many of Taco's images are copyright free. Whenever possible, the company tries to deliver its images by modem. This method also facilitates delivery to European countries without wasting time waiting for mail delivery. In addition to custom artwork, Taco offers pre-made collections. Many collections can also be put together for specific needs. As of this writing, Taco has over 10,000 images (all from this decade, with the exception of a collection of 1800s art).

Taco Clipart Company
1208 Howard Street
Omaha, NE 68102
402/344-7191 or 800/233-TACO
CompuServe ID: 74140,1110

TechPool Studios

The LifeART Super Anatomy Collection
Atmospheres Background Systems

Do you need anatomically correct illustrations? The "LifeART Super Anatomy Collection" provides "the best in anatomic exactness and visual clarity." An excellent resource for those involved in medical, legal, and educational presentations or publications. Topics covered include external views of the body, musculoskeletal, cardiovascular, reproductive, endocrine, gastrointestinal, nervous, and urinary systems, the special senses, joints, and more. Color images can be ungrouped to show underlying structures, or layered and cut away. Other collections include Emergency, HealthCare, and Dental. All collections ship with Transverter to convert EPS to other formats, and to provide several color treatment options. Check out the CorelDRAW! 4.0 CD-ROM for a nice selection of TechPool art.

Tech Pool's "Atmospheres Background Systems" consists of a number of full-page, full-color, and graytone collections of background vector clip art. They include the Watermark special effects tool to provide a professional look to any publication or presentation. Collections include "CityScapes," "Habitats," "Patterns," "Classics," and "Geometrics." Watermark allows color ghosting and graytone contrast controls for any EPS file.

> TechPool Studios
> 1463 Warrensville Center
> Suite 200
> Cleveland, OH 44121
> 216/382-1234

Totem Graphics

Birds
Borders
Deluxe Business Images #1
Deluxe Business Images #2
Domestic Animals
Education
Fish
Food
Flowers
Healthcare
Holidays
Insects
Nautical
Sports
Tools & Hardware
Travel
Wild Animals
Women

These files are gorgeous, full-color EPS images. You might have seen several of Totem Graphics files in the CorelDRAW! version 4.0 CD-ROM disks. Totem's artists have an excellent feel for wildlife illustration. The "Fish" and "Insects" collections are particularly well-executed. Each package includes 96 files and is available in CorelDRAW!, EPSF, and PCX formats.

Totem Graphics, Inc.
6200-F Capitol Blvd.
Tumwater, WA 98501-5288
206/352-1851

U-Design Type Foundry

Bill's American Ornaments
Bill's Barnhart Ornaments 3.0
Bill's Cast O' Characters
Bill's Classic Ornaments
Bill's DECOrations
Bill's Broadway DECOrations
Bill's Tropical DECOrations
Bill's Modern Diner
Bill's Peculiars
Bill's Printers Pals
Bill's Victorian Ornaments
Buddy's Things

Lots of cool stuff from Bill! U-Design specializes in picture fonts with a period feel (as well as unique display fonts). These wonderful decoratives are worth owning. All are value-priced, and many come with bonus fonts such as Bill's Dingbats (which was named by MacUser Magazine as one of their favorite 50 shareware products, as well as one of the 200 best products for the Mac). A catalogue is available.

U-Design Type Foundry
270 Farmington Avenue
Hartford, CT 06105
203/278-3648

Visatex Corporation

The "US Presidents" collection contains portraits of 41 U.S. presidents. "Hollywood Faces" contains portraits of 25 movie stars, including Bogart, Brando, Cagney, and Groucho. These files come in manually dithered grayscale PCX format.

> Visatex Corporation
> 1745 Dell Avenue
> Campbell, CA 95008
> 800/PC2-DRAW or 408/866-6562

Yukio Artwork Archives

This company specializes in aircraft illustrations and rare aviation photographs. "Poster Art" has 20 original layout and format guides, 20 background and modernistic panels, eight typeface letter styles, and more. Be sure to specify the required file format.

> Yukio Artwork Archives
> 2025 Federal Avenue, Suite #2
> Los Angeles, CA 90025

What's on the Disk?

he disk that accompanies this book includes several useful shareware utilities. This appendix briefly describes each program.

To install these utilities, simply open Windows File Manager and double-click on INSTALL.EXE. For more information on these programs and their developers, please consult the README.WRI file, which is copied to your hard drive during the installation process. You also can read more about some of these utilities in Chapter 10, "The Windows DTP Arsenal."

CD4FONTS.WRI

CD4FONTS.WRI (see fig. F.1) is a Windows Write file that contains an alphabetized listing of all the PostScript Type 1 fonts found on the CorelDRAW! CD. The font names are cross referenced with the PFM file needed to install the font on your system.

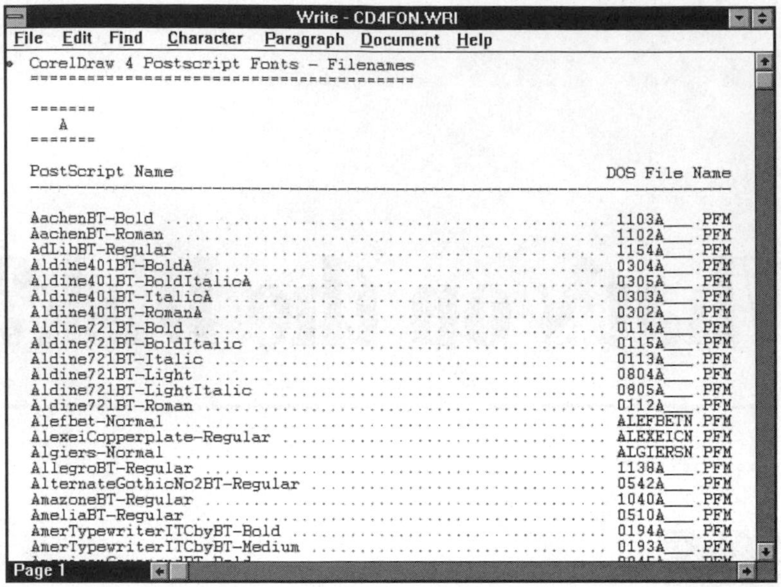

Figure F.1:

CD4FONTS.WRI.

```
┌─────────────────────────────────────────────────────────────┐
│ ─                   Write - CD4FON.WRI                   ▼ ◆ │
├─────────────────────────────────────────────────────────────┤
│ File  Edit  Find  Character  Paragraph  Document  Help        │
├─────────────────────────────────────────────────────────────┤
│• CorelDraw 4 Postscript Fonts - Filenames              ▲     │
│  ==================================================           │
│                                                               │
│  =======                                                      │
│     A                                                         │
│  =======                                                      │
│                                                               │
│  PostScript Name                            DOS File Name     │
│                                                               │
│  AachenBT-Bold ........................... 1103A___.PFM       │
│  AachenBT-Roman .......................... 1102A___.PFM       │
│  AdLibBT-Regular ......................... 1154A___.PFM       │
│  Aldine401BT-BoldA ....................... 0304A___.PFM       │
│  Aldine401BT-BoldItalicA ................. 0305A___.PFM       │
│  Aldine401BT-ItalicA ..................... 0303A___.PFM       │
│  Aldine401BT-RomanA ...................... 0302A___.PFM       │
│  Aldine721BT-Bold ........................ 0114A___.PFM       │
│  Aldine721BT-BoldItalic .................. 0115A___.PFM       │
│  Aldine721BT-Italic ...................... 0113A___.PFM       │
│  Aldine721BT-Light ....................... 0804A___.PFM       │
│  Aldine721BT-LightItalic ................. 0805A___.PFM       │
│  Aldine721BT-Roman ....................... 0112A___.PFM       │
│  Alefbet-Normal .......................... ALEFBETN.PFM       │
│  AlexeiCopperplate-Regular ............... ALEXEICN.PFM       │
│  Algiers-Normal .......................... ALGIERSN.PFM       │
│  AllegroBT-Regular ....................... 1138A___.PFM       │
│  AlternateGothicNo2BT-Regular ............ 0542A___.PFM       │
│  AmazoneBT-Regular ....................... 1040A___.PFM       │
│  AmeliaBT-Regular ........................ 0510A___.PFM       │
│  AmerTypewriterITCbyBT-Bold .............. 0194A___.PFM       │
│  AmerTypewriterITCbyBT-Medium ............ 0193A___.PFM   ▼  │
│                                      0045A   PEM              │
├─────────────────────────────────────────────────────────────┤
│ Page 1        ◆│                                          │◆ │
└─────────────────────────────────────────────────────────────┘
```

Launch

If you'd rather have convenience and efficiency than colorful icons, Launch is the way to go. This application launcher substitutes for Program Manager. The pop-up menu appears whenever you click on the desktop, providing instant access to any program. A host of easily configurable setup options are available.

Cubit Meister

The Cubit Meister utility performs several functions specifically designed for the Windows DTP professional. Cubit Meister converts decimal and fractional inches, millimeters/centimeters, picas/points and points into all the other formats simultaneously. CM also provides an electronic Proportion Scale that calculates proportions even when different measurement systems are entered for the "Original" and "Target" sizes.

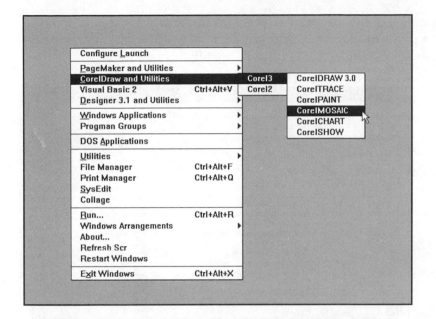

Figure F.2:
Launch.

Figure F.3:
Cubit Meister.

WinPSX

WinPSX is a PostScript soft font downloader that runs under
Windows. It supports Type 1 and Type 3 fonts. Bitstream QEM
PostScript soft fonts are supported under the Type 3 option.
WinPSX enables you to print reports that list available fonts in
the printer and general printer statistics, as well as font samples
of your Type 1 soft fonts.

FontSpec

FontSpec is a TrueType font viewer and type specimen printer.
As a viewer, it displays your TrueType fonts in sizes from 8 to 98

points, using different effects and in various justification modes. In print mode, you can produce quality formatted font specimen sheets in single-, two-column, or full sheets.

Figure F.4:

WinPSX.

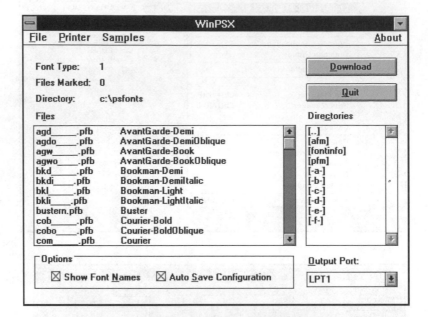

Figure F.5:

FontSpec.

WinZip

WinZip brings the convenience of Windows to the use of ZIP, LZH, and ARC files. You can use WinZip's intuitive point-and-click interface to view, run, extract, add, delete, and test archived files. Optional virus-scanning support is included. The tool bar provides fast access to commonly used actions.

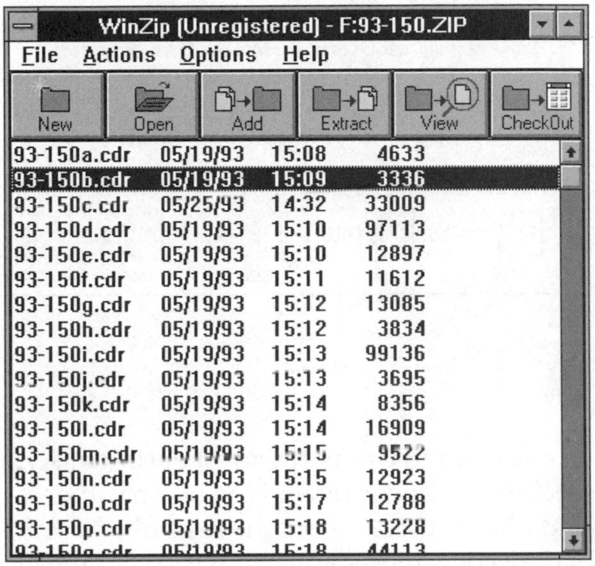

WinZip (Unregistered) - F:93-150.ZIP

File   Actions   Options   Help

New   Open   Add   Extract   View   CheckOut

93-150a.cdr	05/19/93	15:08	4633
93-150b.cdr	05/19/93	15:09	3336
93-150c.cdr	05/25/93	14:32	33009
93-150d.cdr	05/19/93	15:10	97113
93-150e.cdr	05/19/93	15:10	12897
93-150f.cdr	05/19/93	15:11	11612
93-150g.cdr	05/19/93	15:12	13085
93-150h.cdr	05/19/93	15:12	3834
93-150i.cdr	05/19/93	15:13	99136
93-150j.cdr	05/19/93	15:13	3695
93-150k.cdr	05/19/93	15:14	8356
93-150l.cdr	05/19/93	15:14	16909
93-150m.cdr	05/19/93	15:15	9522
93-150n.cdr	05/19/93	15:15	12923
93-150o.cdr	05/19/93	15:17	12788
93-150p.cdr	05/19/93	15:18	13228
93-150q.cdr	05/19/93	15:18	44113

Figure F.6:
WinZip.

AlphaQuote

AlphaQuote is a typesetting estimating and copyfitting program written for the IBM-PC and close compatibles. This DOS program offers an easy, fast, and consistent method of pricing work or comparing the price of desktop publishing with traditional type-setting. You can print attractive reports, save estimates to disk, instantly preview estimates, and calculate from printed pages as well as from a character count.

Figure F.7:

AlphaQuote.

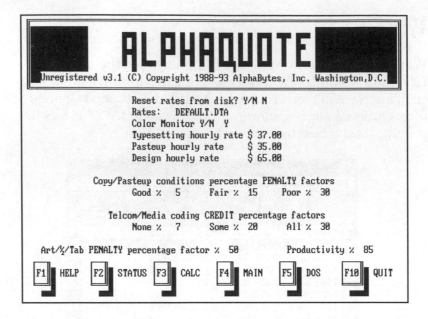

ALPHAQUOTE

Unregistered v3.1 (C) Copyright 1988-93 AlphaBytes, Inc. Washington,D.C.

```
          Reset rates from disk? Y/N N
          Rates:   DEFAULT.DTA
          Color Monitor Y/N  Y
          Typesetting hourly rate $ 37.00
          Pasteup hourly rate     $ 35.00
          Design hourly rate      $ 65.00

     Copy/Pasteup conditions percentage PENALTY factors
          Good %  5        Fair % 15       Poor % 30

        Telcom/Media coding CREDIT percentage factors
            None %  7       Some % 20       All % 30

   Art/½/Tab PENALTY percentage factor % 50        Productivity % 85

   F1  HELP   F2  STATUS  F3  CALC   F4  MAIN   F5  DOS    F10  QUIT
```

SetDRAW

SetDRAW enables you to tweak the most pertinent settings in Draw's five INI files without using Notepad or other text editors with point-and-shoot ease. Not only is the utility simple to use, it is also very safety conscious—you can restore your INI original settings at any time. The program features help at every step, so you rarely need to refer to Corel's documentation.

CorelMOVE! Animation

The CorelMOVE! beach scene designed in Chapter 13 is available on disk from New Riders Publishing. To order this disk, complete and return the order form at the back of the book.

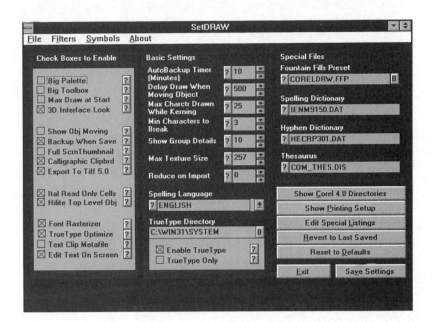

Figure F.8:
SetDRAW.

Index

G

X-Y-Z

Inside CorelDRAW! 4.0, Special Edition
REGISTRATION CARD

Fill out this card to receive information about future CorelDRAW! books and other New Riders titles!

Name _____ **Title** _____

Company _____

Address _____

City/State/ZIP _____

I bought this book because: _____

_____

I purchased this book from:
☐ A bookstore (Name _____)
☐ A software or electronics store (Name _____)
☐ A mail order (Name of Catalog _____)

I purchase this many computer books each year:
☐ 1–5   ☐ 5 or more

I currently use these applications: _____

_____

_____

_____

I found these chapters to be the most informative: _____

_____

I found these chapters to be the least informative: _____

_____

Additional comments: _____

_____

☐ I would like to see my name in print! You may use my name and quote me in future New Riders products and promotions. My daytime phone number is: _____

New Riders Publishing 11711 North College Avenue • P.O. Box 90 • Carmel, Indiana 46032 USA

Fold Here

New Riders Publishing
11711 North College Avenue
P.O. Box 90
Carmel, Indiana 46032
USA

OPERATING SYSTEMS

INSIDE MS-DOS 6

MARK MINASI

A complete tutorial and reference!

MS-DOS 6
ISBN: 1-56205-132-6
$39.95 USA

DOS FOR NON-NERDS

MICHAEL GROH

Understanding this popular operating system is easy with this humorous, step-by-step tutorial.

Through DOS 6.0
ISBN: 1-56205-151-2
$18.95 USA

INSIDE SCO UNIX

STEVE GLINES, PETER SPICER, BEN HUNSBERGER, & KAREN WHITE

Everything users need to know to use the UNIX operating system for everyday tasks.

SCO Xenix 286, SCO Xenix 386, SCO UNIX/System V 386
ISBN: 1-56205-028-1
$29.95 USA

INSIDE SOLARIS SunOS

KARLA SAARI KITALONG, STEVEN R. LEE, & PAUL MARZIN

Comprehensive tutorial and reference to SunOS!

SunOS, Sun's version of UNIX for the SPARC workstation version 2.0
ISBN: 1-56205-032-X
$29.95 USA

To Order, Call 1-800-428-5331

GRAPHICS TITLES

INSIDE CORELDRAW! 4.0, SPECIAL EDITION

DANIEL GRAY

An updated version of the #1 best-selling tutorial on CorelDRAW!

CorelDRAW! 4.0
ISBN: 1-56205-164-4
$34.95 USA

Coming Soon

CORELDRAW! SPECIAL EFFECTS

NEW RIDERS PUBLISHING

An inside look at award-winning techniques from professional CorelDRAW! designers!

CorelDRAW! 4.0
ISBN: 1-56205-123-7
$39.95 USA

CORELDRAW! NOW!

NEW RIDERS PUBLISHING

The graphics approach to using CorelDRAW!

CorelDRAW! 2.01 & 3.0
ISBN: 1-56205-131-8
$21.95 USA

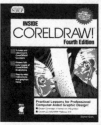

INSIDE CORELDRAW! FOURTH EDITION

DANIEL GRAY

The popular tutorial approach to learning CorelDRAW!...with complete coverage of version 3.0!

CorelDRAW! 3.0
ISBN: 1-56205-106-7
$34.95 USA

To Order, Call 1-800-428-5331

NETWORKING TITLES

#1 Bestseller!

INSIDE NOVELL NETWARE, SPECIAL EDITION

DEBRA NIEDERMILLER-CHAFFINS & BRIAN L. CHAFFINS

This best-selling tutorial and reference has been updated and made even better!

NetWare 2.2 & 3.11

ISBN: 1-56205-096-6

$34.95 USA

MAXIMIZING NOVELL NETWARE

JOHN JERNEY & ELNA TYMES

Complete coverage of Novell's flagship product...for NetWare system administrators!

NetWare 3.11

ISBN: 1-56205-095-8

$39.95 USA

NETWARE: THE PROFESSIONAL REFERENCE, SECOND EDITION

KARANJITSIYAN

This updated version for professional NetWare administrators and technicians provides the most comprehensive reference available for this phenomenal network system.

NetWare 2.2 & 3.11

ISBN: 1-56205-158-X

$42.95 USA

NETWARE 4: PLANNING AND IMPLEMENTATION

SUNIL PADIYAR

A guide to planning, installing, and managing a NetWare 4.0 network that serves the company's best objectives.

NetWare 4.0

ISBN: 1-56205-159-8

$27.95 USA

To Order, Call 1-800-428-5331

WINDOWS TITLES

ULTIMATE WINDOWS 3.1

FORREST HOULETTE, JIM BOYCE,
RICH WAGNER, & THE BSU
RESEARCH STAFF

The most up-to-date reference for
Windows available!

Covers 3.1 and related products

ISBN: 1-56205-125-3

$39.95 USA

INSIDE WINDOWS NT

NEW RIDERS PUBLISHING

A complete tutorial and reference to
organize and manage multiple tasks
and multiple programs in Windows.

Windows NT

ISBN: 1-56205-124-5

$34.95 USA

WINDOWS FOR NON-NERDS

JIM BOYCE & ROB TIDROW

This helpful tutorial for Windows
provides novice users with what they
need to know to gain computer
proficiency...and confidence!

Windows 3.1

ISBN: 1-56205-152-0

$18.95 USA

INTEGRATING WINDOWS APPLICATIONS

ELLEN DANA NAGLER, FORREST HOULETTE,
MICHAEL GROH, RICHARD WAGNER, &
VALDA HILLEY

This book is a no-nonsense, practical
approach to intermediate and advanced
level Windows users!

Windows 3.1

ISBN: 1-56205-083-4

$34.95 USA

To Order, Call 1-800-428-5331

WANT MORE INFORMATION?

CHECK OUT THESE RELATED TITLES:

	QTY	PRICE	TOTAL
CorelDRAW! Special Effects. Learn award-winning techniques from professional CorelDRAW! designers with this comprehensive collection of the hottest tips and techniques! This book provides step-by-step instructions for creating over 25 stunning special effects. An excellent book for those who want to take their CorelDRAW! documents a couple of notches higher. ISBN: 1-56205-123-7.	____	$39.95	_____
Inside CorelDRAW!, Fourth Edition. (covers version 3.0) Tap into the graphics power of CorelDRAW! 3.0 with this bestseller. This book goes beyond providing just tips and tricks for boosting productivity. Readers also receive expanded coverage on how to use CorelDRAW! with other Windows programs! ISBN: 1-56205-106-7.	____	$34.95	_____
CorelDRAW! Now!. Users who want fast access to thorough information, people upgrading to CorelDRAW! 4.0 from a previous version, new CorelDRAW! users—all of these groups will want to tap into this guide to great graphics—now! Developed by CorelDRAW! experts, this book provides answers to everything from common questions to advanced inquiries. ISBN: 1-56205-131-8.	____	$21.95	_____
CorelDRAW! for Non-Nerds. This light-hearted reference presents all the stuff readers need to know about CorelDRAW! to get things done! With quick, easy-to-find, no-nonsense answers to common questions, this book is perfect for any "non-nerd" who wants a fun and easy way to get started using this powerful graphics program. ISBN: 1-56205-174-1.	____	$18.95	_____

Name _____

Company _____

Address _____

City _____ State ____ ZIP _____

Phone _____ Fax _____

☐ Check Enclosed   ☐ VISA   ☐ MasterCard

Card #_____Exp. Date _____

Signature _____

Prices are subject to change. Call for availability and pricing information on latest editions.

Subtotal   _____

Shipping   _____

$4.00 for the first book and $1.75 for each additional book.

Total   _____
Indiana residents add 5% sales tax.

New Riders Publishing   11711 North College Avenue • P.O. Box 90 • Carmel, Indiana 46032 USA

Orders/Customer Service: 1-800-541-6789
Fax: 1-800-448-3804

Master CorelMOVE! with the

Inside CorelDRAW! Animation Disk

This valuable disk contains the completed CorelMOVE! animated sequence that the exercises in Chapter 13 cover. This file comes on a high-density floppy disk and is ready for you to load and use—without spending hours manually creating the drawings. You can use the file to see how a finished CorelMOVE! animation looks and to examine each step along the way, such as positioning elements and editing the frames.

To receive your disk, send the attached coupon and $5.00 to:

New Riders Publishing
11711 N. College Ave.
Suite 140
Carmel, IN 46032

- -

Please send me the *Inside CorelDRAW! Animation Disk*

Name _____

Company _____

Address _____

City _____

State, ZIP _____

Country _____

Phone (include area code) _____

Please include $5.00. (Indiana residents must add 5% sales tax.)

Method of Payment:

____ Check Enclosed

____ Cash

Charge my: ____ VISA ____ MasterCard ____ American Express

Account No. _____ Expires: _____

Signature_____